STANDARD CATALOG OF®
COLT
FIREARMS

BY RICK SAPP

FEATURING PHOTOS
BY PAUL GOODWIN

©2007 Krause Publications

Published by

Gun Digest® Books
An imprint of F+W Publications
700 East State Street • Iola, WI 54990-0001
715-445-2214 • 888-457-2873
www.gundigestbooks.com

Our toll-free number to place an order or obtain
a free catalog is (800) 258-0929.

Library of Congress Control Number: 2007924538

ISBN-13: 978-0-89689-534-8
ISBN-10: 0-89689-534-3

Designed by Elizabeth Krogwold
Edited by Dan Shideler

Printed in China

AUTHOR'S INTRODUCTION

WORKAHOLICS

Developing a book about Colt firearms has been an eye-opening experience. I have always been a particular fan of history and there is plenty of it here – almost two centuries of personality, intrigue and genius.

Most writers begin to spin the Colt narrative at a point where the young Sam, who is perhaps 14 years old, is sitting under a tree. There, he begins to dismantle, and then to reconstruct, an Andy Jackson-era handgun. Perhaps the story is true. It sounds a little too similar to the myth of Isaac Newton's inspiration about the theory of gravity – he is sitting in a garden and a falling apple hits him on the head – for my taste.

In both cases, the problem with these myths is that genius is evident long before the age of 17, before Samuel Colt spent a year at sea and conceptualized, in the whirling ship's capstan, an application to a repeating firearm. And it is not "simple" genius – if something so mysterious and complex could be considered simple – that changes the world. It is genius with some other element: curiosity or opportunity, for instance. It is genius with application that changes the world.

In the case of Colt and Newton – and John Browning, another famous name inextricably linked to the Colt enterprise – that additional element was some inner drive that we have of late labeled "workaholic," as if to be consumed with one's life work or hobby or obsession was a bad thing!

Thank goodness Sam Colt was a workaholic, that he had a vision and enough motivation to "make it happen." It is unfortunate that poor health and an early death at 48 may have been the consequence, but the world is certainly a different place because of his struggles and almost single-minded dedication to succeed.

DEDICATION

So this book is dedicated to all of the workaholics of the world, the men and the women. It is compiled in praise of the folks who are singularly obsessed with changing, building, inventing, writing, moving or perhaps removing something in life. It is written in grateful appreciation of their effort, their insecurities and the passions that often wreck or bring misery to their personal lives. It is put together in awe of the brain with the thorn that cannot rest or give up or retreat.

Whatever term is required to keep the world's workaholics on track regardless of their personal sacrifice – "Seize the day" or "Semper Fi" or "Neither rain nor snow …" or "Go for the gold" – I ask this of the world's workaholics: please keep on keeping on. This world becomes a different and probably a better place because you are consumed by or fixated on your goal.

And ignore the whining and weeping and wailing, the political correctness that is overwhelming us. To hell with the roses and the diamonds. The kids should work for their college education (like the "boy named Sue," they will be better people for it). If the spouse needs help drying the dishes, suggest that she (or he) employ a maid service. And when, not if, your invention, your great American novel, your brilliant idea makes page one of the New York Times and you cash the first royalty check on the way to millions of dollars … savor the moment. And then get back to work!

HISTORY: THE TRUTH IS OUT THERE

This book is about history, but it is about history through the lens of collecting Colt firearms. As such, it encompasses wars and murders – as if they were mutually exclusive – fortunes made, friendships betrayed … in short, the entire spectrum of the human comedy. Nevertheless, this particular compilation is narrowly focused on products, hard goods, and the prices we pay for them.

Before I began studying Colt firearms I had no idea of the controversies, mysteries and unresolved questions surrounding virtually every part of every gun listed in this volume. That amuses and puzzles me, because it seems as though it should be entirely straightforward: X gun was first built in X year with X features for X reasons or to address X needs. But this is an illusion; these determinations only *seem* straightforward. What I have learned this past year is that every facet of every action involved in making something new – even something as hard and factual and physical as a gun – becomes the subject of an historical obsession. Actually, I like that.

Almost nothing is straightforward in collecting Colt firearms – and the older the gun, the more complex its history becomes. Records are incomplete; factories burn; new models are stolen or pirated; guns are faked; financing fails; collectors with dubious character alter guns or just lie; owners die or just change their mind. Critical spellings are typed incorrectly and passed on for generations. People forget. And all this complexity ultimately means that it is more difficult to make a good decision about investing.

Caveat emptor is the Latin expression. Buyer beware. It certainly applies to collecting. Stamps. Antiques. Firearms.

As a historian, I often wish my subjects were easier to understand, would hold still for analysis. I have been fortunate to write books about Lewis and Clark and their expedition to the Pacific; and about Ulysses S. Grant and his journey through the Civil War. And even those incredibly researched and well documented subjects have gray areas, mysteries. Why, for instance, did Meriwether Lewis – Thomas Jefferson's personal secretary and the man Jefferson personally chose to lead the expedition – kill himself … or did he? Why did Grant, such a successful military commander, lead his presidential administration so poorly? Why was Sam Colt's son, Caldwell, such a wastrel and dandy?

All of these questions are what make history and collecting fascinating. We know, as Agent Mulder in *The X Files* television show did, that somewhere "the truth is out there."

DOING OUR HOMEWORK

Normally, by the time we are old enough to invest in a Walker Colt we have heard "do your homework" applied to everything from schoolwork to the purchase of a new car to proposing to a potential spouse. Right from the start, we never liked homework, even though, paradoxically, we have always known that those who did their homework fared better: got a better price or a better grade or were accepted to a better school.

So we know, secretly but absolutely, in our heart of hearts, that we should avoid the impulse to buy that John Wayne Commemorative at a neighborhood gun show. Of course we enjoyed the movie *True Grit*, but it does not make you closer to the quiet man to purchase this gun before checking it out and learning its history and speculating honestly about its potential. (And once we have realized that commemorative guns are somewhat like the endless multitude of fishing lures, designed to attract fishermen as well as fish, we can make intelligent decisions about those quirky limited editions.)

So the truth is out there. Somewhere. As collectors and historians it is our duty to find it.

RICK SAPP

MARCH 2007

GAINESVILLE, FLORIDA

PS: A NOTE ABOUT AUCTION RESULTS:

Throughout this book I have attempted to demonstrate the volatility of the Colt market by including internet auction results where appropriate. Sometimes the auction results gibe with the given value of guns in similar condition; sometimes they do not. Does this mean that the values I have cited are incorrect? No. It does, however, demonstrate the wide variations that sometimes occur in individual real-life auctions. I believe that the values cited in this book represent the average values that the reader will encounter, not only in internet auctions, but in retail gun shops and at local gun shows.

Happy hunting!

CONTENTS

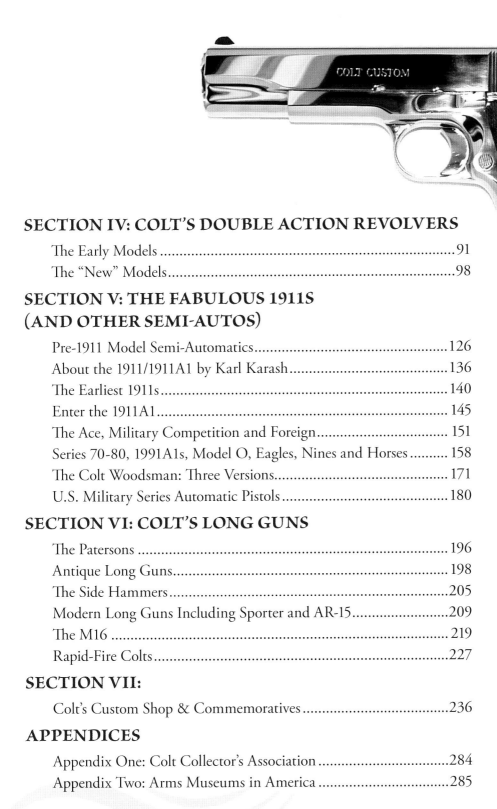

COLT:
TODAY &
TOMORROW

A MESSAGE
FROM COLT'S:

The Future of Colt...
as Colt Sees It

"Our legacy for the twenty first century will rest on how well we lay the groundwork today for creating a company that continues to be responsive to consumer needs, and depends as much on inventiveness and innovation as it does on technology. We are striving to meet this challenge and to guarantee a secure place for Colt in the pages of history as they unfold in the decades to come."

2007 CATALOG, COLT'S
MANUFACTURING COMPANY LLC

With a history as distinguished as any firearms company in the world, Colt's Manufacturing Company LLC today finds itself looking in two directions: forward into the 21st century with new designs and unlimited possibilities, and backward to the 20th and 19th centuries to a record of remarkable achievement, innovative approaches to shooting problems, continuing innovation and, ultimately, strong brand identification and customer loyalty.

Since Samuel Colt opened his Hartford Armory, Colt's (hereinafter referred to simply as Colt) has always operated with the kind of double vision that many companies attempt and few actually achieve. More than 150 years ago, the boy genius Sam Colt realized that a successful and long-lasting American firearms company would need to serve both the military and the civilian marketplace.

Thus, Colt produced arms for every market segment. It built deringers and pocket pistols for personal protection and the famous Single Action Army or "Peacemaker" for military and civilian use. Its management set the stage for a century of innovation by dozens of manufacturers worldwide when it agreed to produce John M. Browning's 1911 automatic pistol and proceeded to manufacture the Gatling gun and the Thompson submachine gun. In the modern era it co-designed the remarkable M16, the staple of U.S. military small arms for almost half a century.

Today, Colt has two principal divisions: its commercial or civilian division (Colt's Manufacturing Company LLC) and its defense contracting division, which encompasses law enforcement, military and private security support (Colt Defense LLC). This sectional approach to the multiple markets that Colt serves is the sign of a nimble and diversified company that is both flexible enough to tackle the challenges of the century ahead … and respectful of its legacy as well.

"I believe the Colt vision now is to reestablish our presence as a significant player in the commercial handgun market," says Mark Roberts, Director of Sales and Marketing for the commercial division. Roberts, who worked on the manufacturing side for six years before moving to marketing, has a well-rounded view of Colt's progress since 1998. He is personally vested in the manufacturer's success.

During the 1990s, Colt as well as most other U.S. firearms manufacturers, found itself facing an increasingly hostile battery of attorneys who represented a small minority of the American public. Supported by numerous well-funded non-profit – and often tax-exempt – organizations such as the *Brady Center to Prevent Gun Violence* or even anti-hunting organizations such as *Defenders of Wildlife* and *People for the Ethical Treatment of Animals,* these attorneys were evidently tasked to "go after the gun industry." In an era when one could receive hundreds of thousands, perhaps millions, of dollars in damages for spilling one's own coffee in one's own lap inside one's own vehicle, the injury was significant in time and resources.

The barrage of anti-gun lawsuits, which culminated (but did not, unfortunately, end) in 1999, forced Colt (and others) to re-evaluate their commercial product lines. Suddenly, another factor was added to the administrative overhead in addition to reliability, marketability, research and testing: additional staff lawyers.

Larry Keane, Senior Vice President and General Counsel to the National Shooting Sports Foundation, estimates lawsuits from municipalities alone cost the industry $225 million. Those costs are on-going. Insurance became a massive burden: not only were policy increases substantial, but deductibles skyrocketed and exclusions compounded – if a manufacturer could find insurance at all. There were less resources for wage increases and new product research. Overall, there was less money for capital investments and both buildings and equipment suffered. According to Keane, "1999 is the year that the entire industry, including Colt's, was almost destroyed."

Primarily as a result of the turbulence in the civilian marketplace, Colt dropped its tiny six-shot Mustang in 1999; dropped its small double-action .380 ACP Pony the following year; and let the 9mm Pocket Nine go in 2001. Other models, fully functional and serviceable guns, fell out of Colt's catalog. Colt, and the industry as a whole, cautiously felt its way forward, but there was a realization that Colt's brand equity, name and legacy – all built carefully over 150 years – made it a special target for anti-gun activists, specialists in appeasement and pacifists of all stripes.

Fortunately, although Colt and other firearms manufacturers briefly went into what Roberts refers to as "something of a hunker down" mode, the damage was not permanent. Life, indeed, has gone on because of simple need and customer demand from both civilians and the military. The international requirement for quality firearms has, if anything, increased, but at Colt the vision had to be renewed. And that could not happen overnight.

Looking at the firearms marketplace, Colt management understands that the world is now a highly competitive and highly integrated place, and that the 21st century already is filled with great gun makers from many nations. Competitive contract bids for new or old designs may be received from almost any corner of the earth.

"A lot of guns are being made now that are very comparable to Colt's," Roberts reflects, accepting the fact that all of Colt's original patents – on guns like the redoubtable 1911, for instance – expired long ago. "So it has been up to us to redefine our vision, our product lines and our quality standards, to insist that, at every level, they become the best in this business."

The results of nearly a decade of thoughtful planning have left Colt – at least on the commercial side – as more of a "niche marketer" than they were in the generation of the World War II veterans. For long-term profitability, it is much more important for a company to carefully study the market before launching a new product line than it was even a dozen years ago. A new firearms concept may now cost millions of dollars and take years of study, and even then may go nowhere … or may be immensely profitable. So production of guns to match every shooting opportunity is not, at present, in the new vision. Shotguns for sporting clays; hunting rifles for big game; new deringers for self-defense – none of these appears to be in Colt's immediate future.

These days, looking at a more dangerous and quixotic international playground than perhaps ever before in Colt's or America's history, Colt has accepted its role as a niche player on the commercial side and as a robust contractor to the U.S. government (and to other, friendly governments as well) on the defense side. Consequently, the majority of Colt's internal resources

and external public relations and lobbying efforts are targeted to meet defense-contracting opportunities.

Still, Colt has a commercial handgun capacity with both legacy and product that remain in high demand. According to Roberts, "Colt's Manufacturing has not defined its niche as bells and whistles, guns with seven sorts of whiz-bang features and any 'gun of the week' syndrome. We believe that at this time, our niche is the basic, mil-spec single-stack .45 and some offshoots of that trusted firearm. We are also committed to maintain a very strong presence in the single-action community with our Model P, the classic Colt Peacemaker. These directions are intended for the Colt purist, the person who likes guns with the refinement, aesthetics and quality they had 40 and 50 years ago." To promote the brand, Colt's continuing task is therefore to maintain a competitive competence in price, quality and distinctiveness.

So, according to Mark Roberts, Colt's commitment to the civilian market remains solid, even if it may not carry as extensive a product line as it once did. For example, the Hartford manufacturer went through a major "commemorative era" from the 1960s to the 1980s wherein dozens of special guns were produced in the "Lawman Series": the 3,000 guns designated the 1967 Bat Masterson Frontier Scout, or the 250 .45 automatics in the 1979 Ohio President's Special Edition. Colt has made a decision to move beyond that market, perhaps finding that the resources invested in building and marketing a few hundred specialized guns, even one for which the pattern was well-established, could not be recouped in profitability and that the dozens of commemoratives produced may, in effect, have softened the brand when the guns did not hold their initial commemorative values.

"Although the manufacturing process is continually changing, we, like other companies that manufacture intricate mechanical instruments continue to look for ways to build excellent, durable parts at less expense," Mark Roberts says. "Basically though, we still operate the way we did a generation ago, with high quality forged steel and machined bar stock, and making very limited use of MIM (metal injection molded) parts. I believe that most people would be truly astonished at the amount of hand finishing and team evaluation that our quality inspectors require for that perfect Colt fit and feel."

THE RAMPANT COLT:
SAM COLT

(1814 - 1862) – American
Genius, American Original

*S*am Colt was a prodigy. In 20 years, he went from penniless to immensely wealthy; from being a literal nobody to consorting with the richest, most famous and, occasionally, the most powerful people in the world. Beginning with a prototype revolver carved from a chunk of wood, he orchestrated a firearms revolution and organized one of the largest and most successful industrial enterprises in America. Almost 200 years after his birth, his story is still amazing and inspiring.

The son of a sometime farmer, sometime small businessman, Samuel Colt was born in Hartford, Connecticut, in 1814. Although his father and stepmother worked hard to give him a good education – his biological mother died when he was just a few years old – at the age of 11, he was indentured as a farm servant. And like most rural youngsters, he was at home with the muzzleloaders of the day.

As a youth, the boy had a profound mechanical curiosity and was greatly influenced by a book titled the *Compendium of Knowledge,* an encyclopedia of a scientific nature. This book contained articles about inventors such as Robert Fulton who – by linking an idea with a challenge, and with the ability to work mechanically with gears, wheels and levers – succeeded in expanding the frontier of human accomplishment. When Sam's father subsequently took over the operation of a Massachusetts textile mill, the young Sam worked there also.

Shortly afterward, Sam Colt spent a year at sea. It may very well have been there, watching the action of the ship's wheel as it spun and locked (or perhaps the capstan, a rotating wheel used to control lines to sails and spars, and to redirect the force of the wind) controlling the sailing ship's movements, that he conceived his idea for spinning or rotating chambers that would hold firearms

The best-known American gunmaker of all time, Samuel Colt (1814-1862).

ammunition. On board the ship, he even worked with the carpenter to carve a realistic model of a six-shooter. The boy was just 18 years old.

Returning to New England, Sam and his father commissioned several gunsmiths to build revolving cylinder firearms to Sam's specifications, but because the Colts lacked the finances to hire truly first-class metalsmiths, these models operated poorly or not at all. One of the first two exploded in Colt's hands. So to raise money to bring his ideas to fruition, the young man took to the road as an entertainer ("Doctor Coult of Calcutta") giving lectures about and demonstrations of laughing gas (nitrous oxide) in fairs and auditoriums from the Mississippi River to Montreal.

The income from his laughing gas tour allowed him to commission excellent working models and engineering drawings of his revolvers. The tour also gave him valuable experience in promotion and marketing, experience he would soon put to the test with his own inventions. At just 21 years of age, in 1835, he sailed to England and France to patent his revolver, fearing that the Europeans would immediately pirate his work. Afterwards, he returned to the U.S. and patented his drawings and ideas at home.

In his book *COLT: An American Legend*, R.L. Wilson reminds us that when Colt organized his first factory in Paterson, New Jersey, in 1836, the president of the U.S. was Andrew Jackson, and that the Union encompassed only 25 states and a vast frontier had been purchased just 33 years before by Thomas Jefferson.

Although that time seems an eternity ago, financing options were about the same. With patents, working models and a personal investment, Colt incorporated as the Patent Arms Manufacturing Company, borrowed enough money to capitalize his factory and begin turning out revolving cylinder handguns, rifles and even shotguns for the cap-and-ball or percussion era that was replacing the older flintlocks.

For a collector, finding a Paterson Colt in a dusty, rarely-visited attic would be better than finding a friendly Irish leprechaun willing to take him to the pot of gold at the end of the rainbow. It did not turn out as well for Colt, however. His Paterson models were functional, even remarkable for the time, but hardly efficient or reliable. In New Jersey, Colt developed and produced three different revolving-cylinder handgun models – pocket, belt and holster; two types of revolving

long rifle – one cocked by a hammer and the other by a finger lever or ring; a revolving carbine; and a revolving-cylinder shotgun. In all cases, gunpowder and bullets were loaded into the front of the cylinder while the primer was inserted into a hollow nipple located on the outside of the cylinder, where it would be struck by the hammer when the trigger was pulled.

But Sam Colt's designs were still immature and the black powder of the day was extremely "dirty," leaving a great deal of fouling that complicated the functioning of moving parts. For these reasons and because of the lack of government orders, Colt closed the doors of his Paterson enterprise in 1842.

Nevertheless, Colt's Paterson plant did in fact produce working models of multi-shot handguns, rifles and shotguns. His guns were used in the Seminole War in Florida and, most important, in the fighting to establish the Republic of Texas that would culminate in the Mexican-American War.

The Paterson failure was not the end of Sam Colt, though. Filled with ideas and with insufficient hours in the day to bring them all to life, he experimented with waterproof ammunition, underwater harbor defense systems via coordinated explosive mines and, with Samuel F.B. Morse, the telegraph. In fact, having narrowly averted a war with Louis Philippe's France in the mid 1830s, the government awarded Colt $50,000 – an immense sum in those days – to further his plans for harbor defense. But hostilities with Mexico, from whom the U.S. demanded a huge chunk of territory, interrupted Colt's East Coast harbor defense efforts and turned him, once again, into a firearms entrepreneur.

It may have been luck, in the form of a couple of famous Texas Rangers, as much as his personal inventive genius that gave Colt a second chance. Captain Samuel Walker was recruiting for the fighting in Texas when he exchanged letters with Colt, whose Paterson guns he had used successfully against the Comanche. Many frontiersmen regarded that southwestern tribe as the finest light cavalry of the era. Working together, Colt and Walker soon developed a fresh design, more powerful and more reliable than Colt's Paterson guns, and Colt induced Eli Whitney, Jr., son of the inventor of the cotton gin, to financially back his enterprise.

Colt sold the subsequent 1847 Walker Colt percussion revolver to the government and to civilians alike. Based on the new designs, these guns were an immediate success and Colt was on his way to fame and fortune. Walker, on the other hand, died the following year, killed by the thrust of a lance during the Battle of Juamantla, near Tlaxcala, Mexico.

By 1851, Colt was organizing and building a modern factory along the Connecticut River in Hartford. Four years later, the factory was fully operational and, incorporated as Colt's Patent Fire Arms Manufacturing Company, was turning out fresh firearms models to supply a national sense of unrest and the flood of immigrants moving west. The California Gold Rush, the Indian Wars and looming sectional conflict that would become the Civil War, or War Between the States, fueled Colt's armory and his almost boundless energy. Soon, a factory in London was also producing the indefatigable Yankee's designs.

In his new factory, which was built to the latest standards of the day, Colt lost no time in specifying interchangeable parts for his firearms, some 80 percent of which were turned out on precision machinery. Because of the undeviating attention Colt – and capable lieutenants such as Elisha K. Root, a long-time friend and highly qualified engineer – paid to the manufacturing process, the Hartford production machinery achieved a remarkably high degree of uniformity for the mid-19th century. Typically, the metal parts of a Colt revolver were designed, molded, machined, fitted, stamped with a serial number, hardened and assembled right there in Hartford.

In the mid-1850s, Colt finished his remarkable factory and topped it with a marvelous blue onion dome resplendent with gold stars. Above it stood a cast bronze "rampant colt," the rearing stallion holding a broken spear – half in its mouth and half in tandem across its legs – that would become the internationally-recognized Colt logo.

Sam also oversaw the building of a mansion, complete with greenhouses and formal gardens, which he named *"Armsmear,"* and he got married. His wife, Elizabeth, the daughter of a New England parson, would be instrumental in guiding the company through turbulent times following his early death in 1862.

Colt, who was by now extraordinarily wealthy and well-connected, took his bride on a six-month tour of Europe. The highlight of couple's honeymoon was undoubtedly their attendance at the coronation of Czar Alexander II in St. Petersburg, Russia. (Sam and

Elizabeth had several children, but only one survived into adulthood. The one surviving boy was named Caldwell. Unfortunately, Caldwell proved to be an heir of no importance, a dilettante yachtsman and skirt-chaser. He was shot to death in 1894 while fleeing from an irate husband in Key West, Florida.)

In the 1850s, Sam Colt was considered one of the 10 wealthiest men in America. The Governor of Connecticut presented him with the honorary title of Colonel of State Militia, probably as payback for political and financial support. Still, Sam's life was anything but calm. Because he gave lavishly engraved sets of firearms inset with gold and silver as gifts to men he believed would look favorably upon his company, he was investigated by the U.S. Congress. Adding to his troubles, several of his children died at birth or shortly thereafter. He also fought his way through numerous lawsuits, all of which sought a slice of the Colt enterprise.

In those days, Colt sold his firearms through a small force of traveling salesmen, known as agents, and between 15 and 20 "jobbers," the old term for wholesalers who sold large quantities of guns to smaller retail outlets such as hardware stores. In addition, the company maintained sales offices in both New York City and London. The sales department also would accept direct orders at the plant, providing they were from someone who was rich and famous, a friend of the Colt family, or a buyer of a large quantity of weapons. This practice would continue long after Sam's death. (In July of 1885, frontiersman and some-time marshal/some-time outlaw W.B. "Bat" Masterson sent Colt his order for a nickel-plated .45 caliber single action revolver. "Make it very Easy on [the] trigger," he wrote under the letterhead of the Opera House Saloon of Dodge City, Kansas. His letter still survives in the Colt archives.)

Sam Colt was later recognized as one of the earliest American manufacturers to fully realize the potential of an effective marketing program that included sales promotion, publicity, product sampling, advertising and public relations. Whether or not any specific bribes were asked or offered is not known, but given the climate of the time, such would not have been unusual.

Samuel Colt's health began to fail late in 1860 as the country moved toward total war. He was tired and overworked. Prior to the actual outbreak of war, Colt continued to ship product to customers in southern

In his lifetime, Sam Colt had produced more than 400,000 firearms.

states; as soon as war was "official," however, Colt supplied only the Union forces. By the end of 1861, the Hartford Armory was operating at full capacity, with more than 1,000 employees and annual earnings of about $250,000.

On January 10, 1862, Sam Colt died at the age of 47. The cause of his death remains obscure even today; contemporary accounts suggest rheumatic fever or possibly pneumonia. In his lifetime, he had produced more than 400,000 firearms. His estate was reportedly worth $15 million, an enormous sum for the time, an amount of money equivalent to more than $350 million by today's economic standards. Following Sam's death, control of the company passed into the hands of his widow, Elizabeth, who had promised that she would carry out her husband's wishes for the future.

Colt died while the Civil War raged – indeed, while the outcome was very much in doubt. On a cold February morning two years after he was buried, the city of Hartford awoke to the news that Colt's factory was in flames. At 8:15 that morning, smoke was reported issuing from the attic wing. Flames spread so rapidly that by 9:00 a.m. Colt's well-known blue and gold onion dome with its trademark rampant colt weathervane had collapsed into the fire. Although the workers battled valiantly to save the building, its machinery and stock, by evening everything was reduced to smoking rubble. The cause of the fire was never determined, but there was some evidence of Confederate sabotage.

Unfortunately Sam had never bothered to insure the ruined building. Elizabeth had done so in a partial manner and she spearheaded reconstruction with the pitiful one-third of replacement value they eventually wrung from the reluctant insurance companies. By 1867 the new armory, now with firewalls three feet thick, was "not only an unsurpassed workshop but, also a monument to the memory of the late Colonel Colt and was fully consistent with Elizabeth's determination to live a life of 'faithful affection' and memory."

Control of the company remained in the hands of Elizabeth and her family until 1901 when she, having no living heirs, sold it to a group of investors. Thus ended the Colt family's direct affiliation with the company that had become, and remains, one of the most widely-recognized in American history.

THE COLT COLLECTOR:
PINNACLES & PITFALLS

*I*f you have ever thought that you might want to begin a collection of Colt (or other) firearms, you are in for a challenging and entertaining learning experience. Surprisingly, you do not have to begin with thousands of dollars to devote to the hobby, either. Over time, you may want to extend your interests to the more fascinating (and expensive) corners of Colt collecting – the earliest models that generally become available seem to be the 1850s Dragoons and Walkers – but whatever you decide, you will want to start quietly and carefully, learning as you go, enjoying the trip.

INTERVIEW WITH A COLLECTOR

To learn more about the fun, fascinating and potentially lucrative hobby of collecting Colt firearms, we turned to an expert, Ed Cox of Fernley, Nevada. Ed is a member of the Colt Collector's Association (www.coltcollectorsassoc.com) as well as the owner of www.antiquegunlist.com and other Internet sites.

RS: Good morning, Ed. How would you describe yourself as a Colt firearms collector?

Ed: I'm not a staunch collector like many people are. I kind of half-way collect and deal, buy and sell. I mean, some of these folks get a gun and just absolutely would not turn it loose for anything. I don't look at it that way. When I'm ready to sell a gun, I put a price on it and if somebody gives me that price then they own it. It's theirs. I think I'm more of a dealer than a collector, but they are all "my Colts" as long as I have them in my possession until I sell them.

RS: How long have you been involved in the gun collecting field?

Ed: Well, I really don't know as far as collecting is concerned…. You know, you start out as a kid shooting and maybe owning a gun and I think at that time it's kind of planted in you that there are

a certain number of guns around, whether they are hunting guns or just pistols that you can take out and shoot. This interest and familiarity with guns just naturally leads into collecting.

These days most people don't have the luxury of growing up with guns, though. It would be nice if people could start collecting a little earlier, but most have to wait until the kids are gone and all the school bills are paid.

RS: How many Colts do you own at the present time?

Ed: Counting the broken ones and the ones I'd never part with and the ones that are for sale, maybe a couple hundred.

RS: How would you describe the impulse to collect?

Ed: Well, I think that for each person it is different. For me, it is the nostalgia of the 1800s. I don't collect anything much into the 1900s, but there are many collectors who specialize in Colt semi-automatics and machine guns and newer stuff. Some people collect only the commemorative issues. So for each person it is different. That kernel of itch and interest pushes us all in a little different direction.

With the antique guns, there is a lot of nostalgia connected to collecting them and they will consistently go up in value more than anything you can think of, including the stock market.

RS: So which of the old Colts do you collect? The Patersons? Percussion Era guns?

Ed: Well, I don't go back that far. A real Paterson in good condition today would probably cost between $200,000 and $300,000. And in the single actions, some of those guns run to $40,000 or $50,000.

I am in the Percussion Era, though, and the Dragoons are a little bit more in my price range. For an authentic Dragoon, you're probably talking about $5,000.

RS: Do you do any cowboy shooting, Ed? Are you a member of the Single Action Shooting Society?

Ed: I don't do any cowboy shooting. Even though I could shoot some of the guns I own, I don't. When you pay a certain amount of money – and some people will disagree with this – you don't want to stick a bullet in it and risk blowing it up. Old guns are made of old steel and I know of people who have bought a single action gun from the 1880s and they just had to shoot it so they put a modern round through it and blew up the gun.

RS: A gun from the 1880s would have been built in the black powder era, wouldn't it, so pressures and proof testing and what-not would be different.

Ed: Now, if you shot that 1880s gun with a light black powder load, you might not have any problem. I have the reloading knowledge and even have all the black powder components here, so I could go out and shoot, but I don't want to. For me, it's more about collecting. I just want to look at this piece. I've got a Burgess rifle sitting above the window here in my office and I look at it all the time and I want to think of what cowboy had this gun; what sheriff or bad guy had this. If the gun could only talk it would probably tell some great stories.[1]

But as far as taking that gun down and putting a bullet in it and shooting, well I could with no problem, but I don't have the desire to do that.

RS: I understand that most dedicated collectors would never shoot the guns in their collection. In fact, with a commemorative gun a single shot would cause minor scratches and detract from its value, and with an antique gun … well, what's the point?

Ed: That's partially true. Parts just are not available for many of these old guns unless a collector can get something hand made and that would simply destroy the gun's re-sale value. So you're right on that account: what would be the point?

With commemoratives, some collectors like them because they want a mint gun in the box and they are certainly not going to run a round through it. They become valuable because Colt just doesn't make these guns anymore.

I prefer the older stuff that I can cock, though, guns that I can oil and take care of short of firing a round through them.

RS: So your guns are mechanically in good condition, but you choose not to shoot them. Do most collectors do maintenance to this extent?

Ed: You still have a lot of people who think that if the gun came to them this way, it's just a "leave it alone" proposition; they don't do anything to it. But you've also got a number of the modern collectors who want the gun working, at least functional even though they won't go out and shoot it. It gives them some satisfaction to know that they could go out and shoot it if they wanted to.

RS: Would you say that it takes several thousand dollars to begin serious collecting?

Ed: No, it doesn't, because even a lot of the early Sturm-Rugers from the '50s are collectible today. A lot of other companies are becoming collectible, too. The Iver Johnsons, for instance, and lots of off the wall guns. Even the so-called "Saturday night specials" are becoming collectible and you can start out buying those guns for $150 to $200.

Colt collecting is like the Cadillac of gun collecting, the ultimate. Colt and Winchester. Not that some of the other guns aren't reaching peaks on rarity and getting up there like Colt. But Colt and Winchester are still the top of the line of collecting, and it seems like everybody wants a Colt or a Winchester. Take Winchester. The old line company is gone now. The manufacturing factory is closed. They're no longer in business. If that happens to Colt, everybody is going to want a piece of the history of Colt and prices for Colt guns are going to go through the roof.

RS: So what do collectors say about Colt? What's the future look like?

Ed: It's hard to say what'll happen to Colt. They still produce guns for us consumers, but it's got to come out of the Custom Shop so that's limited in quantity. It's just depends on their management and ownership. I don't want to speak publicly about Colt, but I don't know where they are going to go, either. Colt is an icon, but I've even seen articles that have said they've gone out of the commercial business. Of course, Colt says it's going to be around a long time, but whether they are or not, I don't know.

RS: When somebody gets into collecting Colt or Smith & Wesson or any other brand, will they get to a point where they want to show off their collection, say at the annual meeting of the Colt Collector's Association … or do most people keep their guns locked away and private for safe keeping?

Ed: The Collector's Association holds a convention somewhere in the U.S. every year. But there again, I live in Nevada and if the convention is in West Virginia, that's a long drive. I'm lucky this year because the convention is in Reno and I'm right here.

As far as showing off fine collections of guns, that's nice, but I know guys who have a lot of guns and they don't show them at all.

I think a lot of collectors don't want to display their guns. They keep them under lock and key. Some of the people who can afford it eventually build some kind of place to show their gun collection. I know guys in the CCA who have vaults and have their guns hanging up on display in there so they can just go in and look up and enjoy them any time they want, but that costs quite a bit of money.

RS: When someone decides to get into collecting, is it customary for them to identify some niche that interests them, and then concentrate on it? I'm thinking, for instance, of collecting all variations of the New Police, or Single Action Army or Pre-1911 Colt Semi-Autos.

Ed: I think the urge to collect stems from someone's background with guns, like in hunting. They find a gun that interests them and they read a little and begin to learn more and, pretty soon, they find another gun that is of similar interest but maybe just a little different and they buy that and read and learn a little more.

It takes a good size library to collect guns. You can't just run out and buy guns without reading and learning about them, and about the marketplace. Now, some people do, but they are the ones who usually get hurt because they don't know what they are buying and they pay too much. Let's face it. You can pay any kind of astronomical price for a gun. If you want it, but the guy who owns it doesn't want to let go of it, he'll put a very high price on it – and if you want it bad enough, you'll have to pay that high price if you want to own it bad enough. I guess, in that way, it's no different than if you collect automobiles.

I do believe that you've got to have an extensive library of books. I've probably got between 50 and 100 books about guns and I've read and studied most of them, especially the parts about what I want to collect or trade. Eventually your knowledge builds from just hanging around collectors, and buying and selling a few guns.

I don't think I started off collecting and decided, "Well, I'm going to just collect Pythons." Of course, I don't collect Pythons. That's a new gun, but some guys do collect them because they like them.

I happen to collect anything chambered for the .41 caliber cartridge. For me, it is just a nostalgic caliber that's not made any more. They don't even produce the ammunition in the United States now, and if you want to fire one of the old .41s, you have to build the ammo yourself. I know of some guys who load the .41 for cowboy action shooting, but it's still an obsolete caliber. I just kind of like it and want to try to collect one of every model Colt produced in that caliber. Some of them are quite rare, too, and then you had the .41 rimfire and the .41 Long, but Colt didn't offer a .41 Long after about 1923. So the history goes back quite a long way for me. And no, they never made a semi-auto in .41 caliber.

RS: You make collecting firearms sound like a pretty fascinating hobby.

Ed: Well, that is what it is for me, because it connects me to a fascination with the cowboy era. Along with that is the Single Action Army revolver and whatever, Wild Bill Hickok and Calamity Jane and Buffalo Bill Cody, but everyone goes their own way for whatever personal reason.

I've collected many things over the years just because I was interested in them, and then got rid of them. But the .41s … I just kind of stayed with them.

So I would say that if you are going to collect anything, you first ought to go out and buy some books on the subject and read them. Now there aren't going to be books on every possible Colt gun that you can collect, but there are some that will kind of help you along. One of them is the book *Colt: An American Legend* by R.L. Wilson that covers just about every gun Colt made up until the mid 1980s, and it's a good book. But then again, if you were going to specialize in collecting the '49 Pocket or the '51 Navy, you'd want to try to find a book specifically on them.

You know, just the accoutrements of black powder, they have a book on that and some people just collect that sort of thing. So it just depends on where your interest lies and finding the book on that. Of course they're always writing new books and one of them may be in an interest you like. And if there isn't a book in the particular area you want, you need to belong to the Colt Collector's Association and get to know the people who have been doing this for a really long time and they will kind of help you out and help you get started with some ideas about what you should do and what you should look out for.

I think collecting should always be … you should always buy the best your money can afford. Buy low end if that is all you can afford, but buy authentic. The older guns are only going to increase in value if you take care of them. Eventually you'll move out of the low end, maybe after buying two or three, and be able to trade up to a more valuable gun.

RS: Is there a certification process for gun appraisers? Even a voluntary system through the CCA, for instance?

Ed: No, there's no certification. I know there are a lot of good people out there who can give you a rough idea on almost any gun, but there really are a few people in any particular field who are specialists and can give you a evaluation of what a particular gun is worth.

You take John Kopec [phone 532-222-4440;

"U.S. Cavalry and Artillery Authentication Service"] who does letters on Single Action Army military guns – well, people like his letters because he wrote the book and he is constantly studying this gun. People like to be able to say, "Kopec said there was nothing wrong with this gun or to watch for such and such …." Because most of the military guns have gone up in value quite drastically, you want to make sure that what you bought, or are just thinking about buying, is authentic and not something put together. Kopec wrote the book on the Single Action Army military guns[2] and there isn't anyone out there who is a lot more knowledgeable about the subject than him.

Now, there are many other guys out there who are specialists in particular types of guns like the percussion Dragoons. You can find these fellows. You just have to hunt for them on line and through the Colt Collector's Association. The CCA is a good source if you are even considering buying an old gun, unless you are buying from an auction house and the auction house would supply its own certificate of authenticity and then stand behind it. Most auction houses will and do. I won't say that all of them do (stand behind or guarantee the authenticity of the product they sell), but generally, if an auction house says that something is genuine or real, they mean it that way. And nowadays, a lot of people are going to auctions to buy.

RS: Is there one best way to buy a collectible gun, a way that is better than others?

Ed: No, but if you are an up and coming collector, you need to find somebody that you can trust and then buy through him for a while and let him help you work your way up the ladder. That way, when you are ready to get out there on your own, you won't get stuck. There are bad guns out there, fakes, guns that have been put together from parts or with new parts or whatnot. So you do have to be careful.

RS: It sounds a lot like stamp collecting, just involving a little more money.

Ed: Yes, I'd say so. Sometimes you reach out there and think you're getting a real good deal and then discover that it wasn't a good deal at all. And you need to be careful of that. I guess that one sour experience can make you cautious, but most of the time the collectors in this field are pretty honest guys who got into it because they love it and making money on it comes round about the fun they have.

RS: Ed, thank you very much for sharing all this with us and I look forward to meeting you at a Colt Collector's Association gathering one of these years.

INTERVIEW NOTES

1. The Colt-Burgess Lever Action Rifle was brought to Colt by gun designer Andrew Burgess and was produced from 1883 to 1885. It was Colt's only attempt to compete with Winchester for the lever action rifle market. It is said that when Winchester started to produce revolving handguns for prospective marketing, Colt dropped the Burgess from its line. The rifle is chambered for .44-40 and has a 25.5 inch barrel with a 15-shot tubular magazine. The Carbine version has a 20.5 inch barrel and a 12 shot magazine. The finish is blued, with a case colored hammer and lever while the stock is walnut with an oil finish. The Colt Hartford address is on the barrel, and "Burgess Patents" is stamped on the bottom of the lever. A total of 3,775 rifles were manufactured: 1,219 with round barrels and 2,556 with octagonal barrels. There were also 2,593 carbines. In "Good" condition with an octagonal or a round barrel, one would expect to pay at least $3,500.

2. With Ron Graham and Kenneth Moore, John Kopec authored "A Study of the Colt Single Action Army Revolver" and printed it privately in 1976. Although it is no longer in print, copies still come available from time to time from Colt enthusiasts and this handbook has itself become collectible.

GUN RATING SYSTEMS

Accurately describing a gun's condition is critical when one evaluates a firearm, because from that evaluation, one will estimate the gun's value. Differences in condition can easily cut the value of a collectible gun in half, or double it. Terms used to evaluate firearms condition have specific meanings.

In the opinion of the editor, all grading systems are subjective. It is my task to offer the collector and dealer a measurement that most closely reflects a general consensus on condition. The system used here seems to come closest to describing a firearm in universal terms. I strongly recommend that the reader acquaint himself with this grading system before attempting to determine the correct price for a particular firearm's condition. Remember, in most cases condition determines price.

NIB—NEW IN BOX

This category can sometimes be misleading. It means that the firearm is in its original factory carton with all of the appropriate papers. It also means the firearm is new; that it has not been fired and has no wear. This classification brings a substantial premium for both the collector and shooter.

EXCELLENT

Collector quality firearms in this condition are highly desirable. The firearm must be in at least 98 percent condition with respect to blue wear, stock or grip finish, and bore. The firearm must also be in 100 percent original factory condition without refinishing, repair, alterations or additions of any kind. Sights must be factory original as well. This grading classification includes both modern and antique (manufactured prior to 1898) firearms.

VERY GOOD

Firearms in this category are also sought after both by the collector and shooter. Modern firearms must be in working order and retain approximately 92 percent original metal and wood finish. It must be 100 percent factory original, but may have some small repairs, alterations, or non-factory additions. No refinishing is permitted in this category. Antique firearms must have 80 percent original finish with no repairs.

GOOD

Modern firearms in this category may not be considered to be as collectable as the previous grades, but antique firearms are considered desirable. Modern firearms must retain at least 80 percent metal and wood finish, but may display evidence of old refinishing.

Small repairs, alterations, or non-factory additions are sometimes encountered in this class. Factory replacement parts are permitted. The overall working condition of the firearm must be good as well as safe. The bore may exhibit wear or some corrosion, especially in antique arms. Antique firearms may be included in this category if their metal and wood finish is at least 50 percent original factory finish.

FAIR

Firearms in this category should be in satisfactory working order and safe to shoot. The overall metal and wood finish on the modern firearm must be at least 30 percent and antique firearms must have at least some original finish or old re-finish remaining. Repairs, alterations, nonfactory additions, and recent refinishing would all place a firearm in this classification. However, the modern firearm must be in working condition, while the antique firearm may not function. In either case the firearm must be considered safe to fire if in a working state.

POOR

Neither collectors nor shooters are likely to exhibit much interest in firearms in this condition. Modern firearms are likely to retain little metal or wood finish. Pitting and rust will be seen in firearms in this category. Modern firearms may not be in working order and may not be safe to shoot. Repairs and refinishing would be necessary to restore the firearm to safe working order. Antique firearms will have no finish and will not function. In the case of modern firearms their principal value lies in spare parts. On the other hand, antique firearms in this condition may be used as "wall hangers" or as an example of an extremely rare variation or have some kind of historical significance.

PRICING SAMPLE FORMAT

NIB	EXC.	V.G.	GOOD	FAIR	POOR
550	450	400	350	300	200

THE COLT ARCHIVE LETTER

Courtesy of Colt's Manufacturing Company LLC: Considered one of the most unique and prestigious services offered by Colt, the Archive Letter is universally recognized as an unparalleled investment in Colt firearms collecting. The Archive Department will search through Colt's vast archives to provide you with accurate and documented details confirming the original specifications and delivery of your particular Colt firearm. You will then receive a personal letter outlining all the fine points of your firearm, written on Archive Department's distinctive stationery, embossed with the official seal and signature of the Colt Historian.

Whether your Colt is a treasured family heirloom or a more recent purchase, a Colt Archive Letter can provide fascinating and valuable information of historical or anecdotal importance. When it is authenticated in this exceptional fashion, the value and collectability of the weapon referred to in a Colt Archive Letter is significantly enhanced.

Colt Archive Letters can finally provide descriptive details about custom engraving and other special features that will ensure the value of the firearm for future generations to treasure.

COLT ARCHIVE SERVICES PRICE LIST (WWW.COLTSMFG.COM/CMCI/HISTORICAL.ASP)

Prices and specifications are current as of April of 2006 and are subject to change without notice.

PERCUSSION MODELS

- $300.00 - 1851 Navy (98,000 to 132,000), 1861 Navy (1 to 12,000) and 1860 Army Revolvers (1 to 140,000). Records are only available on these models within the specified serial number ranges as noted above.
- $200.00 – Some 1849 Pocket Revolvers are available – call prior to ordering (see Premium Pricing for additional charges)

MODEL 1871 TO 1872 OPEN TOP REVOLVER

- $200.00 (see Premium Pricing for additional charges)

SINGLE ACTION ARMY .44 RIMFIRE

- $200.00 (see Premium Pricing for additional charges)

REVOLVERS

* $75.00 – Agent, Army Special, Anaconda, Banker's Special, Border Patrol (c. 1970), Cobra, Commando, Courier, Cowboy, Deringer (4th Model), Lord & Lady Deringer, Detective Special, DS II, Diamondback, Frontier Scout, King Cobra, Marshal, New Frontier .22, Officer's Model, Officer's Model Match, Official Police, Pequano, Pocket Positive, Police Positive, Police Positive Special, Python, Peacemaker .22, Three-fifty-seven Magnum, Trooper, Reproduction Black Powder models (see Premium Pricing for additional charges)
* $100.00 – Aircrewman, Bisley, Border Patrol (c. 1952), Camp Perry, Marine Corps Model, 1889 Navy, New Army, New Line, New Navy, New Pocket, New Police, New Service, New House, New Frontier SAA, Open Top Pocket, Shooting Master, Single Action Army, 1877 Double Action, 1878 Double Action (see Premium Pricing for additional charges)

PISTOLS

* $75.00 – Ace, 38AMU Kit, Challenger, .45-22 Conversion Units, Colt .22 Auto, Government Model .380s, Huntsman, Jr. Colt, Match Target, Mustang .380s, 1903 Pocket Hammer (.38), 1903 Pocket Hammerless (.32), Pony .380 Series 90, Targetsman, Woodsman (see Premium Pricing for additional charges)
* $100.00 – All American, .38 AMU Automatic Pistol, .22-45 Conversion Units, Combat Elite, Commander models, Delta Elites, Double Eagles, Gold Cup, Government Model, National Match, Officer's ACP, .38 Super & Super Match, .38 Special Kit, 1900 Automatic, CZ-40, 1902 Military & Sporting, 1905 Automatic, 1911 & 1911A1 Automatics, M1991A1 Automatics

RIFLES

* $75.00 – Colteer, Courier, Coltsman Bolt Action, Stagecoach
* $100.00 – AR-15 Sporter, Burgess Model, Sharps Rifle (limited records), Lightning Rifles (limited records), Sauer (see Premium Pricing for additional charges)

SHOTGUNS

* $100.00 – 1878 Hammer, 1883 Hammerless (see Premium Pricing for additional charges)

SPECIAL EDITIONS

* $100.00 (see Premium Pricing for additional charges)

COMMEMORATIVES

* $100.00 (see Premium Pricing for additional charges)

NOTES

About Premium Pricing: This pricing is added to the base price of the letter when the following special features are noted:

* Standard engraving – $100.00
* Expert engraving – $125.00
* Master engraving, no gold inlays – $150.00
* Gold inlays with scroll engraving quoted individually
* Unique shipping destination – cost as follows:
  * Company Executives – add $50.00
  * Buffalo Bill, Bat Masterson, etc. – add $200.00
  * Colt family members – add $100.00
  * Retype Service: A previously prepared Colt historical letter can be submitted for verification and reissued in the current owner's name – $35.00
  * Retypes for custom engraved firearms – $50.00

ARCHIVE PHONE SERVICE

This premium service enables our customers to obtain all the pertinent information on 1st Generation Single Actions up to the 343,000 serial number range over the phone. This does not include the Bisley Model. A historical document containing the information will follow within two to three weeks. A MasterCard, Visa, American Express or Discover Card is required as a method of payment for this service. This expedited service is also offered on the 2nd Generation Single Actions. However, we require one day to process these requests.

- 1st Generation Single Action Army Phone Service: $150.00 – up to serial range of 343,000 (see Premium Pricing for additional charges)
- Expedited Phone Service – applies to all other models – Standard letter fee plus additional $100.00: Requires three days to process (see Premium Pricing for additional charges)
- Dates of Manufacture – $25.00
- Identification Service – $50.00: This service provides novice collectors and customers with identification and general information on a specific firearm
- Memorabilia Identification Service - $25.00: This provides novice collectors and customers with identification and general information and approximate value on a specific Colt memorabilia item

DISCOUNTS

A 10% discount will be given to all members of the Colt Collector's Association. (This discount may not be combined with quantity discounts.)

QUANTITY DISCOUNTS:

- Requests for 5-10 historical documents qualify for a 10% discount
- Requests for 11-20 historical documents qualify for a 15% discount
- Requests for more than 20 historical documents qualify for a 20% discount

REFUND POLICY

If we have records available and can attempt the research, but do not locate the firearm in question, a research fee will apply as follows:

- $75 & $100 requests will be charged a $50.00 research fee
- $200 requests will be charged a $100.00 research fee
- $300 requests will be charged a $100.00 research fee

No fee will be charged for Single Actions serialized under 343,000 (which include the Phone Service) that are non-record guns. Please make check or money order payable to Colt Archive Properties. MasterCard, Visa, American Express and Discover Card are accepted for all services

GUN COLLECTION MANAGEMENT PROGRAMS

BY JOHN CARADIMAS, EXCERPTED FROM WWW.M1911.ORG

Once you begin collecting, you may find that index cards with handwritten notes serve just as well to keep track as anything. As your collecting expands, however, as you meet additional collectors and consider tracking purchases and sales prices, the index cards may become more confusing than helpful. At that point, you may want to turn to a specialized computer program.

Several programs have been developed especially for gun collecting: NM Gun Collector, Gun Inventory, GunTracker, GunSafe and KollectAll, among others. [Editor's Note: These and other collection management programs can be located for download or purchase through any web search site such as Google or Dogpile.]

KOLLECTALL

This is a generic "Collection Management Software." It allows you to organize anything that you may be collecting, from books to stamps to guns, with everything in between. The program comes with some predefined "collections," including guns.

Unfortunately, by trying to be all things to all collections and collectors, this program lacks several features of the more specialized programs. This generic philosophy shows up with the lack of dedicated help fields, fields that have predefined values from which to select. Also, the data entry form is organized in a strange way, where the various gun-related fields, which should be grouped together, are spread all over the form, in no rational order, at least for a gun owner. Being the "Jack of all trades" is not always the best approach.

On the other hand, KollectAll allows you to summarize the value of your collection, and to add images of any gun stored in its file. Unfortunately, the images are only loosely connected to the related item, which only shows you the image of that particular item after you have clicked the "Images" tab. From then on, however, you can browse all the images you have stored in the program's files. Finally, the program can show you a list of all your guns.

GUN SAFE

Gun Safe is a dedicated gun collection organizer program, made by Kevin Kelly. Kelly is a shooter and a collector, and he has used his experience to good effect when developing this program.

From the program's main menu, you can select your next step. The data entry screen is very well organized with drop-down menus helping you fill in the various fields. There is a huge manufacturer's list, a list of all possible calibers, a configuration list (single action, double action, pump, semi-auto, etc.), a type list (pistol, revolver, rifle, shotgun, machine-gun, etc.), a stock/grips list (with various stock or grips to select from), a finish list (blue, stainless, Parkerized, etc.) and more.

What's significant is that all these lists are customizable, so you can alter them to suit your needs. For example, if one is collecting only 1911 pistols, you can edit the manufacturers list, to include only 1911 manufacturers. You can edit the caliber list to include only those calibers that a 1911 is available in, and so on. I liked that feature. Such lists exist also in the other data entry screens. In the same screen the user can fill in other useful details, such as manufacturing date, purchasing date, condition, if he has the original box or not, if the item is a C&R or not, where the gun is stored, what accessories he has for that particular firearm and more.

Gun Safe has separate forms for entering purchasing and sale information. There is a list of "Transaction Kinds," from which you can select how the gun was acquired (gun shop, on-line shop, auction, etc) and enter details about the seller. Likewise, there is a separate form for the sale of the gun while another allows you to maintain detailed records of when that particular firearm was maintained and what was done to it at that time. Still another form allows you to enter notes for that particular firearm, very useful for keeping important information, such as favorite loads.

The program has a final data entry screen in which you can enter pictures of that firearm. An unlimited number of pictures can be entered, which however are not directly associated with that particular gun. Even though the program will show you the picture associated with that gun first, it will also continue and show you all other pictures entered in its database, something not very intuitive. You can also, of course, ask to see a complete list of your collection.

Apart from a few minor idiosyncrasies, the program is very nice and should cover the needs of the average gun owner. What serious collectors will miss is the ability to see the total value of your collection, something Gun Safe does not offer.

GUNTRACKER 2.4

This program will appeal to the serious gun collector. Included is a database with almost every possible firearm manufacturer (something tells me that the maker of this program is licensing the Blue Book of Values database). For each manufacturer, the program includes an incredible number of predefined models (every model that this particular manufacturer has ever produced). There are so many manufacturers and models and model variations that it is easy to become frustrated with the details.

The program does not force you to select from its internal database, by browsing through the models produced by a specific manufacturer. You can use the Search function to narrow your selection. And you can enter a firearm record without using the built-in database; so the user can select his method of data entry.

The data entry form has all the fields that a gun owner or a collector will need. In addition to the usual fields of maker, model, serial number, etc. the program allows you to enter the current value of the firearm as well as the price paid for it. It also allows scheduling the next maintenance session, to enter an insured value, storage location and a personal rating. This program allows you to associate pictures with each firearm, and the images for each firearm are associated to that particular firearm alone (a nice touch). It also allows you to enter notes about the gun.

From the data entered, the user can get a variety of reports, such as a Full Collection Report, or a Scheduled Maintenance Report or a report of firearms per storage location. A "Wanted" report shows which firearms you have defined as desirable. Finally, a customized report option is available, but I didn't have the time to try this out.

Overall, this is a program for the serious gun collector, a bit too difficult to use for the average Joe who owns some firearms and wants to have an electronic reference for them.

NM GUNCOLLECTOR

Once you start the program, its title changes to NM Firearms. It comes with a full installation procedure and it is quite intuitive to use. There are some tabs on the top, from where you select what you want to see, and a few buttons, like "Add Item," "Delete Item," etc.

On a data screen, wherever you see a down-arrow next to a field, there is a hidden list of options you can use. For example, if you click on the arrow next to "Manufacturer," a list of manufacturers will appear, from which you can select the one who made your firearm. Manufacturers, types and calibers are already predefined, but you may want to alter the lists to suit your needs. For example, I personally would edit the manufacturer list and leave in only the ones who produce M1911 pistols.

The Receipt tab allows you to enter information related to the seller of that firearm, while Disposition is the area where you enter information about whom you sold it to. In these screens you can enter the amount of money you paid for the gun and the amount of money you got when you sold it.

A separate tab allows you to enter pictures of the selected firearm, an unlimited number of pictures can be entered and the program includes a nice feature to show you those pictures in thumbnail form. There is a "Statistics" tab where you can see a list of your whole collection, together with the total values etc. Finally, there is a "Lists Edit" tab, from which you can alter the predefined lists that appear in certain fields in the data entry screen.

One unique feature of this program is the fact that it incorporates a bar code feature, which allows you to print bar code labels for your firearms. The program also allows you to maintain firearm records as if you were an FFL dealer or a C&R collector, and it will generate the BATFE required lists for you, warning you several days before your license expires etc.

Using this program, one appreciates its simplicity and also its flexibility and power. What I liked is how easy it is to enter the information for each firearm you own, and how easy it is to change the predefined lists of values. An M1911 collector can easily erase all the other calibers, for example, except the ones related to the 1911.

Overall, for the average shooter, this is a very nice program to manage his collection.

FIREARMS
ENGRAVING & GUN VALUES

BY JIM SUPICA, OLD TOWN STATION, LTD., COLLECTIBLE FIREARMS (WWW.ARMCHAIRGUNSHOW.COM)

(ORIGINALLY PUBLISHED IN NRA'S INSIGHTS MAGAZINE)

What in the world could make a gun worth more than a new car? Or worth more than a new house, for that matter? In most cases, when a gun is hammered "sold" for five or six figures at one of the high-end auction houses, part of the answer is "engraving." But if that is the case, how come that engraved commemorative you saw at the last gun show was offered for less than a standard model? To explain this situation, let's take a look at the history of firearms engraving, and the market for old and new engraved guns today.

THE ORIGIN OF ENGRAVING

The origin of decorated arms is lost in the mists of pre-history. The role of man's earliest weapons in providing food and ensuring his survival made them some of the earliest and most important tools. The impulse to decorate and personalize them must have accounted for some of humankind's first artistic endeavors.

As societies and their technology evolved, the bond between art and arms logically continued. Whether for a king or a tribal chieftain, weaponry represented the means to acquiring and holding political power, and the enhancement of these to suit the status of the owner was a given. What are a scepter and crown, if not vestigial arm and armor?

Whatever the origins, by the time the first firearms were developed, the tradition of decorating arms (and armor) had long been established. The earliest matchlocks were more or less standard military issue tools (used by commoners), and hence not often decorated. However as wheellocks and then flintlocks evolved, some of the finest artistic efforts of the Post-Medieval Epoch, the 16th, 17th and 18th centuries, were applied to them.

A strong firearms engraving tradition grew in Europe, with separate and identifiable German, French and British styles evolving. The French engraved arms of the Louis XIII and XIV era (roughly 1610 to 1715) are justly famous as masterpieces.

Before the industrial revolution and efficient mass production utilizing interchangeable parts, each gun was hand crafted individually. During this flintlock and early percussion era, the vast majority of firearms included some sort of decoration. Usually this took the form of engraving designs, patterns or images directly on the metal of the lock, barrel and hardware, along with carving and possibly inlaying the wood of the stock. Only military issue weapons of the era tended to lack this type of embellishment, and even these can often be found with an individuals initials carved into the stock or scratched into the metal, probably during a long night's encampment.

In America of the 1800s, the production of firearms represented the cutting edge of evolving technology and art. As Eli Whitney introduced mass production techniques, Whitney firearms were among the first products so made.

When Samuel Colt introduced the first perfected repeating firearms, his percussion revolvers, he also continued the tradition of decorated arms by rolling various scenes onto the cylinders, including a dragoon battle, a naval engagement and a stagecoach holdup on various models. In addition to these standard mass produced scenes, Colt also offered individually engraved pieces, either custom ordered or made by Colt for presentation to prominent individuals to promote the firm's wares.

THE GOLDEN AGE OF ENGRAVING

The second half of the 19th century, from just before the Civil War to the turn of the century is considered the "Golden Age" of firearms engraving. During this period, nearly all of the major gun manufacturers offered fancy engraved firearms for their well-heeled or more discerning customers, with Colt, Winchester and Smith & Wesson particularly utilizing the services of the master engravers of the era.

This is the period when a distinctly American style of engraving came into its own. It evolved from the Germanic vine scroll style brought to this country by the great masters of the era: Louis D. Nimschke, Gustave Young (Jung) and Conrad Ulrich. The style incorporated larger, more flowing scrollwork, and came to be most associated with Nimschke. Today, it is often called "Nimschke style" or perhaps "New York style" engraving. The next generation of great engravers included the sons of Young, the sons and grandsons of Ulrich, and Cuno Helfricht, along with many other master engravers.

Some of the driving forces behind this artistic explosion were the practice of giving "presentation" arms to influential friends, and the great national and international expositions of the era. During and after the Civil War, it was customary to express appreciation to civic or military leaders, or to a valued business associate or loved family member, by giving a specially engraved firearm. Sometimes this involved a simple inscription of the recipient's and possibly the giver's names, but it sometimes included extensive decoration. The great expositions were "fairs" where manufacturers would display their best products, and the arms makers vied with each other to produce the most strikingly eye-catching artworks.

ENGRAVING IN RECENT HISTORY & TODAY

Firearms engraving declined during the first half of the 20th century, although it was kept alive by such great engravers as R.J. Kornbrath. However, the years following World War II saw a resurgence of the interest in engraving, both contemporary work and collectible classic firearms art.

In the 1960s and '70s, there was a trend of mass-produced decorated firearms, probably most notably the many "commemoratives" marketed by Colt and Winchester. Rather than individual hand-crafted pieces, thousands of identically decorated guns would be sold commemorating an individual, event, or even a general "concept," such as "Antlered Game." During this period, organizations such as Ducks Unlimited or various law enforcement agencies would also commission special limited runs of mass produced decorated firearms.

The 1980s and '90s saw a resurgence of truly exceptional engraving. The custom departments at Smith & Wesson and Colt, along with several gifted private engravers in America and Europe (Perazzi shotguns, for example, from Botticino, Italy) are currently producing working firearms that rival and in some cases surpass the "Golden Age" masterpieces.

Given this rich history, and the undeniable timeless appeal of decorated arms, how does one establish a value for an engraved gun? Let's take a look at some of the choices.

COMMEMORATIVE ISSUES

These guns tend to be valued for their scarcity as collectibles or for their general eye appeal. If individual hand engraved guns are considered and evaluated as unique works of art, these mass produced pieces are perhaps more similar to limited edition prints of artwork or other items intentionally made to be collectibles, such as limited edition Christmas ornaments. The various price guides such as *Blue Book of Gun Values or Standard Catalog of Firearms* provide a good indication of the retail price of these arms. Generally speaking, the fewer produced, the older the commemorative, and the more attractive the decoration, the greater the value.

To command close to full "book" value, a commemorative type arm *must* be in NIB or "new in the box" condition, definitely unfired and preferably without the action having ever been worked! (Due to manufacturing tolerances, such actions as rotating the cylinder of a revolver or working the lever of a rifle can create minute scratches in the finish that will reduce the desirability of a collectible commemorative). Once a commemorative has been fired, its value begins to rapidly decline towards that of a standard non-decorated example of the same model. A commemorative that shows extensive wear will often bring much less than a plain model with similar wear.

Although the interest in commemoratives declined in the 1970s and 1980s, probably due to over-production, today's market shows some signs of renewed interest.

INSCRIBED PIECES

A gun which has no decoration other than an individual's name or other inscription may bring more or less than a similar gun without any special marking. There are two factors that determine the value, historical significance and authenticity.

Of these factors, authenticity of the inscription will make or break the piece. Unfortunately, out and out fraudulent inscribed guns are not that uncommon. Often, the documentation accompanying the piece and providing some "provenance" of the authenticity of the inscription will be a deciding factor.

Once determined to be authentic, the premium that an inscribed piece brings will be determined by its historical significance. As can be imagined, a modern gun that just has "someone else's name" on it will generally be less desirable for a shooter than a plain gun, and may be worth less because of the inscription. On the other hand, authentically inscribed guns which can be proven to have been owned by a famous (or infamous) individual can bring astronomical prices for the history they embody.

Any authentic inscription that is more than 100 years old will generally add some interest and value to a gun.

MODERN ENGRAVED GUNS

Engraved firearms have to be evaluated as individual works of art. Some of the factors that must be considered include skill of workmanship, extent of coverage, artistic appeal and uniqueness. Factory engraving will bring a premium over engraving of unknown origin. Sparse coverage brings less than full coverage.

For example, Smith & Wesson offers three standard levels of engraving. Their "C" is 1/3 coverage, with recent pricing ranging in the $800 to $1,250 range, depending on the size of the gun (this is the engraving charge, and does not include the base price of the gun). The S&W "B" engraving is 2/3 coverage and runs in the $1,300 to $1,500 range, while full or "A" coverage engraving costs around $1,400 to $1,900.

Colt's custom engraving runs the opposite direction. Colt's "A" engraving is the least coverage, and the scale runs up to "D" grade full coverage. Colt also offers varying qualities of engraving: Standard, Expert and Master. According to the *Blue Book of Gun Values* recent pricing for Colt's top of the line Master grade engraving, signed by the master engraver, on a Colt Single Action Army was $1,163 for A; $2,324 for B; $3,487 for C; and $4,647 for D.

These values are for standard scrollwork patterns. Special jobs requiring artistic talent in the development of a unique design can run considerably more.

A major determining factor on non-factory engraved guns is the reputation and skill of the engraver. As with other artists, the acknowledged masters of the form will bring substantial premiums over unknown engravers. When dealing with an unknown engraver, the quality of the work will determine its final value. The finest engraving is always done with hand tools, chisel and hammer. Crudely done engraving can actually lessen the value of a firearm.

ANTIQUE ENGRAVING

Older engraving is valued in a similar way to modern engraving: the artistic quality, extent of coverage and reputation of the engraver are of greatest importance. However, most 19th century engraving was not signed by the engraver, and attribution to a particular hand is much more art than science, and that art has been mastered by only a few students after many years of study.

Fortunately, factory records for firms such as Winchester, Colt and Smith & Wesson are intact and originality of engraving on a particular serial numbered gun can often be determined by a search of the records. On the other hand, much 19th century engraving was ordered by the distributors, such as giant M.W. Robinson, rather than the manufacturers. Sometimes, a factory notation that a gun was shipped to a distributor "soft" or "in the white" indicates that the gun was intended to be engraved. Some of the finest engraved guns were commissioned by distributors or even by individual owners. When considering paying a premium for old engraving, it's a very good idea to get an expert opinion on the authenticity and quality.

Ultimately, gun value and engraving come down to individual taste. Most shooters and firearms enthusiasts find that sooner or later they get the hankering for a "fancy" gun. Even individuals who may not be interested in guns can appreciate the artistry of a beautifully engraved firearm.

FOR ADDITIONAL INFORMATION

The recently published book *Steel Canvas* by R. L. Wilson features a fascinating and authoritative discussion of arms engraving along with beautiful photographs of some of the finest firearms ever made. Earlier works by the same author include Winchester Engraving, Colt Engraving, and Nimschke's pattern book published as L.D. Nimschke, Firearms Engraver. Firearms Engraving as Decorative Art by Frederic Harris provides an interesting discussion of the origins of engraving motif's in oriental art along with a theory about identifying individual engravers by a detailed study of their cutting style.

COLT COLLECTOR'S ASSOCIATION, INC. 2006 "SHOW GUN"

As an example of the quality of engraving on specialty Colt firearms available to and desired by avid collectors, the Colt Collector's Association, Inc. offered the following revolver as the "Show Gun" during its annual three day show in Louisville, Kentucky in October, 2006. This gun is the highest example of gun engraving and decoration today and the gun is so designed for display only. It will never be fired and the action will, in all likelihood, never be worked and this will prevent any scarring of the internal mechanisms.

The following description was prepared for the CCA Internet site by 2006 CCA Louisville Show Gun Project Manager Earl L. Whitney and can be found through the CCA Internet site at www.coltcollectorsassoc.com/index.htm. The Show Gun Committee was composed of Project Manager Earl L. Whitney, Project Manager; David Grunberg, Technical Advisor; Michael W. Dubber, Artistic Engraver Coordinator; Joe Canali, Firearm Coordinator; and Dr. Tom Covault, Firearm Coordinator.

THE SHOW GUN

The 2006 CCA Louisville Show Gun was designed after the .22 RF Flattop Target Model of the 1888 to 1895 period. Less than 925 Flattop Target Models were built by Colt during that period and less than 92 in the .22 RF caliber. According to historical research this is the only Colt Flattop Target Model made with an 8.5 inch barrel.

- Colt Single Action Army
- Flattop Target Model
- .22 RF caliber
- 8.5 inch barrel
- Deluxe Exhibition Grade engraving by Michael W. Dubber
- Colt oxide black finish
- Carved ivory one piece grips: The left side has a thoroughbred racing horse with the Kentucky Derby winner's garland of roses. The right side shows the profiles of Kentucky native sons Daniel Boone and James Bowie.
- Serial number #CCA2006 engraved on a 24k gold inlaid plate.
- Signed under barrel "M. W. Dubber Engr." this firearm is also signed on the back of the cylinder. All gun parts are marked with MWD.
- Museum Exhibition Grade case: Mission style finish English oak roll top desk with one drawer, full top beveled glass viewing area and French fit red velvet cloth.
- Master engraved Exhibition Grade argentium silver die cut description plate for the display case having the Kentucky theme.
- Six custom made .22 RF blank gold plated cartridges by Michael W. Dubber.
- Engraver's leather journal showing construction of the CCA Show Gun with photos, compact disk, master plates showing patterns, drawings, prototype laser art on ivory pieces and other items used in the production of this firearm.
- Five piece accessory set, ivory handles with lased art "Serpentine Colt" logo, oxide black and gold plate finish, 24k gold inlaid and scroll engraved oil bottle. The ferrules on the accessories are scroll engraved and gold plated.
- A three quarter scale ivory handle Bowie Knife with oxide black raindrop Damascus blade, 24k raised inlay feather pattern design on the guard and the bolster.
- Lased art ivory handles showing Serpentine "COLT" on the right panel and "CCA—LOUISVILLE—2006" banner on the left panel.
- Ivory plaque carving of the Colt factory dome

ENGRAVING DESCRIPTION

The 2006 Louisville Show Gun is a "Colt Single Action Army Flattop Target Model" with serial number #CCA2006. The gun is Exhibition Grade embellished by Colt Master Engraver Michael W. Dubber with 100 percent coverage in American style scroll engraving: 24k gold lines and vignettes, 24k gold and pure platinum raised and flush inlays with period Kentucky state and historical themes.

- Custom Exhibition Grade engraved in the American Scroll pattern
- 24k gold Kentucky state map on the flattop panel. Raised inlay with single

star for the state capital at Frankfort.

- 24k gold fifteen stars flush inlaid on flattop represent Kentucky becoming the 15th state in the Union in 1792.
- 24k gold "CCA LOUISVILLE 2006" banner raised inlay on left side of barrel
- 24k gold "CCA2006" serial number engraved on a flush gold inlaid plate
- 24k gold and platinum "MY OLD KENTUCKY HOME" (the Kentucky state song) with an artistic musical scale and images flush inlaid in gold and platinum on the right side of the barrel.
- 24k gold "The Blue Grass State" in 24k gold flush letters on back strap
- 24k gold Fort Knox in raised image with flush inlaid 24k gold letters "Ft. Knox" on back strap
- 24k gold and platinum northern cardinal, the Kentucky state bird, is inlaid in 24k raised gold with platinum branch on the trigger guard
- 24k gold trigger guard inlaid in flush 24k gold borders and vignettes
- 24k gold ejector housing with highly decorative filigree vignette ejector rod operating piece is lightly engraved in a geometric pattern
- 24k gold back strap and butt strap outlined in decorative flush borders and tracery
- 24k gold front sight fitted with a solid gold adjustable insert, front site is flush engraved and inlaid in gold vignette
- 24k gold rear sight is inlaid with 24k gold aiming notch
- 24k gold horseshoe in raised 24k gold inlay on the muzzle end of the barrel
- 24k gold Colt patent address flush letters with gold border and tracery
- 24k gold .22 RF in flush gold inlay gold banner
- 24k muzzle end flush inlaid wide and narrow bands with gold and platinum tracery flowing forward
- 24k gold bands, one wide and one narrow, flush inlaid on the receiver end barrel
- 24k gold frame trimmed in flush gold borders and vignettes. Vignettes have raised 24k gold dots on the ends.
- 24k gold hammer, gold sides and top are flush inlaid in decorative gold borders and vignettes
- 24k gold Kentucky Derby rose, the official flower of the Kentucky Derby, raised inlay on right side of frame in front of the cylinder

- 24k gold and platinum Churchill Downs spire, raised inlaid on left side of the frame in front of the cylinder, the official trademark of Churchill Downs, home of the Kentucky Derby, the first race each year of horse racing's "Triple Crown" circuit.
- 24k gold Rampant Colt trademark on frame raised gold inlay and flush 24k patent dates
- 24k gold Kentucky thoroughbred horse, the Kentucky state horse, raised inlay on recoil shield finished in Italian Bulino style detail
- 24k gold and platinum Bowie Knife on right side of frame 24k handle raised inlay and Bowie blade pure platinum raised inlay
- 24k gold and platinum Kentucky gray squirrel, raised inlay of pure platinum finished in fine line detail with 24k gold raised acorns on loading gate
- 24k gold two raised acorns with engraved oak leaf in recoil shield recess
- Six gold plated custom made .22 RF cartridges
- Trigger: front has been finished with hand cut checkering
- Cylinder is flush inlaid in one wide and one narrow gold line
- Cylinder rear line is flush engraved in "feather pattern" design
- Cylinder flutes are outlined in flush 24k gold line
- Cylinder flutes are flush scroll engraved at the front
- Cylinder front engraved in scroll pattern
- Cylinder pin is inlaid with a raised gold dot with star pattern engraving on end
- Turned boss is engraved in rope pattern
- Qualified screws
- The following screws are engraved:
    o Three mainframe screws
    o Butt screw
    o Front trigger guard screw
    o Ejector rod housing screw

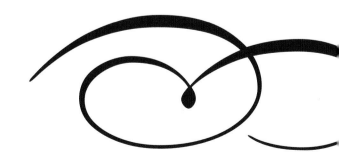

COLT'S PERCUSSION REVOLVERS

THE PATERSON REVOLVERS

*S*am Colt accomplished amazing things in his life. Born in 1814, he spent a year at sea and then, at what we today would consider the tender age of 18, began touring the United States and Canada as a showman. He adopted the stage identity "Dr. Coult of Calcutta" and entertained crowds with laughing gas.

The gas was a means to an end, however, as his act raised funds to hire gunsmiths in Albany, Baltimore and Hartford. These gunsmiths eventually produced a plethora of firearm designs. This, too, was a wondrous accomplishment considering the relative complexity of the revolvers and the relatively primitive state of the machinery of mass production.

In 1835, Colt traveled to Europe where he obtained patents in England and France – the countries, it was generally believed, most likely to pirate his ideas if he first patented in the United States. (In those days it took weeks, not hours, to visit those countries in person.) His first U.S. patent was granted on February 25, 1836, and the next month, he chartered the Patent Arms Manufacturing Company in Paterson, New Jersey, with sales offices and showroom in New York City.

The Paterson-based Patent Arms Manufacturing Company lasted six years. Problems with mechanical reliability caused by immature designs and dirty powder often caused the guns to fail when tested. Although Colt repeaters, both handguns and rifles, did prove themselves in the Indian Wars in Florida and Texas, they did not win government approval or patronage, and the Patent Arms Manufacturing Company ceased operations in 1842.

PROTOTYPES

Sam Colt commissioned a number of prototypes from gunsmiths in Albany, Baltimore (John Pearson), and Hartford between 1832 and 1836: nine rifles, one shotgun and 16 pistols. The value of these prototypes on the open market would be extremely high – perhaps in the hundreds of thousands of dollars – and cannot be hypothetically evaluated.

The muzzleloading revolving rifles operated by pulling a large lever, which turned the cylinder and cocked the internal hammer. They fired, of course, when the trigger was pulled. Anson Chase and W.H. Rowe of Hartford built the 1832 takedown model. The barrel assembly unscrewed by hand from the frame.

The cylinders of prototype rifles were enclosed, both front and rear, by flash plates. Upon firing, the plate could – and sometimes did – deflect flame from burning powder downward to set off other loads. These "flash plates" were deleted from production models. The inlaid stocks are checkered. The guns lacked forearms; if the off hand supported the gun in traditional style – i.e., directly below the barrel – it would almost certainly be burned by expanding gas.

John Pearson built a number of Colt prototypes in 1835. The size of these prototypes ranged from 4 lb., 4 oz. for the hefty .53-caliber martial pistol, with its barrel machined and bored from rifle stock, to diminutive .33-caliber pocket pistols. Some of these pistols included integral bayonets, which allowed the user to defend himself with the pistol when it was empty. Barrel assemblies were later stamped "S. COLTS PATENT FEBR. 25 1836." Trigger assemblies were built either to drop down upon cocking the hammers or fold down manually.

THE ANSON CHASE EXPERIMENTAL

This gun is probably one of the very first of the Colt prototypes. It already has the general configuration that Colt ultimately built into his 1836 Patent. Of course, it has a trigger guard and regular trigger, showing that Colt thought of these features at a very early date. This gun was probably built from 1831 to 1832. The gun's features include: .50 caliber, a five shot straight round cylinder, a 10.25 inch octagonal barrel, round trigger guard, blade and hammer notch sights and a rounded butt. The overall length of the gun is 14.25 inches. This prototype has been held in the Colt factory collection.

CUTLASS OR KNIFE PISTOL

One of the last of the Paterson experimental pistols, Colt designed a double action Knife Pistol as a combination Bowie knife and repeating pistol. Because of pre-Civil War black powder's unreliability, this pistol could have proved handy in close-quarters combat. The exposed trigger served to cock, revolve the cylinder and fire the gun. The extended, sweeping "knuckle bow" trigger housing protected the hand from sword cuts and served as a loading lever when lowered. These specifications were: six shot, .38 cal. with a six-inch barrel.

EXC.	V.G.	GOOD	FAIR	POOR
–	–	30,000	15,000	-

EXPERIMENTAL DAGGER REVOLVER

This pistol was made between 1832 and 1835, just before Colt took out patents and before the Paterson factory was in operation. The dagger was never included in any of the regular production guns, but it appears in patent drawings. Shields covering the nipples and chamber mouths were also discarded before production guns were built. The gun was 7.25 inches in length with a 3.875-inch octagonal barrel. Built in .32 caliber, the straight round cylinder carried five shots. Because the design was for a folding trigger, there was no trigger guard. Sights were a mid-barrel blade and a hammer notch. The butt was rounded. This prototype has been held in the Colt factory collection.

COLT'S PROMOTION MODEL REVOLVER

This beautifully engraved firearm, now a part of the Colt Memorial Collection in the Wadsworth Athenaeum in Hartford, Connecticut, was built in 1835. Sam Colt was, after all, as much a promoter as he was an inventor and this gun bridged those sides of his personality. It measured 7.25 inches length overall and had a rounded butt. The .40-cal., 3.25-inch barrel was octagonal and the straight round cylinder held five shots. Sights were a small front blade and rear notch at the intersection of the barrel and frame. It had a folding trigger without a trigger guard.

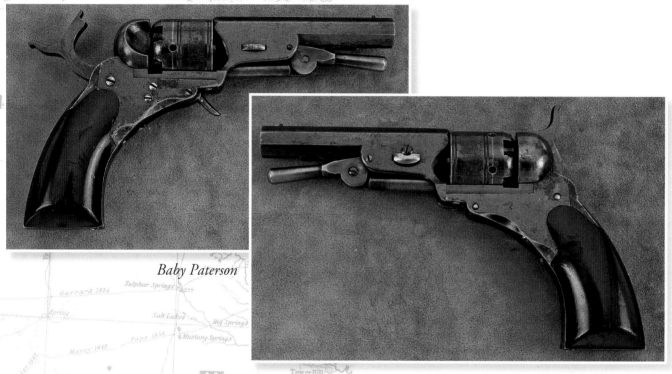

Baby Paterson

PRODUCTION GUNS

MODEL NO. 1 POCKET OR BABY PATERSON

Built beginning in 1837, the Baby Paterson was the first production revolver manufactured by Colt in Paterson. It was intended to serve the carriage trade or military officers who needed a deringer-size, concealable revolver. The single action Model 1 or Pocket Model with folding trigger is the most diminutive in the Paterson line. The standard model has no attached loading lever. Chambering is .28 cal. Percussion; cylinder capacity is five shots. Barrel lengths vary from 1.75 to 4.75 inches. The finish is all-blued, with varnished walnut or fancier grips. It has a roll-engraved centaur motif cylinder scene, and the barrel is stamped "PATENT ARMS MFG. CO. PATERSON N.J. COLT'S PT." Serial numbers are not visible without dismantling, but each is numbered, #1 through #500.

EXC.	V.G.	GOOD	FAIR	POOR
-	-	30,000	12,500	-

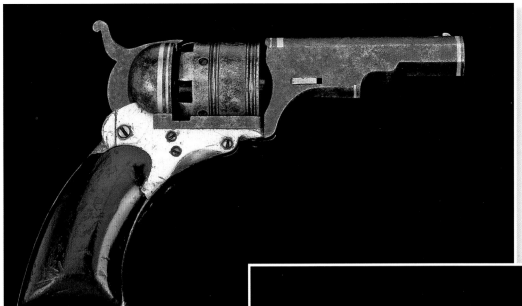

Belt Model Paterson

MODEL NO. 2 BELT PATERSON

Manufactured from 1837 to 1840, the Belt Model Paterson is a larger revolver than the Model 1, with a straight grip and an octagonal barrel that is 2.5 to 5.5 inches in length. Chambered for .31 cal. percussion, the Belt Model holds five shots and has a folding, drop-down trigger. The finish is all-blued, with varnished walnut grips. There is no attached loading lever. It has a roll-engraved centaur motif cylinder scene, and the barrel is stamped "PATENT ARMS MFG. CO. PATERSON N.J. COLT'S PT." Serial numbers, which are shared with the #3 Belt Model, range from #1 to #850.

EXC.	V.G.	GOOD	FAIR	POOR
-	-	50,000	20,000	-

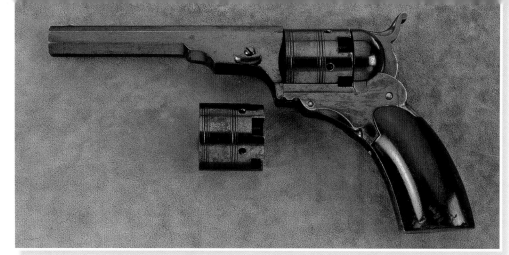

Belt Model Paterson #3.

MODEL NO. 3 BELT PATERSON

revolver is similar to the Model #2 except that grips are curved or flared outward at the bottom to form a more hand-filling configuration. When cocked, the trigger dropped down automatically into firing position. It has a roll engraved centaur motif cylinder scene, and the barrel is stamped "PATENT ARMS MFG." A few guns feature attached loading levers, but these are extremely rare and, when found, add approximately 35 percent to the base value. Cased, matched pairs are extremely rare and consequently, extremely valuable. The .31 cal. Model #3s were also serial numbered in the same #1 to #850 range.

EXC.	V.G.	GOOD	FAIR	POOR
-	-	75,000	30,000	-

MODEL NO. 5 TEXAS PATERSON

Also known as the Holster Model, this is the largest and most sought-after of the Paterson Colts. It saw use by both the military and civilians on the American frontier. Chambered for .36-cal. percussion, the Model 5 holds five shots; it has an octagonal barrel that varies from 4 to 12 inches in length. Rare models have an attached loading lever, which was retro-fitted after 1839. The finish is blued, with a case-colored hammer. Grips are varnished walnut although ivory and mother-of-pearl were popular options. Some models feature optional silver-band decorative inlays. The cylinder is roll engraved and the barrel is stamped "PATENT ARMS MFG. CO. PATERSON, N.J. COLT'S PT." Most Texas Patersons are well used and have a worn appearance. One in Exc. or V.G. condition would be highly prized. A verified military model would be worth a great deal more than a standard model, so qualified appraisal would be essential. An attached loading lever brings approximately a 25 percent premium. Manufactured from 1838 to 1840, the serial number range is #1 to #1000.

EXC.	V.G.	GOOD	FAIR	POOR
-	-	125,000	50,000	-

Texas Paterson

Model #4 Ehler's Pocket Paterson.

MODEL NO. 4 EHLERS POCKET PATERSON

John Ehlers was a major stockholder and treasurer of the Patent Arms Mfg. Co. When it went bankrupt, he seized the company's assets and inventory. These .28 cal. five shot revolvers were Pocket Model Patersons that were not finished at the time. Ehlers had them finished, shortened the frame by 3/16 of an inch and then marketed them himself. Each featured an attached loading lever and the centaur scene on the cylinder. The abbreviation "MFG. CO." was deleted from the barrel stamping. Produced from 1840 to 1843, a total of about 500 revolvers were involved in all of the Ehlers variations

EXC.	V.G.	GOOD	FAIR	POOR
-	-	50,000	20,000	-

MODEL NO. 5 EHLERS BELT PATERSON

This was the second of Ehlers efforts to recoup his losses from the Colt manufacturing bankruptcy and it derived from the No.2 Belt Pistol. The caliber was .31; the frame was shortened by 0.1875 inch and while cylinder lengths vary, cylinders feature the centaur scene. Attached loading levers were standard. The Ehlers Belt Models fall within the same 500 revolver lot and they are quite rare

EXC.	V.G.	GOOD	FAIR	POOR
-	-	50,000	20,000	-

WALKERS AND DRAGOONS

Struggling to refine his designs and begin manufacturing again, Samuel Colt was handed a gift in 1846 in the form of Captain Samuel H. Walker. A veteran of the frontier fighting with Mexico and Native Americans, particularly the fierce and combative Comanche in Texas, Walker attracted a great deal of attention in the national press … and he had become a Colt believer.

According to R.L. Wilson's *Colt: An American Legend*, Captain Walker and the subsequent six-shot percussion revolvers Colt produced were the "key to the mint." Although quite large, these handguns were immediately successful and by 1847, both orders and favorable publicity were flooding Sam Colt's mailbox. It was this gun that allowed Colt to return in triumph to Hartford, the city of his birth, and begin an industrial enterprise that, before his early and untimely death in 1862, became an empire.

Although the Mexican War ended in 1848, Europe and the U.S.A. were beset by troubles that caused demand for Colt's now operationally-correct revolvers to skyrocket: the Crimean War, the California Gold Rush and, as farmers, adventurers and pioneers pushed west, the escalating Indian Wars.

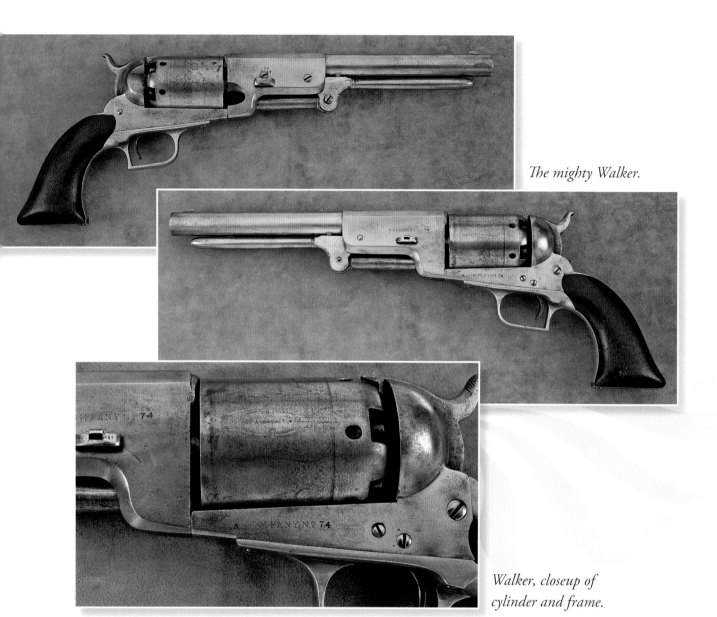

The mighty Walker.

Walker, closeup of cylinder and frame.

WALKER MODEL

This revolver is named for Captain Samuel H. Walker, hero of combat in Texas and Mexico, where he was killed by a lance at the battle of Juamantla. More important, perhaps, Walker worked personally with Sam Colt, to design this new gun – and did not, as far as is known, request that his name be attached to patents or checks for royalties. The Walker is a massive revolver. It weighs 4 lb., 9 oz. and has a nine inch part round, part octagonal barrel. The cylinder holds six shots and is chambered for .44 cal. percussion. One thousand Walker Colts were manufactured in 1847, and nearly all of them saw extremely hard use. Originally this model had a roll engraved cylinder, military inspection marks and barrel stamping that read "ADDRESS SAML. COLT-NEW YORK CITY." Practically all examples

noted have had these markings worn or rusted beyond recognition. Because from a collector's point of view the Walker may be the most desirable and sought after Colt, and because of the extremely high value of a Walker in any condition, qualified appraisal is definitely recommended. These revolvers were serial numbered A-, B-, C- and D-Company #1 to #220, and E-Company #1 to #120.

EXC.	V.G.	GOOD	FAIR	POOR
-	-	300,000	150,000	50,000

CIVILIAN WALKER

This limited edition model is almost identical to the military model, but has no martial markings. Guns carry serial numbers #1001 through #1100.

EXC.	V.G.	GOOD	FAIR	POOR
-	-	300,000	150,000	50,000

Whitneyville-Hartford Dragoon.

WHITNEYVILLE-HARTFORD DRAGOON

This six shot, .44-cal. percussion revolver is often referred to as a Transitional Walker. Although it is still a large gun, using some leftover Walker parts, it is shorter and lighter and handles easier than a Walker. It has a 7.5-inch part-round, part-octagonal barrel and the frame, hammer and loading lever are case colored. The remainder is blued, with a brass trigger guard and varnished walnut grips. Some of the parts used in its manufacture were left over from the earlier Walker production run. The Whitneyville-Hartford has a roll engraved cylinder scene and the barrel is stamped "ADDRESS SAML. COLT NEW YORK CITY." Only 240 were made in late 1847 and serial numbers run from #1100 to #1340. This is an extremely rare model, and much care should be taken to authenticate any contemplated acquisition.

EXC.	V.G.	GOOD	FAIR	POOR
-	-	60,000	35,000	18,500

FIRST MODEL DRAGOON

The First Model is a large, six-shot, .44-cal. percussion revolver that weighs 4 lb. 2 oz. It has a 7.5 inch part round, part octagonal barrel. The frame, hammer and loading lever are case colored; the remainder is blued with a brass grip frame and square backed trigger guard. The trigger guard is silver plated on the Civilian Model. Another distinguishing feature of the First Model is the set of oval cylinder stop notches. The cylinder is roll engraved and early production cylinders were not blued, but left "in the white." The barrel stampings read "ADDRESS SAML. COLT NEW YORK CITY" and "COLT'S

PATENT" appears on the frame. On Military Models the letters "U.S." also appear on the frame. Although the serial number range is from #1341 to #8000, about 7,000 were built from 1848 to 1850.

MILITARY MODEL

EXC.	V.G.	GOOD	FAIR	POOR
-	-	40,000	20,000	3,500

CIVILIAN MODEL

EXC.	V.G.	GOOD	FAIR	POOR
-	-	35,000	18,000	3,000

WALKER REPLACEMENT/FLUCK DRAGOON

This extremely rare Colt (300 produced) is sometimes referred to as the "Fluck" in memory of the man who first identified it as a distinct and separate model. They were produced in about 1848 by Colt as replacements to the military for Walkers that were no longer fit for service due to mechanical failure. These were large, six-shot, .44-cal. percussion revolvers with 7.5-inch part round, part octagonal barrels. The

Walker Replacement/Fluck Dragoon.

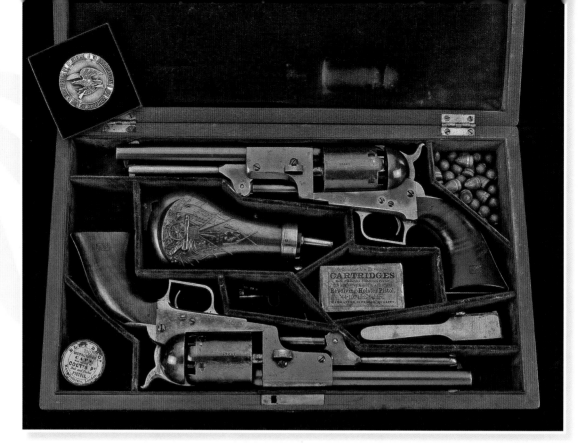

Second Model Dragoon.

frame, hammer and loading lever are case colored; the remainder is blued. The grips, which are longer than other Dragoons and similar to the Walkers, are varnished walnut and bear the ordnance inspector's mark "WAT" (for W.A. Thornton) inside an oval cartouche on one side and the letters "JH" on the other. The frame is stamped "COLT'S/PATENT/U.S." The letter "P" appears on various parts of the gun. Serial numbers ran from #2216 to #2515. This is another model that should definitely be authenticated before any acquisition is made.

EXC.	V.G.	GOOD	FAIR	POOR
-	-	45,000	25,000	6,000

SECOND MODEL DRAGOON

Most of the improvements that distinguish the Second Model from the First Model are internal and thus not readily apparent. It was still a six-shot, .44 cal. pistol with a 7.5-inch barrel. Although it retained the square back trigger guard, an obvious external change was that rectangular cylinder-stop notches replaced First Model's oval stops. There is a Civilian Model, a Military Model and an extremely rare variation that was issued to the militias of New Hampshire and Massachusetts (marked "MS."). Serial numbered #8000 to #10700, total production of this model was approximately 2,700 revolvers in 1850 and 1851. Once again, caution is advised in acquisition.

NOTE: This advertisement appeared during the Spring of 2007 at *AntiqueGunList.com*:

"Colt 2nd model U.S. Dragoon, 6-1/2 inch barrel, serial number 88XX manufactured 1850. This is a rough old Dragoon that took a lot of work to get in working order again. It is a real Dragoon with a good barrel address, patent and U.S. stamps. The barrel was shortened long ago. The serial numbers match on the frame barrel and cylinder (I found an 8). The trigger guard and back strap are serial number 76XX and the hammer is original. It has several new screws because we had to drill out the old ones. The wedge is a replacement. The action is very good and locks up correctly. The grips fit nicely and appear to be original the back strap and trigger guard. There is a lot of pitting on the cylinder so as mentioned I could only find the number 8 on it. The bore still has good rifling, roughness about a 5-6. Overall condition fair. $2,550."

MILITARY MODEL

EXC.	V.G.	GOOD	FAIR	POOR
-	-	40,000	30,000	3,000

MILITIA MODEL

EXC.	V.G.	GOOD	FAIR	POOR
-	-	45,000	30,000	3,000

CIVILIAN MODEL

EXC.	V.G.	GOOD	FAIR	POOR
-	-	35,000	25,000	3,500

*Third Model
Dragoon.*

THIRD MODEL DRAGOON

This is the most common of all the large six-shot, .44-cal. Colt percussion revolvers. Approximately 10,500 were manufactured from 1851 through 1861. It is quite similar in appearance to the Second Model, retaining the 7.5 inch barrel and rectangular cylinder stop slots, the most obvious external difference being the round trigger guard. The Third Model Dragoon was the first Colt revolver to come with an optional detachable shoulder stock. There are three basic types of stocks, and all are quite rare as only 1,250 were produced. There are two other major variations to note, the "C.L." Dragoon, which was a militia issue model and is rare, and the late issue model with an 8-inch barrel. These have serial numbers above #18000, and only 50 were produced. Qualified appraisal should be secured before acquisition as many fakes abound.

MILITARY MODEL

EXC.	V.G.	GOOD	FAIR	POOR
-	-	30,000	17,500	3,000

SHOULDER STOCK CUT REVOLVERS

EXC.	V.G.	GOOD	FAIR	POOR
-	-	35,000	20,000	3,000

SHOULDER STOCKS

EXC.	V.G.	GOOD	FAIR	POOR
-	15,000	8,000	4,000	2,000

C.L. DRAGOON

Hand engraved, not stamped.

EXC.	V.G.	GOOD	FAIR	POOR
-	-	57,500	17,500	3,000

CIVILIAN MODEL

EXC.	V.G.	GOOD	FAIR	POOR
-	-	27,500	15,000	2,500

EIGHT INCH BARREL LATE ISSUE

EXC.	V.G.	GOOD	FAIR	POOR
-	-	42,500	25,000	3,000

*Third Model Dragoon
with canteen buttstock.*

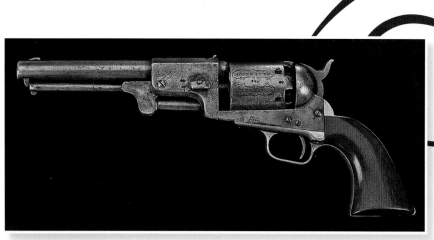

Hartford English Dragoon.

HARTFORD ENGLISH DRAGOON

Still a six-shot, .44-cal. pistol with a 7.5 inch barrel, this is a variation of the Third Model Dragoon. The only notable differences are British proofmarks and the distinct #1 to #700 serial number range. Other than these two features, the description of the Third Model would apply. These 4-lb., 2-oz. revolvers were manufactured in Hartford but were finished at Colt's London factory from 1853 to 1857. Some bear the hand engraved barrel marking "ADDRESS COL. COLT LONDON." Many of the English Dragoons were elaborately engraved, and individual appraisal would be a must. Two hundred revolvers came back to America in 1861 to be used in the Civil War. As with all the early Colts, caution is advised in acquisition.

EXC.	V.G.	GOOD	FAIR	POOR
-	-	25,000	12,000	3,000

MODEL 1848 BABY DRAGOON

This is a small five-shot, .31-cal. pocket-size percussion revolver. It has an octagonal barrel that varies in length in 1-inch increments from three to six inches. Most were made without an integral loading lever, although some with loading levers have been noted. The frame, hammer and loading lever (when present) are case colored; the barrel and cylinder are blued. The grip frame and trigger guard are silver-plated brass. Barrels are stamped "ADDRESS SAML. COLT/NEW YORK CITY". Some have been noted with the barrel address inside brackets. The frame is marked "COLT'S/PATENT." The first 10,000 revolvers have a squared-back trigger guard, rounded cylinder stops and the Texas Ranger and Indian roll engraved cylinder scene; later guns have a stagecoach holdup scene. This is a popular model, and many fakes have been noted. Although approximately 15,500 were manufactured between 1847 and 1850, the serial range is only between #1 and #5500.

TEXAS RANGER/INDIAN SCENE

EXC.	V.G.	GOOD	FAIR	POOR
-	-	12,000	6,500	2,000

NOTE: Attached loading lever add 15 percent.

STAGECOACH HOLDUP SCENE

EXC.	V.G.	GOOD	FAIR	POOR
-	-	13,000	7,000	2,000

Baby Dragoon, 3-inch barrel.

Baby Dragoon, 4-inch barrel.

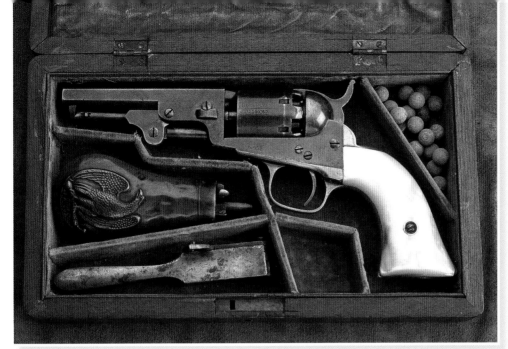

Model 1849 Pocket, blued with ivory grips.

POCKET AND ARMY, NAVY

With success on the U.S. military front based on production of his Walkers and Dragoons, Samuel Colt's fortunes improved immediately. Thus it was an easy decision to enter the civilian market with a repeating handgun, a smaller version of the massive Walker. The first Pocket models became the hugely popular 1849s and they were so identical to the earlier guns – except in physical size – that they were often referred to as "Colt's Baby Dragoons."

The subsequent six-shot Navy revolvers also proved to be popular and the combination sales of these two pistols during the early '50s made Colt's business financially secure. Colt even opened a manufacturing facility in London to complement his Hartford plant and to forestall European imitators and infringements on his patents.

Unfortunately for today's collectors, parts were often interchanged between Hartford and London, even shipped back and forth across the Atlantic, and switched between models as orders were written. This makes precise identification quite difficult and opens the door for argument and perhaps even a little mystery.

MODEL 1849 POCKET

This is a small, five- or six-shot, .31 cal. percussion revolver. It has an octagonal barrel that varies from three to six inches in length in one-inch increments.

Model 1849 Pocket, nickel finish.

Most, but not all, had loading levers and weighed a mere 1 lb., 11 oz. with the 6-inch barrel. The frame, hammer and loading lever are case colored; the cylinder and barrel are blued, the cylinder having rectangular stop slots and a stagecoach holdup roll scene. The grip frame and rounded trigger guard are made of brass and are silver plated. There are both large and small trigger guard variations noted.

This is the most plentiful of all the Colt percussion revolvers. Approximately 325,000 were manufactured during a 23-year period, from 1850 to 1873, and serial numbers run from about #14400 and up. There are more than 200 variations of the 1849 Pocket, and one should consult an expert for individual appraisals. Many fine publications specialize in the field of Colt percussion revolvers and these would be most helpful identifying variations. The values represented here are for the standard model.

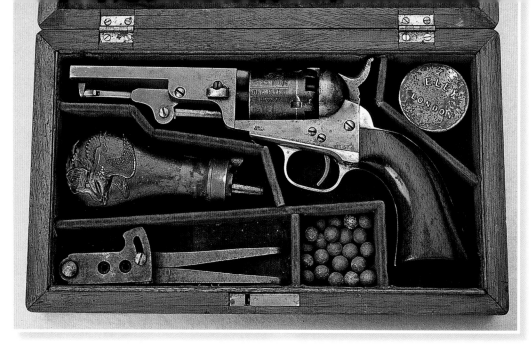

*Model 1849
Pocket, cased
with accessories.*

NOTE: This advertisement appeared in the Spring of 2007 at *AntiqueGunList.com*:

"*Colt 1849 Pocket Model, 31 cal., 4 inch barrel, 5 shot, SN 136XXX 1859. It has all matching numbers including the rammer but the wedge is un-numbered and appears not to be an original Colt wedge. It is loose but will not come out without removing the wedge screw. The action is tight and correct, no looseness between frame and barrel. The cylinder has about 70% scene and the screws are all good. The frame and barrel are smooth and not pitted, hints of color. The 2 line New York address, serial numbers and patent stamp are all sharp and readable. The back strap and trigger guard have 30% silver remaining. The original grips appear to have been re-varnished as they are in excellent condition with no chips or cracks. Overall condition very good. $1,295.*"

As did the following advertisement. Note that the gun and its presentation are very different from the previous, yielding a very different asking price:

"*Cased 1849 Colt Pocket Model, 5 inch barrel, 2 line New York address, SN 144XXX 1858, wood case and accessories. I will start with the fact that it appears this cased 49 had some moisture damage at one time. I believe that is why it was re-lined as a French fitted case, very well done and not recently. The lid does not close all the way down on the right corner, warped slightly, sets up about a 1/4 inch, but fixable. There are two spots of pitting on the 49 on the right side where it touched the case. Those are the negatives mentioned up front. I believe this Colt has always been cased. It has 85% scene, 80% safety pins remaining, 80% thin barrel blue, 50% frame and rammer case colors and 80% silver on the trigger guard and back strap. All the serial numbers match including the rammer and wedge. The action is correct, the bore is a shiny 8 to*

9 and the barrel address and patent stamps are sharp. The original grips have only a small amount of edge wear with no chips or cracks and 98% of the varnish remaining. The flask is a double faced Eagle with pistol and flask. It is in fine condition with no dents or seam openings. I see these flasks out there in this condition for $450 to $700. The Colt stamped bullet mold has most of the original blue on the inside and thin blue on the outside and does not appear to have been used. The percussion tin is empty but it is an early Eley, London marked tin. The unopened ammo pack is in excellent condition. I feel that the wood case is an original case with restoration. I have more pictures of the case and accessories, if interested I will email them to you. An early 49 pre Civil War cased Pocket model with nice accessories at a fair price. Overall condition very good plus to fine. $3,995."

EXC.	V.G.	GOOD	FAIR	POOR
-	-	1,800	1,200	300

Model 1849, Wells-Fargo marked.

London Model 1849 Pocket.

LONDON MODEL 1849 POCKET

Identical in configuration to the standard 1849 Pocket Revolver, the London-made models have a higher quality finish and their own serial numbers range from #1 to #11000. They were manufactured from 1853 through 1857. The '49 London Pocket features a roll engraved cylinder scene and the barrels are stamped "ADDRESS COL. COLT/LONDON." The first 265 revolvers produced, known as "early models," have brass grip frames and small, round trigger guards. They are quite rare and worth approximately 50 percent more than the "standard model," which has a steel grip frame and large oval trigger guard. Note that parts were interchanged between Hartford and London and thus, the presence of a London barrel stamping does not preclude its production in Hartford and vice versa. British versus U.S. proofing stamps are a clue to origin.

EXC.	V.G.	GOOD	FAIR	POOR
-	-	1,800	1,200	300

MODEL 1851 NAVY

This is undoubtedly the most popular percussion revolver Colt produced in the medium size and power range. It is a six-shot, .36-cal. percussion revolver with a 7.5 inch octagonal barrel and an attached loading lever weighing 2 lb., 10 oz. with the 6 inch barrel. The basic model has a case colored frame hammer and loading lever, with silver-plated brass grip frame and trigger guard. Early model trigger guards were squared and later models were rounded. Grips are varnished walnut. Colt manufactured more than 215,000 in Hartford and 42,000 in London between 1850 and 1873.

The basic Navy features a roll-engraved cylinder scene of a battle between the navies of Texas and Mexico and is marked with the date May 16, 1843. There are three distinct barrel stampings: serial numbers #1 to #74000, "ADDRESS SAML. COLT NEW YORK CITY"; serial numbers #74001 to #101000 "ADDRESS SAML. COLT HARTFORD, CT."; and serial numbers

Model 1851 Navy .36.

Model 1851 Navy, Third Model.

#101001 to #215000 "ADDRESS SAML. COLT NEW YORK U.S. AMERICA." The left side of the frame is stamped "COLT'S/PATENT" on all variations. This model is also available with a detached shoulder stock, and values for the stocks today are nearly as high as for the revolver itself. The number of variations within the 1851 Navy designation – more than 100 from the Hartford and London factories, including one with a 12 inch barrel and peep sights – makes it necessary to read specialized text available on the subject. We furnish values for the major variations but again caution potential purchasers to acquire careful appraisals before a purchase.

NOTE: This advertisement for an 1851 Navy recently appeared at *AntiqueGunList.com*:

"1851 Navy, U.S. marked and militarily issued, 90XXX range (1860) and matching except for wedge (which is missing) and arbor pin (which probably was matching but has been shortened and thus SN is gone). Extremely desirable large-guard iron strapped Navy-Navy variation and having the Hartford address, which is very good as are the frame markings and serial numbers. The Naval battle cylinder scene is virtually all gone except for the serial line and some faint traces of the wave bottoms at the rear portion of the cylinder. Overall, the metal is quite nice and smooth with no appreciable heavy pitting and perhaps just some VERY minor insignificant freckling here and there. Color is basically a thin dark grey-brown over most of the surface with some patches of lighter grey on the frame area. Grips are VG, look to be the originals to this gun, but do have one mentionable chip at a toe edge on the right grip, which is visible in the one photo. Mechanically it seems to operate OK and the bore is quite decent, but the hammer spur will need to be rebuilt at the top (or hammer replaced) as it is missing about 1/2" of the thumb piece checkered portion. And as mentioned, the arbor pin (cylinder axle pin) has also been shortened and should also be replaced so as to use a standard replacement wedge. Currently, it has a small brass wedge, which does work to hold the barrel in place but quite obviously is incorrect. All in all, it is a VERY scarce and desirable military issued Navy-Navy (these iron strapped variations having been issued to the Navy and the brass strapped versions issued to the Army), and certainly WELL worthy of some minor refurbishing and restoration. Normally, these iron strapped Hartfords are priced beginning in the two to three thousand (and up) range for a similar conditioned military Navy; this one is well below that figure. And for the medium-grade collector of Navies or Civil War Martial Revolvers, this is a VERY good value and a VERY difficult gun to ever come across anywhere but the most advanced gun shows or auctions. Read the Swayze book on the Colt 1851s for a full description and rarity of this variation ...and some good in-depth research might also uncover the ship or unit it was issued to originally as well as the battle records. Good+ $1,850."

SQUARE BACK TRIGGER GUARD, 1ST MODEL
Barrel wedge above the screw. Serial numbered #1 to #1000.

EXC.	V.G.	GOOD	FAIR	POOR
-	-	35,000	25,000	5,500

SQUARE BACK TRIGGER GUARD, 2ND MODEL
Screw above barrel wedge. Serial numbered #1001 to #4200

EXC.	V.G.	GOOD	FAIR	POOR
-	-	25,000	10,000	2,500

SMALL ROUND TRIGGER GUARD, 3RD MODEL
Serial numbered #4201 to #85000.

EXC.	V.G.	GOOD	FAIR	POOR
-	-	5,000	2,500	500

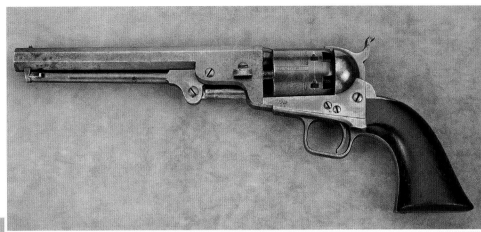

Martially-Inspected Model 1851 Navy.

LARGE ROUND TRIGGER GUARD, 4TH MODEL

Serial numbered #85001 to #215000.

EXC.	V.G.	GOOD	FAIR	POOR
-	-	4,500	2,200	500

MARTIAL MODEL

"U.S." stamped on the left side of frame; inspector's marks and cartouche on the grips.

EXC.	V.G.	GOOD	FAIR	POOR
-	-	12,000	4,000	1,000

SHOULDER STOCK VARIATIONS

1st and 2nd Model Revolver cut for stock only. Expert appraisal is recommended prior to a sale of these very rare variations.

STOCK ONLY

EXC.	V.G.	GOOD	FAIR	POOR
-	-	8,000	4,000	1,250

3RD MODEL CUT FOR STOCK.

REVOLVER ONLY.

EXC.	V.G.	GOOD	FAIR	POOR
-	-	9,500	4,000	1,250

STOCK

EXC.	V.G.	GOOD	FAIR	POOR
-	-	7,000	3,750	1,000

LONDON MODEL 1851 NAVY

These revolvers are physically similar to those made in the U.S. with the exception of the barrel address, which reads "ADDRESS COL. COLT LONDON" and British proofmarks are stamped on the barrel and cylinder. Approximately 42,000 were made between 1853 and 1857 with their own serial number range from #1 to #42000. There are two major variations of the London Navy, and again a serious purchaser would be well advised to seek qualified appraisal as fakes have been noted.

NOTE: At an auction at the Center of New Hampshire Holiday Inn, in Manchester, New Hampshire in October, 2006 James D. Julia Auctions sold an "Outstanding cased engraved Colt Model 1851 London Navy Revolver in the English Series serial number #194 for $27,000.

This very contrasting – at least in price – advertisement appeared in the Spring of 2007 at *AntiqueGunList.com*:

London Model 1851 Navy.

"Colt Percussion 1851 Navy, 36 cal., SN 13XXX manufactured in 1855. This is one of the 1851 Navies ordered by the British government for the Army in the Crimea in 1855. It has the WD under Broad Arrow stamped on the left side of the barrel with NO British proof stamps on the cylinder. The numbers all match including the rammer and wedge and are sharp and readable. This Navy was used and did not sit in a drawer or Military locker. The cylinder scene on all London Navies is lighter than the US manufactured Navies. Due to use, this one has 30% remaining with a sharp serial number. The patent stamp and barrel address are crisp and all readable. It has the domed screws heads as all London Navies should have with all being in good condition except for the wedge screw, which has the bottom potion of the head missing. There are small areas of salt and pepper pitting on the cylinder. The barrel has some thin blue and some stronger blue in protected areas. The frame, trigger guard and back strap appear to have been cleaned at some time. The action is tight and correct; the bore has strong rifling and is a 7-8. The original grips have no cracks, one medium dent in the middle of the left side and fit well. The holster is NOT part of the sales price. Overall condition very good. $2,895."

1ST MODEL

Serial numbered #1 to #2000 with a small round brass trigger guard and grip frame. Squareback guard is worth a 40 percent premium.

EXC.	V.G.	GOOD	FAIR	POOR
-	-	4,250	1,750	700

2ND MODEL

Serial numbered #2001 to #42000, steel grip frame, and large round trigger guard.

EXC.	V.G.	GOOD	FAIR	POOR
-	-	4,000	1,500	600

HARTFORD MANUFACTURED VARIATION

Serial numbers in the #42000 range.

EXC.	V.G.	GOOD	FAIR	POOR
-	-	4,500	3,000	600

SIDE HAMMER HANDGUNS

Sometimes a practical and farsighted innovation makes the grade and sometimes it does not, for no special reason other than it does not catch the eye or the imagination of the public. Although they featured a uniquely new solid frame with screw-in barrel, spur trigger, hammer on the right side and E.K. Root's new creeping loading lever, Sam Colt's percussion Side Hammer Pocket Revolvers, manufactured from 1855 to 1870, were never extremely popular.

Although the civilian market was apparently becoming saturated with handguns, when Colt's extended patent expired manufacturers such as Remington quickly entered the market. Smith and Wesson, a true competitive thorn in Colt's paw since its inception in the mid-1800s, was not far behind.

Development of the Side Hammers – there were both pistols and long guns – is often linked in time to the dramatic expansion of the Colt factory in Hartford. (The famous blue dome with its inlay of gold stars, rebuilt after the disastrous 1864 fire, can still be seen today.)

Model 1855 Colt-Root pocket revolver.

MODEL 1855 "ROOT" POCKET

The "Root," as it is popularly known because of the "creeping loading lever" patented by long time Colt engineer and friend E.K. Root, was the only solid frame revolver ever produced during Colt's lifetime. It has a spur trigger, walnut grips and the hammer is mounted on the right side of the frame. The standard finish is a case colored frame, hammer and loading lever, with the barrel and cylinder blued. It is chambered for both .28 cal. and .31 cal. percussion. Each caliber has its own serial number range: #1 to #30000 for the .28 cal. and #1 to #14000 for the .31 cal. Although only 40,000 of these pistols was produced, the model nevertheless consists of seven basic variations, and the serious student should avail himself of publications that deal with this particular model in depth. Colt produced the Side Hammer Root from 1855 to 1870.

MODELS 1 AND 1A SERIAL #1 TO #384

3.5-inch octagonal barrel, .28-cal., roll engraved cylinder, Hartford barrel address without pointing hand.

EXC.	V.G.	GOOD	FAIR	POOR
-	-	6,000	3,500	1,200

MODEL 2 SERIAL #476 TO #25000

Same as Model 1 with pointing hand barrel address.

EXC.	V.G.	GOOD	FAIR	POOR
-	-	1,800	1,200	500

MODEL 3 SERIAL #25001 TO #30000

Same as the Model 2 with a full fluted cylinder.

EXC.	V.G.	GOOD	FAIR	POOR
-	-	1,800	1,200	500

MODEL 3A AND 4 SERIAL #1 TO #2400

.31 cal., 3.5 inch barrel, Hartford address, full fluted cylinder.

EXC.	V.G.	GOOD	FAIR	POOR
-	-	2,500	1,500	600

MODEL 5 SERIAL #2401 TO #8000

No trigger guard. A .31 cal. pistol with 3.5 inch round barrel, address "COL. COLT NEW YORK."

EXC.	V.G.	GOOD	FAIR	POOR
-	-	1,800	1,200	500

MODEL 5A SERIAL #2401 TO #8000

Same .31 cal. as Model 5 with a 4.5 inch barrel.

EXC.	V.G.	GOOD	FAIR	POOR
-	-	3,200	1,600	600

MODELS 6 AND 6A SERIAL #8001 TO #11074

Same as Model 5 and 5A with roll engraved cylinder scene.

EXC.	V.G.	GOOD	FAIR	POOR
-	-	1,800	1,200	500

MODELS 7 AND 7A SERIAL #11075 TO #14000

Same as Models 6 and 6A with a screw holding in the cylinder pin.

EXC.	V.G.	GOOD	FAIR	POOR
-	-	3,500	2,200	800

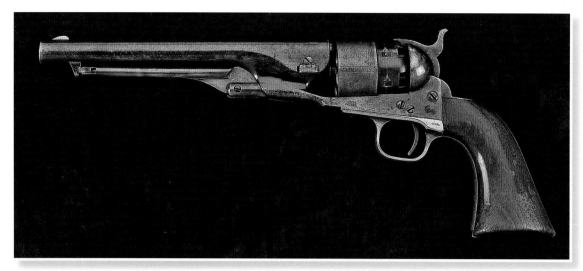

Model 1860 Army .44.

1860 MODELS ARMY, NAVY AND POLICE PERCUSSION PISTOLS

It would be an understatement to maintain that the Civil War was a boon to firearms manufacturers such as Colt's Patent Fire Arms Mfg. Co. Indeed, Colt's thrived during the conflict, employing two ten-hour shifts and as many as 1,500 men, while more than a half million Americans died on the battlefield and more than a million were disabled for life. That is an inescapable, if terrible and unfortunate, condition of war. Colt also thrived in spite of a disastrous 1864 fire, probably the result of sabotage by Confederate sympathizers, and the subsequent rebuilding.

Lt. Colonel Samuel Colt, who would perhaps today be described as a workaholic, and was certainly the most energetic genius, died on January 10, 1862, having directed the design and manufacture of his final series of handguns. His 1860 Series – many adaptable for attachable shoulder stocks – sold more than 280,000 between 1860 and 1873, and were the last new percussion introductions in the Colt line.

MODEL 1860 ARMY REVOLVER

This model was the third most produced of the Colt percussion handguns and, with 127,156 delivered, was the primary revolver used by the Union Army during the Civil War. The 1860 Army is a six shot .44 caliber percussion revolver weighing 2 lb., 10 oz. It has either a 7.5- or an 8-inch round barrel with an integral loading lever. The frame, hammer and loading lever are case colored; the barrel and cylinder (either fluted, which is scarce, or round, which have the roll-engraved naval combat scene) are blued. The trigger guard and front strap are brass, and the backstrap is blued steel. Grips are the characteristic Colt one piece walnut. Early models have barrels stamped "ADDRESS SAML. COLT HARTFORD CT." Later models are stamped "ADDRESS COL. SAML. COLT NEW-YORK U.S. AMERICA." And "COLT'S/PATENT" is stamped on the left side of the frame; ".44 CAL.," on the trigger guard. The cylinder is roll engraved with a naval battle scene. Between 1860 and 1873, Colt manufactured 200,500 of these 1860 Army Revolvers. Serial numbers began at #1.

NOTE: This advertisement appeared in the Spring of 2007 at *AntiqueGunList.com*:

"Colt 1860 Army, 8 inch barrel, 44 cal., Civilian, manufactured 1868 SN 171XXX. This is a nice '60 Army from the 1860s. The barrel address and patent stamp are sharp, the cylinder scene is at least 90% with a readable Engagement line. The cylinder has 30% blue and safety pins remaining. The frame has 70% case colors, the hammer has 80% and the rammer has 20%. The screws are all in good condition with blue remaining. The serial numbers all match except the wedge, which is numbered but not matching. The action is crisp and tight and the bore is a shiny 9. The barrel has 40% shiny blue remaining and the back strap has 30%. The metal is smooth, no pitting only minor dings around the right wedge opening. The original grips have 20% varnish, an old repair to the left front toe, no cracks, minor dings and fit tight. Overall condition fine to excellent. $3,650."

MARTIAL MARKED MODEL

EXC.	V.G.	GOOD	FAIR	POOR
-	-	7,500	3,500	900

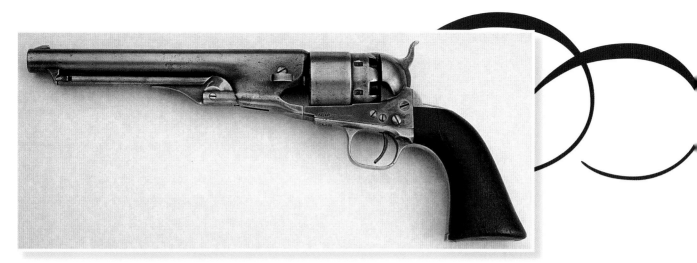

Model 1860 Civilian Model.

CIVILIAN MODEL

This model is found in either three or four screw variations and it may or may not be cut for a shoulder stock. Civilian models are usually better finished.

EXC.	V.G.	GOOD	FAIR	POOR
-	-	6,000	3,000	800

FULL FLUTED CYLINDER MODEL

Approximately 4,000 Army Models were made with full fluted cylinders, sometimes called the Cavalry Model. With 7.5- and 8-inch barrels, they appear in the first 8,000 serial numbers.

EXC.	V.G.	GOOD	FAIR	POOR
-	-	15,000	7,000	2,000

SHOULDER STOCK 2ND TYPE (FLUTED CYLINDER MODEL) OR SHOULDER STOCK 3RD TYPE (STANDARD MODEL)

NOTE: Expert appraisals should be acquired before a purchase. These are rare accoutrements. Scarcity precludes estimating values.

MODEL 1861 NAVY REVOLVER

The 1861 Navy is a six-shot, 7.5-inch round barreled, .36-cal. percussion revolver. The frame, hammer and attached loading lever are case colored, while the barrel and cylinder are blued. The grip frame and trigger guard are silver plated brass. The grips are of one piece walnut. The cylinder has the standard Colt roll engraved naval battle scene, and the barrel stamping is "ADDRESS COL. SAML. COLT NEW-YORK U.S. AMERICA." The frame is stamped "COLT'S/PATENT" with "36 CAL." on the trigger guard. There are not many variations within the 1861 Navy model designation, as less than 39,000 were built between 1861 and 1873. Their serial numbers begin at #1.

NOTE: This advertisement appeared in the Spring of 2007 at *AntiqueGunList.com*:

"*Colt Percussion 1861 Navy, 7-1/2 inch barrel, 36 cal., manufactured 1865 SN 26XXX. There were only approximately 38K, '61 Navies manufactured between 1861-73. I bought this Navy recently at an estate sale belonging to … an old time collector and it has not been out for sale for 30 to 40 years. This is a nice example with 90 to 95% cylinder scene, 90% safety pins and a fully readable Engagement line on the edge of the cylinder. The*

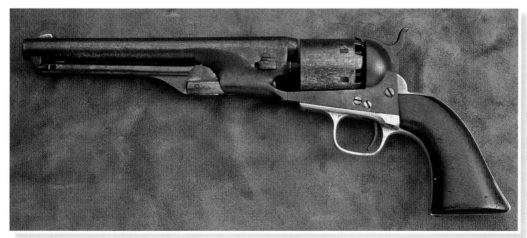

Model 1861 Navy.

action is tight and correct and the bore is a shiny 9+. There are traces of case color on the frame, hammer and loading lever and bright case inside the frame when the cylinder is removed. It has original blue in protected areas on the barrel. The metal is smooth with some handling dings and NO pitting. All the serial numbers match including the wedge. The screws are all good with some having original blue remaining. The original grips have no cracks or chips, one dented area on the upper left side and fit like a glove. There is a name scrolled into the trigger guard in front of the trigger, "Cayeta," and two small dotted letters or numerals behind the hammer on the back strap. Overall condition fine. $3,150."

CIVILIAN MODEL

EXC.	V.G.	GOOD	FAIR	POOR
-	-	7,500	3,500	900

MILITARY MODEL

Marked "U.S." on frame, inspector's cartouche on grip; 650 were marked "U.S.N." on the butt.

EXC.	V.G.	GOOD	FAIR	POOR
-	-	18,000	5,500	1,800

SHOULDER STOCK MODEL

Only 100 3rd type stocks were made. They appear between serial #11000 and #14000. These are very rare revolvers. Caution should be exercised when purchase is considered.

REVOLVER

EXC.	V.G.	GOOD	FAIR	POOR
-	-	17,500	5,000	1,500

STOCK

EXC.	V.G.	GOOD	FAIR	POOR
-	-	9,500	4,250	1,000

NOTE: Expert appraisals should be acquired before a purchase. These are rare accoutrements.

FLUTED CYLINDER MODEL

Approximately the first 100 were made with full fluted cylinders.

EXC.	V.G.	GOOD	FAIR	POOR
-	-	45,000	7,500	2,000

NOTE: Expert appraisals should be acquired before a purchase. These are very rare.

MODEL 1862 POCKET NAVY

This is a small five-shot, .36-cal. percussion revolver that resembles the configuration of the 1851 Navy. It has either a 4.5-, a 5.5- or a 6.5-inch octagonal barrel with an attached loading lever. The frame, hammer and loading lever are case colored; the barrel and cylinder are blued. The grip frame and trigger guard are silver plated brass; and the one piece grips are varnished walnut. The Colt stagecoach holdup scene is roll engraved on the cylinder. The frame is stamped "COLT'S/PATENT" and the barrel, "ADDRESS COL. SAML. COLT NEW-YORK U.S. AMERICA." About 19,000 were manufactured between 1861 and 1873. Pocket Navy revolvers are serial numbered in the same range as the Model 1862 Police. Because a great many were used for metallic cartridge conversions, they are rare today. The London Address Model with blued steel grip frame would be worth more than the standard model.

NOTE: This advertisement appeared in March of 2007 at *GunBroker.com*:

"Colt 1862 Pocket Navy engraved. This is one of the best looking Colt Pocket Navys I have seen. The engraving covers the frame and approximately half of the barrel. The backstrap and trigger guard also have good coverage. The hammer and the loading lever have a good amount of engraving as well. I recently had this Pocket Navy examined by an author of one of the well known Colt Pocket Pistol books. He told me he was certain the pistol was engraved in house by one of the Ulrich brothers. The

Model 1862 Pocket Navy.

1862 Police Revolver.

blue is mostly gone on this pistol. I don't know if it didn't have blue or was cleaned. The edges are still sharp and the lettering is sharp and easy to read. Nearly all of the silver is still present on the backstrap and trigger guard. The hammer and the frame still retain a very good amount of case color. What can you say about the color of nicely aged ivory grips. These grips fit as you would expect factory fitted grips to fit. This pistol boasts all matching numbers including the grips. The wedge does not have a number, but appears to be 100% original. The bore shows use, but is in good condition. Check out the pictures of the cylinder scene. The scene is great. It is one of the few pistols I have seen that you can actually tell what is on the cylinder. This Colt 1862 Engraved Pocket Navy functions flawlessly. The lockup is very tight and everything is as you would expect it to be. This is a very rare and tastefully done Colt 1862 Engraved Pocket Navy. Bid with confidence. A three day look is fine. Please ask questions prior to bidding. Prefer guaranteed funds. Shipping is $50 USPS, registered mail. This is an antique so shipping is to your door. Have fun!"

Bidding for this antique firearm closed at $7,100 but did not reach the seller's reserve.

STANDARD PRODUCTION MODEL

EXC.	V.G.	GOOD	FAIR	POOR
-	-	3,000	1,200	500

NOTE: Longer barrels will bring a premium over the 4.5 inch length.

MODEL 1862 POLICE REVOLVER

This is a slim, attractively designed revolver that some consider the most aesthetically pleasing of all the Colt percussion designs. It has a five-shot, half-fluted cylinder chambered for .36 cal. and is offered with a 3.5-, 4.5-, 5.5- or 6.5-inch round barrel. The frame, hammer and loading lever are case colored; the barrel and cylinder, blued. The grip frame is silver plated brass; and the unitary, one piece grips are varnished walnut. The barrel is stamped "ADDRESS COL. SAML. COLT NEW-YORK U.S. AMERICA" and the frame has "COLT'S/ PATENT" on the left side. One of the cylinder flutes is marked "PAT. SEPT. 10 1850." Nearly 28,000 Police Revolvers were manufactured between 1861 and 1873. Many were converted to metallic cartridge use, so they are quite scarce on today's market. The London Address Model would be worth approximately twice the value of the standard model. Police with 3.5 inch barrels, known as the Trapper's Model, are extremely rare and possibly only 50 were built.

NOTE: The following advertisement appeared in the Spring of 2007 at *AntiqueGunList.com*:

"Colt Percussion, 1862 Pocket Police, 4-1/2 inch barrel, fluted cylinder, 36 cal., SN 17XXX manufactured 1863. An excellent example of a Civil War era Colt Pocket Police with all matching numbers including the wedge. This Colt has seen very little use in 144 years. It has NO pitting, a few small nicks on the cylinder and barrel only. There is No pitting on the hammer, recoil shield or nipples. The action is tight as new and the bore is a shiny 9+ with only a couple of very light rough spots. The screws retaining light blue, they are in excellent condition and do not appear to have been removed. The frame has 85% case, the rammer has 80% and the hammer has 95% case. The cylinder and barrel have thin blue on almost all areas darker in the protected locations. The serial numbers, patent stamps and barrel address are sharp and crisp with no wear. The back strap and trigger guard have 20 to 30% thin silver remaining. The fine original grips have 98% of the varnish, no chips or cracks and only minor dings in the varnish. A great example of a Civil War Colt Pocket in overall fine to excellent condition. $3,695."

STANDARD PRODUCTION MODEL

EXC.	V.G.	GOOD	FAIR	POOR
-	-	2,250	1,000	400

NOTE: Longer barrels will bring a premium over the 3.5- or 4.5-inch length.

SECTION III

COLT'S REVOLVERS & THE METALLIC CARTRIDGES

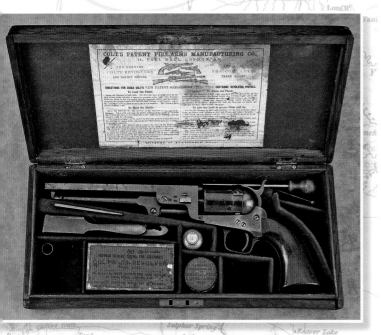

Model 1851 Navy Thuer Conversion.

METALLIC CARTRIDGE CONVERSIONS

*T*he transitional era from muzzleloading to breechloading was not the Colt's company's finest hour. That was still to come. In fact, hemmed in by Smith & Wesson's exclusive rights to the Rollin White patent for bored-through chambers to accommodate breechloading metallic cartridges, Colt struggled to maintain the lustre of its name and market share. It was not until 1869 that the White patent expired, and even then, Colt was not prepared with new models.

So from the waning of the percussion era until 1872 Colt took in non-firearm manufacturing business (even manufacturing sewing machines) and worked feverishly on new firearm designs. In the four years between the end of the Civil War and 1869, when it became clear that breechloading cartridges were the future and would soon replace all of their designs, Colt struggled with diminishing sales of its muzzleloading guns.

Between 1869 and 1972, Colt produced a number of models that are variously considered "conversions." These weapons were Colt percussion revolvers that were reworked to accommodate metallic cartridges. None can be considered entirely successful.

*Model 1860 Army
Thuer Conversion.*

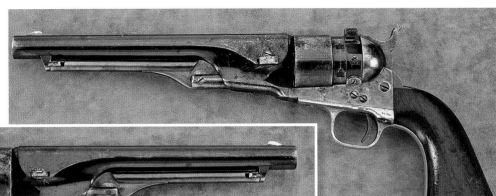

THUER CONVERSION

Although quite simplistic and not commercially successful, the Thuer Conversion (named after gunsmith and patent holder F. Alexander Thuer) was brought out in 1869 and remained in the line until 1872 for a total of about 5,000 guns. It was the strongest attempt by Colt to circumvent former employee Rollin White's patent (which had been sold to Smith & Wesson) and to convert remaining Colt percussion revolvers to the new metallic cartridge system. This conversion was designed around the proprietary, tapered Thuer cartridge and consisted of a ring that replaced the back part of the cylinder, which had been milled off. The ring is stamped "PAT. SEP. / 15. 1868." The ejection position is marked with the letter "E." These conversions have rebounding firing pins and were milled to allow loading from the front of the revolver cylinder. All Thuer Conversions were six-shot revolvers. This conversion was undertaken on the six different models listed; and all other specifications, finishes, markings, etc., not directly affected by the conversion would be the same as previously described. From a collectible and investment standpoint, the Thuer Conversion is very desirable. About 5,000 revolvers were altered in the years 1869 to 1870. Competent appraisal should be secured if acquisition is contemplated.

MODEL 1849 POCKET CONVERSION (.31 CAL.)

EXC.	V.G.	GOOD	FAIR	POOR
-	-	12,500	4,000	2,000

MODEL 1851 NAVY CONVERSION (.36 CAL.)

EXC.	V.G.	GOOD	FAIR	POOR
-	-	15,000	5,000	2,000

MODEL 1860 ARMY CONVERSION (.44 CAL.)

EXC.	V.G.	GOOD	FAIR	POOR
-	-	17,500	6,000	2,000

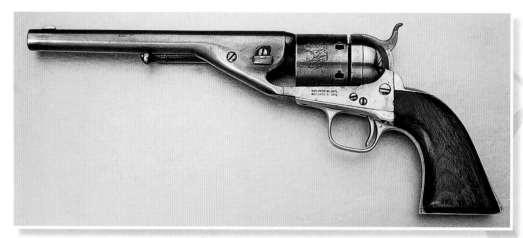

Model 1861 Navy Thuer Conversion.

Richards Conversion 1860 Army.

MODEL 1861 NAVY CONVERSION (.36 CAL.)

EXC.	V.G.	GOOD	FAIR	POOR
-	-	17,500	6,000	2,000

MODELS 1862 POLICE CONVERSION (.36 CAL.)

EXC.	V.G.	GOOD	FAIR	POOR
-	-	11,500	3,500	1,500

MODEL 1862 POCKET NAVY CONVERSION (.36 CAL.)

EXC.	V.G.	GOOD	FAIR	POOR
-	-	11,500	3,500	1,500

NOTE: Blued models will bring higher prices than nickel models in the same condition.

RICHARDS CONVERSION, 1860 ARMY REVOLVER

The Richards Transformation was Colt's second attempt at metallic cartridge conversion and it met with quite a bit more success than the Thuer Model. The Richards Conversion was designed for the .44 Colt cartridge and has a six-shot cylinder and an integral ejector rod to replace the loading lever that had been removed. The other specifications pertaining to the 1860 Army Revolver remain as previously described if they were not directly altered by the conversion. The Richards Conversion adds a breechplate with a firing pin and its own rear sight. Approximately 9,000 of these conversions were manufactured on the basis of a number of the old caplock designs and parts between 1873 and 1878: the .44-caliber M1860 revolver (1,153 converted for the army in 1871), the .36-cal. M1851 and M1861 and 368 .38-cal. rimfire adaptations, which went to the navy in 1873.

NOTE: The following advertisement appeared in the Spring of 2007 at *AntiqueGunList.com*:

"Colt Model 1862 Pocket Navy Conversion, 38 RF

cal., 3 inch barrel, manufactured 1875 SN #20XXX. These are called "type 4" in the fine book New Model Police & Pocket Breech Loading Pistols, pages 70-75. Approximately 2,000 were manufactured with only 410 made with 3 inch barrels and 60% of those were nickel finish. Which leaves around 165 that were blue and case in serial range #19900 to #21200. Only 4% were made in center fire. This one has 90% barrel blue with 60% being shiny blue. The cylinder has 15% shiny blue. The frame has 70% case colors, the hammer has 80% and the back strap and trigger guard have 20% silver remaining. The action is correct and the bore is a shiny 9.5. The cylinder has 90% scene and the screws are all good. The one-line barrel address is all there but as noted in the book they are lightly stamped. The patent stamps are crisp with dashes and all the numbers match. The grips have 70% of the varnish and no chips or cracks. This is a hard to find Pocket Navy conversion in a rare barrel length. Overall condition fine. $3,150."

And The following advertisement appeared in the Spring of 2007 at AntiqueGunList.com:

"Colt Conversion 1860 Army Richards, all matching numbers 3288, 6 inch barrel with original sight moved back. This is in as-found condition; I am leaving the TLC to the next collector. The cylinder scene is light and has a readable matching serial number, as does the Richards recoil ring assembly. There is 40%+ nickel remaining. The bore is good and it functions correctly with all the clicks. The original grips have no cracks; wear to both front toes and a small chip on the left up by the frame. The barrel address and patent date are sharp as are all the serial numbers with the cylinder being light. It is not a rusted metal surface Colt, fairly smooth overall with some minor salt and pepper pits on the cylinder and recoil shield. The ejector head is homemade as is the wedge. It has some screws that need to be replaced. The ejector housing looks to have had a weld repair long ago on the bottom portion. Overall condition fair to good. $1,495."

CIVILIAN MODEL

EXC.	V.G.	GOOD	FAIR	POOR
-	-	5,250	2,000	600

MARTIAL MARKED VARIATION

This variation is found with mixed serial numbers and a second set of conversion serial numbers. The "U.S." is stamped on the left side of the barrel lug, and inspector's cartouche appears on the grip. This is a very rare Colt revolver. Blued models will bring higher prices than nickel models in the same condition.

EXC.	V.G.	GOOD	FAIR	POOR
-	-	15,000	7,000	2,000

TRANSITION RICHARDS MODEL

This variation is marked by the presence of a firing pin hammer. Blued models will bring higher prices than nickel models in the same condition.

EXC.	V.G.	GOOD	FAIR	POOR
-	-	6,000	3,000	1,200

RICHARDS-MASON CONVERSION, 1860 ARMY

This conversion, directed perhaps by William Mason, a talented firearms designer who also worked on the Single Action Army and the double action trigger mechanism of the Lightning revolver, is different from the Richards Conversion in a number of apparent aspects. The barrel was manufactured with a small lug much different in appearance from that seen on the standard 1860 Army. The breechplate does not have its own rear sight, and there is a milled area to allow the hammer to contact the base of the cartridge. These conversions were also chambered for the .44 Colt cartridge, and the cylinder holds six shots. There is an integral ejector rod in place of the loading lever. The barrels on some are stamped either "ADDRESS COL. SAML. COLT NEW-YORK U.S. AMERICA" or "COLT'S PT. F.A. MFG. CO. HARTFORD, CT." Patent dates 1871 and 1872 are stamped on the left side of the frame. The finish of these revolvers, as well as the grips, was for the most part the same as on the unconverted armies, but for the first time, nickel plated guns are found. There were approximately 2,100 of these conversions produced in 1877 and 1878. Blued models will bring higher prices than nickel models in the same condition.

NOTE: The following advertisement appeared at AntiqueGuns.com in March of 2007:

"Colt Richards Conversion of a Colt 1860 Army with wonderful old ivory grips. Grips show aging lines on bottom and slightly undersized, but ivory can shrink, I believe these have just shrunk. The gun shows 95% original nickel with scattered peppered spots of staining, crisp like new mechanics, in .44 CF, 53xx matching on bottom of gun and on cylinder. I could not pop wedge, bright excellent bore with fine patches of dusty residue. Excellent overall."

The seller requested an opening bid of $8,900.

EXC.	V.G.	GOOD	FAIR	POOR
-	-	6,000	2,500	800

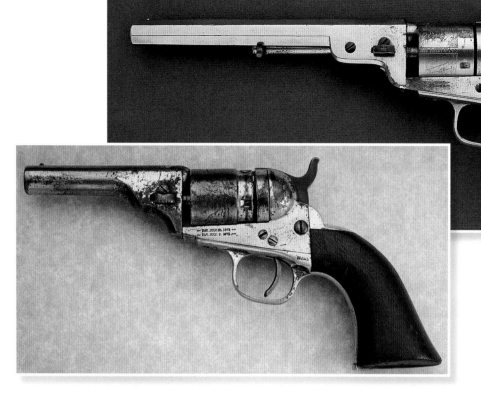

Model 1851 Richards-
Mason Conversion.

Model 1862 Pocket Navy Conversion.

RICHARDS-MASON CONVERSIONS 1851 NAVY

These revolvers were converted in the same way as the 1860 Army previously described, the major difference being the caliber, .38 rimfire or centerfire. Finishes are mostly the same as on unconverted revolvers, but nickel plated guns are not rare.

PRODUCTION MODEL SERIAL NUMBERS #1 TO #3800

EXC.	V.G.	GOOD	FAIR	POOR
-	-	4,500	2,000	800

U.S. NAVY MODEL SERIAL NUMBERS #41000 TO #91000

"USN" stamped on butt; steel grip frame. Blued models will bring higher prices than nickel models in the same condition.

EXC.	V.G.	GOOD	FAIR	POOR
-	-	7,000	3,000	1,000

NOTE: A Navy Conversion was recently listed as follows on *AntiqueGuns.com*:

"Colt Richards Conversion, blued with 90% varnish to grips, light edge wear. Cylinder shows 95% strong naval scene, 80% rainbow hues on frame, 75% deep barrel blue. This is an exceptional conversion, it has #32xx matching on bottom of gun, matching on cylinder with assembly number on breech block. Fine to excellent overall."

The seller requested a starting bid of $8,000.

RICHARDS-MASON CONVERSION 1861 NAVY

The specifications for this model are the same as for the 1851 Navy Conversion described above, with the base revolver being different. 2,200 were manufactured in the 1870s.

STANDARD PRODUCTION MODEL SERIAL NUMBERS #100 TO #3300

EXC.	V.G.	GOOD	FAIR	POOR
-	-	4,250	1,500	500

U.S. NAVY MODEL SERIAL #1000 TO #9999

EXC.	V.G.	GOOD	FAIR	POOR
-	-	6,500	3,500	1,000

Blued models will bring higher prices than nickel models in the same condition.

NOTE: The following gun was posted for sale at *AntiqueGuns.com* in the Spring of 2007:

"Colt M-1861 Navy Conversion to .38 CF. It comes with a factory letter and when in original percussion had been shipped to the US Naval Yard in New York City. The gun was later converted and has about 50% barrel blue, traces of case color on frame, strong case color on hammer. It has about 50% cylinder scene, the screw in front of wedge is replaced, numbers on bottom of gun all match. The wedge appears better than rest of gun and so appears to have been replaced. #9xxx on TG, Barrel and Frame, number on backstrap is 2550. #4236 on cylinder, I take it this was common on arsenal refitted guns."

The seller requested an opening bid of $5,700.

Model 1862 Police Conversion, nickel finish, in Excellent+ original condition.

Model 1862 Police Conversion, nickel finish, with period holster.

MODEL 1862 POLICE AND POCKET NAVY CONVERSIONS

The conversion of these two revolver models is the most difficult to catalogue of all the Colt variations. About 24,000 of these were produced between 1873 and 1880. There are five basic variations with a number of minor variations. The confusion is usually caused by the different ways in which these were marked. Depending upon what parts were utilized, caliber markings could be particularly confusing – and wrong. One must also consider the fact that many of these conversion revolvers found their way into secondary markets, such as Mexico and Central and South America, where they were either destroyed or received sufficient abuse to obliterate most identifying markings. The five basic variations are all chambered for the .38 rimfire or .38 centerfire cartridge. All held five shots, and most were found with the round roll engraved stagecoach holdup scene. The half-fluted cylinder from the 1862 police model is quite rare on the conversion revolver and not found at all on some of the variations. The finishes on these guns were pretty much the same as they were before conversion, but it is not unusual to find nickel plated specimens. Blued models will bring a premium over nickel in the same condition.

The basic variations are listed.

ROUND BARREL POCKET NAVY WITH EJECTOR

EXC.	V.G.	GOOD	FAIR	POOR
-	-	3,500	1,600	800

3.5 INCH ROUND BARREL WITHOUT EJECTOR

EXC.	V.G.	GOOD	FAIR	POOR
-	-	2,500	1,000	300

4.5 INCH OCTAGONAL BARREL WITHOUT EJECTOR

EXC.	V.G.	GOOD	FAIR	POOR
-	-	3,000	1,200	400

MODEL 1862 POCKET NAVY OCTAGON BARREL WITH EJECTOR

EXC.	V.G.	GOOD	FAIR	POOR
-	-	3,250	1,500	600

For half-fluted cylinder add 20 percent.

MODEL 1862 POLICE ROUND BARREL WITH EJECTOR

EXC.	V.G.	GOOD	FAIR	POOR
-	-	3,250	1,500	600

Blued models will bring higher prices than nickel models in the same condition.

NOTE: The following advertisement appeared in the Spring of 2007 at *AntiqueGunList.com*:

"Colt Conversion, 3-1/2 inch Round Barrel , 38 RF cal., late 1870s, SN 2XXX. These 3 1/2 inch round barrels were manufactured and shipped from 1875-86. There were 10,125 manufactured according to the fine book Colts New Model Police and Pocket Breech Loaders, page 76, almost all in .38 rim fire. This is a fine example of a low serial number round barrel, as the serial range for new guns is #1750 to #5450. It appears unfired as the bore is a shiny 10 with strong rifling and no nickel loss at the muzzle. The screws do not appear to have been removed as they are all in fine condition with most of their original finish. It has 100% cylinder scene and all the serial numbers match. The patent dates and barrel address are sharp and crisp, the hammer has most of the case colors and the trigger has good blue. The back strap and trigger guard have 95% silver. The frame, barrel and cylinder have no nickel loss only some minor scratches and dings in the nickel. The action is tight and crisp. The grips have no cracks, all of the varnish but peculiarly there are 2 small kill type notches on the right front bottom edge, maybe for identification. Overall condition excellent. $2,850."

DERINGERS TO NEW MODELS

Just as the decade before the Civil War was an era of great unrest in the U.S., the post war years were also socially complicated. The frontier was expanding toward its logical end, immigrants were flooding into the cities, and the southern states were restive and hostile under reconstruction policies. In such an environment, personal confrontations were commonplace.

Thus, it may not be entirely curious that the first Colt firearm designed specifically for the metallic cartridge was a single shot deringer, a weapon designed for concealment and personal protection. Breechloading pocket deringers became popular in the mid 1860s when the .41 chambering became the most popular big-bore rimfire cartridge generally available.

Colt's purchase of Brooklyn deringer manufacturer National Arms Co. in 1870 and the subsequent design of its "New Line" models based on William Mason's patents made Colt a solid player in the small pistol market and also pushed the company forward into an age of diversification.

All Colt deringers were designed to load by

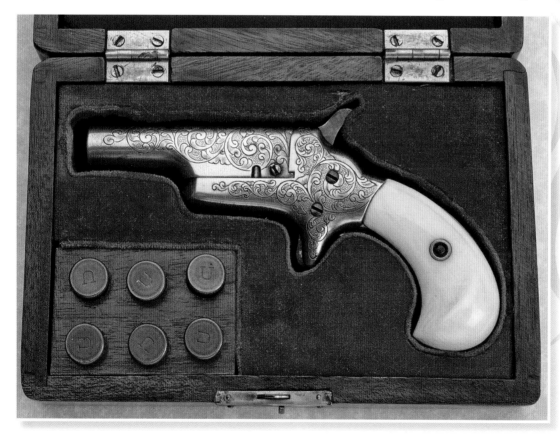

First Model Deringer.

pivoting the deringer barrel. On the National models, for example, the barrel pivots nearly 90 degrees to the left (i.e., from 12:00 to 9:00) around a pin beneath the breech; on the Third Model, the barrel swings to the right.

NOTE: A surprising number of Colt deringers are still found in their original boxes, even older models. This can add 100 percent to the value of the pistol.

COLT'S DERINGERS

FIRST MODEL DERINGER

After Colt purchased Brooklyn's National Arms Co. for its deringer designs, the company built this small (under seven ounces), all-metal single-shot chambered for .41 rimfire. The 2.5-inch barrel pivots sideways for loading. The 4.9-inch-long gun is engraved with a scroll pattern and has been noted blued, silver or nickel plated. The barrel is stamped "COLT'S PT. F.A. MFG. CO./HARTFORD CT. U.S.A/ No.1." Under the release catch, ".41 CAL." is stamped on the frame. The grips were forged integrally with the butt. There were approximately 6,500 of this model manufactured from 1870 to 1890. It was the first single-shot pistol Colt ever produced.

EXC.	V.G.	GOOD	FAIR	POOR
-	-	2,500	1,200	400

NOTE: The following advertisement for a National No. 1, the predecessor of Colt's First Model Deringer, appeared in the Spring of 2007 at *ArmChairGunShow.com*:

"National Arms - No. 1 Moore's pattern Deringer - scarce 2" barrel - .41 rimfire - Very good condition. - Lightly cleaned light gray barrel; mellow patina brass frame; fine markings & engraving. - This model was produced through the 1860's, first by Moore, then by National, with the pattern then acquired by Colt for their Model 1 Deringer, beginning in 1870. Total production by National was probably around 3,000, very few of those in this rare short barrel configuration. Serial number #830. $1,500." AND The following advertisement appeared subsequently on the same Internet site for a Colt manufactured No. 1: Colt - 1st Model Deringer Brit proofed .41 rimfire. About excellent condition. Barrel 90%, frame 60 to 70% original nickel; excellent markings; excellent bore & mech. Serial number #771. $1,950."

SECOND MODEL DERINGER

Although this model has the same odd shape as the First Model, it is readily identifiable by the checkered, varnished walnut grips (replacing the integrally forged grips of the First Model) and the "NO. 2" on the barrel after the address. It is also .41 rimfire and has a 2.5 inch barrel that pivots in the same manner as the First Model. Sources disagree on the number manufactured, but it is probable that about 6,500 of these were manufactured between 1870 and 1890.

EXC.	V.G.	GOOD	FAIR	POOR
-	-	2,000	900	400

NOTE: The following advertisement appeared in the Spring of 2007 at *AntiqueGunList.com*:

"National No.2 41RF Deringer, with good bore, good action and some thin traces of nickel plate still remaining on the brass factory engraved frame. The barrel is a dark grayish color and has some moderate wear and minor freckle scattered pitting; the hammer has some deeper pitting as can be seen in the photos below. The address is dim but mostly readable (these were never deeply struck like the later Colt Deringers were) and the grips are very good with no serious wear or damage. The National was the successor to the Moore Deringer of Civil War vintage (1860-1865), and then National was bought out by Colt Firearms in 1870, which then continued this line of Deringers with the Colt name. The Nationals were made between 1865-1870 with about 12,000 produced. VG $775."

THIRD MODEL DERINGER

Designed by F. Alexander Thuer, who was also responsible for Colt's first breechloading metallic cartridge conversion, the Third Model appeared in the Colt line in 1875 and remained popular until 1912. Thus, it is often referred to as the "Thuer Model." It is chambered for the .41 rimfire cartridge (a few were chambered for .41 centerfire), weighs slightly less than 6.5 oz., is a fraction under five inches long and has a 2.5-inch barrel that pivots to the left (not down) for loading. Its frame ran forward under the barrel, carrying a vertical barrel pivot screw which allowed the horizontal, rather than vertical pivoting. An ejector pin pushed the empty case out of the chamber at the end of the opening movement.

The earliest guns had a prominent bolster around the barrel pivot screw, and the sheath that protected the trigger was vertical instead of angled forward. The Third Model has a more balanced appearance than its predecessors, and its commercial success (45,000 produced between 1875 and 1910) reflects this. The barrel is stamped "COLT" in small block letters on the first 2,000 guns. The remainder of the production

House Model Revolver.

features "COLT" in large italicized print. ".41 CAL." is stamped on the left side of the frame. This model will be found with the barrel blued or plated in either silver or nickel and the bronze frame plated. Grips are varnished walnut.

FIRST VARIATION, EARLY PRODUCTION

This has a raised area on the underside of the frame through which the barrel screw passes, and the spur is not angled. Small block "COLT" lettering on barrel.

EXC.	V.G.	GOOD	FAIR	POOR
-	-	6,500	2,200	1,000

FIRST VARIATION, LATE PRODUCTION

This is similar to early production but has large italicized "COLT" on barrel.

EXC.	V.G.	GOOD	FAIR	POOR
-	-	3,250	1,500	600

PRODUCTION MODEL

EXC.	V.G.	GOOD	FAIR	POOR
-	-	800	400	200

Blued models will bring a premium over nickel in the same condition.

NOTE: The following very different listings appeared in March of 2007 at *AntiqueGuns.com*:

"*Colt #3 Single Shot Deringer in .41 RF, the gun has been lightly cleaned overall, grips have been very lightly sanded and do not fit the gun perfectly, Colt on barrel shows show light wear. Traces of silver on brass, very good overall.*"

The seller set the starting bid at $375.

"*Colt #3 Minty Single Shot Pistol, 95% grip varnish, 98% silver on frame, 98% barrel blue, 98% deep case color on hammer, egg shell blue on screws, light wear to high points of grips, excellent plus overall. The bore is dusty and needs a scrubbing. The bore is dirtier than I would like to see it and frankly that concerns me, a gun this minty should have a MINT bore, and the crude inside the bore could be just dust, but it appears more than that. Anyone serious in this gun, if you win the gun, we will get the consignor to clean the bore before you send funds. If the bore does not clean to minty, then the gun has probably been refinished, but color looks perfect to me on this gun.*"

The seller asked for a starting bid of no less than $2,300.

HOUSE MODEL REVOLVER

There are two basic versions of this model, both of which are chambered for the .41 rimfire deringer cartridge. The four shot version is known as the "Cloverleaf" due to the deeply fluted shape of the cylinder when viewed from the front. Each cylinder was recessed to conceal the cartridge rim and was loaded from the right side simply by manually rotating the cylinder until it was clear of the frame. A sheath kept the cartridges in place as the cylinder rotated and could be swung aside for loading. Alternately, the cylinder could be removed from the frame entirely and the empty cased poked out by an ejector rod housed inside the cylinder arbor pin. Approximately 7,500 of the nearly 10,000 House revolvers were of this four-shot configuration. They were offered with a 1.5- or 3-

inch barrel. The 1.5 inch length is quite rare, and some octagonal barrels in this length have been noted. Grips were usually rosewood, although walnut examples are known. Marked "PAT. SEPT. 19, 1871" on the topstrap of the frame. The earliest hammers had a high spur, but this was later changed to one less likely to catch in the pocket.

The five shot round cylinder or second version of the House Model accounts for the rest of the production. It is found with serial numbers over #6100 and is offered with a 2.875 inch length barrel only. This model is stamped on the top strap "PAT. SEPT. 19, 1871." It has brass frames that were sometimes nickel plated. The barrels are found either blued or plated. The grips are varnished walnut or rosewood. There were only about 2,500 of these revolvers built from 1871-1876.

CLOVERLEAF WITH 1.5 INCH ROUND BARREL

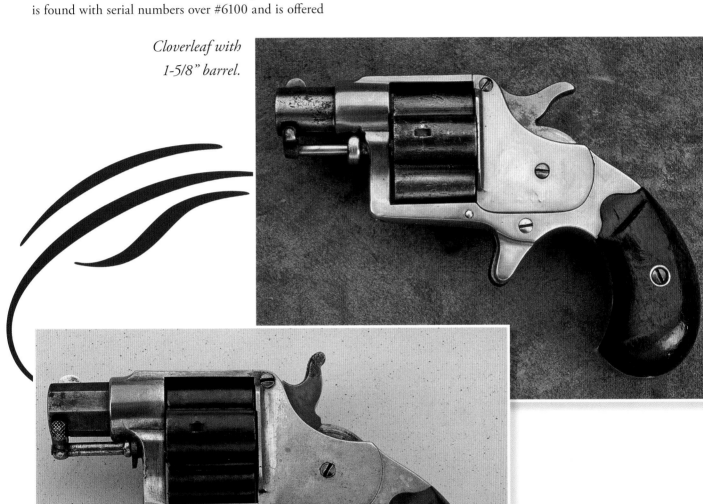

Cloverleaf with 1-5/8" barrel.

Cloverleaf with 1" octagonal barrel.

Cloverleaf with 3" barrel.

EXC.	V.G.	GOOD	FAIR	POOR
-	-	3,000	1,250	400

NOTE: Blued models will bring a premium over nickel in the same condition.

CLOVERLEAF WITH THREE INCH BARREL

EXC.	V.G.	GOOD	FAIR	POOR
-	-	1,500	500	200

HOUSE PISTOL WITH FIVE SHOT ROUND CYLINDER

EXC.	V.G.	GOOD	FAIR	POOR
-	-	1,300	500	200

NOTE: The following advertisement appeared in the Spring of 2007 at *ArmChairGunShow.com*:

"Colt - House Pistol .41 rimfire, 2.5" barrel. Good condition. Pepper-spotted gray metal with some pinpoint pits; medium patina brass frame; good markings. Almost working with very weak lockup. Sound worn wood grips. Serial number #710. $450."

COLT'S EARLY CARTRIDGE REVOLVERS

MODEL 1871-1872 OPEN TOP

This model was the first revolver Colt manufactured especially for a metallic cartridge. It was not a conversion. Although it was not commercially successful and was not accepted by the U.S. Ordnance Department, it paved the way for the Single Action Army that came out shortly thereafter, which was an immediate success. The U.S. Army had decided as early as 1868 to adopt only a solid frame revolver design, yet Colt offered another open top gun design in the hope of gaining the military contract. Chambering a special 44-23-200 cartridge (not the .44 Henry rimfire, as is so often claimed), it

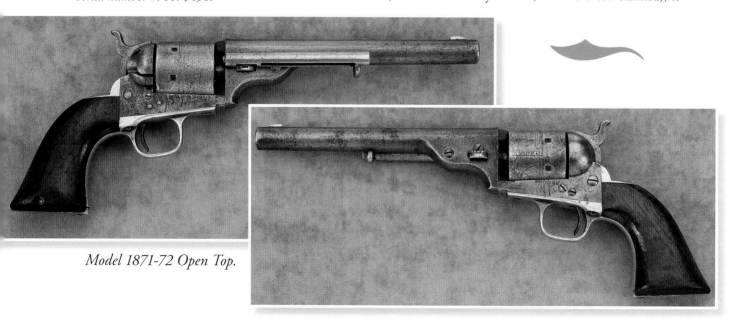

Model 1871-72 Open Top.

was speedily rejected. Eventually, after better designs were introduced, many of these were nickel plated, fitted with ornate pressed meal or carved ivory grips, and sold in Mexico. Uniquely for a cartridge Colt, the rear sight lay on the rear end of the barrel block ahead of the cylinder. The pistol featured 7.5 or 8 inch round barrels and a six shot cylinder. The grip frame and some internal parts were, however, taken from the 1860 Army and the 1851 Navy.

This model is all blued, with a case-colored hammer. There are some with silver plated brass grip frames, but most are blued steel. The unitary one piece grips are varnished walnut. The cylinder is roll engraved with the naval battle scene. The barrel is stamped "ADDRESS COL. SAML. COLT NEW-YORK U.S. AMERICA." The later production revolvers are barrel stamped "COLT'S PT. F.A. MFG. CO. HARTFORD, CT. U.S.A." The first 1,000 revolvers were stamped "COLT'S/PATENT." After that, 1871 and 1872 patent dates appeared on the frame. There were about 7,000 of these revolvers manufactured in 1872 and 1873. Blued models will bring higher prices than nickel models in the same condition.

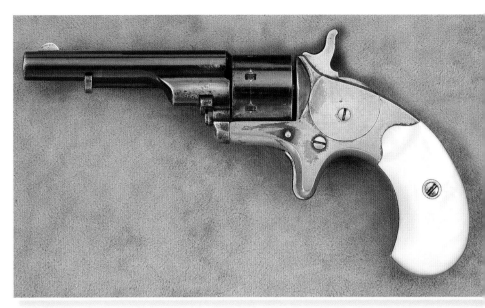

Open Top .22 Pocket Revolver.

1860 ARMY GRIP FRAME

EXC.	V.G.	GOOD	FAIR	POOR
-	-	10,000	3,000	800

1851 NAVY GRIP FRAME

EXC.	V.G.	GOOD	FAIR	POOR
-	-	11,500	4,000	1,200

NOTE: The following advertisement appeared at *AntiqueGuns.com* during the Spring of 2007:

"Colt Model 1871 Open Top .44 caliber revolver with Army Grips, smooth brown, heavy patina over an old arsenal re-blue. The guns shows 40% scene; matching numbers on bottom of gun, grips show long use, very good overall. The bore is dark and shall spotting the entire length."

The seller requested a minimum opening bid of $3,800.

OPEN TOP "OLD LINE" POCKET

This is a .22-cal. rimfire, seven-shot revolver that was offered with a barrel either 2.4 or 2.9 inches in length.

With more than 114,000 manufactured between 1871 and 1877 (although it was certainly considered obsolete by 1873), the model was a commercial success. A great many more would undoubtedly have been sold had not cheap foreign copies begun to flood the market at that time, forcing Colt to drop this model from the line.

This revolver has a silver or a nickel plated brass frame, and a nickel plated or blued barrel and cylinder. The grips are varnished walnut or rosewood, and the butt was of the bird's head design. Loading could be accomplished with the help of a groove cut in the rear right side of the frame, behind the cylinder. The earliest guns had an ejector rod on the right side of the barrel, but this was abandoned in 1874 and the cylinder actually had to be removed to expel its contents. The cylinder bolt slots are found toward the front on this model. "COLT'S PT. F.A. MFG. CO./HARTFORD, CT. U.S.A." is stamped on the barrel and ".22 CAL." on the left side of the frame.

EARLY MODEL WITH EJECTOR ROD

EXC.	V.G.	GOOD	FAIR	POOR
-	-	1,750	800	400

PRODUCTION MODEL
WITHOUT EJECTOR ROD

EXC.	V.G.	GOOD	FAIR	POOR
-	-	600	300	150

Blued models will bring a premium over nickel in the same condition.

NOTE: The following advertisement appeared in the Spring of 2007 at *AntiqueGunList.com*:

New Line .22 Revolver, 2nd Model.

"Colt Open Top, 22 cal., serial number #56XXX, manufactured 1871 to 1877. This is a nice little Colt OT with a tight action and a very good bore, a 9. The nickel finish is about 95%, the grips are in fine condition with no cracks or chips and 95% varnish. The hammer and trigger have good fire-blue color. The two-line address and caliber stamps are sharp. Overall condition fine. $550."

And this classified advertisement appeared at *GunBroker.com* in May of 2007:

"You are bidding on a Colt Open Top Pocket revolver in .22 caliber. This is a 7 shot revolver made between 1871 and 1877. There were approx. 114,000 made. SN 9xxxx. This has a 3.375 inch barrel. I would put it in Very Good condition for its age. Seems fine mechanically although I have not fired it. The grips are walnut and appear to be original to the gun. A few small dings, but no cracks or chips. The nickel plating is in pretty good shape along the barrel and cylinder, with some fading so that you can see the brass along either side of the trigger, worse on the right side. The hammer and trigger are case colored and are mostly a deep blue now. No major pitting is noted. The cylinder is tight and indexes properly. The spring is strong. The same serial number is stamped on the butt and under the barrel, it is in two lines under the barrel. Stamped on top of the barrel is a Maltese Cross followed by COLT'S PAT FA MFG Co and another cross, then underneath that HARTFORD CT U.S.A. I believe that this is an excellent example of an American Legend antique firearm."

Seller opened bidding at $375 with a Buy-It-Now price of $635. It went unsold.

THE NEW LINES

NEW LINE .22

The "Little Colt" or "Baby Colt," a promotional name coined by distributor Benjamin Kittredge of Cincinnati, was the smallest-framed version of the five distinct New Line Revolvers. It has a seven shot cylinder and a 2.25 inch barrel that was originally cylindrical, but was later changed to have flattened sides. The frame is nickeled brass, and the balance of the revolver is either nickel plated or blued. The grips are rosewood. "COLT NEW .22" is found on the barrel; and ".22 CAL.," on the frame. The barrel is also stamped "COLT'S PT. F.A. MFG.CO./HARTFORD, CT. U.S.A." There were two models during the period of manufacture. The first had short cylinder flutes and locking recesses just behind them, while the second (1876) had the locking recesses on the rear face of the cylinder and lengthened the flutes accordingly. Approximately 55,000 of these were made from 1873 to 1877 and serial numbers begin with #1. Colt stopped production of its New Lines rather than try to compete with the cheap "Suicide Specials."

1ST MODEL (SHORT CYLINDER FLUTES)

EXC.	V.G.	GOOD	FAIR	POOR
-	-	600	300	150

2ND MODEL (LONG CYLINDER FLUTES)

EXC.	V.G.	GOOD	FAIR	POOR
-	-	500	250	125

Blued models will bring higher prices than nickel models in the same condition.

New Line .32 Revolver.

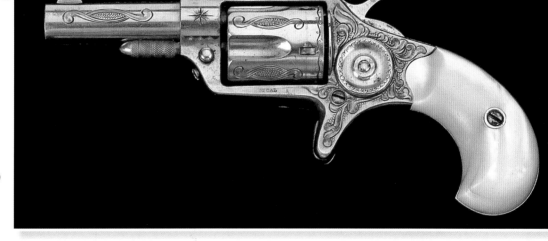

New Line .30
Revolver.

NOTE: The following ad appeared at *AntiqueGuns.com* in the Spring of 2007:

"*Colt New Line .22 Cal with 90% grip varnish, it has upright hammer with deep case color on hammer. The cylinder and barrel have 40% deep blue, functional, fine overall.*"

The seller requested $450 as a minimum opening bid.

NEW LINE .30

The five-shot "Pony Colt" is a larger version of the .22 New Line. As with all the New Line Pocket Models, loading was accomplished by sliding cartridges by the groove and unloading by removing the cylinder. The basic difference is size, caliber, caliber markings and the offering of a blued version with case colored steel frame. Approximately 11,000 were manufactured from 1874 until 1876.

EXC.	V.G.	GOOD	FAIR	POOR
-	-	600	300	150

Prices above are for nickel finish. Blued models will bring a premium of 100 percent.

NOTE: The following advertisement was featured at *AntiqueGuns.com* in March of 2007:

"*Colt New Line .30 cal with 2.5 inch barrel, retains 30% medium to thin blue overall, the hammer shows some rainbow hues, action is slightly funky. It appears a spring was replaced with a home made spring. Very good overall.*"

The seller requested that bidding start at $360.

NEW LINE .32

The five-shot "Ladies Colt" is the same basic revolver as the .30 caliber except that it is chambered for the .32 cal. rimfire or centerfire and is so marked. Eleven thousand of this model were manufactured from 1873 until 1884. The gun was commonly offered with a 2.25-inch barrel and, rarely, a 4-inch barrel. The 4-inch variation would be worth nearly twice the value of a standard model.

EXC.	V.G.	GOOD	FAIR	POOR
-	-	600	300	150

Prices above are for a nickel finish. Blued models will bring a premium of 100 percent.

NOTE: The following New Line .32 was recently listed for sale at *AntiqueGunList.com*:

"Colt New Line 32 cal. CF, nickel with hard rubber grips, SN 20XXX. This is an interesting New Line. The barrel address is stamped COLTS PT.F.A.MFG. CO HARTFORD, CT. U.S.A. Second models should have a 1874 patent date, this one does not. It does not have the etch[ed] panel or caliber stamps either. There are 3 British [proof] stamps on the gun. They are on the barrel, one cylinder flute and on the frame. This may be possibly a German [proof] stamp also. The barrel address is clear and the grips are excellent. The hammer, cylinder pin and screws have almost all of the Peacock blue color. The nickel is not peeling; it has discoloration and some dullness. Mechanically correct and very tight. The bore is a shiny 9. Overall condition fine. More pictures available on request. $575."

NEW LINE .38

Approximately 5,500 of this model, the "Pet Colt," were manufactured between 1874 and 1880. It is chambered for either the .38 rimfire or centerfire, and later models accepted the .38 Short Colt. Barrels are so marked. With a 2.25-inch barrel, the New Line .38 weighed a mere 13.5 oz. This model in a 4-inch barrel would also bring twice the value of the shorter-barreled version.

EXC.	V.G.	GOOD	FAIR	POOR
-	-	800	400	200

Blued models will bring a premium over nickel in the same condition.

NOTE: The following advertisement appeared in the Spring of 2007 in *AntiqueGunList.com*:

"Colt Deringer .38 New Line 80% nickel with a good Colt New .38 etched panel good markings excellent working condition 2 piece walnut grips good bore Serial #433X $1,150."

NEW LINE .41

This is the "Big Colt," as it was sometimes known in advertising of its era. It is chambered for .41 rimfire or centerfire and is so marked. After about 1877, this five-shot pocket revolver was also offered in .41 Long Colt centerfire. For collectors, the large caliber of this variation makes it the most desirable of the New Lines. Approximately 7,000 of this model were manufactured

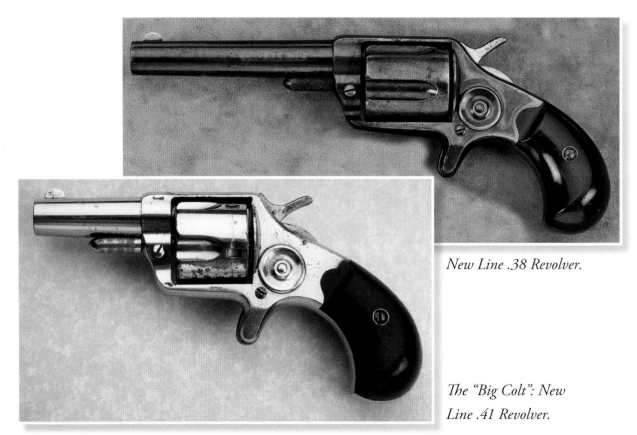

New Line .38 Revolver.

The "Big Colt": New Line .41 Revolver.

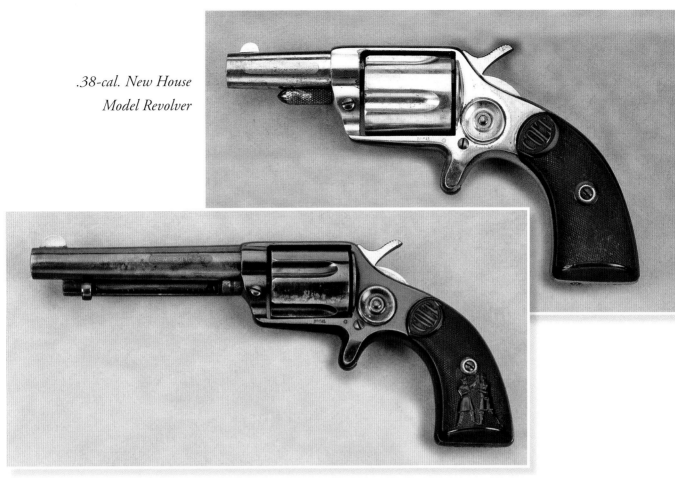

.38-cal. New House Model Revolver

New Police "Cop & Thug" .38 revolver. Note tableaux on grip.

from 1874 to 1879. With the 2.25-inch barrel, the weight is about 12 oz. A gun with a 4-inch barrel would be worth a 100 percent premium.

EXC.	V.G.	GOOD	FAIR	POOR
-	-	900	400	200

Prices above are for nickel finish. Blued models will bring a premium of 100 percent.

NEW HOUSE MODEL

This five-shot revolver is similar to the other New Lines except that it features a square butt instead of the bird's head configuration, a 2.25-inch round barrel without ejector rod, and a thin loading gate. It is chambered for the .32 (rare), .38 and .41 centerfire cartridges. The cylinders had long flutes with the locking notches on the rear face and a lock screw that passed laterally through the frame held the cylinder axis pin. The sheathed trigger was retained and the top strap was forged as part of the frame. The finish was either full nickel plated or blued, with a case colored frame. The grips are walnut, rosewood or (for the first time on a Colt revolver) checkered hard rubber, with an oval around the word "COLT." The barrel address is the same as on the other New Lines. The frame is marked "NEW HOUSE," with the caliber. About 4,000 were

manufactured between 1880 and 1886. The .32 caliber model would bring a 10 percent premium.

EXC.	V.G.	GOOD	FAIR	POOR
-	-	1,000	450	250

Prices above are for nickel finish. Blued models will bring a premium of 100 percent.

NOTE: The following advertisement appeared in the Spring of 2007 at *AntiqueGunList.com*:

"Colt Deringer .38 Colt New House about 50% original blue left excellent working condition good bore fire blue on the back of the hammer. Two piece hard rubber grips the rest of the gun is kind of turning patina. Good circle with the horse in it, too. Serial #226XX $1,750."

And The following advertisement appeared in March of 2007 at *AntiqueGuns.com*:

"Colt New House .38 C, Cop and Thug, in scarce blue with 95% coverage in deep blue, bright excellent bore. Serial number stamped on base of butt is #19947. Crisp like new action, marked, Watson Bros., 4 Pall Mall, London. Excellent plus overall."

The seller opened bidding at $4,000.

NEW POLICE

This was the final revolver in the New Line series. It is chambered for .32, .38 and .41 centerfire caliber.

The .32 and .41 are quite rare. It is offered in barrel lengths of 2.25, 4.5, 5.5 and 6.5 inches. An ejector rod is found on all but the 2.5 inch barrel. The finish is either nickel or blued and case colored. Grips are hard rubber with a scene of a policeman arresting a criminal embossed on them; thus, the model became known to collectors as the "Cop and Thug" model. (New Police models exported to England were fitted with plain wooden grips.) The barrel stamping is as the other New Lines, and the frame is stamped "NEW POLICE .38." Approximately 4,000 of this model were manufactured between 1882 and 1886.

LONG BARREL MODEL WITH EJECTOR

EXC.	V.G.	GOOD	FAIR	POOR
-	-	3,250	1,400	700

The .32- and .41- caliber versions of this model will bring a 40 to 50 percent premium. Blued models and models with 5.5- or 6.5-inch barrels will also bring a premium. Short barrel model will bring about 50 percent of the listed prices.

THE MOST FAMOUS GUN IN HISTORY: MODEL OF 1873,

SINGLE ACTION ARMY (SAA)

The Colt Single Action Army (SAA) or Peacemaker, as it is sometimes referred to, is one of the most widely collected and recognized firearms in the world. With few interruptions or changes in design, it has been manufactured from 1873 until the present. It is still available on a limited production basis from the Colt Custom Shop.

According to Ian Hogg and John Walter writing in *Pistols of the World*, the SAA "was the successor to the Open Top, developed from 1871 to '72 from all the Colt revolvers that had gone before. It was developed specifically to meet the requirements of the US Army and incorporate the latest metallic-cartridge technology.

"However, although initially produced for the army, the success of the SAA was so great that it became the symbol of the Old West: the immortal cowboy's gun. Production began in 1873 and continued until 1940, by which time 310,386 guns (excluding Flat Top and Bisley patterns) had been made. A few guns were assembled from existing parts during World War II, but

work then ceased until popular demand persuaded Colt to recommence manufacture in 1955.

"The SAA revolvers made prior to World War II were offered in thirty chamberings, from .22 Short rimfire to .476 Eley, though the popularity of each varied. By far the most common was .45 Long Colt, amounting to 150,683 examples – nearly half the total. The popularity of Winchester rifles "Out West" persuaded Colt to chamber revolvers for the most popular WCF ("Winchester Central Fire") cartridges. These included .32-20 WCF, .38-40 WCF and .44-40 WCF, the total numbers of SAA in each category amounting to 29,812, 38,240 and 64,489 respectively. The only other chambering to be applied to more than 10,000 guns was .41 centerfire.

"At the other extreme, there were only nine in .38 S&W, four .45-caliber smoothbores, two each in .32-44 and only a single factory-original SAA in .32 RF and .380 Eley. However, it must be remembered that not only have guns been rebarreled and re-chambered down the years, but there is also a healthy market for fakes!

"Few guns have had such an extended production run, and few revolvers have exceeded the total numbers of the SAA. In addition to Colt's own production, reduced almost to nothing in recent years, there have been many copies. A few guns were made in Spain prior to the Spanish Civil War, often showing important differences in detail, but nostalgia and the "fast-draw" craze created such a demand for single-action Western-style revolvers that they have been made in huge quantities – particularly in Italy by Armi San Marco and Uberti. Others have been made in Switzerland by Hammerli (subsequently passed to Interarms in the USA) and in Germany by Sauer and Schmidt. The SAA has also provided the inspiration for a legion of adaptations."

Peacemaker variations are myriad. It has been produced in 30 different calibers and barrel lengths from 2.5 to 16 inches, with 4.75-, 5.5- and even 7.5-inch variations according to a shooter's taste as these guns could be personally ordered if the shooter was well known. The standard finish is blued, with a case colored frame. Many are nickel plated. Examples have been found silvered and even gold plated, and in combinations thereof. The finest engravers in the world have used the SAA as a canvas to display their artistry. The standard grips from 1873 to 1883 were walnut, either oil stained or varnished. From 1883 to approximately 1897, the standard grips were hard rubber with an eagle and shield logo. After this date, at serial number #165000, the hard rubber grips featured the Rampant Colt. Many specially order grips were available, notably pearl and ivory, which were often checkered or carved in ornate fashion.

In its heyday, the SAA was inexpensive and reliable, though only an inexperienced shooter carried the hammer (which had a fixed firing pin) down on a loaded chamber. The mechanism was so simple that there was comparatively little to break, and anything that did fail could be repaired by even the most inexperienced gunsmith. The only accessory commonly offered with the gun was a turnscrew, and even that was not essential.

The variables involved in establishing values for the Peacemaker are extreme. Added to this, one must also consider historical significance, since the SAA played a big part in the formative years of the American West. Fortunately for those among us interested in the SAA, there are a number of fine publications that deal exclusively with this model. It is our strong recommendation that they be acquired and studied thoroughly to prevent extremely expensive mistakes.

Colt's factory records are nearly complete for the SAA, so do your research before purchasing one of the rare or valuable specimens.

For our purposes we will dissect Colt's Single Action Army production as follows:

- Antique or Black Powder, 1st Generation, 1873 to 1898, serial number #1 to #175000. The cylinder axis pin is retained by a screw in the front of the frame.
- Pre-WWII, 1899 to 1940, 1st Generation, serial number #175001 to #357859. The cylinder axis pin is retained by a spring loaded button through the side of the frame. This method is utilized on the following models, as well.
- Post-WWII 2nd Generation, 1956 to 1978, serial number #0001SA to #99999SA.
- 3rd Generation, 1978 to present, beginning with serial #SA1001. A breakdown of production by caliber will follow. It is important to note that the rarer calibers and the larger calibers bring higher values in this variation.

NOTE: As a general rule, nickel plated guns bring a *deduction* of 20 to 30 percent. For revolvers with 4.75 inch barrels, add 10-15 percent. For checkered grips add 20 percent.

The following is an example from the Summer, 2007 listings at *ArmChairGunShow.com* of the fascination that collecting antique Single Action Army Colts can elicit, even when provenance isn't 100 percent certain:

"Tom Mix attributed - martial Colt Single Action Army - w/ holster rig and badge; also 101 Ranch and Buffalo Soldier associated .45 Colt; 5"+ cut barrel. About good condition. Gray-brown patina, well worn w/ light roughness; traces of nickel on backstrap. Good markings include 'U.S.' frame and '101' stamped large on right side of frame, and mixed numbers, frame #3852, trigger guard K inspected #138257, backstrap #30028, barrel obscured but may be 5646. Appears as an Artillery Model with some replaced parts, including ejector rod head and screw, firing pin, & trigger. Old replaced German silver front sight. Cylinder pin screw broken off. Working; strong rifling with light pitting throughout bore. Stag grips with Tom Mix's Lazy T M bar brand relief carved on top of left panel.

"With lightweight early double loop holster & cartridge belt with billet marked '44C/DENVER MFG. CO. MAKERS/24.' Also star in shield 'SPECIAL OFFICER' marked silver badge with '101' scratched at bottom tip of shield on front & center of star in back.

"Listed in a recent Julia Auction catalog, 'This revolver was reportedly given to Tom Mix by an African-American special deputy who worked at the 101 Ranch around the turn of the 20th Century. This revolver was reportedly issued to troops of the 10th Cavalry. It is well known that Tom Mix was an employee of the 101 Ranch and subsequent to his becoming famous, a frequent guest there' Discussion with helpful Julia representatives indicated the previous owner, who had a special interest in African-Americans in the West, has purchased the gun and rig with the understanding that these assertions were true. He decided to sell it after he was unable to uncover more information on that aspect of the attribution. Accompanied by an unidentified clipping illustrating the gun and identifying it as 'issued to all black cavalry unit in Colorado. Later was carried by Black Special Officer on 101 Ranch.' Also a document discussing Mix's work on the 101 from 1906 through 1911. The provenance on this fascinating colorful ensemble is far from nailed down, but offers intriguing possibilities for further research, with overlapping layers of historical significance. $7,500."

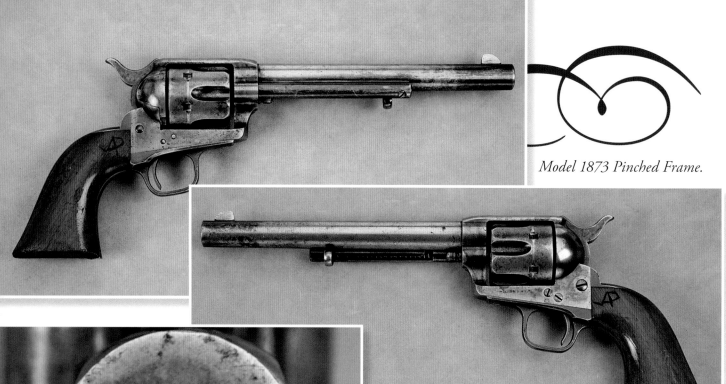

Model 1873 Pinched Frame.

Here's something you don't see every day: a Model 1873 Pinched Frame with serial number 14.

THE ANTIQUE SINGLE ACTION ARMY

FIRST YEAR PRODUCTION "PINCHED FRAME" 1873 ONLY

It is almost necessary to categorize this variation on its own. It is one of the rarest and most interesting of all the solid frame SAAs, not to mention that it is the first. On this model the top strap is "pinched" or constricted approximately one-half inch up from the hammer to form the rear sight. This "V" groove runs the length of the topstrap, above the cylinder. The reason for the frame change came in 1872 at the recommendation of Capt. John Edie, a government inspector and president of a board of officers, who thought that the full-fluted top strap would be a big improvement in the sighting capabilities of this revolver. The highest surviving serial number having this feature is #156, the lowest #1.

Model 1873 Pinched Frame, top view. Note "pinch" in topstrap that fiorms rear sight, just to the left of the hammer face.

Model 1873 Early Military Model, left view.

Model 1873 Early Military Model, bottom view.

From these numbers, it is safe to assume that the first run of SAAs were all of this pinched-frame design. There is no sure way to tell how many there were, though, since Colt apparently did not serial number the frames exactly in the order that they were manufactured. An educated guess would be that there were between 50 and 150 pinched frame guns in all, and that they were all made before the middle of July 1873. The barrel length of the first model is 7.5 inches; the standard caliber .45 Colt; and the proper grips were of walnut. The front sight, brazed to the muzzle, is a plain flat blade and on some models is German silver. Because so few were produced, this model will rarely be encountered; and if it is, it should never be purchased without competent inspection and appraisal.

EXC.	V.G.	GOOD	FAIR	POOR
-	85,000	55,000	32,000	10,000

EARLY MILITARY MODEL 1873 TO 1877

The serial number range on this first run of military contract revolvers extends to #24000. The barrel address is in the early script style with the # symbol preceding and following. The frame bears the martial marking "US," and the walnut grips have the inspector's initials stamped inside a cartouche, often accompanied by the date of inspection. The front sight is steel as on all military models. Guns with 7.5-inch barrels were initially issued to mounted units, and full length guns are now often known as "Cavalry Models." The caliber is .45 Colt, and the ejector rod head is the bull's eye or donut style with a hole in the center of it. The finish features the military polish and case colored frame, with the remainder blued. Authenticate any potential purchase, because many spurious examples have been noted. The Sioux Indian campaign of 1876 saw its first use in a major military operation. In the battle of the Little Bighorn, George Custer's troops were armed with the Model 1873 revolver.

EXC.	V.G.	GOOD	FAIR	POOR
55,000	45,000	35,000	17,000	6,000

Certain three digit and four digit serial numbers will command a substantial premium. Seek an expert appraisal prior to sale.

NOTE: The following advertisement appeared at *AntiqueGuns.com* in March of 2007:

"US Cavalry Colt SA 7.5 inch barrel, serial number #27xx matching, Ainsworth, 3rd shipment of first contract of Colt SA revolvers. Shipped on January 3, 1874 to San Antonio Arsenal for use by the 4th Cavalry; 1,000 guns were in shipment. All correct, but well used Ainsworth with full compliment of inspector initials, partial visible cartouches on left grip, no cartouches on right grip. Mottled gray overall with patches of fine pinpricks, probably from a deteriorating holster. Traces of thin blue in protected places of metal, grips have been lightly sanded. It appears to be all correct, but has not been viewed by [firearms appraiser John] Kopec, from all I can tell. Very good overall."

The seller started bidding at $12,500 and would sell immediately for $14,500.

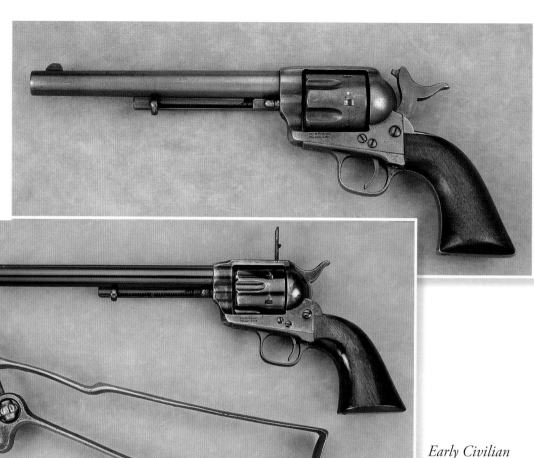

*Model 1873
.44 Rimfire,
left view.
Note rimfire
hammer.*

*Early Civilian
Model SAA
"Buggy Rifle"
with shoulder
stock. Very rare.*

EARLY CIVILIAN MODEL 1873-1877

This model is identical to the .45-cal. Early Military Model but has no military acceptance markings or cartouches. The Civilian Model has a higher degree of polish than is found on the military models, and the finish on these early models could be plated or blued with a case colored frame. The SAA was always regarded as a tool and, although many ornate presentation or "commemorative issue" examples have been made, the standard revolver was almost always plain and unadorned. Some could have the German silver front sight blade. The early bull's eye ejector rod head is used on this model. This model also has a script barrel address. The grips are standard one piece walnut. Guns fitted with ivory grips are worth a premium.

EXC.	V.G.	GOOD	FAIR	POOR
35,000	28,000	16,000	12,000	6,000

Certain three-digit and four-digit serial numbers will command a substantial premium. Seek an expert appraisal prior to purchase.

NOTE: The following advertisement appeared in the Spring of 2007 at *AntiqueGunList.com*:

"Colt Single Action Army, 7 1/2 inch barrel, 45 cal., U.S. Cavalry, Henry Nettleton, buy-back, SN 54XXX, shipped to Kittredge Cin. Ohio 3-11-80. Colt bought Cavalries back from the Army when there was a surplus, nickeled them, stamped 45 cal. on the trigger guard and sold them to the civilian market. The Kopec letter says nickel and the Colt letter says blue. I believe this one was nickeled as I have had several of the H.N. buy-backs over the years and all were nickeled. I have also had numerous nickeled Colt's that the Colt letter said they were shipped blue, a very common Colt letter error. This is a good example of a U.S. H.N. Cavalry with all the correct stamping excluding the U.S. Many of the H.N. were not stamped with the U.S. and this one does not show that it was removed. It has the H.N. stamp on all the parts including the hammer, P stamp on the barrel and cylinder. It is a smooth metal gun, appears to have had some cleaning, front sight has been slimed down some. The barrel address, patent dates,

Model 1873 .44 Rimfire, bottom view.

inspectors stamps are all sharp and readable as are all the serial numbers in 5 locations. The bore has good rifling, a 7-8, and the action is tight and correct. The original Colt grips show wear to the corners and fit tight. Today's prices on a Kopec letter are $300 and a Colt letter is $100, so figure that into the price of this Colt. It is a good example of a desirable inspector right in the Indian Wars time period at a reasonable price. Overall condition very good. $4,950.".

44 RIMFIRE MODEL, 1875-1880

Made to fire the .44 Henry rimfire cartridge, this model Colt was to be used as a compatible companion sidearm to the Henry and Winchester 1866 rifles used extensively during this era. However, this pistol did not enchant the public and the .44 rimfire was doomed to economic failure as soon as it appeared on the market. By that time, it had already been established that large caliber centerfire cartridges were a good deal more efficient than their rimfire counterparts. Large caliber rimfires were deemed obsolete before this Colt ever hit

the market. The result was that Colt's sales representatives sold most of the production to "Banana Republics" in South and Central America, where the guns received much abuse. Most had the original 7.5-inch barrels cut down; and in use, nearly all were denied even the most basic maintenance. Thus, model survival rate was low. All this adds to its desirability as a collector's item, however – and makes the risk of acquiring a fake that much greater.

The .44 Rimfire is unique in that it was the only SAA variation to have its own serial number range, starting with #1 and continuing to #1892, the latest known surviving specimen. The block style barrel markings were introduced during this production run. At least 90 of these revolvers were converted by the factory to .22 rimfire, and at least one was shipped chambered for .32 rimfire. These guns had "COLT'S FRONTIER SIX-SHOOTER" on the left side of the barrel, but the mark was applied by an acid etching process and was not particularly durable. These guns included a high proportion of nickel plated examples, and some were decorated with Mexico's famous eagle and snake emblems in the grips.

EXC.	V.G.	GOOD	FAIR	POOR
45,000	37,000	20,000	8,000	3,500

NOTE: The following advertisement appeared at *AntiqueGunList.com* in the Spring of 2007:

"Colt SAA 4-3/4x44WCF, 127XXX (1888) and most likely being one of the very VERY first with the roll-die COLT FRONTIER SIX-SHOOTER barrel logo. Correct two-line barrel address (a little faint with wear) and having a decent bore. The action is good, but somewhat sticky as if it has had some internal parts replaced without a good final tuning-up ...and if this was to be used as a shooter, the action should be smoothed up (and checked out) by a competent gunsmith. It does have all the positions on the hammer. The Eagle grips do look to have some legitimate wear, but I am pretty sure that they are good reproductions. Metal has some minor freckle-pitting scattered here and there and has a dark greyish patina overall. This configuration (the short barreled 44/40) was immortalized in the 1970s Marty Robbins C&W song called 'Mr. Shorty' where he describes the gun as a short-barreled bad forty-four ...and says, '...the forty-four spoke and sent powder and smoke ...and seventeen inches of flame' (...a VERY descriptive line!) It is getting pretty hard to find these 1880s Single Actions at prices under two thousand twenty-five hundred anymore, and this is a modest, but decent little gun. About VG $2,095."

Model 1873 Late Military Model.

LATE MILITARY MODEL 1878-1891

The later Military Models are serial numbered to approximately #136000. They bear the block style barrel address without the # prefix or suffix. The frames are marked "US," and the oil stained walnut grips are impressed with the inspector's cartouche and initials. The finish is the military style polish, case colored frame and the remainder is blued. This was the standard sidearm during the Indian campaigns until about 1890. The earliest guns lacked caliber marks, but owing to a steady increase in options, these were added to the barrel or frame after about 1880. On the military marked Colts, it is imperative that potential purchases be authenticated as many fakes have been discovered.

EXC.	V.G.	GOOD	FAIR	POOR
30,000	22,000	12,000	8,000	5,000

Revolvers produced from 1878 to 1885 will command a premium. Seek an expert appraisal prior to sale.

NOTE: The following advertisement appeared at AntiqueGunList.com in the Spring of 2007:

"Colt S/A, 7-1/2"X44WCF, circa 1887 (#123XXX) and having a smooth crisp action, all the clicks on the hammer, and a decent 44/40 bore. VG Eagle grips with moderate wear, smooth metal showing some rounding to the sharp edges and some faint traces of an old cold blue ...but mostly being a neutral greyish color. The etched CFSS[Colt's Frontier Six Shooter] panel is LONG gone, but the remaining markings are all decent ....and all things considered, it is still a VERY collectible and decent S/A in VG condition. $3,045."

ARTILLERY MODEL 1895-1903

A number of "US" marked SAAs were returned either to the Colt factory or to the Springfield Armory, where they were altered and refinished. These revolvers have 5.5-inch barrels and any combination of mixed serial numbers. They were remarked by the inspectors of

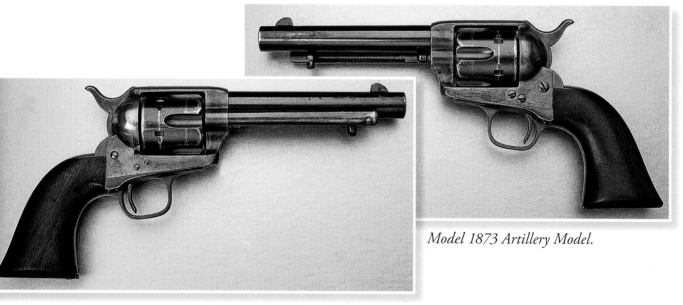

Model 1873 Artillery Model.

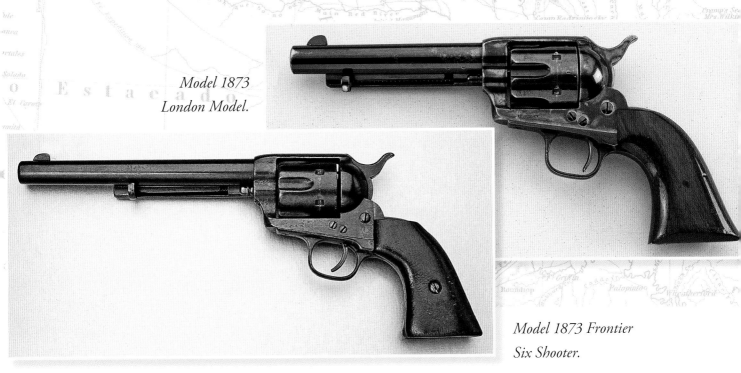

Model 1873
London Model.

Model 1873 Frontier
Six Shooter.

the era and have a case colored frame and a blued cylinder and barrel. Some have been noted all blued within this variation. This model, as with the other military marked Colts, should definitely be authenticated before purchase. Some of these revolvers fall outside the 1898 antique cutoff date that has been established by the government and may not be quite as desirable to investors. They are generally worth approximately 20 percent less.

EXC.	V.G.	GOOD	FAIR	POOR
18,000	12,500	8,000	4,000	3,000

NOTE: The following advertisement appeared at AntiqueGunList.com in the Spring of 2007:

"Colt S/A 4-3/4 x 44WCF, c1896 (162XXX serial range) and having the plain hard rubber grips (Eagle-less) which show quite a bit of wear to the checking. Also, this has the later style plunger pin release and is a VERY early specimen to have that feature. Faint traces of original blue where the barrel meets the frame and around the trigger bow junctions and some THIN cloudy grays on the frame of faded C/H, but basically a thin patina gun with minor scattered pitting. Mechanically it is tight, but has the 2nd notch worn on the hammer, and should have this professionally freshened up if the gun were to be shot much. The bore is very good, but there is a dent on the left side front of the barrel that does show on the inside slightly, and this COULD affect accuracy (....assuming anyone considers these as being accurate weapons!) The patent markings are very good ...as is the correct two-line address, the side roll die logo is a bit fainter. Overall this is a decent little short barrelled forty-four, and has the earliest plunger frame that I have had in quite a while. $2,295."

LONDON MODEL

These SAAs were manufactured to be sold through Colt's London Agency. The barrel is marked "COLT'S PT. F.A. MFG. CO. HARTFORD, CT. U.S.A. DEPOT 14 PALL MALL LONDON." This model is available in various barrel lengths. They are generally chambered for .45 Colt, .450 Boxer (729 guns built for this cartridge), .450 Eley (2,697 built), .455 Eley (1,150 built) and, rarely, .476 Eley (161 built), the largest caliber of all the SAA chamberings. A good many of the London Models were cased and embellished, and they should be individually appraised. This model must be authenticated as many spurious examples have been noted.

EXC.	V.G.	GOOD	FAIR	POOR
22,000	15,000	10,000	4,500	2,000

Revolvers chambered for .476 Eley will command a 100 percent premium.

FRONTIER SIX SHOOTER 1878-1882

Several thousand SAAs were made with the legend "COLT'S FRONTIER SIX SHOOTER" acid etched into the left side of the barrel instead of being stamped. This etching is not deep, and today collectors will become ecstatic if they discover a specimen with mere vestiges of the etched panel remaining. These acid etched SAAs are serial numbered #45000 to #65000. They have various barrel lengths and finishes, but all are chambered for .44-40 caliber.

EXC.	V.G.	GOOD	FAIR	POOR
42,500	22,000	14,000	8,000	6,000

Model 1873 Sheriff's/Storekeeper's Model.

SHERIFF'S OR STOREKEEPER'S MODEL 1882-1898

Although this model was manufactured with a short barrel (2.5 to 4.75 inches long), most have 4-inch barrels. It features no ejector rod or housing, and the frame is made without the hole in the right forward section to accommodate the ejector assembly. The Sheriff's or Storekeeper's Model is numbered above serial #73000. It was manufactured with various finishes and chambered for numerous calibers. This model continued after 1898 into the smokeless or modern era. Examples manufactured in the pre-war years are worth approximately 20 percent less. Although faking this model is quite difficult, it has been successfully done.

EXC.	V.G.	GOOD	FAIR	POOR
40,000	27,500	15,000	9,000	4,500

FLATTOP TARGET MODEL 1888-1896

This model, originally designed for target shooting, is highly regarded and sought-after by collectors. It is not only rare (between 900 and 925 were manufactured) but is an extremely attractive and well finished variation. The most readily identifying feature of the flattop is the lack of a groove in the top strap and the sight blade dovetailed into the flattop. The ejector rod and its case were also frequently removed, the owners preferring to remove the cylinder to reload. The Flattop is chambered for 22 different calibers from .22 rimfire to the large .476 Eley. The .22 rimfire (93 known), .38 Colt (the most popular model with 122 known guns), .41 centerfire (91 known), .45 Long Colt (100 known), .450 Boxer (89 known) and .450 Eley (84 known) are the predominant chamberings. A single gun was chambered for the .44

Model 1873 Flat-Top Target.

Bisley Model.

S&W Special. The 7.5 inch barrel length is the most commonly encountered, although lengths from 4.25 to 9 inches have been recorded.

The serial number range is primarily between #127000 and #162000, but some have been found in higher ranges. The finish is all blued, with a case colored hammer and its checkered grips are either hard rubber or walnut. The front sight has a removable blade insert. The values given are for a standard production model chambered for the calibers previously mentioned as being the most common. It is important to have other calibers individually appraised as variance in values can be quite extreme.

EXC.	V.G.	GOOD	FAIR	POOR
35,000	25,000	15,000	8,000	4,000

Nickel plated versions of this model will command a premium.

BISLEY MODEL 1894-1915

This model was named for the target range in Great Britain, where National Target Matches have been held since the 19th century. The model was designed as a target revolver, a direct descendant of the Flattop Target, with an odd humped back grip that was supposed to better fill the hand while target shooting. It is also easily identified by the wide, low profile hammer spur (a "dished" spur); a wide, checkered and markedly curved trigger; and the name "BISLEY" stamped on the barrel. Bisley production fell within the serial number range #165000 to #331916. There were 44,350 made.

The Bisley was offered in 16 different chamberings from .32 Colt to .455 Eley. The most common calibers were .32-30, .38-40, .41, .44-40 and .45 Colt. The barrel lengths are 4.75, 5.5 and 7.5 inches. The frame and hammer are case-colored; the remainder, blued. Smokeless powder models produced after 1899 utilized the push button cylinder pin retainer. Grips are checkered hard rubber. This model was actually designed with English sales in mind. Though it did sell well there, American sales accounted for most of the Bisley production. The values we provide here cover the standard calibers and barrel lengths. Rare calibers such as the two smoothbore guns, one found chambered for .44 and two in .45, and/or other notable variations can bring greatly fluctuating values, and qualified appraisals should be secured in such cases.

EXC.	V.G.	GOOD	FAIR	POOR
10,000	7,000	4,000	2,500	1,200

Bisley Flat-Top
Target Model.

Model 1873 Standard
Civilian Production
Model, 1876-1898.

Bisleys manufactured before 1898 are worth approximately 50 percent more.

NOTE: The following advertisement appeared at ArmChairGunShow.com in the Spring of 2007:

"Colt Bisley - Single Action Army - factory letter - .32WCF (.32-30); 4.75" barrel. About excellent condition. Nice old honest Colt, with nearly all the original nickel remaining, but a bit tough to evaluate since the nickel has turned milky and is widely covered with pinpoints of roughness and small bubbles; maybe 95% plating coverage remains. Fine markings; good mech; light roughness in bore Moderately worn hard rubber grips. Factory letter shows one gun shipment in this configuration to Wyeth Hardware of St. Louis on 9/22/04. Serial number #251050. $2,650."

BISLEY MODEL FLATTOP TARGET 1894-1913

This model is quite similar to the Standard Bisley Model, with the flattop frame and dovetail rear sight feature. It also has the removable front sight insert. The Bisley Flattop has a completely blued finish with case colored hammer only and is available with a 7.5-inch barrel. Smokeless powder models produced after 1899 utilized the push-button cylinder pin retainer. Calibers are the same as the standard Bisley with 14 different chamberings. Colt manufactured 976 of these revolvers. The advice regarding appraisal would also apply.

EXC.	V.G.	GOOD	FAIR	POOR
25,000	16,000	9,500	3,500	1,800

Nickel plated models will definitely command a premium.

STANDARD CIVILIAN PRODUCTION MODELS 1876-1898

This final designated category for the black powder or antique SAAs includes all the revolvers not previously categorized. They have barrel lengths of 4.75, 5.5 and 7.5 inches and are chambered for any one of 30 different calibers. The finishes could be blued, blued and case colored, or plated in nickel, silver, gold or combinations thereof. Grips could be walnut, hard rubber, ivory, pearl, stag or bone. The possibilities are practically endless. Values given here are for the basic model, and we again strongly advise securing qualified appraisal when not completely sure of any model variation.

For Standard Civilian Production Models with screw in frame, serial number to #163000 add a 25 to 100 percent premium depending on year built. Seek expert appraisal prior to sale.

EXC.	V.G.	GOOD	FAIR	POOR
27,000	18,000	12,000	8,000	3,000

NOTE: The following advertisement appeared in the Spring of 2007 at *AntiqueGunList.com*:

"Colt SAA 1st Generation .44-40 7 ½" barrel this gun has been totally restored and engraved nickel plated with one piece ivory grips fit the gun perfectly this is an etched panel barrel factory letter states .44-40 7 ½" barrel nickel finish shipped February 25. 1889 to E.C. Meacham Arms Company St Louis Missouri. Serial number #11279XX. $4,550."

And this ad showed up at *AntiqueGuns.com* in March of 2007:

Pre-war Model 1873.

"*Colt Single Action 4.75 inch barrel, .45 LC, serial numbered #94XXX with an 1883 manufacturing date and having a good bore and action although it is missing the second position on the hammer and therefore it probably should have the sear notch freshened up (or re-cut) if it were to be shot very much. The exterior has at least 20 to 30% thinning nickel remaining and mixing with grey steel and some kind of swirly looking scattered rag pitting (or holster pitting) from long storage in either a damp holster or a rag that was often wet. The Eagle style grips do show medium to heavy wear, and are rather ill-fitting to this particular revolver and thus are no doubt replaced from another gun ... but at least they are the correct style for this era. Correct two-line barrel address, and while this is not a higher end major collection Single Action, it is rather uncommon to be a short barrel in this early 1880s vintage, and is still a desirable revolver. Like most all mid-range value S/As, it probably has had its share of cosmetic restorations and changed parts and therefore, while this gun is (of course) satisfaction guaranteed, I cannot unequivocally state that it is without some of those commonly encountered cosmetic enhancements or restorations. About G+/VG.*"

The seller asked for bidding to start at $2,100 and would sell immediately for $2,475.

The Colt's Single Action Army Revolvers discussed to this point are considered to be in the federally designated antique category. The arbitrary cutoff date of 1898 was established perhaps because it related to the change over from black to smokeless powder. Thus any weapon manufactured prior to this date is considered an antique.

As an antique, a pre-1898 weapon is not subject to the restraints placed on collectors and dealers by the Gun Control Act of 1968. This is important because firearms falling into this category will usually bring higher prices from investors who do not relish paperwork on collectible investments. There will be those who

disagree, but our experience nevertheless suggests that it is correct.

MODERN ERA SINGLE ACTION ARMY

Rather than diminish with time, the fame of the Peacemaker has grown with the years. Colt's Single Action Army or SAA was the "Gun that Won the West" as much as the Winchester 1873 Carbine. Often, the two were carried in tandem: the rifle for longer range and a .44-caliber SAA the up-close-and-personal stopper.

The myth and tradition of the SAA has been perpetuated by film and television. After all, they were carried by Wild Bill Hickok and Buffalo Bill Cody and General George Patton. Actors such as the redoubtable Gene Autry carried the SAA on screen. According to Robert "Doc" O'Meara, writing in *The Guns of the Gunfighters: Lawmen, Outlaws and Hollywood Cowboys*, Autry carried a single, nickel plated SAA with either a 4.75 or 5.5 inch barrel and, of course, ivory or mother-of-pearl grips.

A surprising number of Colt pistols are still found in their original boxes, even older models. This can add 100 percent to the value of the pistol, especially if the box is in good shape.

SAAS PRIOR TO AND DURING WORLD WAR I

STANDARD PRODUCTION PRE-WAR MODELS

The 1899 cutoff has been noted as a government-accepted date dividing antique from modern era guns. Nevertheless, the actual beginning production date

Pre-war Model 1873 with long-fluted cylinder.

for smokeless powder models was 1900. Thus, pre-World War I Colts are quite similar to the antiques: finishes, barrel lengths, grips, mechanics of the action and so on. Calibers are also similar, with the exception that obsolete calibers were dropped and new versions added. The most apparent physical difference between smokeless and black powder models is the previously discussed method of retaining the cylinder axis pin. Pre-World War Colts used a spring-loaded button through the side of the frame. The black powder models used a screw in the front of the frame. The values furnished for this model designation are for these standard models only. The serial number range on the pre-war SAAs is from #175001 to #357859. Variations can have marked effects on value fluctuations, and qualified appraisal should be secured.

EXC.	V.G.	GOOD	FAIR	POOR
11,500	6,750	4,000	2,500	1,500

NOTE: The following advertisements were placed in the Spring of 2007, the first at *AntiqueGunList.com* and the second at *ColtAutos.com*:

"*Colt SAA 4 ¾" Barrel 38-40 blue and case color in protected areas good markings on barrel back strap & trigger guard in excellent working condition good bore this gun was manufactured in 1911 requires FFL ask all questions sold as is. Colt Letter shipped October 18, 1911 to Richard and Conover Hardware Co Oklahoma City, Oklahoma Serial #3199XX $2,950.*"

"*Single Action Army - caliber: .38wcf (.38/40), serial number #251506, price: $1,500. Description: a fine 1909*

Colt Single Action. This gun has been re-blued but looks old, possibly factory, and comes with a beautiful set of stag grips faded to proper color for the age. They are fitted perfectly. The piece has a 5 inch barrel and all numbers (barrel, frame, and grip) match. The loading gate has a different number but looks as old as the gun. All marking are sharp and clear and none of the screws show tampering. Bore is excellent and bright with no pitting. A gun like this in original finish would sell for $3,500 to $4,000 but you have the chance to buy a good solid Colt SAA for less than half of market price."

LONG FLUTED CYLINDER MODEL 1913-1915

The Colt company never threw anything away. That credo was never more evident than with this model. These long flute cylinders were actually left over from the model 1878 Double Action Army Revolvers. Some bookkeeper in the hierarchy at Colt had an inspiration that probably drove the gunsmiths slightly mad: to make these cylinders fit the SAA frames. There were 1,478 of the long flutes manufactured. They are chambered for the .45 Colt, .38-40, .32-20, .41 Colt and .44 Smith & Wesson Special. Offered in the three standard barrel lengths, they were especially well polished, having what has been described as Colt's "Fire Blue" on the barrel and cylinder. Frame and hammer are case colored and they are fitted with checkered hard rubber grips. These firearms are particularly fine examples of Colt's craft. Today, these models are rare.

EXC.	V.G.	GOOD	FAIR	POOR
15,000	8,500	6,000	3,250	2,000

2nd Generation Model 1873 SAA.

2nd Generation Sheriff's Model SAA.

POST-WORLD WAR II MODELS

STANDARD POST-WAR MODEL 1956-1975

In 1956 the shooting and gun collecting fraternity succeeded in convincing Colt that there was a market for a reintroduced Single Action Army. The revolver was subsequently brought back in the same external configuration. The only changes were internal. Specifications as to barrel length and finish availability were the same and calibers available were .38 Special, .357 Magnum, .44 Special and .45 Colt. The serial number range of the reintroduced 2nd Generation, as it is sometimes known, is from #000ISA to #73000SA.

Values for the standard post-war Colts are established by four basic factors: caliber (popularity and scarcity), barrel length, finish and condition. Shorter barrel lengths are generally more desirable than the 7.5 inches. The .38 Special is the rarest caliber, but the .45 Colt and .44 Special are more sought after than the .357 Magnum. Special feature revolvers, such as the 350 factory engraved guns produced during this period, must be individually appraised. Today's world ivory situation has also become quite a factor in determining value, as ivory grips are found on many 2nd Generation SAAs. These factors have been considered and evaluations presented for this model as accurately and clearly as possible. Remember as always, when in doubt secure a qualified appraisal before making an offer.

For 4.75-inch barrel add 25 percent; 5.5-inch barrel add 15 percent; nickel finish add 20 percent; ivory grips add $250.

7.5 INCH BARREL MODEL

.38 SPECIAL

NIB	EXC.	V.G.	GOOD	FAIR	POOR
2,450	1,850	1,200	900	700	600

.357 MAGNUM

NIB	EXC.	V.G.	GOOD	FAIR	POOR
1,850	1,350	900	750	700	650

.44 SPECIAL

NIB	EXC.	V.G.	GOOD	FAIR	POOR
2,950	2,250	1,750	1,100	1,000	750

.45 COLT

NIB	EXC.	V.G.	GOOD	FAIR	POOR
2,000	1,650	1,400	1,000	900	750

NOTE: The following advertisement appeared in the Spring of 2007 on *AntiqueGunList.com*:

"Colt SAA 2nd generation .38 Special manufactured 1956. 90% plus blue and case color. In excellent working condition. Original two-piece hard rubber grips; good markings this gun is FFL or C&R. Ask questions. Gun sold as is. Serial number #836XSA. $1,995."

SHERIFF'S MODEL 1960-1975

Between 1960 and 1975, approximately 500 Sheriff's Models were manufactured. They have 3-inch barrels and no ejector rod assemblies. The frames were made without the hole for the ejector rod to pass through. They were blued, with case colored frames; 25 revolvers

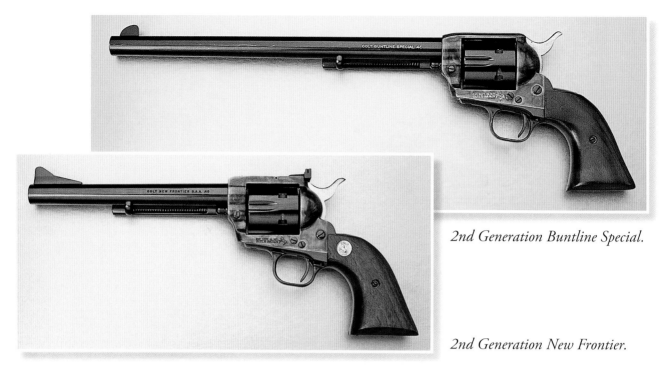

2nd Generation Buntline Special.

2nd Generation New Frontier.

were nickel plated and would bring a sizable premium if authenticated. Barrels are marked "COLT SHERIFF'S MODEL" and serial numbers have an "SM" suffix. They are chambered for the .45 Colt cartridge.

For nickel plated finish add 20 percent.

NIB	EXC.	V.G.	GOOD	FAIR	POOR
3,000	2,200	1,800	1,200	850	600

BUNTLINE SPECIAL 1957-1975

The "Buntline Special" was named after a dime novelist named Ned Buntline (real name Edward Z.C. Judson), who supposedly made a gift of a special long-barreled Colt revolver to Wyatt Earp, Bat Masterson, Charlie Bassett, Neal Brown and Bill Tilghman, all "Old West" lawmen. The story is probably another Old West myth as no Colt records exist to lend it credence. None of the supposed gift guns have been located, and Judson is probably still rolling in his grave, not in Tombstone or Abilene, but in Stamford, New York, chuckling about the "mystery."

For whatever reasons, the Buntline has acquired a reputation far in excess of its importance, numbers or usefulness. True, guns of this type were exhibited at the Centennial Exhibition in Philadelphia in 1876, but they were "Buggy Rifles" with folding rear sights and skeleton stocks. It is probable that others were made for the 1878 St. Louis Exposition.

Nevertheless, the Colt factory decided to take advantage of the market – no doubt urged on by casual collectors and the success of Sturm, Ruger and the Great Western Arms Company – and produced the

12-inch barreled SAA from 1957 to 1974, ultimately manufacturing, so strong is the mystique of the Buntline legend, approximately 3,900. They are chambered for the .45 Long Colt cartridge and offered in the blued and case-colored finish. Only 65 Buntlines are nickel plated, making this an extremely rare variation that definitely should be authenticated before purchase. Walnut grips are most common, but they were also offered with the checkered hard rubber grips. The barrels are marked on the left side "COLT BUNTLINE SPECIAL .45." (Note: A few 3rd Generation Buntlines were manufactured in the late 1970s, but aside from serial numbers they are difficult to distinguish from their predecessors as any revisions were internal rather than apparent.) For nickel finish add 60 percent.

NIB	EXC.	V.G.	GOOD	FAIR	POOR
2,250	1,650	1,250	850	600	500

NEW FRONTIER 1961-1975

This was the target model of the post-war Single Action Army, capitalizing upon the presidential campaign slogan of John F. Kennedy in 1960 *("We stand at the edge of a New Frontier")*. The New Frontier is readily identified by its flattop frame, adjustable rear sight and high front sight. Colt manufactured approximately 4,200 chambered for the .357 Magnum, .45 Colt, .44 Special (255 produced) and occasionally (only 49 produced) in .38 Special. A few were chambered for .44-40. The 7.5-inch barrel length is by far the most common, but the 4.75- and 5.5-inch barrels (even 70 guns with 12-inch "Buntline barrels," see below) were

3rd Generation SAA.

also offered. The standard finish was case colored and blued. Nickel plating and full blue were offered but are rarely encountered. Standard grips were walnut. The barrel is stamped on the left side "Colt New Frontier S.A.A." The serial has the "NF" suffix.

NIB	EXC.	V.G.	GOOD	FAIR	POOR
1,850	1,400	1,000	800	600	500

For 4.75-inch barrel add 25 percent; 5.5-inch barrel add 20 percent; full blue add 50 percent; .38 Special add 50 percent; .44 Special add 30 percent;. 44-40 add 30 percent.

NEW FRONTIER BUNTLINE SPECIAL 1962-1967

This model is rare, because Colt only manufactured 70 during this five-year period. They are similar to the standard Buntline with a 1- inch barrel, but are chambered only for .45 Colt.

NIB	EXC.	V.G.	GOOD	FAIR	POOR
4,000	3,000	2,000	1,500	1,000	700

3RD GENERATION SAAs

3RD GENERATION SAA 1976 TO 1981

In 1976 Colt made some internal changes in the SAA. The external configuration was not, however, altered. Serial numbering began in 1976 with #80000SA, and in 1978 reached #99999SA. At this time the suffix became a prefix, and the new serial range began with #SA01001. This model's value is determined in much the same manner as was described in the section on the 2nd Generation SAAs; caliber, barrel length, finish, grip and condition are once again the five principal determinants of value in the collector market. The prevalence of specially ordered guns was great during this period, and many more factory engraved SAAs were produced in Colt's Custom Shop than formerly in the modern era.

3rd Generation Model 1873 SAA Cavalry Model.

3rd Generation Model 1873 SAA Artillery Model.

3rd Generation Sheriff's Model.

It is strongly advised that any firearms that deviate from the standard be appraised by a competent authority. There are, frankly and unfortunately, too many fraudulent Colt SAAs in circulation and the financial risks are great. In addition, many of the fine replica guns can fool the unwary.

7.5-INCH BARREL

.357 MAGNUM

NIB	EXC.	V.G.	GOOD	FAIR	POOR
1,400	1,150	895	750	600	500

.44-40

NIB	EXC.	V.G.	GOOD	FAIR	POOR
1,500	1,250	900	750	600	500

.44-40 BLACK POWDER FRAME (SCREW RETAINING CYLINDER PIN)

NIB	EXC.	V.G.	GOOD	FAIR	POOR
1,700	1,400	1,150	1,000	800	600

.44 SPECIAL

NIB	EXC.	V.G.	GOOD	FAIR	POOR
1,400	1,200	900	700	550	500

.45 COLT

NIB	EXC.	V.G.	GOOD	FAIR	POOR
1,500	1,300	900	750	600	500

For 4.75-inch barrel add 25 percent; 5.5-inch barrel add 10 percent; nickel plating add 10 percent; ivory grips add $250.

SHERIFF'S MODEL 3RD GENERATION

This model is similar to the 2nd Generation Sheriff's Model. Serial numbers and the fact that this model is also chambered for the .44-40 are the only apparent differences. Colt offered the 3rd Generation Sheriff with interchangeable cylinders – .45 Colt/.45 ACP or .44-40/.44 Special – and a 3-inch barrel The blued and case colored finish was standard.

NIB	EXC.	V.G.	GOOD	FAIR	POOR
1,050	875	750	600	450	400

For interchangeable cylinders add 30 percent; nickel plated finish add 10 percent; ivory grips add $250.

BUNTLINE SPECIAL 3RD GENERATION

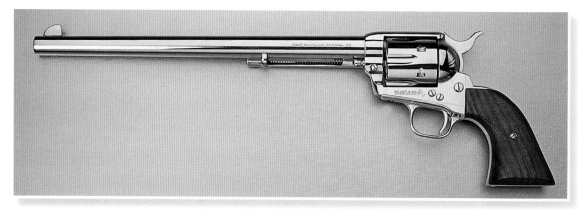

3rd Generation SAA Buntline Special, nickel finish.

3rd Generation Buntline
Special, blued finish with
factory engraving.

3rd Generation
New Frontier.

The same essential configuration as the 2nd Generation with the 12-inch barrel. Standard finish blued and case colored. It is chambered for .45 Colt and has checkered hard rubber grips.

NIB	EXC.	V.G.	GOOD	FAIR	POOR
1,050	875	750	600	450	400

For nickel finish add 20 percent.

NEW FRONTIER 3RD GENERATION

Again, the newer model is similar in appearance to 2nd Generation guns. Third Generation New Frontiers have five-digit serial numbers whereas 2nd Generation guns have only four-digit numbers. That and the calibers offered are basically the only differences. Third Generations are chambered for the .44 Special and .45 Colt and are rarely found in .44-40. Barrel lengths are 7.5 inches standard, with the 4.75- and 5.5-inch lengths rarely encountered.

NIB	EXC.	V.G.	GOOD	FAIR	POOR
950	725	650	550	500	400

For .44-40 add 20 percent; 4.75-inch barrel add 35 percent; 5.5-inch barrel add 25 percent.

NOTE: The following advertisement was placed on GunBroker.com in March, 2007:

"Colt New Frontier Single Action Revolver in .45 Colt caliber. Blued steel finish with beautifully color case hardened frame and walnut grips. Features a 7.5-inch barrel and an adjustable rear sight. New in the box with all factory documentation. A gorgeous piece recently purchased from an estate. It appears unfired and unturned. Serial number is #07694NF. The only defect noted is a small, barely noticeable hair-thin scratch on the cylinder which is visible in the third photograph." The gun attracted a high bid of $950 but failed to meet reserve.

If you wish to procure a factory letter authenticating a Single Action Army, you may do so by writing: Colt Historian, P.O. Box 1868, Hartford, CT 06101. There is a charge of $50 per serial number for this service. If Colt cannot for some reason provide the desired information, $10 will be refunded. Enclose the Colt model name, serial number and your name and address, along with the check.

Frontier Scout with duotone finish.

Frontier Scout with extra .22 Magnum cylinder in original factory box.

SCOUT MODEL SAAs

FRONTIER SCOUT 1957-1971

Introduced to meet public demand for a smaller and lighter Single Action Army – and perhaps inspired by Sturm, Ruger's Single Six .22 – this is a scaled-down version of the SAA chambered for .22 LR (beginning in 1957) with an interchangeable .22 WMR or Magnum cylinder (introduced in 1959). It was offered with a 4.25-, 4.75- or a 9.5-inch Buntline style barrel, and an alloy frame that cut about 8 oz. from the standard SAA weight.

First-year production frames were duotone with the frame left in the white and the balance of the revolver blued. All blued models and wood grips became available in 1958. In 1961 the duotone model was dropped from production. In 1964 dual cylinders were introduced. These revolvers have "Q" or "F" serial number suffixes. In 1960 the "K" series Scout was introduced and featured a heavier frame, nickel plating and wood grips. The majority of commemorative revolvers are of this type. This series was discontinued in 1970. Prices are about 15 percent higher than for the "Q" and "F" series guns.

FRONTIER SCOUT 22 BUNTLINE: The "Buntline Special" version of the Frontier Scout.

NIB	EXC.	V.G.	GOOD	FAIR	POOR
550	425	200	175	125	90

For the 9.5-inch Buntline add 50 percent; for extra cylinder, add 10 percent.

PEACEMAKER SCOUT & NEW FRONTIER

Similar to the Frontier Scout with a steel, case colored or blued frame. Fitted with old style black plastic eagle grips. Barrel lengths offered were 4.75, 6 or 7.5 inches in the so-called "Buntline" model. It also has an interchangeable .22 Magnum cylinder. Most of these revolvers had a "G" suffix although some built in 1974 had a "L" suffix. From 1982 through 1986, a New Frontier with cross-bolt safety was offered. This model is often referred to as the "GS" series. This revolver was offered with adjustable sights only. No Peacemakers were offered in this series.

NIB	EXC.	V.G.	GOOD	FAIR	POOR
550	475	300	200	150	100

Peacemaker Scout.

New Frontier Scout.

NOTE: The following advertisement appeared on *GunBroker.com* in March, 2007:

"You are bidding on a Colt New Frontier 22 revolver. The revolver has a 22 Mag cylinder and 4.4 inch barrel. Case colored frame and black grips. Grips have minor wear and scratches on butt. Very minor pitting on top on frame and one very minor spot on cylinder. Revolver has an L prefix serial number."

The seller opened bidding at $495 but failed to attract a bid.

FRONTIER SCOUT MODEL SAA 1962-1971

This is basically a scaled-down version of the Single Action Army chambered for .22 LR rimfire cartridges. It was offered with a 4.75-, 6- or 7-inch barrel. The earlier production has case colored frames with the remainder blued; later production, probably beginning in 1971, is all blued. Grips are checkered hard rubber.

NIB	EXC.	V.G.	GOOD	FAIR	POOR
400	275	200	150	100	75

NOTE: The following advertisement on *GunsAmerica.com* appeared in March, 2007:

"Frontier Scout .22 Mag, 4.75 inch bbl., bright Alloy frame, serial number #110XXXF, about 1961, black plastic grips, unfired. You won't find a single blemish on this piece. With original box. Original owners son wrapped a single band of duct tape around box, other than that, this package is Mint. Asking $650."

CURRENT PRODUCTION: 1982 TO PRESENT

STANDARD SINGLE ACTION ARMY

The SAA, it is perhaps sad to note, has all but faded from the firearms picture except in movies (although most actors are generally unconscious about what weapon they are wielding) and cowboy shooting action competition. This model is currently available as a specially ordered custom shop proposition. The cost is great; the availability is low. The heyday of one of the most venerable firearms of them all is pretty much at an end.

The currently-produced SAAs have been available in .32-20, .38 Special, .357 Magnum, .38-40, .44-40, .44 Special, .45 ACP and .45 Colt. Barrels are available in 3-inch through 10-inch lengths. The finishes are nickel plated and blued, with case-colored frames. Current SAAs feature the 2nd Generation-style cylinder bushing. Standard composite grips have an eagle design. The current dealer price ($1,075 to $1,225) and suggested retail price ($1,380 to $1,530) vary with feature and option. A variety of custom options such as unsigned standard American scroll engraving are available from the factory. This model is available on special order only.

Current-production SAAs were formerly available only through the Colt Custom Shop. As of 2007 Colt is offering the SAA as a standard-production item in the following configurations. All have fixed sights.

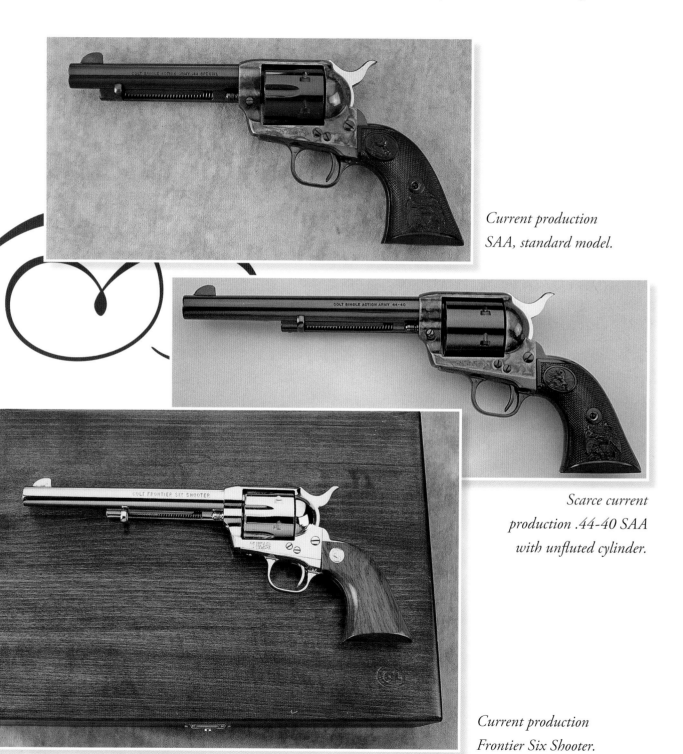

Current production SAA, standard model.

Scarce current production .44-40 SAA with unfluted cylinder.

Current production Frontier Six Shooter.

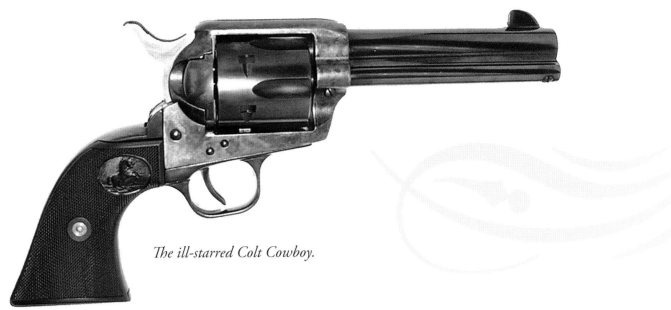

The ill-starred Colt Cowboy.

Model #	Caliber	Bbl. Length	Finish
P1540	.32-20	4¾"	Colored Case/Blue
P1541	.32-20	4¾"	Nickel
P1550	.32-20	5½"	Colored Case/Blue
P1551	.32-20	5½"	Nickel
P1570	.32-20	7½"	Colored Case/Blue
P1571	.32-20	7½"	Nickel
P1648	.38 Spl	4¾"	Colored Case/Blue
P1649	.38 Spl	4¾"	Nickel
P1658	.38 Spl	5½"	Colored Case/Blue
P1659	.38 Spl	5½"	Nickel
P1678	.38 Spl	7½"	Colored Case/Blue
P1679	.38 Spl	7½"	Nickel
P1640	.357	4¾"	Colored Case/Blue
P1641	.357	4¾"	Nickel
P1650	.357	5½"	Colored Case/Blue
P1651	.357	5½"	Nickel
P1670	.357	7½"	Colored Case/Blue
P1671	.357	7½"	Nickel
P3840	.38-40	4¾"	Colored Case/Blue
P3841	.38-40	4¾"	Nickel
P3850	.38-40	5½"	Colored Case/Blue
P3856	.38-40	5½"	Nickel
P3870	.38-40	7½"	Colored Case/Blue
P3876	.38-40	7½"	Nickel
P1940	.44-40	4¾"	Colored Case/Blue
P1941	.44-40	4¾"	Nickel
P1950	.44-40	5½"	Colored Case/Blue
P1956	.44/.40	5½"	Nickel
P1970	.44-40	7½"	Colored Case/Blue
P1976	.44-40	7½"	Nickel
P1840	.45 LC	4¾"	Colored Case/Blue
P1841	.45 LC	4¾"	Nickel
P1850	.45 LC	5½"	Colored Case/Blue
P1856	.45 LC	5½"	Nickel
P1870	.45 LC	7½"	Colored Case/Blue
P1876	.45 LC	7½"	Nickel

COWBOY (CB1850)

Introduced in 1998, this model is a replica of the Single Action Army that features a modern transfer bar safety system. It is offered with a 5.5 inch barrel and chambered for .45 Colt. Fixed sights and walnut grips. Blued barrel with case colored frame. The weight is about 42 oz. Parts for the Cowboy were manufactured mostly in Canada and finished and assembled in the United States. The Cowboy was also the subject of an ugly lawsuit between Colt and the now-defunct American Western Arms (AWA).

NIB	EXC.	V.G.	GOOD	FAIR	POOR
650	500	375	300	225	150

SINGLE ACTION ARMY "THE LEGEND"

A limited edition revolver built to commemorate Colt's official sponsorship of the PRCA, the Professional Rodeo Cowboy's Association, production was limited to 1,000. Chambered for .45 Long Colt fitted with a 5.5-inch barrel. Nickel finish Buffalo horn grips with gold medallions. Machine engraved and washed in gold.

NIB	EXC.	V.G.	GOOD	FAIR	POOR
2,750	2,250	-	-	-	-

NOTE: The following advertisement appeared on GunsAmerica.com in the Spring of 2007:

"Colt Legend Rodeo Standard. New in box with sleeve and additional factory display case. $2750 plus shipping."

SECTION IV

COLT'S DOUBLE ACTION REVOLVERS

Model 1877 Lightning Storekeeper's Model in .38 Colt.

Contrary to popular belief, the double action revolver was not long in arriving at Colt's factory. Indeed, 20 years before his death in early 1862, before Hartford Armory was even dreamed of, Sam Colt secretly tinkered with plans for building a double action handgun.

Nevertheless, Colt remained a lifelong opponent of double action trigger mechanisms. Stung by criticism of his designs, particularly from Britain, Colt had often stated publicly that the extra effort required to cock the trigger and rotate the cylinder prevented a steady aim. This may have been true of blueprints originating in the 1850s, but the Beaumont-Adams was just one of the efficient double action revolvers being made during the life of Colt's London factory, and it might have been expected that the principles would be adopted in the United States. Dead by his 48th year, Sam Colt scarcely had time to witness the emergence in America of revolvers such as the Cooper, made in quantity in Philadelphia. The Cooper fitted a double action trigger within external lines that were ("no doubt deliberately," write Ian Hogg and John Walter in *Pistols of the World*) surprisingly similar to the Colt "Pocket Model" cap locks.

The quantity of black powder residue after firing a typical cap-and-ball revolver may have inhibited Colt himself from moving forward with this style of action; it was not until the advent of the self contained breechloading cartridge that the Colt Armory began to

Model 1877 Thunderer in .41 Colt.

Model 1877 Thunderer Storekeeper's Model.

experiment seriously with double action mechanisms.

Apparently, the success of rival designs convinced Colt management that a double action gun was necessary to retain a hold on the commercial market in North America. Designs that had been prepared by William Mason, dating back to 1871, were hurriedly perfected and the new double action Colt was advertised for the first time on January 1, 1877.

So less than 15 years after the colonel's death, Colt was developing its double action Model 1877, popularly known as the Lightning. This was still about 20 years before smokeless powders became available in quantity to the general public. Nevertheless, the concept of the double action – that with the pull of the trigger a shooter could rotate the cylinder, and cock and fire the hammer – was appealing once shooters realized that it could be fired accurately, and the double action handgun gradually replaced, by the turn of the century, the venerable but old-fashioned single action.

The mechanical action of the early double action Colts was complicated and some of the individual components seemed only marginally strong enough to withstand continual use. However, there is no solid evidence that gunsmiths found them unrepairable, and the manufacture of 166,849 DA revolvers from 1877 to 1909 shows that they were virtually as popular as the SAA.

The ease with which these early Colt double actions could be fired commended them to discerning gunmen such as William Bonney ("Billy the Kid") and that true killer, the incorrigible Texan, John Wesley Hardin (although he also enjoyed shooting people with a .44 caliber 1860 Army). So with Colt's hold on the domestic market prior to 1900, it is not difficult to see why these models survived for so long. Almost all of the guns chambering the .38 or .41 Colt cartridges were marked "COLT D.A.38" (or ".41") in a panel on the left side of the barrel, though about 200 were made for the .32-20 WCF round prior to 1897. Others will be found with the pre-1891 London address (14 Pall Mall) on top of the barrel.

THE EARLY MODELS

MODEL 1877 LIGHTNING AND THUNDERER

The Model 1877 was Colt's first attempt to manufacture a double action revolver and – surprise! – it shows a striking resemblance to the Single Action Army. Sales of this model were brisk, with over 166,849 produced between 1877 and 1909. Chambered for two different cartridges, the .38 Colt was known as the "Lightning," and the .41 Colt was the "Thunderer," apparently names bestowed on the pistols to give them

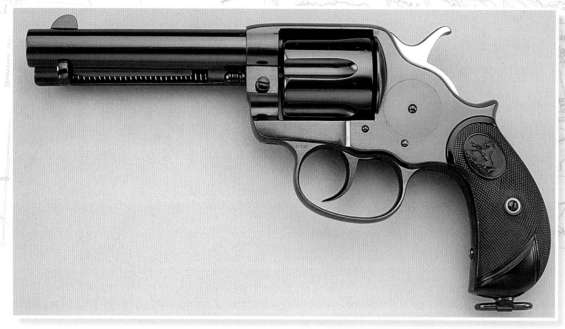

Model 1878 Double Action .45.

advertising appeal by that redoubtable distributor from Cincinnati, Ben Kittredge. The standard finishes are blued, with case colored frame and nickel plate. The bird's head grips are of checkered rosewood on the early guns and hard rubber after 1882 on the majority of the production run. Barrel lengths most often encountered are 2.5 and 3.5 inches without an ejector rod, and 4.5 and 6 inches with the rod. Individual cartridges were inserted in the cylinder through a pivoting loading gate on the rear right side of the frame, and expelled by using the ejector (if fitted) on the right side of the barrel to push them back out individually through the gate. Other barrel lengths from 1.5 through 10 inches were offered. Triggers were set almost centrally within the guard. The Model 1877 holds six shots in either caliber.

There were quite a few variations found within this model designation. Values furnished are for the standard variations. As antiques, guns made before 1898 would be more desirable from an investment standpoint.

WITHOUT EJECTOR, 2.5 AND 3.5 INCH BARREL

EXC.	V.G.	GOOD	FAIR	POOR
3,000	2,000	1,000	500	350

WITH EJECTOR, 4.5 AND 6 INCH BARREL

EXC.	V.G.	GOOD	FAIR	POOR
3,000	1,800	1,000	750	450

For blued guns add 25 percent. Premium for a shorter barrel than 2.5 inches; add 50 percent;.41 Caliber Thunderer add 10 percent. For a barrel longer than 6 inches add 50 percent. London barrel address, add 20 percent. In the rare .32 caliber add 50 percent. Rosewood grips add 10 percent.

NOTE: These advertisements for Model 1877 Lightning and Thunderer were placed in the Spring of 2007 on *AntiqueGunList.com*:

"Colt DA 1877 Lightning 90% plus blue with 70% case turning brown excellent 2 piece original to the gun hard rubber grips nice fire blue on hammer trigger and some left on screws excellent bore with excellent markings all matching this is probably one of the best blued and case colored Lightning I have had. Serial number #1262XX. $3,850."

"Colt DA 1877 Thunderer Model. This gun has been made up a long time ago it is a .41 caliber with a 6 ½" barrel one line barrel address with RAC & a P on the frame is stamped U.S. on one side on the other side is stamped RAC has a square butt with one piece wood grips RAC on the wood grips has an RAC stamped on the cylinder this actually looks like a small cavalry model a silver gray brown gun in excellent working condition. Serial number #79515. $1,650."

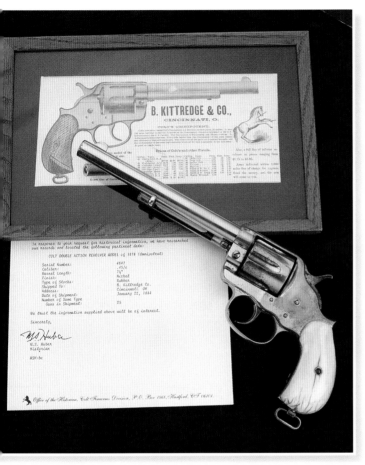

"*Omnipotent,*" i.e.,
"*all-powerful.*"

Model 1878 Frontier "Omnipotent."

MODEL 1878 ARMY & FRONTIER

This is a large and somewhat ungainly looking revolver, but it was fairly well received commercially because it is chambered for the large calibers that were popular in that era. Although heavier and stronger than its predecessors, the 1878 "Army & Frontier" Model had a weak main spring – needed to allow self cocking – and was prone to misfires and accidental discharges, the reasons behind its rejection by the Army when first offered in 1879. Still, it was a better combat weapon than the Lightning or Thunderer, easier to repair and more resistant to misuse and dirt. It has a solid frame with a removable trigger guard. The cylinder does not swing out, and there is a thin loading gate. It has bird's

head grips made of checkered hard rubber; walnut would be found on the early models. The finish is either blued and case colored or nickel plated.

It will be noted that the Model 1878 has no bolt notches in its cylinder. This is because in William Mason's design, the cylinder is locked by a rather complicated arrangement of the hand and trigger. The Model 1878 holds six shots, and the standard barrel lengths are 4.7, 5.5 and 7.5 inches with an ejector assembly, and 3, 3.5 and 4 inches without. With the 7.5-inch barrel, the weight was 39 oz. The standard chamberings for the Model 1878 are .32-20, .38-40, .41 Colt, .44-40 and .45 Colt. Colt manufactured 51,210 between 1878 and 1905 and a number were built with special barrel lengths from 2.5 to 12 inches. A very few "hammerless" Army & Frontier revolvers were also made, the hammer hidden by a separate shroud. Antique models made before 1898 would be more desirable from an investment standpoint.

MODEL 1878 FRONTIER STANDARD

EXC.	V.G.	GOOD	FAIR	POOR
4,200	3,000	1,200	800	400

Add a 15 percent premium for blued revolvers. Add 10 to 50 percent premium for calibers other than .44-40 or .45.

NOTE: The following advertisement was featured in the Spring of 2007 on *AntiqueGunList.com*:

"*Colt DA 1878 Frontier 4.75 inch barrel .38-40 brown silver gray gun in good working condition good barrel address and .38 WCF original 2 piece hard rubber grips has some cracks in the grips this gun was shipped to R. Kupferschmidt Company in Memphis Tennessee July 20, 1900 in a one gun shipment Serial #420XX. $1,450.*"

MODEL 1878 FRONTIER OMNIPOTENT

This is a special order version of the model above with the name "Omnipotent" stamped on the barrel. (In a happy turn of events, the name "Omnipotent" has recently been resurrected by United States Fire Arms for a single-action .45 styled after the Model 1878.)

EXC.	V.G.	GOOD	FAIR	POOR
16,000	10,000	6,000	3,000	1,000

*Model 1878
Sheriff's Model.*

*Model 1902 "Philippine"
or "Alaskan" Model.*

SHERIFF'S MODEL

A "snubby" version of the 1878 chambered for .44-40 or .45 Colt with barrel lengths of 3.5 or 4 inches.

EXC.	V.G.	GOOD	FAIR	POOR
6,000	4,000	2,000	1,000	800

NOTE: The following advertisement for a Sheriff's Model appeared at AntiqueGuns.biz in March, 2007.

"Colt 1878 Double Action Sheriff's Model from the Stagecoach Museum Gun Collection. $22,500. This very rare Colt Double Action revolver was manufactured in 1882 in .44-40 caliber. An accompanying Colt Factory Letter indicates that it was originally shipped to Hibbard, Spencer, and Bartlett, in ejector-less Sheriff's configuration. Later this revolver became part of the famous Stagecoach Collection (item #479) and is so documented by serial number and is pictured on page 129 & 152 in the well known 'Stagecoach Collection' book. This revolver comes with a rare copy of this book signed by the three buyers of the Stagecoach Collection and inscribed to the late Colt expert and author, Keith Cochran. A second inscription to the current owner of this rare piece is also inscribed 20 years later by two surviving buyers.

"This revolver comes with its original 1880's Sheriff's holster with iron star and its display mahogany case with 12 period cartridges, display cartridge box, original Screwdriver, 1880's Compass, Oil Bottle, 1890's HSB Watch Fob, and a very rare original Deputy Prohibition Commissioner Badge. It carries the HWS collection seal and brass #479 museum inventory tag."

MODEL 1902 PHILIPPINE OR ALASKAN

This U.S. Ordnance contract model is a variant of the Model 1878. It has a 6-inch barrel and is chambered for .45 Colt. The finish is blued, and there is a lanyard swivel on the butt. It bears the date "1902" and "U.S." on every pistol and the U.S. inspector's mark "RAC" for Rinaldo A. Carr. The 1902 is sometimes referred to as the "Philippine" or the "Alaskan" model. The trigger guard is quite a bit larger than standard, allowing a two-finger pull or the trigger to be pulled while wearing thick gloves. Master gunsmith David Chicoine, however, maintains that the purpose of the enlarged trigger guard was to accommodate a slightly longer trigger, the purpose of which was to provide more leverage in an attempt to ameliorate the gun's notoriously heavy trigger pull. Colt ultimately produced 4,600 of these guns serial numbered from #43401 to #48097.

EXC.	V.G.	GOOD	FAIR	POOR
5,500	3,500	1,800	1,000	600

NOTE: The following advertisement appeared on *ArmChairGunShow.com* in the Spring of 2007:

"Colt - US Model 1902 - so-called Philippine model - .45 Colt - Good condition. - Dark gray patina with scant traces of original finish and some pitting over one cylinder chamber; legible markings including U.S. military marks. Almost working, need mech. tuning. Lightly worn hard rubber grips, w/ repair to rear of right panel. Oversized trigger and guard are typical of this military model from the era of the Philippine insurrection. Serial number #45419. $1,350."

NAVY MODEL 1889

The advent of efficient automatically-extracting revolvers, actively promoted by Smith & Wesson, slowly eroded markets that had previously been dominated by Colt. A search for a design that combined ease of use with strength of construction resulted in the introduction of a cylinder mounted on a yoke that could be swung laterally outward when the recoil shield on the left side of the frame was pulled backward to disengage the lock.

Colt's William Mason had filed a patent on such a design as early as 1881, though he was not the first in that field. Winchester's Stephen Wood had obtained protection for swinging cylinder designs as early as 1876. Colt investigated features patented in 1884 by Horace Lord and Carl Ehbets, including a cylinder that swung on the top strap and a trigger guard that swung down – forward – and then clockwise – to open the action and eject the cases. In fact, few avenues were untouched by Colt's engineers in a most comprehensive exploration of exploitable designs. Finally, in 1888, a patent protecting the finalized yoke-mounted cylinder design was obtained.

Although Smith & Wesson's competing design, the "Hand Ejector," became more or less the standard for this sort of revolver, the fact remains that Colt's swing-out revolver preceded it by at least 7 years and proved its strength and superiority over the top-break revolvers made famous by Smith & Wesson.

The 1889's cylinder revolved counterclockwise and was locked by a pawl engaging notches in the cylinder's rear face. The frame was deepened at the front, and the lower run beneath the cylinder was squared at the front edge, giving an appearance of solidity and strength. However, the method of locking the cylinder during the firing cycle was relatively poor. It was substantially revised before the improved New Army & Navy appeared in 1892.

CIVILIAN MODEL

The 1889 Navy is an important model from a historical standpoint as it was the first double action revolver Colt manufactured with a swing-out cylinder. About 31,000 were produced between 1889 and 1894. The Model 1889 is chambered for .38 and .41 Colt cartridges. The uniquely counter-clockwise rotating

Model 1889, nickel finish.

cylinder without stop slots on this model holds six shots and it is offered with a 3, 4.5 or 6 inch barrel. (The cylinder of all other Colt double action revolvers revolves in a clockwise fashion.) The finish was either blued or nickel plated. Grips are checkered hard rubber with the "rampant colt" in an oval molded into them. Patent dates 1884 and 1888 appear in the barrel marking, and the serial numbers are stamped on the butt. Serial numbers begin with #1 and continue to about #31000, for those revolvers built in 1894.

Add premium for blued models. For 3-inch barrel add 20 percent.

EXC.	V.G.	GOOD	FAIR	POOR
3,000	1,500	1,000	600	300

NOTE: The following advertisement appeared at *GunsAmerica.com* in March of 2007:

"This is a Colt model 1889 New Navy .41 Colt double action revolver. It has a 4.5 inch barrel with excellent bore. It has black textured grips. Excellent overall condition. (sn#203xx)."

The seller's asking price was $799.

MARTIAL MODEL

This variation is chambered for .38 Colt and has a 6-inch barrel. It was offered only with a blued finish and had "U.S.N." stamped on the butt. Most of the Navy models were later altered at the Colt factory to add the Model 1895 improvements. An original unaltered specimen would be worth as much as 50 percent premium over the altered values listed. Serial numbers were in the #1 to #5000 range.

EXC.	V.G.	GOOD	FAIR	POOR
9,000	5,000	2,500	1,000	500

NEW ARMY AND NAVY MODEL 1892

Army trials between 1890 and 1891 revealed the weakness of the Model 1889's locking system. It allowed the cylinder to rotate when the gun was holstered or if the shooter attempted to turn the cylinder as the trigger was being pulled. Combining the trigger with the cylinder-rotating pawl, and adding a double locking bolt, necessitating an extra set of bolt stop notches in the periphery of the cylinder, addressed the problem. The locking bolt dropped clear as soon as the hammer lifted to cock, and the pawl engaged the ratchet on the rear of the cylinder to begin rotation.

Often, the manufacturer's marks will include reference to patent protection granted in 1884, 1888 or 1895, and this helps date individual guns if other indicators, serial numbers, for example, are unclear. The New Army and Navy Models were superseded by the New Service Model in 1908.

CIVILIAN OR COMMERCIAL MODEL

This model is similar in appearance to the 1889 Navy, because the first 4,700 were modified from the 1889 Navy. The main differences are improvements to the lock-work function. It has the double bolt stop notches, a double cylinder locking bolt and shorter flutes on the cylinder mentioned above. The .38 Smith & Wesson and the .32-20 were added to the .38 Colt and .41 Colt chamberings. The checkered hard rubber grips are standard, with plain walnut grips found on some contract series guns. Barrel lengths and finishes are the same as described for the Model 1889, 2 to 6 inches in one-inch increments. The patent dates 1895 and 1901 appear stamped on later models. Colt manufactured 291,000 of these revolvers between 1892 and 1907, and serial numbers begin with #1. Guns made before 1898 are considered antiques and are more desirable from an investment standpoint. For 3-inch barrel add 20 percent.

EXC.	V.G.	GOOD	FAIR	POOR
2,000	1,200	500	300	100

NOTE: The following advertisement was featured in the Spring of 2007 on *AntiqueGunList.com*:

"Colt DA 1892 U.S. 6" barrel .38 Colt has been re-blued not all of the 2 line address can be seen. Last patent date on the barrel is '88. Barrel crane, cylinder, latch are serialized to the gun. All other markings in excellent shape. On the butt says U.S. Model 1892. It has 2 piece wood grips in excellent working condition Serial number #486. $795."

MODEL 1892 U.S. NAVY – MARTIAL MODEL: BUTT INCLUDES "U.S.N." AND ANCHOR

EXC.	V.G.	GOOD	FAIR	POOR
3,500	2,750	1,500	1,000	750

MARTIAL MODEL (BUTT INCLUDES "U.S./ARMY")

The initial army purchase was for 8,000 Model 1892 revolvers, almost all of which were altered to add "Model 1894" improvements. Unaltered examples will bring a premium.

EXC.	V.G.	GOOD	FAIR	POOR
3,500	2,000	800	600	400

Model 1892 New Army .38.

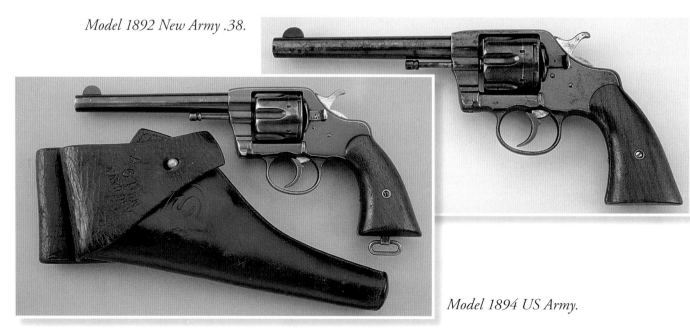

Model 1894 US Army.

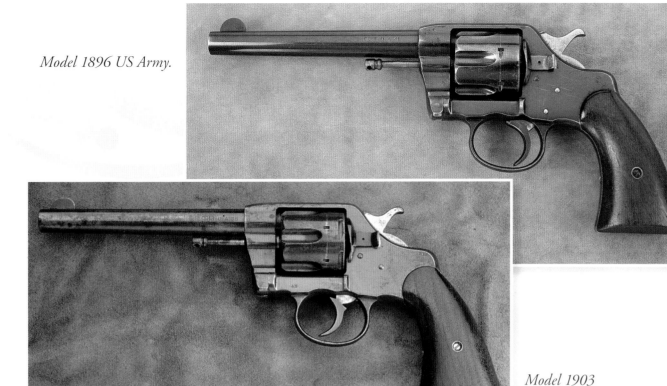

Model 1896 US Army.

*Model 1903
US Army.*

MODEL 1894/1896 ARMY MODEL

In continual use, the 1892 Colts were found to have serious weaknesses. The cylinder still revolved counterclockwise, which, as the mechanism opened to the left, tended to push the yoke/cylinder unit out of the frame as the trigger was pressed. Wear eventually prevented the chamber from aligning properly with the bore, and shooting became progressively less accurate.

Although changes were made, there is still some doubt whether the model designation was changed. This arises because the marks on the butt, which are separated into short lines, can be read as either "U.S. Army Model 1896," for example, or "U.S. Army Model," "1896." The first instance would suggest that the date is part of the designation, whereas the second could simply be a generic army model description with a separate date of acceptance. There is no doubt that the 1894 model is a separate pattern, but the status of others is less clear.

So, in essence, this is an improved Model 1892 with a better locking mechanism for the cylinder. Many Model 1892s were converted in this manner. By the middle of 1897, all U.S. troops were issued the Model 1894 revolver, which has the distinction of being the first U.S. military handgun to use smokeless powder cartridges.

Confusion exists as to the difference between the various Colt swing-out revolvers of this period. Here is some clarification:

- The Model 1896 was identical to the Model 1894, as discussed above.
- The Model 1901 was the same as the Model 1894 with the addition of a lanyard swivel.
- The Model 1903 was identical to the Model 1894 with a smaller bore diameter (9.068mm) and a modified grip.

NOTE: The following advertisement was featured in the Spring of 2007 on *AntiqueGunList.com*:

"Colt DA 1903 U.S. 6" barrel .38 Colt 50% blue in excellent working condition 2 piece Walnut grips RAC stamped on the but. Good inspector marks on the gun. The butt of the gun stamped U.S. Army Model 1903 with serial number. Has lanyard ring. Serial number #2098XX $795."

And this advertisement was featured on *GunBroker. com* in March, 2007:

"Colt Double Action New Army .38 LC. Serial number #65399, mfg 1895, last patent date on BBL '95. Action works well, reasonably tight, RAC (Rinaldo A. Carr) inspections on grips & frame, exc brite bore. 40-50% blue remains. Good representative example. Antique, FFL not required, S&H 17.50." Bidding closed at $550.

EXC.	V.G.	GOOD	FAIR	POOR
3,500	2,000	800	600	400

Model 1905
Marine Corps
Model.

MODEL 1905 MARINE CORPS

This model is a variation of the 1894 New Army and Navy Model. It was derived from the late production with its own serial range #10001 to #10926. With only 926 produced between 1905 and 1909, it is quite rare on today's market and is eagerly sought after by Colt Double Action collectors. This model is chambered for the .38 Colt and the .38 Smith & Wesson Special cartridges. It holds six shots, has a 6-inch barrel, and is offered in a blued finish only. The grips are checkered walnut and are quite different from those found on previous models. "U.S.M.C." is stamped on the butt; patent dates of 1884, 1888, and 1895 are stamped on the barrel. 125 of these revolvers were earmarked for civilian sales and do not have the Marine Corps markings; these will generally be found in better condition. Values, however, are similar.

EXC.	V.G.	GOOD	FAIR	POOR
4,500	3,500	2,000	1,500	750

New Service, blued finish, .38 Special.

New Service, nickel
finish, .38 Special.

Colt New
Service .38-40.

New Service Target.

New Service
Military in
.45 ACP/.45
Auto Rim.

THE "NEW" MODELS

NEW SERVICE MODEL

This model, intended as a military weapon from the outset, was in continual production from 1898 through 1944. It is chambered for 11 different calibers: .38 Special, .357 Magnum, .38-40, .44 Russian, .44 Special, .44-40, .45 ACP, .45 Colt, .450 Eley, .455 Eley and .476 Eley. The New Service is offered in barrel lengths from 2 to 7.5 inches, either blued or nickel plated. Checkered hard rubber grips were standard until 1928, and then checkered walnut grips were used with an inset Colt medallion. This was the largest swing out, clockwise rotating cylinder double action revolver that Colt ever produced, and approximately 356,000 were manufactured over the 46 years they were made. There are many different variations of this revolver, and one should consult carefully before making a purchasing decision.

EARLY MODEL, #1 TO #21000

EXC.	V.G.	GOOD	FAIR	POOR
1,000	650	350	200	125

EARLY MODEL TARGET, #6000 TO #15000

Checkered walnut grips, flattop frame, 7.5" barrel.

EXC.	V.G.	GOOD	FAIR	POOR
3,000	1,500	550	300	200

IMPROVED MODEL, #21000 TO #325000

Has internal locking improvements.

EXC.	V.G.	GOOD	FAIR	POOR
850	550	300	175	150

IMPROVED TARGET MODEL, #21000 TO #325000

EXC.	V.G.	GOOD	FAIR	POOR
2,250	1,500	550	300	200

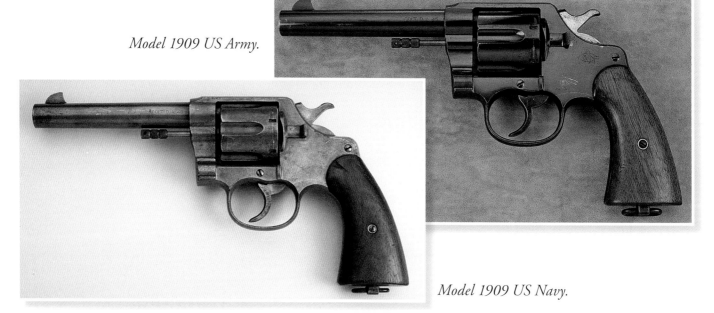

Model 1909 US Army.

Model 1909 US Navy.

U.S. ARMY MODEL 1909, #30000 TO #50000

5.5 inch barrel, .45 Colt, walnut grips, "U.S. Army Model 1909" on butt. About 18,000 were produced.

EXC.	V.G.	GOOD	FAIR	POOR
3,500	2,000	800	300	200

U.S. NAVY MODEL 1909

Same as above with "U.S.N." on butt. About 1,000 produced with serial numbers between #50000 and #52000.

EXC.	V.G.	GOOD	FAIR	POOR
3,500	2,000	1,000	350	250

U.S. MARINE CORPS MODEL 1909

Checkered walnut grips, "U.S.M.C." on butt. Serial numbered between #21000 and #23000, about 1,200 were built.

EXC.	V.G.	GOOD	FAIR	POOR
4,500	2,750	1,350	650	450

NOTE: The following advertisement from the Spring of 2007 appeared at *ArmChairGunShow.com*:

"Colt - New Service - Chief of Police presentation revolver with shooting award nightstick - .38 WCF; 7.5" barrel. - Excellent condition. - Great historic law enforcement set. 24" turned hardwood nightstick has a silver presentation plaque reading "Presented by Chief McFarland to C.C. HEDRICK - Best Score at Police Shooting Tournament Dec. 24 1898". Revolver sideplate is inscribed, "Presented to C.C. HEDRICK 1930". Previous owner reports that Hedrick had become Chief of Police in Leavenworth, Kansas during his career, and that this revolver was a presentation upon retirement. Research in progress. Sideplate appears to have been refinished, probably after inscription. Grip straps are turning plum.

Elsewhere this revolver retains 97% of original blue; with markings, bore, mechanics and grip all excellent. Serial number #271584. $3,950."

And the following advertisement appeared in the Spring of 2007 at *AntiqueGunList.com*:

"Colt DA 1909 New Service Navy in .45 LC these are very rare guns silver gray gun markings on the barrel are weak markings on the butt are strong good USN anchor and number in excellent working condition I believe this gun has been buffed and some blue put on it 2 piece wood grips this is an FFL or C&R ask all questions sold as is. Serial number #58X. $1,250."

U.S. ARMY MODEL 1917

Smooth walnut grips, a 5.5-inch barrel, .45 ACP. Model designation stamped on butt and barrel. The Model 1917 differed from the Model 1909 in that it had a shorter cylinder for half moon clips for the .45 ACP cartridge, a wider cylinder stop lug on the sideplate, and a tapered barrel instead of a straight barrel. Blued, unpolished finish. Serial numbered between #150000 and #301000 as about 150,000 were purchased by the military.

EXC.	V.G.	GOOD	FAIR	POOR
1,250	850	500	300	225

NOTE: The following advertisement appeared at *ArmChairGunShow.com* in the Spring of 2007:

"Colt - US Army Model 1917 - .45 ACP; 5.5" barrel. Good condition. Maybe 30% original blue, balance mottled plum and gray; legible markings; barrel. Serial number does not match. Very good mechanics and bore. Smooth worn military grips. Serial number #39860. $595."

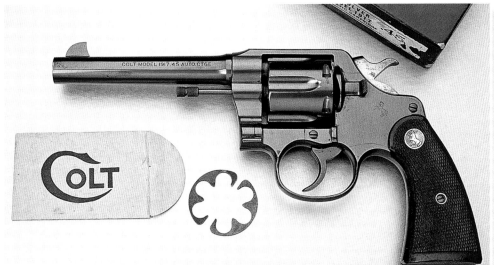

*Model 1917
Civilian.*

*Colt Shooting
Master.*

MODEL 1917 CIVILIAN, #335000 TO #336000

Approximately 1,000 made in .45 ACP only from Army parts overrun, either blued or nickel finished. A few were built for target shooting, with long barrels and adjustable rear sights set in flattop frames. No military markings.

EXC.	V.G.	GOOD	FAIR	POOR
750	550	400	250	200

LATE MODEL NEW SERVICE, #325000 TO #356000

Checkered walnut grips and internal improvements.

EXC.	V.G.	GOOD	FAIR	POOR
850	650	400	200	125

SHOOTING MASTER, #333000 TO #350000

Known in the Colt factory as "Model J," this gun was introduced in August 1900 and was built in small numbers until World War II began. It had a round-butt grip frame, checkered walnut grips with Colt medallion, a 6- or 7.5- inch barrel, "Colt Shooting Master" on barrel, and a flattop frame with target sights. The earliest guns had broad-grip butts, but a narrow pattern subsequently became standard; the original pattern was then reduced to the status of an option. It also featured a hand-honed action, an adjustable rear sight in the flattop frame and a prominent front sight with the blade pinned in its seat. Chambered for the .357 Magnum, .38 Special, .44 Special, .45 Long Colt, .45 ACP and .455 Eley. Add 100 percent premium for .357 Magnum, .44 Special, .45 ACP, and .45 Colt. Deduct $100 for the .38 Special.

EXC.	V.G.	GOOD	FAIR	POOR
1,750	1,200	850	400	300

MAGNUM MODEL NEW SERVICE, OVER #340000

Chambered for .357 Magnum, .38 Special.

EXC.	V.G.	GOOD	FAIR	POOR
950	600	350	250	200

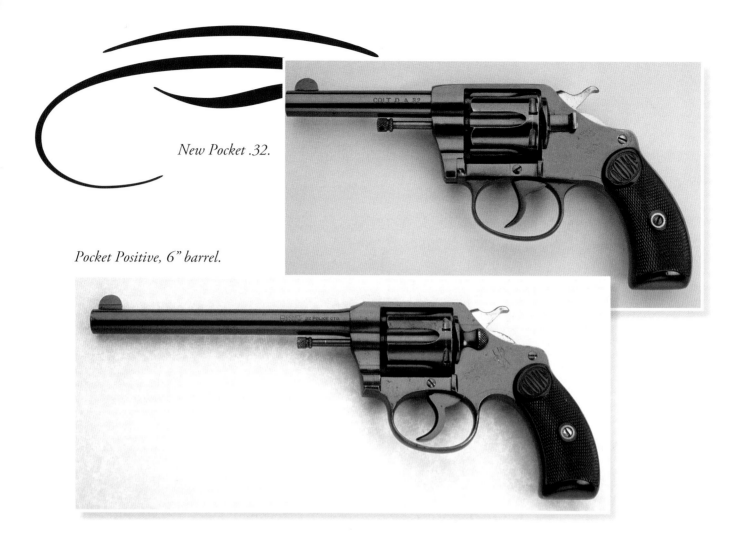

New Pocket .32.

Pocket Positive, 6" barrel.

NEW POCKET MODEL

This was the first small frame, swing out cylinder, double action pocket revolver made by Colt. The concept was a personal defense weapon, and it was built on the 1892 type army revolver with the Model "A" frame. Its most notable improvement was the introduction of a clockwise-rotating cylinder, which tended to push into the frame as the trigger was pressed. It is chambered for .32 Colt and .32 Smith & Wesson (not interchangeably). It holds six shots and is offered with barrel lengths of 2.5, 3.5, 5 and 6 inches. The finish is blued or nickel plated, and the grips are checkered hard rubber with the oval Colt molded into them. "COLT'S NEW POCKET" is stamped on the frame, thus making it readily identifiable. 1884 and 1888 patent dates are stamped on the barrel of later production guns. There were approximately 30,000 of these revolvers manufactured between 1893 and 1905. Antiques made before 1898 are, of course, more desirable. Serial numbers begin with #1. For early production without patent dates add 25 percent. For the 5 inch barrel add 10 percent.

EXC.	V.G.	GOOD	FAIR	POOR
600	450	300	250	150

POCKET POSITIVE

This gun owed its introduction to the development of the "positive lock" mechanism (patented 1905) that ensured that the firing pin could not strike the cartridge unless the hammer had been drawn back to full cock. Externally this is the same revolver as the New Pocket, but it has the positive lock feature. Barrels measured 2 to 6 inches long and calibers were in a variety of .32 centerfires (e.g., .32 Short Colt, .32 Long Colt, .32 New Police, .32 S&W, and .32 S&W Long). It was manufactured between 1905 and 1945 and serial numbers for the 130,000 production run begin where the New Pocket numbers end. It took four years to use all of the older New Pocket .32 and .38 frames. Thereafter, production bore "POCKET POSITIVE" barrel rolls. A few Pocket Positives were made with spurless hammers, allowing them to be carried in a pocket in great safety, but it is not known whether this alteration was undertaken in the Hartford factory.

EXC.	V.G.	GOOD	FAIR	POOR
500	375	275	225	125

NOTE: The following advertisement appeared in the Spring of 2007 on *ArmChairGunShow.com*:

"Colt - Pocket Positive - .32 Police; 3.5" barrel. 85% blue; barrel markings are a bit weak, a possible sign of refinish, but the blue looks original to me. If redone, it was long ago and expertly. Good mechanics, timing a bit off, fine bore. Chips to toes of moderately worn grips. Serial number #54971. $325."

NEW POLICE MODEL

This model appears similar to the New Pocket Model and the frame is stamped "NEW POLICE." It is chambered for the .32 Colt, .32 Colt New Police and .32 Smith & Wesson cartridges. The barrel lengths are 2.5, 4 or 6 inches in length, while finishes are blued or nickel plated. From 1896 to 1907, Colt manufactured 49,500 of this model. The New York City Police Department purchased 4,500, and the backstraps are so marked. There was also a target model of this revolver built in the 1890s, which features a 6-inch barrel with a flattop frame and target sights, of which 5,000 were produced. New York Police marked add 20 percent. Target model add 30 percent.

EXC.	V.G.	GOOD	FAIR	POOR
400	250	200	150	100

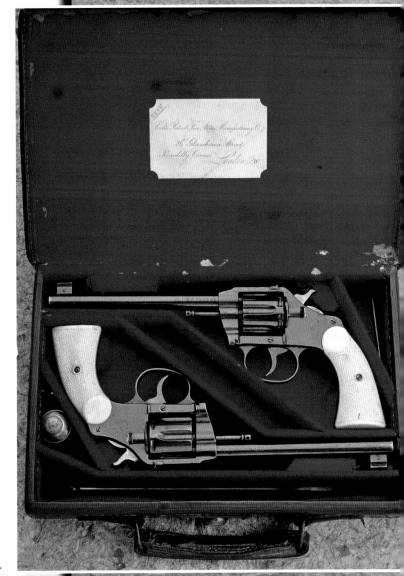

New Police .32.

New Police Target.

Army Special in factory box.

*Officer's Model
Target, 1st Issue.*

ARMY SPECIAL MODEL

This is a heavier framed, improved version of the New Army and Navy revolver. The shape of the frame is modernized, the front face being sloped back and the lower run deeply curved over the trigger guard. More of the trigger is exposed, and the cylinder rotation is changed to clockwise, thus pushing the cylinder into the frame. The hammer was given a loosely pivoting firing pin. It is chambered for the .32-20, .38 Colt, .38 Smith & Wesson and .41 Colt. The Army Special is offered with either a 4.5- or 6-inch barrel. The finish is blued or nickel-plated, and the grips are checkered hard rubber. The serial number range is #291000 to #540000, and the guns were manufactured between 1908 and 1927. "Army Special" is roll engraved on the left side of the barrel.

EXC.	V.G.	GOOD	FAIR	POOR
550	400	250	200	150

NOTE: The following advertisement appeared on *GunBroker.com* in March of 2007:

"Colt Army Special .38 Special Revolver. Serial number # 541997. 4" barrel. Overall, gun is in very good condition. Some wear on the finish around the barrel. Bore is in very good condition and gun is tight. Wood grips have some wear on them, but not bad. Includes a pistol rug." Bidding started at $199.99.

OFFICER'S MODEL TARGET 1ST ISSUE

This revolver, actually part of the New Army and Navy Series of 1892 to 1908, is chambered for the .38 Special cartridge. It has a 6 inch barrel and is blued, with a slightly modified flattop frame, checkered walnut grips (without medallions) and adjustable rear target sights. Colt manufactured this model from 1904 to 1908, but production based on orders has been described as "meager."

EXC.	V.G.	GOOD	FAIR	POOR
1,000	750	350	300	200

NOTE: The following advertisement appeared on *GunBroker.com* during Spring of 2007:

"Colt First model Officers Model double action 38 special, original, bluing is about 40%, Grip show some wear and nicks on both grips, checkering shows wear. Some minor pitting behind the hammer, cylinder great. Screws and pins untouched bore excellent, 6-inch barrel fixed sights. Serial number #6540."

The seller began the auction at $200.

Officer's Model with heavy barrel.

Officer's Model Target, 2rd Issue.

Camp Perry single-shot target pistol.

OFFICER'S MODEL TARGET 2ND ISSUE

This model is similar to the 1st Issue and built on the same "41-caliber frame" but is offered in .22 LR and .32 Police Positive, as well as in .38 Special. It also is furnished with a 4-, 4.5-, 5-, 6- or 7.5-inch barrel in .38 Special only. It had checkered walnut grips and was customarily available blued. Colt manufactured this model between 1908 and 1940, and it was intended for target shooting rather than for general purposes.

EXC.	V.G.	GOOD	FAIR	POOR
700	550	300	250	150

NOTE: The following advertisement appeared on *ColtAutos.com* during February of 2007:

"Officers Model Target in 22 LR. Mfg. 1930 with 6 inch barrel, serial number #52052, wood checkered grips with medallions. No rust or pitting, just normal holster wear. Adjustable front and rear sites, mint bore and cylinders. Overall finish rating is 90+. Price includes shipping to the lower 48 only. Can ship to C & R. $750."

CAMP PERRY SINGLE-SHOT

Colt named this model after the site of the U.S. Target Competition held annually at Camp Perry, Ohio.

The Camp Perry is the only single-shot Colt built on a revolver frame and it was Colt's first attempt to enter the specialized target shooting market. Prototypes were tested in the Camp Perry matches as early as

Officer's Model Match.

1920, but the guns were not marketed commercially until the beginning of 1927. This gun was created by modifying an Officer's Model frame to accept a special, flat single-shot chamber block instead of a cylinder. The barrel ran back into the block, and the entire unit pivoted to the left side and downward for loading. For weight, this target pistol came in at about 35 oz., which was supposed to accustom the shooter to the weight of the full bore Officer's Model. Few purchasers were convinced of these merits, however, and sales did not fulfill marketing projections.

The manufacture of replacement parts ceased in February, 1939, but new guns were still being offered when the U.S. entered World War II. The pistol is chambered for .22 LR and is offered with an 8- (early production) or a 10-inch (later production) barrel. The improved 10-inch barrel, introduced in 1934, featured a recessed head chamber to allow high power ammunition to be used. The firing mechanism was also improved, gaining a straighter trigger lever and a faster lock time. The finish is blued, with checkered walnut grips. The name "Camp Perry Model" is stamped on the left side of the chamber; the caliber is on the barrel. About 2,500 of these target competition and shooting practice revolvers were manufactured between 1920 and 1941. Add 100 percent premium for a 10-inch barrel. Add 50 percent premium for original box.

EXC.	V.G.	GOOD	FAIR	POOR
2,500	1,750	950	600	400

OFFICER'S MODEL MATCH

Introduced in 1953, this model is similar to the Officer's Model Target and chambered for either .22 caliber or .38 Special with 6 inch barrel. The revolver is fitted with a heavy tapered barrel and wide hammer spur, with adjustable rear sight and ramp front sight. It was sold with checkered walnut target grips. A blued finish is standard. It was discontinued in 1970. Very popular for competitive shooting, the Officer's Model Match could be fired either double or single action and was available in long-action (standard) or short-action configurations. Values for the .22 caliber version are listed. Officer's Model Match in .38 caliber will bring approximately 20 percent less.

EXC.	V.G.	GOOD	FAIR	POOR
750	600	450	350	250

.22 CALIBER IN SHORT ACTION – SINGLE ACTION ONLY

EXC.	V.G.	GOOD	FAIR	POOR
1000	750	600	500	350

NOTE: The following advertisement appeared on *ColtAutos.com* in August of 2006:

"Colt Officers Model - Caliber: .22, serial number #18552, Price: $ 700. Description: This is perhaps the finest Officers Model I have had the pleasure to own. This gun has no wear marks except muzzle crown and that is minimal. This gun was in a collection and I suspect was never shot, and if so less than 250 rounds. The grips are flawless, Screws are perfect. A really nice piece."

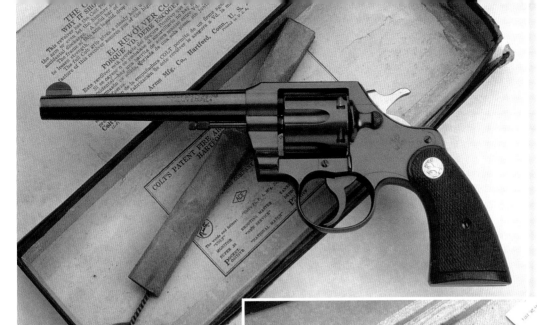

*Official Police,
heavy barrel.*

*Police: the Official
Police Mark III.*

OFFICIAL POLICE

A popular revolver, which remained in the Colt line for many years, the Official Police was manufactured from 1927 to 1969 and more than 425,000 were built. Still, it was nothing more than the Army Special of 1908 under a new name. Few purchases were being made by the military in the mid-1920s, but as large numbers of pistols were being bought by police forces, a change in name improved the gun's marketing potential. It is chambered for .32-20 and .41 Colt, but these calibers were discontinued in 1942 and 1930, respectively. The .38 Special was chambered throughout the production run: a .22 LR was added in 1930 with about 30,000 total produced. This model holds six shots, has a squared butt, and is offered with 2-, 4-, 5- and 6-inch barrels. The 2-inch barrel version had a slender round heel butt and the rear sight notch was a broad Partridge type square notch. Heavy-barrel versions were also offered. The top strap was matte, the trigger checkered during production and the chambers of post-1934 guns were recessed to protect the cartridge case rims. The grips are checkered walnut or plastic. The finish is either blued or nickel plated.

The final incarnation of the Official Sharp-eyed viewers will recognize the Official Police as one of the two sidearms carried by Deputy Barney Fife on *The Andy Griffith Show*. (The other was a S&W Model 10.)

For nickel plating add 10 percent. .22 LR add 20 percent.

EXC.	V.G.	GOOD	FAIR	POOR
400	300	250	200	150

NOTE: The following advertisement appeared on *ColtAutos.com* in October of 2006:

"Official Police .38 Special, serial number #539810, Price: $375.00 - plus $20 s&h. Description: Blue 38spl, 6 inch barrel, walnut grips with rampant Colt, NRA 90% overall condition, a super nice revolver, desires an excellent home."

OFFICIAL POLICE MARTIAL MODEL

This gun was purchased by the military during World War II in barrel lengths of 4, 5 and 6 inches. It has a polished blue finish, is chambered for the .38 Special, and has checkered walnut grips. About 5,000 were bought by the army and another 5,000 by the Defense Supply Corporation.

EXC.	V.G.	GOOD	FAIR	POOR
750	600	400	300	150

Official Police,
Lend-Lease
martial version.

Colt Commando Model.

COMMANDO MODEL

This gun represents a special wartime order for factory guards and other security forces placed by the U.S. Government in November, 1942. This model, for all intents and purposes, is an Official Police chambered for .38 Special, with a 2-, 4- or 6-inch barrel. The Commando is Parkerized and barrel stamped "Colt Commando/.38 Special." It had no checkering on the cylinder latch or trigger and a matte finish on top of the frame. Checkered plastic grips. There were approximately 50,617 manufactured between 1942 and 1945 for use during World War II and serial numbers begin with #1. Add 30 percent for 2 inch barrel.

EXC.	V.G.	GOOD	FAIR	POOR
850	750	400	200	100

Colt Marshall.

Rare Colt Marshall factory snubbie.

Detective Special, 1st Issue.

MARSHAL MODEL

This is an Official Police that is marked "COLT MARSHAL" on the barrel and has an "M" suffix in the serial number. It has a 2- or 4-inch barrel and a rounded butt. The finish is blued. There were approximately 2,500 manufactured between 1954 and 1956, non-consecutive serial numbers ending with an M from #833352-M to #845317-M.

EXC.	V.G.	GOOD	FAIR	POOR
500	400	300	250	150

NOTE: The following advertisement appeared on *GunsAmerica.com* in the Spring of 2007:

"Colt Marshal Model in Nickel. .38 Special, 4 inch barrel, round butt, with "Colt Marshal" on the barrel. Wood grips, and made in 1954-1956. Condition is excellent with 95% nickel. No box or other paperwork. Can sell to California interested collectors through a two party transfer. I am located in Fresno, Calif. I am selling for $1,100.00."

COLT .38 SF-VI

Introduced in 1995, this model is essentially a Detective Special in stainless steel with a new internal mechanism. It has a transfer bar safety mechanism and, fitted with a 2 inch barrel, the cylinder holds six rounds of .38 Special. A 4-inch barreled version in bright stainless steel is also available. The weight is 21 oz. and overall length is 7 inches.

NIB	EXC.	V.G	GOOD	FAIR	POOR
400	325	275	225	150	100

COLT .38 SF-VI SPECIAL LADY

Introduced in 1996, this is a 2 inch barrel version similar to the above model with the addition of a bright finish and bobbed hammer. Weight is 21 oz.

NIB	EXC.	V.G	GOOD	FAIR	POOR
400	325	275	225	150	100

DETECTIVE SPECIAL 1ST ISSUE

This model is actually a duplication, as it is nothing more than a Police Positive Special with a 2 inch barrel standard. It was originally chambered for .32 New Police, .38 New Police (which were discontinued in the 1930s) and .38 Special, which continued until the end of the production run. A few were built with a shrouded hammer, giving them the usual "hammerless" appearance. The finish is blued, and it is offered with wood or plastic grips. Manufactured 1927-1946..

EXC.	V.G.	GOOD	FAIR	POOR
900	650	275	175	100

Detective Special, 2nd Issue.

Detective Special, 3rd Issue.

Detective Special 3rd Issue, nickel finish.

MARTIALLY MARKED

Chambered for the .38 Special and fitted with a 2-inch barrel. Blued finish with checkered cylinder latch and trigger. Checkered walnut grips. About 5,000 were purchased by the military, mostly for military intelligence and police units.

EXC.	V.G.	GOOD	FAIR	POOR
650	500	300	150	100

DETECTIVE SPECIAL 2ND ISSUE

This is basically a modernized, streamlined version of the 1st Issue. It is similar except that it has a 2- or 3-inch barrel and plastic (1947-1954) wraparound checkered walnut (1955-1972) grips and is chambered for .38 Special. It was finished in blue or nickel plate. Manufactured 1947-1972. Add $25 for nickel finish.

NIB	EXC.	V.G.	GOOD	FAIR	POOR
375	275	225	175	125	75

DETECTIVE SPECIAL 3RD ISSUE

Similar to 2nd Issue but with shrouded ejector rod. Manufactured 1973-1986.

NIB	EXC.	V.G.	GOOD	FAIR	POOR
375	275	225	175	125	75

The following advertisement appeared on *GunsAmerica.com* in the Spring of 2007:

"We have a really nice Colt double action revolver in this third-issue Detective Special in .38 Special with a two inch barrel. Blue Pachmayer compact grips with Colt emblem. Comes in box with instruction manual. Appears unfired. 99% plus overall condition. Asking $499."

DETECTIVE SPECIAL II (DS-II), AKA 4TH ISSUE

Introduced in 1997, this version of the Detective special features new internal lockwork and a transfer bar safety mechanism. It is fitted with a 2-inch barrel, has a capacity of six rounds, and is chambered for the .38 Special. In 1998 this model was offered chambered for the .357 Magnum as well. Rubber combat style grips are standard. Weight is approximately 21 oz. Stainless steel finish.

NIB	EXC.	V.G.	GOOD	FAIR	POOR
450	350	275	225	-	-

COLT MAGNUM CARRY

Introduced in 1998 and discontinued around 2000, this model is essentially a renamed Detective Special II. Stainless steel finish. Weight is 21 oz.

NIB	EXC.	V.G.	GOOD	FAIR	POOR
450	350	275	-	-	-

Original Fitz Special.

A pair of Banker's Specials in .22 (left) and .38.

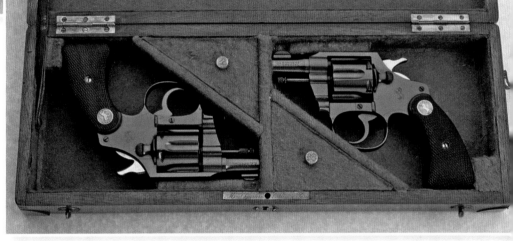

NOTE: The following advertisement appeared in *GunsAmerica.com* in March of 2007:

"Model SD2020 – A stainless steel Detective Special Magnum Carry .357 Magnum with two inch barrel and rubber grips. This gun has been customized by Cylinder & Slide (over $600 in custom work). Trigger has been rounded and polished. Action job. Hammer bobbed and a front night sight. Excellent shooter. This is a very rare gun and hard to find. Only made one year. Asking $1,145."

FITZ SPECIAL (AKA FITZ-COLT)

Developed by showman, ballistic expert and Colt employee named John Henry Fitzgerald (sometimes given as Fitz-Gerald), and intended to slip into his pants pockets, this gun was a modified Detective Special. Only about a hundred were built, all with 2-inch barrels. They feature a bobbed hammer and a clipped trigger guard so that the trigger finger would slide immediately to the trigger. Original Fitz-Colts are highly prized by collectors, but many imitations – often by garage mechanics – have been noted. In use,

they were dangerous unless handled by someone with experience.

NIB	EXC.	V.G.	GOOD	FAIR	POOR
1,200	800	-	-	-	-

BANKER'S SPECIAL

Designed for "easy carrying and quick access … primarily for bank employees," the U.S. Postal Service equipped its railroad mail clerks with this revolver, as did several police forces of the day. The Bankers Special is a 2-inch barreled, easily concealed revolver. Chambered for .38 Special with 1.25-inch cylinder and offered primarily in blued finish, although a few nickel plated guns have been found in private collections. It was also offered in .22 rimfire. The grips are rounded but full-sized, and Colt utilized this feature in advertising this model. The U.S. Postal Service equipped its railway

Colt Cobra in .22 rimfire.

Cobra, 2nd Issue.

mail clerks with this model. Reportedly there were approximately 35,000 manufactured between 1926 and 1943, although serial numbers are all in the six-figure range and later examples have been noted (see below). Nickel models will command a premium, as will a Banker's Special in .22 caliber.

EXC.	V.G.	GOOD	FAIR	POOR
1,200	800	300	250	150

NOTE: The following listing appeared at *GunsAmerica.com* in the Spring of 2007 with an interesting "made in" date:

"Banker's Special in .38 Special. Made 1950 per Colt factory letter shipped to police department of Salem, Mass. inscribed on backstrap. Asking $1,695."

COBRA 1ST ISSUE

Manufactured between 1950 and 1973, the Cobra is simply an aluminum alloy framed lightweight version of the Detective Special. This lightweight frame resulted in a reduction of 7 oz. in weight to only 15 oz. The Cobra is chambered for .32, .38 Special and .22 LR.

This model is available in either a round-butt or square-butt version with a 4 inch barrel only.

EXC.	V.G.	GOOD	FAIR	POOR
500	300	225	150	100

NOTE: The following advertisement appeared at *GunsAmerica.com* in the Spring of 2007:

"Beautiful 1st Edition Colt Cobra 6 shot .38 Special revolver, blue frame. Original walnut grips with Colt Medallion, Graded "NRA 100% Condition." Price includes two day delivery, shipping, handling, insurance, signature confirmation, packaging, a tracking number plus no sales tax to non-KY Residents. Asking $799."

COBRA 2ND ISSUE

The same as the 1st Issue in .38 Special only. It is a streamlined version with wraparound walnut grips and shrouded ejector rod. For nickel plating add 30 percent.

EXC.	V.G.	GOOD	FAIR	POOR
400	300	225	150	100

Police Positive.

Police Positive Target.

POLICE POSITIVE

Developed in answer to a demand for a more powerful version of the .32 caliber Police Positive, firing a heavier bullet with better ballistics, this .38 caliber revolver was scarcely larger, physically, than its predecessor. Except for the 1.25-inch cylinder (instead of 1.63 inches), this is externally the same as the New Police with the addition of the positive lock feature and the two new chamberings, the .38 New Police and the .38 Smith & Wesson. About 200,000 were manufactured from 1905 to 1947 and serial numbers begin at about #49500. These guns were sold to many police forces, especially in the Americas, and others were acquired by European military purchasing commissions (including the British) from 1938 to 1941.

Note that several thousand factory seconds in .32 caliber were barrel-marked "Pequano" (for the Spanish *pequeño*) and sold to Puerto Rico, Central and South America, the Philippines, Thailand and, at the start of WW II, to Britain. It is generally thought that the Pequano guns were "2nd Quality," i.e., not up to Colt's usual production standards. Barrels were from 2 to 6 inches long and serial numbers ranged from #226000 to #237000. Most of these pistols were used hard and, like most Colt's sold to or through foreign countries, few have been returned to the U.S.; therefore no value has been established. When they do appear for sale, they go for whatever the market will bear, generally peaking at around $1000 in the better condition grades.

EXC.	V.G.	GOOD	FAIR	POOR
400	300	250	200	150

NOTE: The following three advertisements appeared on *ArmChairGunShow.com* in the Spring of 2007. They illustrate three different configurations, qualities and sale prices.

"Colt - Police Positive - .32 Police – 6 inch barrel - Fine condition. - About 70% original bright blue, turning gray on barrel and grip straps; excellent markings. - Excellent bore & mech. - Right heel chip glued, otherwise fine C logo grips. About 1914. Serial number #117854. $345."

"Colt - Police Positive - marked "B". - .32 cal. - 2-3/8" barrel. - Very good condition. - About 70% original blue, balance crisp plum metal; excellent markings include large "B" between Police/Positive and "32" on right side of barrel, as described for Pequano 2nd quality models. Fine mechanics and bright bore; fine C hard rubber grips. One of the scarce B marked 2nd quality Police Positives, similar to some later production which were marked Pequano to sell in the Latin American market. About 1910. Serial number #81463. $485."

"Colt - Police Positive Special revolver - .38 Colt Special; 5" barrel. - About as-new condition. Almost 100% original finish; about perfect throughout. Superior specimen. About 1928. Serial number #371338. $800."

POLICE POSITIVE TARGET

This is basically the same as the New Police Target with the positive lock feature. Introduced in 1905 and built for 20 years as factory models "G" (centerfire) or "H" (rimfire). It is chambered in .22 LR and .22 WRF,

*Police Positive
Special in .32-20.*

*Police Positive Special
in .38 Special.*

as well as the other cartridges offered in the earlier model. It had a 6-inch barrel and adjustable rear sights. In October 1925, the original patterns were replaced by factory model "C," which was made until 1943. Triggers were checkered, the top strap was matted and, after 1934, the chambers were recessed to protect the case rims. About 28,000 were built.

Note that a .22 caliber Police Positive chambered for the .22 Short and Long cartridge may be seen with British proofs. Several such revolvers were sold to London Armory in this configuration during the late 1920s. A NIB example recently sold for $1,200.

EXC.	V.G.	GOOD	FAIR	POOR
650	550	400	300	200

POLICE POSITIVE SPECIAL

This model, built from 1907 to 1973, is very similar to the Police Positive. Also known as factory model "D," this was the first small-frame swing cylinder revolver to be made for a powerful cartridge and became a very popular police weapon. It has a slightly larger frame to accept the longer cylinder needed to chamber more powerful cartridges such as the .32-20 and .38 Special, in addition to the original chamberings. Barrel lengths varied from 1.25 to 6 inches, the 4-inch version being the most common. More than 750,000 were manufactured from 1907 to 1973.

Police Positive Mk V.

EXC.	V.G.	GOOD	FAIR	POOR
350	275	225	150	100

NOTE: The following advertisement appeared at *GunsAmerica.com* in the Spring of 2007:

"Police Positive Special - A 1960 production, 38 Special, 4 inch Police Positive Special rated at 99% plus condition. Include is the correct box but no manual. Asking $565."

POLICE POSITIVE SPECIAL MARK V

Introduced in 1994, this is an updated version of the Police Positive Special. This model features a 4-inch barrel with underlug and rubber grips and fixed sights. The butt is rounded. The revolver is rated to fire .38 caliber +P rounds. The overall length is 9 inches and weight approximately 30 oz.

NIB	EXC.	V.G.	GOOD	FAIR	POOR
350	250	200	150	100	85

Colt Border Patrol.

Colt Aircrewman.

BORDER PATROL

This model is quite rare, as Colt manufactured only 400 of them in 1952. It is basically a Police Special with a heavy duty 4-inch barrel. It is chambered for the .38 Special and was built to be very strong and resistant to rough treatment, what one might expect on the U.S. border with Mexico. The finish is blued and serial numbered in the #610000 range.

EXC.	V.G.	GOOD	FAIR	POOR
5000	3000	2000	1000	500

AGENT 1ST ISSUE

This revolver is basically the same as the 1st Issue Cobra with a shortened grip frame or "short butt." This was done to make the Agent more concealable. Colt built the Agent 1st Issue from 1955 until 1973.

EXC.	V.G.	GOOD	FAIR	POOR
400	300	200	125	100

NOTE: The following advertisement appeared on *GunsAmerica.com* in March of 2007:

"Agent - Nice used revolver with a 2-inch barrel and chambering for .38 Special. 6 shot. No trades or deals. Asking $429."

AGENT L.W. 2ND ISSUE

This is a streamlined version with the shrouded ejector rod. In the last four years of its production, it was matte finished. Colt manufactured this model between 1973 and 1986.

EXC.	V.G.	GOOD	FAIR	POOR
350	250	200	175	150

AIRCREWMAN

This model was specially fabricated for U.S. Air Force pilots who carried it for personal protection. At 11 oz., it is extremely lightweight because both the frame and the cylinder are made of aluminum alloy. It has a short, easily manageable 2-inch barrel and is chambered for a distinctive .38 Special "M41" military cartridge with a chamber pressure of 16,000 pounds per square inch. The finish is blued, with checkered walnut grips. There were approximately 1,200 manufactured in 1951, and they are marked "U.S." or "A.F." for serial numbers #1 through #1189. (Note: Some disagreement exists whether this model is properly called "Aircrewman" or "Air Crewman." We have used the former here, as it appears on the barrel roll-stamping.)

EXC.	V.G.	GOOD	FAIR	POOR
4,500	2,500	1,500	800	250

Colt Courier.

Colt Trooper.

COURIER

This is another version of the aluminum alloy Cobra. It features a shorter grip frame and a 3-inch barrel. This model is chambered for .32 and .22 rimfire. There were approximately 3,000 manufactured in 1955 and 1956. For .22 rimfire add 20 percent.

EXC.	V.G.	GOOD	FAIR	POOR
850	750	600	500	350

NOTE: The following advertisement appeared at *GunsAmerica.com* in the Spring of 2007:

"This Extremely Rare Lightweight Colt Courier Revolver appears unfired. It is one of just 3,000 made between 1953 and 1956, hardly ever seen, and estimated in 98 to 99% condition. This mint example is chambered in the unusual .32 Colt New Police caliber. There is a very slight turn ring, and the alloy cylinder has taken a slight patina in contrast to the flawless black frame and barrel. No box or papers - but a Collector's treasure. Asking $895."

TROOPER

Not a variant on an earlier model, this gun was designed specifically by Colt to fill the need for a large, heavy duty, powerful holster revolver that was also extremely accurate. Nevertheless, the frame and general design were almost identical to the Police Special and sales remained good until production ended. It was built with a prominently ramped front sight and an adjustable target rear sight. It was offered with a 4- or 6-inch barrel and blued or nickel finishes with checkered walnut grips. "Colt Trooper" and the caliber are found on the left side of the barrel. The Trooper is chambered for the .38 Special/.357 Magnum, and there is a .22 rimfire version for the target shooter. This model was manufactured between 1953 and 1969 with initial serial numbers #1 to #84616, followed by #906351 to #938520, and finally #J1001 and up.

EXC.	V.G.	GOOD	FAIR	POOR
400	250	200	150	100

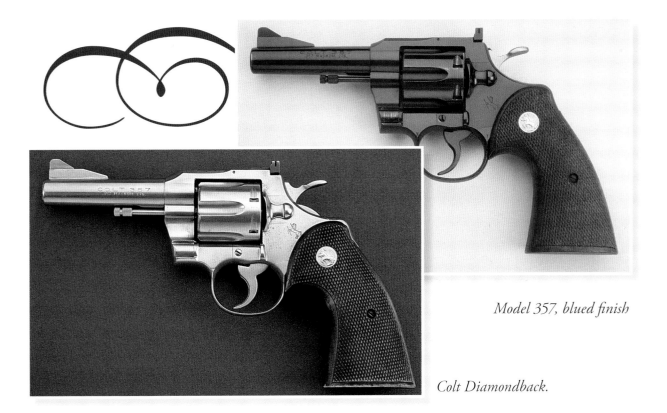

Model 357, blued finish

Colt Diamondback.

NOTE: The following advertisement appeared on *GunsAmerica.com* during the Spring of 2007:

"Colt Trooper First Generation in .38spl 4" barrel. Gun is in excellent condition good clean bore, Like New. SN#91728x. Asking $555."

.357 MAGNUM

This is a deluxe version of the Trooper. It is offered with a special wide spur target wide hammer, large target-type grips and .357 Magnum chambering. The sights are Accro target. It features a 4- or 6-inch barrel and a blued finish. Manufactured between 1953 and 1961, fewer than 15,000 were produced. (Note that the name is sometimes given as "Colt Three-Fifty-Seven.")

EXC.	V.G.	GOOD	FAIR	POOR
500	350	300	200	150

DIAMONDBACK

This model is a medium-frame, duty-type weapon suitable for target work. It has the short frame of the Detective Special with a ventilated rib atop a 2.5-, 4 /-or 6-inch barrel. It is chambered for .38 Special and .22 rimfire. The finish is blued or nickel plated, with checkered walnut grips inset with the Colt medallion. The Diamondback features adjustable target sights, wide

Model 357, nickel finish.

target hammer, shrouded ejector rod and steel frame of the Python. It was manufactured between 1966 and 1986. For .22 caliber or 2.5-inch barrel add 30 percent. Add $300 for nickel finish.

NIB	EXC.	V.G.	GOOD	FAIR	POOR
850	750	450	300	250	150

NOTE: The following advertisement appeared on *ColtAutos.com* in the Spring of 2007:

"This is a beautiful Diamondback in .22 LR. Gun shows almost 100% perfect deep Colt blue. There is the slightest hint of a turn ring on the cylinder, otherwise this gun is perfect. Unfortunately, no box. Price: $1,250."

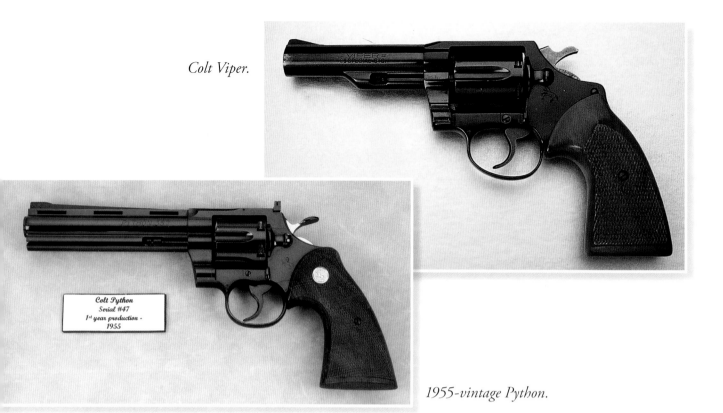

Colt Viper.

1955-vintage Python.

Colt Python
Serial #47
1st year production -
1955

VIPER

This is an alloy framed revolver chambered for the .38 Special. It has a 4-inch barrel and was manufactured between 1977 and 1984. The Viper is essentially a lightweight version of the Police Positive.

NIB	EXC.	V.G.	GOOD	FAIR	POOR
450	375	200	175	125	100

PYTHON

Manufactured since 1955, the Python is the Cadillac of the Colt double action line and was the first revolver to show a substantial change in design since the early 1900s. It is chambered for the .357 Magnum cartridge, holds six shots, and has been offered with a heavy barrel in lengths of 2.5, 3, 4, 6 and 8 inches. This revolver weighs 41 oz. with the 4-inch barrel and is offered finished in high polished Colt Royal Blue, nickel-plate, matte finish stainless steel or what is known as "The Ultimate," a high polished stainless steel. The grips are checkered walnut. The Python has a flat-faced hammer and a floating firing pin in the frame. It is possible that the nickel-plated specimens may bring a 10 percent premium, but in our experience this is not always the case as many potential purchasers have a definite preference for the blued finish. Perhaps because of its reputation for smooth operation and excellent quality, this gun was reintroduced into the Colt product line in 2001 as the Python Elite. The Python was discontinued along with all of Colt's other double action revolvers in 1999. It was available through the Colt Custom Shop until 2003, when even this version was discontinued.

NIB	EXC.	V.G.	GOOD	FAIR	POOR
1400	1100	800	550	400	225

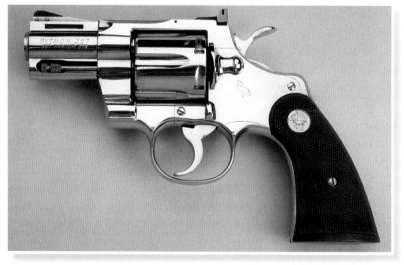

Python snubbie, nickel finish.

Python Elite.

Python Target Model.

MATTE STAINLESS STEEL

NIB	EXC.	V.G.	GOOD	FAIR	POOR
1450	1150	850	600	500	275

"THE ULTIMATE" BRIGHT STAINLESS

NIB	EXC.	V.G.	GOOD	FAIR	POOR
2000	1500	1050	800	-	-

PYTHON ELITE

Reintroduced in 2001, this model features a stainless steel satin finish or blued finish. Adjustable red ramp front sight. Chambered for .357 Magnum with custom, checkered wood grips and choice of 4- or 6-inch ventilated barrel. The weight is about 43 oz. Discontinued 2003.

NIB	EXC.	V.G.	GOOD	FAIR	POOR
2500	2000	1700	-	-	-

NOTE: The following advertisement appeared on *GunBroker.com* in March of 2007:

"*Colt Python Elite .357 Magnum brite stls. This is a VERY nice gun. Only a faint almost invisible line where the cylinder has been turned. It is hard to tell this has been fired at all! This is a Python Elite with a finish that is like a mirror. The grips on this gun are better than any I have seen in years ...look at the swirls of light and dark ...not easy to come by! This gun is in the factory box and has the owner's manual.*"

The gun sold for $3,020.25.

PYTHON .38 SPECIAL

Built from 1955 to 1956, this is a heavy, 8-inch barreled Python chambered for the .38 Special only. It was a limited production venture that was not a success, perhaps because, if users were going to carry a revolver this large, they wanted more stopping power than the .38 would deliver. It was offered in blue only.

EXC.	V.G.	GOOD	FAIR	POOR
700	595	400	300	225

Python Hunter.

Metropolitan Mk III.

PYTHON HUNTER

The Hunter was a special 8-inch .357 Magnum Python offered for one year, 1981, only. The grips are neoprene with gold Colt medallions. An extended eye relief Leupold 2X scope and accessories, such as a fitted, Halliburton extruded aluminum case, were offered for sale packaged as a "Hunter Kit." A complete kit with instructional materials would be expected to sell for an additional 10 to 20 percent.

NIB	EXC.	V.G.	GOOD	FAIR	POOR
1,200	1000	850	600	400	300

NOTE: The following advertisement appeared at *GunsAmerica.com* in the Spring of 2007:

"We have a Colt Python Hunter that is in .357 Magnum. The revolver has a deep blue finish on it. The mental has turned sort of plum colored because of the high nickel content in the metal. The pistol has a hard case and a Leupold 2x scope mounted on top. The revolver has a 6 inch barrel. The price of the revolver is $1799 shipped to the continental USA."

COLT GRIZZLY

This Python variant was manufactured in 1994 with only 2000 units produced. It is basically a matte stainless Python chambered in .357 Magnum with a 6-inch barrel and unfluted cylinder. The Grizzly was shipped with a Python user's manual.

NIB	EXC.	V.G.	GOOD	FAIR	POOR
4000	3000	-	-	-	-

METROPOLITAN MARK III

The Mark III series was designed to replace many of the existing but older Colt revolvers, introducing features such as stainless steel springs, surface hardening of all major parts and a general improvement in manufacture and finish. This revolver is basically a heavier-duty version of the Official Police. It is chambered for .38 Special and fitted with a 4-inch heavy barrel and walnut grips. It is finished in blue only and was manufactured from 1969 to 1972.

NIB	EXC.	V.G.	GOOD	FAIR	POOR
400	300	150	125	100	75

NOTE: The following advertisement appeared on *GunsAmerica.com* in the Spring of 2007:

"This is a Colt Metropolitan Mark III in .38 Special. It has beautiful bluing (close to 99%) but some wear at the muzzle, and most of the case hardening remains on the hammer. The action is very smooth and the rifling is great. It has a set of walnut bull's eye type grips, but is crying for a set of Pachmyers. LOL. This gun is pretty and mechanically excellent; it was well kept. The only downfall of this classic Colt revolver is that someone lightly scribed some personal info on the right side frame below the cylinder. Asking $250."

Lawman
Mk III.

LAWMAN MARK III

This model is offered chambered for the .357 Magnum with a 2- or 4-inch barrel. It has checkered walnut grips and is either blued or nickel plated. Colt manufactured the Lawman between 1969 and 1983.

EXC.	V.G.	GOOD	FAIR	POOR
350	300	200	150	100

NOTE: The following advertisement appeared at *Gunsammerica.com* in the Spring of 2007:

"This Colt Lawman MKIII is a 6 shot revolver that shoots the .357 magnum round. It has a 4 inch barrel and has a nickel finish and wooden grips. This revolver is used but is in excellent condition. Asking $499.99."

Trooper Mk III,
early packaging.

TROOPER MARK III

This revolver was intended to be the target-grade version of the Mark III series. It is offered with a 4-, 6- or 8-inch ventilated rib barrel with a shrouded ejector rod similar in appearance to the Python. It is chambered for the .22 LR and the .22 Magnum, as well as .357 Magnum. It features adjustable target sights,

Trooper Mk III, later packaging.

checkered walnut target grips and is either blued or nickel plated. This model was manufactured between 1969 and 1983.

NIB	EXC.	V.G.	GOOD	FAIR	POOR
550	475	350	200	150	100

NOTE: From *GunsAmerica.com* in the Spring of 2007 come these two advertisements:

"Colt Trooper MK III .357 Magnum with 6 inch barrel, blue finish, Excellent condition. Price includes two day delivery, shipping, handling, insurance, signature confirmation, packaging, a tracking number plus no sales tax to non-KY Residents. Satisfaction guaranteed. Asking $519."

"Trooper MKIII "Sky Marshal" .38 revolver with 2 inch barrel and short butt. Produced to use pre-loaded plastic cylinders with plastic bullets, they were made to be carried by Federal Sky Marshals on airliners during the late 1960s [when sky-jacking was in terrorist vogue]. The plastic bullets would not penetrate the hull of the plane, yet would disable a hijacker. This one includes the Colt

box and is like new. It retains 99% of the orig. blue; excellent checkered walnut stocks with gold rampant Colt medallions. (Included is some historical background paperwork on an earlier Sky Marshal that we had.) Serial number #0121xxU. Asking $1,495."

LAWMAN MARK V

This gun was essentially a version of the Mark III with an improved trigger mechanism. It also entailed a redesigned grip, a shorter lock time, and an improved double action. It was manufactured 1982 to 1985. Add 25 percent for nickel finish.

NIB	EXC.	V.G.	GOOD	FAIR	POOR
700	550	350	200	150	100

TROOPER MARK V

This version of the Trooper Mark III was manufactured between 1982 and 1985. It incorporated the same improvements as those appearing in the Lawman Mark V. Add 25 percent for nickel finish.

NIB	EXC.	V.G.	GOOD	FAIR	POOR
700	550	350	200	150	100

Colt Boa.

BOA

This is basically a deluxe version of the Trooper MK V. It has the same features plus the high polished blue found on the Python. Colt manufactured 1,200 of these revolvers in 1985, and the entire production was purchased and marketed by Lew Horton Distributing Company in Southboro, Massachusetts.

NIB	EXC.	V.G.	GOOD	FAIR	POOR
2500	1950	1050	700	-	-

NOTE: The following advertisement appeared on *GunBroker.com* in March of 2007:

"Colt BOA .357 Magnum, 6 inch barrel, blue, RR/ WO sights. New in the original box with all papers and hang tag, SCARCE!!!!!!!!"

Bidding eventually peaked at $2700 but the seller's reserve was not met.

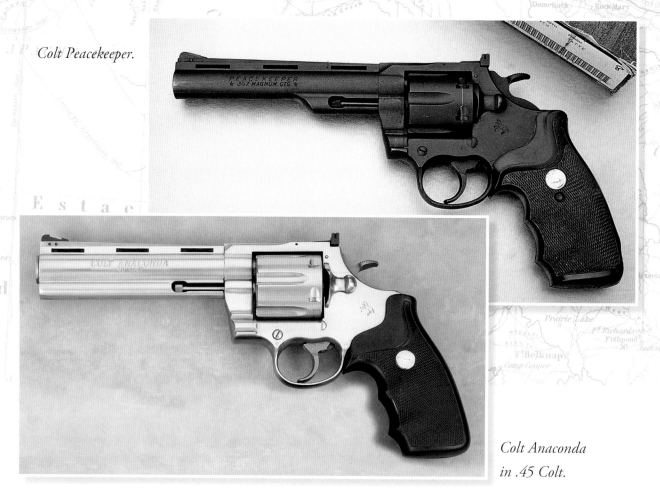

Colt Peacekeeper.

*Colt Anaconda
in .45 Colt.*

PEACEKEEPER

Introduced to replace the Lawman Mark V, this model was similar to the King Cobra and designed as a duty weapon with target capabilities. It is offered with a 4- or 6-inch barrel chambered for .357 Magnum. It features adjustable sights, half length ejector rod shroud and neoprene combat-style grips. The gun was sold with a matte blued finish. The Peacekeeper was manufactured between 1985 and 1987.

NIB	EXC.	V.G.	GOOD	FAIR	POOR
375	275	225	200	150	100

KING COBRA

This stainless steel model of the basic Python model has become the workhorse of the Colt revolver line. The King Cobra has a forged steel frame and barrel, a full length ejector rod housing and ultra-short hammer fall. The barrel is fitted with a solid rib. This model is equipped with an adjustable, white outline rear sight and a red insert front sight. Colt black wraparound neoprene combat style grips (they include finger grooves in the front edge) are standard. The blued model was abandoned in the early 1990s. In 1998 all King Cobras were drilled and tapped for scope mounts.

BLUED

NIB	EXC.	V.G.	GOOD	FAIR	POOR
450	350	300	250	200	100

STAINLESS STEEL

Offered in 4 or 6 inch barrel lengths. In 1997 this model was introduced with optional barrel porting.

NIB	EXC.	V.G.	GOOD	FAIR	POOR
475	350	300	250	200	125

HIGH POLISH STAINLESS STEEL

NIB	EXC.	V.G.	GOOD	FAIR	POOR
500	450	400	300	250	125

NOTE: The following two advertisements appeared on *GunBroker.com* in March of 2007:

"Colt King Cobra, .357 Magnum, 4 inch stainless steel. New in the original box with all papers!"

Bidding eventually peaked at $900 but the seller's reserve was not met.

"Colt King Cobra, .357 Magnum, Legacy Edition, 6 inch gold plated, scarce limited edition, new in the original box!"

The gun sold for $1995.

Colt Anaconda in .44 Magnum.

ANACONDA

This double action .44 Magnum revolver was introduced in 1990, the latest Colt variation in its "snake line." Offered with 4-, 6- or 8-inch barrel, it was intended for hunters and silhouette shooters.

The 4-inch model weighs 47 oz., the 6-inch model weighs 63 oz. and the 8-inch model weighs 59 oz. It was offered with a 6- or 8-inch barrel in a matte stainless steel finish revolver chambered for the .44 Magnum cartridge. The .45 Colt chambering was introduced in 1993. It was constructed of matte finished stainless steel and has black neoprene finger groove combat grips with "gold" Colt medallions. Furnished with either adjustable rear sight and ramp front sights or special scope mount. The Anaconda was discontinued in 1999 but reintroduced in 2001 in .44 Magnum with 4-, 6- or 8-inch barrel. In 1996 a Realtree model was offered with an 8 inch barrel, but this was only manufactured in small numbers and was chambered for the .44 Magnum cartridge. In 1998 the Anaconda was drilled and tapped for scope mounts and buyers had the option of barrel porting. All Anacondas were discontinued for good in 2003.

.44 MAGNUM

NIB	EXC.	V.G.	GOOD	FAIR	POOR
1,100	750	600	450	300	200

.45 COLT

NIB	EXC.	V.G.	GOOD	FAIR	POOR
1250	500	400	300	250	200

REALTREE CAMO MODEL— ADJUSTABLE SIGHTS

NIB	EXC.	V.G.	GOOD	FAIR	POOR
1200	625	500	400	300	200

REALTREE CAMO MODEL—SCOPE MOUNTS

NIB	EXC.	V.G.	GOOD	FAIR	POOR
1,300	800	650	500	400	250

NOTE: The following advertisement appeared on *GunBroker.com* in March of 2007:

"Colt Anaconda .45 caliber double action revolver new and unfired. Serial number #MM36989. Six inch vented rib barrel, transfer bar safety system, six round capacity, stainless steel finish. Black neoprene combat grips with Colt medallion. Red ramp front sight and white rear adjustable sight. Full length ejector rod housing. Colt factory sleeve, carton, owner's manual and warranty card. Manufactured January 1993. Collector grade with no scratches or rub marks. Condition is 100% new."

Bidding started at $1,470.

COLT KODIAK

This Anaconda variant was manufactured in 1994 with only 2000 units produced. It is basically a matte stainless Anaconda chambered in .44 Magnum with a 6-inch barrel and unfluted cylinder. The Kodiak was shipped with an Anaconda user's manual.

NIB	EXC.	V.G.	GOOD	FAIR	POOR
2000	1600	-	-	-	-

SURVIVOR OR MULTI-CALIBER

Introduced into the Colt product line in 1999, this model is based on the Phillips & Rodgers multi-caliber design. This revolver has the capability of using 11 different cartridges in the same cylinder. They are: 9x18, 9x19, 9x23, 9mm, 9 Ruger, 9mm Largo, .380, .38 Super, .38 Special, .38 Special +P and .357 Magnum. The barrel length is 3 inches and the capacity is five rounds. Rubber combat style grips with finger grooves and a fixed rear sight. Machined stainless steel. Weight is about 22 oz. Only one was ever produced; its value is anyone's guess.

THE FABULOUS 1911s
& OTHER SEMI-AUTOS

PRE-1911 SEMI-AUTOMATICS

The Colt Firearms Co. was the first of the major American gun manufacturers to take the semi-automatic pistol seriously. This pistol design was becoming popular among European gun makers in the late 1880s and early 1900s. In the United States, however, building upon the legends of the frontier, the "Wild West," the revolver was firmly ensconced as the accepted design.

Colt realized that if the semi-auto could be made to function reliably, it would soon catch on. Thus, Colt executives negotiated with noted inventors of the day, primarily John M. Browning, to secure or perhaps lease the rights to manufacture their designs. Colt also encouraged the creativity of its own employees with bonuses and incentives and, through this innovative thinking, soon became the leader in semi-auto pistol sales, a position that they have never fully relinquished – at least in name and reputation – to any other American gun manufacturer.

Semi-automatic pistols from Colt represent an interesting field for the collector of Colt handguns. There have been sufficient variations (almost too many, some would argue) with high enough production figures to make it worthwhile to seek them out. In addition, there are now a number of authoritative books specifically about Colt semi-automatics, and anyone wishing to

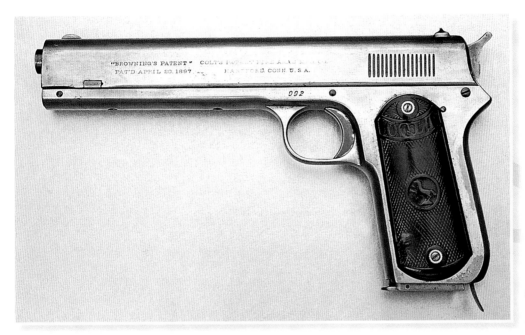

Colt Model 1911.

do so would be able to learn a great deal about them. Collector interest is high and continues to build in this field, and values are definitely on the rise.

MODEL 1900

Although it was little more than a developmental model, this was the first of the Colt automatic pistols and was advertised with a five shot per second firing rate. It was thus not surprising that a total of 3,500 were produced. Still, the Model 1900 was not a very successful design. It was quite clumsy and out of balance in the hand; nevertheless, during Army trials it proved to be reliable.

This gun has a detachable magazine that holds seven cartridges and the barrel is 6 inches in length, giving the gun an overall length of 9 inches and a weight, according to the original instruction sheet (a copy of which could, in the Spring of 2007, be found on Sam Lisker's web site, *ColtAutos.com*) of 35 oz. The action was locked by two transverse ribs on the upper surface of the barrel engaging in two grooves machined in the upper surface of the slide. The barrel was held to the frame by two links, one at the front and one at the rear, until recoil moved it back and down, parallel with the frame, until the lugs disengaged from the grooves. This left the slide free to move back, extracting the empty case, and to chamber a fresh round on the return stroke. Shortly before the forward movement ended, the links raised the barrel until the lugs once again engaged the slide recesses. This is a characteristic John Browning

design, and it has persisted, with various refinements, up to the present day.

Otherwise, look for a case hardened hammer and rear sight safety assembly, and serrations conveniently located at the rear of the slide on all but a few guns made for military trial. These military pistols had serrations at the front of the slide to facilitate charging the gun with the left hand by pushing instead of pulling. The case-colored hammer had a flat cocking spur. This gun is chambered for the .38 Rimless smokeless cartridge. The finish of the Model 1900 is blued, with a safety/sight combination.

The combination rear sight and safety catch proved to be too delicate, though, so most of the guns made after 1902 had a plain rear sight and the safety mechanism was simply eliminated. The grips are either plain walnut for the military field trials or, when sold commercially, checkered walnut or hard rubber.

The left side of the slide is stamped "Browning's Patent" with the 1897 patent date. Colt sold 200 pistols to the Navy and 300 to the Army for field trials and evaluation. The remaining 3,000 or so – estimates of the numbers sold to the military vary – were sold on the civilian market. This model was manufactured from 1900-1903.

Many of the original 1900 pistols had the original unitary sight/safety converted to the later Model 1902 configuration. Although they proved to be more functional, to collectors, these are worth about 50 percent less than unconverted pistols.

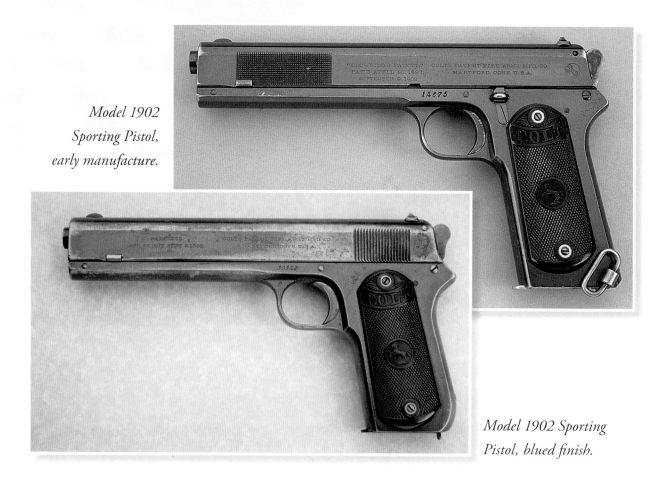

Model 1902 Sporting Pistol, early manufacture.

Model 1902 Sporting Pistol, blued finish.

STANDARD CIVILIAN PRODUCTION

EXC.	V.G.	GOOD	FAIR	POOR
7,500	5,000	3,000	1,250	750

U.S. NAVY MILITARY MODEL (200)

Serial numbers #1001 to #1250 with navy numbers "U.S.N. 1" to "U.S.N. 250" on the left side of the frame.

EXC.	V.G.	GOOD	FAIR	POOR
7,500	6,000	5,000	2,500	1,000

U.S. ARMY MILITARY MODEL – 1ST CONTRACT (100)

EXC.	V.G.	GOOD	FAIR	POOR
22,000	18,000	10,000	4,000	2,000

U.S. ARMY MILITARY MODEL – 2ND CONTRACT (200)

EXC.	V.G.	GOOD	FAIR	POOR
20,000	16,000	8,000	3,000	1,500

MODEL 1902 SPORTING PISTOL

The so-called "Sporting Pistol" was an improved version of the Model 1900. The most notable mechanical changes were the introduction of an inertial firing pin and a hold-open latch that slid vertically in a channel in the left side of the frame. These features were patented by Browning in September of 1902.

The 1900-type firing pin was long enough to rest on the primer as the slide closed and represented a source of potential danger if an accidental discharge occurred. Shortening the pin ensured that it only had to pass through its bush to strike the cap when propelled by the hammer.

The 1902 Sporting Pistol is chambered for the .38 Rimless smokeless cartridge, has a seven round detachable magazine and a 6-inch barrel and weighed 35.5 oz. overall. The overall length was 8.9 inches. It is blued, with checkered hard rubber grips featuring the "rampant colt" molded into them. The first guns had checkered or "diced" serrations at the front of the slide, but these were subsequently replaced by the more familiar rear-of-slide grooves.

When you examine the 1902 Sporting Model, look for the rounded butt, rounded hammer spur, dovetailed rear sight and the 1897 to 1902 patent dates. Colt

Model 1902
Sporting Pistol,
nickel finish.

1902 Military Pistol,
Very Good condition.

manufactured 6,927 of these pistols between 1902 and 1908: 1902 – 625 serial numbered from #4275 to #4900, 1903 – 1,500 from #4901 to #6400, 1904 – 1,300 from #6401 to #6700, 1905 – 1,100 from #7701 to #8800, 1906 – 1,300 from #8801 to #10100 and 1907 – 1090 from #10101 to #10999 and from #30000 to #30190.

Here is a fascinating note about a Colt Model 1902 from Sam Lisker's web site at *ColtAutos.com* and the very thing that makes collecting Colt firearms worthy of a lifetime of study:

EXC.	V.G.	GOOD	FAIR	POOR
3,500	2,000	1,250	750	450

MODEL 1902 MILITARY PISTOL

EXC.	V.G.	GOOD	FAIR	POOR
3,500	2,000	1,250	750	450

STANDARD MODEL WITH REAR OF SLIDE SERRATED

EXC.	V.G.	GOOD	FAIR	POOR
2,500	1,750	1,000	500	400

U.S. ARMY MARKED, #15001 TO #15200 WITH FRONT SERRATIONS

EXC.	V.G.	GOOD	FAIR	POOR
6,000	5,000	2,500	1,250	600

MODEL 1902 MILITARY PISTOL

This is a somewhat larger, heavier pistol than the 1902 Sporting Pistol. It has the same .38 ACP chambering, though, and a 6-inch barrel and detachable magazine holding eight rounds. The grip is larger and squared off to accommodate the larger magazine, and it has a lanyard swivel on the butt. Overall length is 9 inches and weight 38 oz.

1902 Military Pistol, Excellent condition.

Although it was designed to be a military pistol and approximately 18,068 were manufactured between 1902 and 1928, the vast majority was sold to civilians. Early models featured serrations at the front of the slide. The squared-off butt had a lanyard ring. The army eventually purchased about 200 of these guns for field trials in January of 1902, but the caliber was judged to be too light and the cavalrymen in particular expressed a strong preference for revolvers. Serial numbering began in 1902 at #15001 and continued until 1929, ending at #43266.

EARLY MODEL WITH FRONT
OF SLIDE SERRATED

EXC.	V.G.	GOOD	FAIR	POOR
3,500	2,250	1,250	750	450

STANDARD MODEL WITH REAR
OF SLIDE SERRATED

EXC.	V.G.	GOOD	FAIR	POOR
2,500	1,750	1,000	500	400

U.S. ARMY MARKED

#15001 to #15200 with front serrations (200 built)

EXC.	V.G.	GOOD	FAIR	POOR
15,000	12,500	5,000	2,000	600

NOTE: The following advertisement appeared in the Spring of 2007 on Sam Lisker's *ColtAutos.com* website:

"*1902 Military* - Caliber: .38 automatic, serial number #43136, Price: $1,200, Description: Would say 75% to 85% finish. No rust. Black plastic Colt grips. Lanyard ring left side bottom rear. Has mag, but it is not orig. Good bore, shoots well. Have 1 box Peters 38 auto (rustless) left included."

MODEL 1903 HAMMER POCKET PISTOL

This was the first automatic pocket pistol Colt produced. It is essentially identical to the 1902 Sporting Model but has a shorter slide, thus reducing its weight to 31.5 oz. The barrel length is 4.5 inches instead of 6 inches, giving it a 7.5-inch length overall, but it, too, is chambered for the .38 Rimless smokeless cartridge. It is blued, with a case-colored hammer and checkered hard rubber grips that have the "rampant colt" logo molded into them. The detachable magazine holds seven rounds. There were approximately 31,229 of the Pocket Pistols manufactured between 1903 and 1947. Serial numbering began in 1903 with #19999 and continued through 1927 with #47227.

EXC.	V.G.	GOOD	FAIR	POOR
1,100	850	650	350	200

Model 1903 Hammer Pocket Pistol.

NOTE: The following advertisement appeared in the Spring of 2007 on Sam Lisker's *ColtAutos.com*:

"1903 Automatic Colt - Caliber: 38 rimless smokeless, serial number #36895, Price: $1,350.00, Description: Colt Model 1903 pocket (4.5 inch bbl) Hammer Automatic Pistol mfg 1916 only 26,000 produced. Blued case hardened hammer, hard rubber grips has rampant Colt the name Colt and checkering. Slide marked Automatic Colt calibre 38 Rimless Smokeless/patented Apr 20 1897 Sept 9 1902 Colts Pt. F.A. Mfg. Co. Hartford Ct U.S.A. and rampant colt has 2 magazines 100% original bluing at 85% + some patina."

MODEL 1903 HAMMERLESS .32 POCKET PISTOL

This was Colt's second pocket automatic and it, too, was another of John Browning's designs. The name of this model may be misleading, as it is not a true hammerless design but actually featured a concealed hammer.

Chambered for the .32 ACP cartridge, the '03 Hammerless eventually became one of Colt's most successful pistols. Initially the barrel length was four inches but this was soon shortened by a quarter of an inch. The detachable magazine holds eight rounds. The standard finish is blue, but quite a few were nickel plated and many of these nickeled pistols had pearl grips. The early model grips are checkered hard rubber with the "rampant colt" logo molded into them. In 1924 the standard grips were changed to checkered walnut with inset Colt medallions. It has a slide stop and a grip safety. Colt manufactured 572,215 civilian versions of this pistol and approximately 200,000 more for military contracts. This model was manufactured between 1903 and 1945.

A number of these pistols were shipped to the Philippine Army and other foreign military forces, but no clear record of these shipments exists. However, about 24,000 Colt Hammerless pistols were sold to Belgium between 1915 and 1917 and the serial numbers for these pistols are available (see Brunner, *The Colt Pocket Hammerless Automatic Pistols*). In addition, several thousand Colt .32 pocket pistols, as well as Colt .25 and .380 pocket models, were shipped to England during World War I. During World War II, Colt supplied about 8,000 Colt pocket pistols in various calibers to England, and these had a blued or Parkerized

Model 1903 Hammerless
.32 Pocket Pistol.

Model 1905 .45
Automatic Pistol.

finish marked "U.S. PROPERTY." For early Model 1897 patent date add 40 percent. Nickel plated with pearl grips add $100. For 4-inch barrel to serial #72000 add 20 percent.

EXC.	V.G.	GOOD	FAIR	POOR
550	500	450	300	200

NOTE: The following advertisement appeared in the Spring of 2007 on *Sam Lisker's ColtAutos.com*:

"1903 - Caliber: .32 auto, serial number #38756, Price: $999.00, Description: a very nice factory nickel Colt 1903 Pocket Hammerless. Overall a top notch 95 to 97% with ZERO flaws. Has factory nickel magazine and barrel (both, also in excellent condition) and checkered wood grips. This is a fairly rare gun in this condition. I haven't seen another in person that was even close to this good a condition."*

U.S. MILITARY MODEL M

This gun was chambered for .32 ACP caliber only, and serial numbers began with the prefix M. It is marked with "U.S. Property" on the frame and has a blued or Parkerized finish. Pistols issued to General Officers and blued models command a premium.

EXC.	V.G.	GOOD	FAIR	POOR
1,500	950	500	300	250

MODEL 1905 .45 AUTOMATIC PISTOL

The Spanish American War and the "learning experiences" fighting the Moros in the Philippine campaign taught the U.S. Army a lesson about stopping power, or the lack of it. As a result of action in the Pacific and inadequate results with the .38, the Army was convinced that it needed a more powerful handgun cartridge. This led Colt to the development of a .45 caliber cartridge suitable for the semi-automatic pistol. The Model 1905 and the .45 rimless smokeless round were the result.

In actuality, this cartridge was not nearly powerful enough to satisfy the need, because it was not sufficiently more powerful than the .38 to satisfy soldiers in the field facing determined opponents. This cartridge soon led to the development of the .45 ACP, however.

Nevertheless, Colt believed that this pistol/cartridge combination would be a success and geared up for mass production. But the model was not a hit, possibly because it has no safety except for the floating inertia firing pin. It also retained the two-link dropping-barrel that swung the barrel down and back, parallel to the axis of the bore.

The 1905 Automatic was tested extensively against guns such as the Luger and the Savage, performing well

*Model 1908
Hammerless .380
Pocket Pistol.*

enough to become the favorite in run off trials with the Savage after DWM withdrew the .45 cal. Luger from competition. Subsequently, the Army actually bought only 200 of the 33 oz. guns, and these were delivered in March 1908.

Total production was only about 6,210 from 1905 to 1911, which must have been a huge disappointment to Colt. The pistol has a 5-inch barrel, a detachable seven shot magazine and is blued, with a case-colored hammer. It weighed 32.5 oz. and was 8 inches in overall length. The grips are checkered walnut. The hammer was rounded on the first 3,600 pistols, but was changed to a spur hammer on later models. The right side of the slide is stamped "AUTOMATIC COLT/CALIBRE 45 RIMLESS SMOKELESS." The 200 military models have grip safeties only.

A small number (believed to be approximately 440 pistols cut for stocks and 408 shipped with stocks) of these pistols had the backstrap of the butt slotted to accept a shoulder stock. The stocks were made of leather and steel and doubled as a holster and this effectively converted it to a carbine. These pistols have been classified "Curios and Relics" under the provisions of the Gun Control Act of 1968.

CIVILIAN MODEL

EXC.	V.G.	GOOD	FAIR	POOR
6,000	4,500	2,750	950	400

MILITARY MODEL, SERIAL #1 TO #201

Known as the 1907 Contract Pistol, the Military Model .45 has a lanyard loop, a loaded chamber indicator, spur hammer and a grip safety and bears the inspector's initials "K.M."

EXC.	V.G.	GOOD	FAIR	POOR
18,000	16,000	8,500	2,500	950

MODEL 1907 .45 ACP

This seven-shot semi-auto chambered for .45 ACP weighed 33.5 oz. It was fully blued and came with checkered walnut two piece grips. The 5-inch barrel gave it an 8.125 inch overall length. Only 207 were produced and shipped between March and October of 1908. A single officer presided over the inspection of the Model 1907 Contract pistols. All of the pistols bear the initials "K.M." for Major Kenneth Morton. These initials are hand stamped into the upper leg of the trigger guard on the left side. Major Morton assumed the post in April of 1907 and acted as the inspecting and accepting officer throughout the fiscal year 1907 to 1908.

EXC.	V.G.	GOOD	FAIR	POOR
18,000	16,000	8,500	2,500	950

MODEL 1908 HAMMERLESS .380 POCKET PISTOL

This model is essentially the same as the .32 Pocket Pistol, chambered for the more lethal .380

Model 1908 Hammerless .25 ACP.

ACP, also known as the 9mm Browning short. Other specifications are the same. Although Colt manufactured approximately 138,000 in this caliber for civilian sales, they were less popular than their smaller cousins. An unknown number were sold to the military.

STANDARD CIVILIAN MODEL

For nickel with pearl grips add $100.

EXC.	V.G.	GOOD	FAIR	POOR
800	650	475	350	250

MILITARY MODEL

Some have serial prefix "M." Each is marked "U.S. PROPERTY" on the frame. Blued finish. None of these pistols was originally Parkerized.

EXC.	V.G.	GOOD	FAIR	POOR
2,500	1,750	750	500	300

MODEL 1908 HAMMERLESS .25 POCKET PISTOL (VEST POCKET)

MODEL 1908 HAMMERLESS 25 IN BOX: Model 1908 Hammerless .25 in factory box.

The 1908 Hammerless is another Browning design, and Fabrique Nationale manufactured this pistol in Belgium as the 6.35mm FN-Browning Model 1906 or "Baby Browning," before Colt picked up the rights to build it in the U.S. In Europe, it proved to be exceptionally popular, but many American owners found its short butt difficult to hold and maneuver satisfactorily.

This was the smallest automatic that Colt made. It is chambered for the .25 ACP, and hence had a light recoil. The 1908 has a 2-inch barrel, and is 4.5 inches long overall. At only 13 oz., this is a true pocket pistol. It was amply provided with safeties, the original grip and manual locks being joined after gun #141000 in 1916 by a magazine safety system designed by George Tansley. The detachable magazine holds six shots. The 1908 Hammerless is offered in blue or nickel-plate, with grips of checkered hard rubber and, on later versions, checkered walnut. It has a grip safety, slide lock and a magazine disconnector safety. By Colt's standards, this model was a commercial success with approximately 409,000 manufactured between 1908 and 1941.

A small number of these pistols were bought by the OSS (Office of Strategic Services, America's forerunner to the Central Intelligence Agency) during World War II from retailers or distributors. These pistols are probably not martially marked. Beware of fakes that are marked by an engraving tool.

CIVILIAN MODEL

EXC.	V.G.	GOOD	FAIR	POOR
600	400	300	200	100

MILITARY MODEL

"U.S. Property" marked on right frame. This model is very rare.

EXC.	V.G.	GOOD	FAIR	POOR
3,750	3,000	1,000	450	300

NOTE: The following advertisement appeared on *GunsAmerica.com* during the Spring of 2007:

"Model 1908 .25ACP REDUCED! Colt Vest Pocket Model 1908 Hammerless 25acp 2 inch barrel, Nickel finish, Genuine Ivory grips with silver medallions (recent production not factory originals, Nice bore! Made in 1911. Nickel finish 95% + Consignment, sorry no trades! WAS $995 REDUCED $895."

MODEL 1909 .45

A successor to the 1905, this was the first of the Browning Colts to use the improved depressor system patented by Browning in February 1911 (although protection had actually been sought 18 months previously). Browning replaced the cumbersome parallel-motion depressor of the 1905 with a single link beneath the breech and guided the movement of the barrel by inserting a barrel bushing in the front end of the slide.

When the pistol is ready to fire, two lugs on the top of the barrel above the chamber engage recesses cut in the under-surface of the slide. The front of the barrel is supported in the bushings at the muzzle and the rear of the barrel is held up by a pivoting link, attached to the barrel at the top and the slide stop pin at the bottom.

Then, when the gun fires, recoil moves the barrel and slide backwards. As the barrel runs back, it begins to pivot the actuating link around the slide stop pin and the top of the link, which describes an arc, pulls the rear of the barrel down until the locking lugs disengage the slide. The barrel then comes to a halt, but the slide continues to move back, allowing the extractor to pull the empty case from the chamber, the spent case to be ejected, and the hammer to be cocked.

At the end of the recoil stroke, a return spring beneath the barrel, compress during the opening movement, expands to drive the slide forward. This action strips a fresh cartridge out of the magazine and into the chamber, allows the link to swing the rear of the barrel back u and into engagement with the slide, and runs the locked parts back into battery. The hammer remains cocked and the pistol is ready to fire again.

A manual safety catch lies on the frame and a grip safety – in the form of a movable plate – is let into the rear of the butt. Unless the hand grips the butt securely enough to release the grip safety, the weapon cannot be fired.

This system soon proved to be sturdy and reliable, although, because the barrel began to tilt before the bullet left the muzzle, there were concerns that the accuracy would fall short of the original "parallel motion" system. However, as with many firearms theories, practical experience showed that there was no noticeable difference.

The 1909 shares the external appearance of the 1905, with the grip almost perpendicular to the bore axis, but has a variety of refinements. In addition to the new method of depressing the barrel, these included revisions to the grip safety mechanism and the replacement of the butt heel magazine catch with a crossbolt through the frame behind the trigger. The guns were 8.125 inches long, had 5-inch barrels and weighed about 36 oz. empty. Their detachable box magazines held seven rounds. Total production of this model was only 23 guns with serial numbers running from #0 to #23.

EXC.	V.G.	GOOD	FAIR	POOR
600	400	300	200	100

MODEL 1910 .45

Only a handful of these guns were built, and they were essentially modified 1909s with the grip raked backwards at a 74-degree angle rather than the earlier 84 degrees. According to many sources, this made the pistol "point more naturally" and it was used on all subsequent models. A prototype was demonstrated to the Army in February of 1910. Only eight guns were acquired for trials, although a perfected version with an additional manual safety catch performed well enough to allow the basic design to be adopted. It was a seven-shot semi-auto, with a 5-inch barrel for an overall length of 8.47 inches. It weighed 36.2 oz. A total of only eight guns (some sources report 12 guns total), fully blued with checkered walnut grips, were produced and shipped between 1910 and 1911.

EXC.	V.G.	GOOD	FAIR	POOR
1,200	900	400	200	100

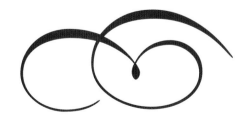

Model 1911, early commercial model.

THE MODEL 1911/1911A1

(MODEL DESIGNATIONS AND PRICES BY KARL KARASH)

This section of the price guide primarily refers to Colt 1911 and 1911A1 Commercial Government Models. What follows is a listing of the major variations that collectors have divided the total collectible pistol production into, along with the current market prices of these respective variations. This is prefaced by a few introductory comments that the editors hope will help guide the new enthusiast through the hazards of collecting. A recommended reading and reference book listing and a detailed explanation of the condition categories are provided. A method of determining the percentage of remaining finish will be detailed. Finally, a brief history of the Colt Commercial Model pistol and a list of the important factors that determine the value of a commercial Government model pistol are included.

The popularity of the Military Colt 1911/1911A1 and its Commercial Government Model sisters has recently risen to unheard-of levels. The reasons for this popularity ares probably due to a number of causes. Among those are: the relatively recent release of such superb movies as *Saving Private Ryan, We Were Soldiers, Band of Brothers* and *The Lost Battalion*; the availability of massive amounts of World War II historical features

on The History Channel; the widespread use of the internet, and the internet auctions as a tool for buying and selling collectable pistols; and perhaps a general realization that the heroes of WWII are rapidly leaving us behind.

Serious 1911/1911A1 collectors usually try to accumulate the best, the most comprehensive and the most complete collection. Yet most collectors only want to have one or two GI (Government Issue) or Government model pistols, and not even necessarily an original pistol, because they probably intend to shoot it …a lot. Beginners often begin by wanting a pristine, completely original pistol that they can shove in a holster and toss behind the seat of their pickup truck. Rapidly rising prices, however, have caused many of these folks to re-examine whether they want to pay for an original mint-condition pistol and then beat it up. Others want a collection of completely original pistols in as pristine condition as is possible that they will probably never shoot let alone touch without wearing white gloves. The vast majority of modern collectors want pistols in original condition and in as good condition as they can afford.

All of these "demand factors" have recently driven up the selling prices of collectible (original) Military and Commercial Government Model 1911/1911A1 pistols to unheard-of levels. Prices realized on internet auctions seem to break new records daily. These auctions are especially troubling to older collectors who are accustomed to one-on-one buying and selling at gun shows and gun stores. Pistols sold via internet auctions usually have one or more pictures that can range from seemingly crystal clear (although perhaps digitally enhanced) to very fuzzy. The pictures are often of poor quality, and hide as much as they reveal. The conventional hands-on transaction where the buyer uses his knowledge and examines the pistol live, has been replaced by a virtual electronic process that is filled with risk for the buyer and seller alike. Nonetheless, the popularity of these auctions seems to be increasing, and the prices realized seem to be setting records. Live auctions, too, are still popular and also are realizing record prices, although probably not to the level of the internet.

The dramatic increase in collecting is a result of interest from new and inexperienced collectors. (We were all inexperienced once.) These new (and often young) collectors usually take to the internet like a duck to water. Sometimes the new collector finds himself in over his head but, unlike a duck, he doesn't float. Experienced collectors know that there are a large number of refinished, restored, cold blued, altered, faked or just plain "messed with" pistols that will be represented as original. Often these undesirables can only be distinguished by a *hands-on* inspection. Indeed the army of new collectors has attracted its own group of sellers with questionable ethics who trail behind, hoping to pick off an especially inexperienced or over eager straggler. This unsavory lot has sprung forth hoping to pass off a non-collectible, often-altered pistol as if it was an original item. Usually the seller will attempt to take advantage of the inexperienced buyer by "spinning a yarn," as well as claiming knowledge of what an original should be. Greed has not gone out of fashion.

Caveat emptor. Selling collectibles is usually treated as a "buyer beware" situation and legal redress is often impractical. In-depth knowledge and experience are the only weapons collectors have to protect themselves from predators waiting to pounce. Before buying a pistol, one must consult the books and attend the auctions. Spend time at gun shows. Talk to and get to know other collectors.

Above all, the inexperienced collector must look at original pistols, as many as possible, and hold them in your hands (white gloved, of course). Learn what they look like. Carrying around a pair of white cotton gloves in a plastic bag is a good way to show collectors that you are serious and will not leave fingerprints on

their pistols. Never pass up the opportunity to look at a collection. And never forget that an original pistol may be worth thousands of dollars, while a similar refinished pistol would be worth only a utility shooter price.

Also remember that the recent, widespread collector interest has generated greatly inflated prices, as well as widespread counterfeiting and fakery. Only through education – and, unfortunately, a buying mistake or two – can the collector avoid truly costly blunders.

There are four reference books on the Colt .45 auto pistol that are so indispensable to collecting .45s that they must be mentioned by name: *Colt .45 Service Pistols, Models of 1911 and 1911A1*, Colt .45 Government Models (Commercial Series) and the Collectors Guide to Colt .45 Service Pistols, Models of 1911 and 1911A1, all written by Charles Clawson; and U.S. Military Automatic Pistols 1894-1920 by Edward S. Meadows. The Meadows book is still available and is an excellent reference on 1911 pistols through 1920. Clawson has just reprinted his Collectors Guide to Colt .45 Service Pistols, Models of 1911 and 1911A1, but his other two books are out of print and have become difficult to find – even via the internet.

Note that because these pistols are primarily collector's items, and because originality and condition are the two factors that determine a pistol's collector value, condition categories here differ from the stated categories used elsewhere in the book. Prices are for pistols with all-original parts and the factory original finish. Broken parts, replaced parts, gunsmithing, and cold blue touch ups require appropriate deductions from the prices listed. Refinished pistols can be considered to be in or below poor condition or as non-collectible shootable pistols. Arsenal reworks are generally refinished and while they are considered collectible pistols, they have their own categories that have values much lower than original pistols.

We define condition categories in terms of the percentage of original finish remaining. Excellent = 96-98 percent original finish; Very Good = 90-95 percent original finish; Good = 70-91 percent original finish; Fair = 45-69 percent original finish; and Poor = less than 45 percent original finish. All of these prices assume a completely original pistol and any deviation from originality requires an adjustment (a deduction) to the price. A replaced (non-original) part will reduce the value of the pistol more than the cost of the part because another part that is contemporary to the pistol will never be an "original" part for this pistol.

Note that National Rifle Association standards of condition are considerably different from the condition standards of collectible 1911/1911A1 pistols. The NRA standards allow a sliding scale of originality, repairs, number of replaced parts, originality of finish, operability, cracks, pitting present and even rust.

Collectors of antique firearms more or less expect the guns they find to be repaired, refinished, rusted, and generally abused. However, serious collectors of modern firearms, and the 1911/1911A1 is a modern firearm, regardless of the year it was manufactured, generally expect to find original unaltered pistols, and they expect to find a high percentage of original finish remaining. This is largely because a significant percentage of these pistols still exist today in original condition.

Many pistols however are not in original condition and they may become the collector's ideal for the generations to come after most of today's original collector pistols have gone out of circulation. Perhaps then the general NRA grading standard will be useful to 1911/1911A1 collectors for grading their mismatches, repaired, rusted and refinished guns. Until then, the grading standard will assume a completely original pistol with original finish (whatever remains is original). Any deviation from this will cause the value to be sharply degraded.

There is one item that 1911/1911A1 collectors, especially military collectors, must give some slack on – the condition of the bore. Most early ammunition was highly corrosive and the majority of otherwise high-end collectible pistols show corrosion of the bore. Therefore a collectible 1911 will remain collectible in spite of a corroded bore. The selling price will of course suffer.

The amount of original finish can be accurately estimated by comparing the amount and thickness of the remaining finish on each part of the pistol's surface with its portion (expressed as a percentage) of the total surface area. Then one would add the remaining percents. Thinning finish only counts for a portion of area covered. For example, if the finish on the front strap covers the entire surface, but the finish is only half as dense or thick as new finish, the contribution to the total is half of 7.6 percent, or 3.8 percent, and if the remainder of the pistol was as new, the pistol would have 100 percent minus 3.8 percent or 96.2 percent finish. (This sounds like a science, but it is truly an art.)

The biggest mistake that beginners make is to disregard rust and other, similar defects, subsurface reddening (subsurface rust) patina, scratches and other

defects that were not on the pistol as it left the factory. None of these are original and must be deducted as missing finish. Any pitting must, of course, be noted because its presence reduces the value of the pistol more than would simple worn finish. The second most common mistake is to consider thin worn blue as if it was original blue. Blueing that is only half as thick and as deep as original blueing gives one a 50 percent pistol.

The U.S. Military Model of 1911 was developed by a combination of the genius of John M. Browning plus a lot of interaction and feedback from the Ordnance Department. John T. Thompson Lt. Colonel of the Ordnance Department informed Colt's Patent Firearms Manufacturing Company on March 29, 1911 that the (M1911) self-loading pistol had passed all prescribed tests (*Editors note*: and by doing so, was adopted by The Department), and The Department requested a quote on 30,262 pistols. The price that was finally agreed on was $14.25 for a pistol and one magazine. Additional magazines were to be 50¢ each.

The first 40 1911 pistols were assembled on December 28, 1911, with an additional 11 pistols assembled the next day. The first shipment, a single wooden case of M1911 pistols serial numbered from 1 to 50, was made on January 4, 1912, from the Colt's factory in Hartford, Connecticut to the Commanding Officer, Springfield Armory. This single crate, marked on the outside: "Serial Numbers 1 Through 50," has become "the stuff that (M1911 collector's) dreams are made of."

The M1911 pistol was the most advanced self-loading pistol of its time and, in the eyes of many, it and its hundreds of imitators have remained so virtually to this date. Yet while this is probably an exaggeration, elements of its design have become adopted in most subsequent self-loading designs.

While hundreds of minor manufacturing and ergonomic changes have been made, only one functional change was made to the M1911 during its manufacture from 1911 to 1945. Removal of the original dimpled magazine catch required pushing the entire catch body into the frame far enough that the fingers could grasp and turn the protruding portion until the tooth of the catch lock left its groove in the receiver. Upon coming free, the catch lock and spring (propelled by the energy stored in the spring,) often flew out of sight and landed in a mud puddle. In a moment of stress, this could be a deadly flaw.

At about serial number #3190, the design was changed and a slot was cut in the magazine catch body as well as in the head of the magazine catch lock. This greatly facilitated the disassembly of the pistol as well as reduced the chances of losing a part. However two safety devices invented by Colt's Chief Engineer William L. Swartz (these devices, a firing pin block and a sear safety device, are known collectively as the "Swartz Safeties") were adopted only in Commercial Government models in 1938. Yet Colt's manufacturing changes, Ordnance Department-mandated changes (including 1911/1911A1 improvements), marking, commercial derivatives, and part variations used during manufacture by the various suppliers, amounted to more than 200 variations, enough to keep even the most ardent collector in pursuit for decades.

The Colt Government model is functionally identical to the Military model except for finish and markings. Commercial pistols received a higher polish finish as well as their own appropriate markings and serial number range. Collectible commercial (Government Model) pistols are usually in excellent or better condition and they are expected to be in better condition than Military pistols.

The commercial or civilian version of the 1911 .45 is distinguishable by the "C" prefix in the serial number. This model commenced production in 1911 with serial number C1 and was superseded in 1924/1925 by the Model of 1911A1. The improvements built into the Model of 1911A1 were gradually phased into the pistols in the range #C131000 to #C138000. However the four major changes (shortening the trigger, arching the mainspring housing, lengthening the grip safety, and adding the frame finger cutouts) did not occur until about #C136000. The finish of the early pistols (under serial number #C4500 to #C5500) is a brilliant mirror-like high polish blue. Pistols under about #C4500 had most of the visible small parts finished in a spectacular brilliant blue that can best be compared to the blue in a peacock's tail feathers. Pistols after about #C5500 generally had less of a degree of polishing than the earlier pistols.

The 1911 checkered walnut grips feature a raised uncheckered diamond relief around the screw holes. The 1911 has a thin front sight blade, long trigger, short spur on the hammer, and short tang on the grip safety. (The hammer spur was later lengthened at about serial number #C100,000.) The mainspring housing is flat, and there is no finger cut on the frame behind the

trigger. The pistol is chambered for the .45 ACP and has a seven round detachable magazine. Pistols between about #C3000 and #C5000 had fully blued barrels and were marked "Government Model" on the right front of the frame. From the beginning until about #C3000 and after about #C5000, the barrel area visible through the ejection port was left "in the white." The "Government Model" marking was moved to above the trigger on the right side at about #C5000. All Government Model 1911s generally had a "Verified Proof" mark on the upper left trigger guard bow.

There are an extremely large number of variations of this model if all of the part, finish, and marking changes are included. The major variations are listed, but even now new information is surfacing and there may be as yet unknown variations. Be cautious of absolute statements, because these pistols were made in a real factory with real shipping schedules where "exceptions to the rule" often occurred. Be extra cautious with near new pistols, as restored pistols usually appear near new.

Boxes: For high-condition commercial pistols, original numbered factory boxes (most original Colt factory boxes were serial numbered on the bottom with pencil) will usually add a significant premium to the selling price of a pre-war pistol. Likewise, the instruction sheet, hang tag, numbered test target, and factory supplied screwdriver and cleaning rod will also bring premiums. Often original boxes are tattered and broken but still bring a significant premium. The "original box" premium can be anywhere from a few dollars to 30 percent of the selling price, depending on the condition and appearance of the box and accessories, as well as the rarity of the pistol. Boxes alone often sell for hundreds of dollars at auctions. One does not need a lot of imagination to see these orphan boxes becoming reborn into "original" pistol-box combinations; so be cautious. High-end collectors of commercial pistols often value the combination of a box and pistol that appear to match at a significant premium over a pistol alone, yet one must be as cautious about purchasing a boxed pistol with accessories that may have been assembled recently as one is with guns themselves. Prices listed herein are for pistols without boxes or any other accessories.

Provenance: Collectors of commercial pistols have historically placed great value on the provenance of a pistol. If it can be documented that the previous owner was a famous or, even better, infamous person, the selling price of a pistol can increase several fold.

Nowhere is this notion more deeply imbedded than with the collectors of the Colt Single Action Army. Pistols documented as belonging to famous outlaws or Texas Rangers usually bring huge premiums over the equivalent undocumented pistol. However, there is currently little agreement as to what constitutes value regarding provenance of modern pistols.

Factory Options: Colt's price lists offered a number of special options that the pistol could be ordered with such as fancy stocks, (carved, ivory and special woods,) special finishes, (nickel, gold or silver-plating), special sights (Kings, special custom wide sights), special engraving, special targeting and selection, and custom metal checkering. These custom features will often bring a premium, and sometimes a large premium, especially if documented. These premiums apply mostly to the fine condition pistols because some options, such as nickel plated finish, look much worse when worn than do blued finishes.

Colt Factory Letter: A Colt factory letter currently costs $100 minimum. It includes: Name and address shipped to, finish, (the letter usually lists blue if no other notation is made in the factory records), type of stocks (the letter lists "Not Listed" if no other notation is made in the factory records), number of guns in shipment, barrel length, (the letter usually lists 5 inches) and any specially ordered features such as adjustable sights. Unless a pistol was shipped directly to a famous person, the Colt letter will be of little help tying it to a famous person because the majority of domestically shipped pistols were shipped to hardware stores or similar establishments. The notation of special features can authenticate a custom feature if it was installed at the factory, however not all special features were apparently listed in Colt factory records, and work done on repair orders would not be listed in the letter as Colt repair records have been lost. Conversely, any custom feature not noted in the letter would ordinarily be condemned to aftermarket status. A factory letter that shows a tie to a famous person or a set of installed special features can be a big win, but the vast majority of pistols were ordinary pistols sent to ordinary places. The small amount information supplied in the Colt factory letter can usually be obtained from one of the references cited, especially for a military pistol, but for commercial pistols with any features that are out of the ordinary, it is probably the only method of documenting them.

The designations "1911" and "1911A1" are military designations and were not used by Colt in advertising literature to describe the Commercial Government models. However, it has become common practice among most collectors, as well as the general public, to refer to Colt pre-1924 commercial version as the Colt "1911 Commercial Government Model," as well as to refer to the post 1924 version as the Colt "1911A1 Commercial Government Model."

Conversely, Military models are referred to as the "1911 Military Model" and the "1911A1 Military Model" with no "Colt" prefix, as they were both made by more than one manufacturer.

Furthermore, the "Colt's Patent Firearms Manufacturing Co." referred to itself as "Colt's" while "Colt" became common usage.

The common language designations will be used here with apologies to the purists. Prices listed are intended to represent the average selling price, not the asking price. However, please remember that many of the variations are so rare that not a single one may have sold in the last couple of years and the corresponding prices that are listed are best estimates. Considerable thought has gone into most of them, but they are estimates nonetheless.

THE EARLIEST 1911S

American manufacturers, who were then preoccupied with revolvers, largely ignored the advent of the automatic pistol in Europe in the 1890s. Colt was the exception, realizing that the pistol could easily rival the revolver if it could be made to operate reliably. Thus, the company took an interest in the development of automatic pistols from the start, gaining a lead over its leading American gunmaking rivals that lasted until the mid 1950s.

Among the earliest designs was an interesting blow-forward design patented in 1895 by Carl Ehbets, but the first to show genuine promise was a small Browning blowback demonstrated in the summer of 1895. It was successful enough to encourage the inventor to deliver three additional guns early in 1896 – each of which operated in a different manner! Eventually, John Browning received a variety of patents in April 1897.

Ironically, the original small-caliber blowback design, which had no future as a military weapon, was abandoned in favor of a recoil-operated locked breech design. Exploitation of the blowback was left

to *Fabrique Nationale d'Armes de Guerre* (FN) though Colt's management ultimately had a change of heart and began production of adapted FN style guns in 1903.

The recoil operated gun originally chambered a rimmed .38 caliber revolver cartridge, but it was soon adapted to semi-rim ammunition loaded with smokeless propellant. Demonstrated to the U.S. Army towards the end of 1898, it was developed to become the "Model 1900." This eventually led to the .45 ACP Model 1911, which has enjoyed the longest production run of any automatic pistol in history.

The Colt 1911 in all its variations, models and improvements from inception is perhaps one of the most remarkable firearms in the history of gunpowder. More than five million have been produced, the largest production volume of any Colt handgun. In accepting it for general government use in 1911, the board of military officers said that with the 230 grain bullet tested, at 800 fps muzzle velocity, the Colt 1911 was the most powerful, accurate and rapid firing pistol that had ever been produced.

All collectors know the outline of the 1911 story. That it was the result of a combination of genius – John M. Browning and the Colt factory and engineers – and that the years of this cooperation, 1897 to 1911, were undoubtedly some of the most creative and, ultimately, most profitable in the Colt's story. Thus, until patent markings were dropped in the 1940s, the Browning name is stamped on Colt semi-autos.

Writing in the mid 1980s, R.L. Wilson estimated that no more than 10 percent of Colt's semi-autos were fit for collection, the other 90 percent having been fired to the point that they needed repair and re-bluing, and as such were no longer of collectible grade. Still, 10 percent of more than 5,000,000 of this style handgun is a whole lot of steel!

Since it was the federal government that ultimately made the Model 1911 the standard of the world, it is to the April 1, 1911 *Army and Navy Journal* that we give the last – and first – word on the remarkable Colt's 1911:

"The board therefore recommends that the Colt caliber .45 automatic pistol of the design submitted to the board for test be adopted for use by foot and mounted troops in the military service in consequence of its marked superiority to the present Service revolvers and to any other known pistol, of its extreme reliability and endurance and of its fulfillment of all essential requirements."

EARLY 1911 COMMERCIAL GOVERNMENT MODEL

These semi-autos have serial numbers through about #C4500, high polish on all parts and fire-blue finish on the trigger, slide stop, thumb safety, hammer pins, ejector and stock screws. Pistols in the latter part of the serial range did not have fire blued stock screws. Pistols through about serial number #C350 had the dimpled magazine catch. The main spring housing pin was rounded on both ends in the pistols through about serial #C2000. Keyhole (punch and sawcut) magazines were shipped on pistols through serial #C3500.

EXC.	V.G.	GOOD	FAIR	POOR
6,000	3,600	2,200	1,400	900

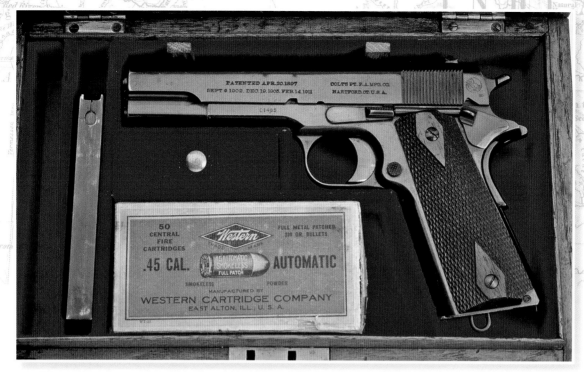

Model 1911 Commercial Government, un-numbered slide.

NOTE: For three digit serial numbers add 20 percent. Two digit serial numbers add 40 percent. For finish 99-100 percent add 30 to 50 percent.

STANDARD 1911 COMMERCIAL MODEL WITH UN-NUMBERED SLIDE

Above about serial number #C4500 with un-numbered slide to approximately #C127300. No fire blue. Polished finished but not mirror finish. Loop magazine until about #C90000. A number of small variations exist within this wide serial range such as slide nomenclature and exact positioning of the "rampant colt," but none currently receives any particular premium. For a 99-100 percent finish add 20 to 50 percent.

EXC.	V.G.	GOOD	FAIR	POOR
3,500	2,100	1,500	900	700

NOTE: The following advertisement was placed on *ArmChairGunShow.com* in the Spring of 2007:

"Colt - 1911 - Commercial Model - .45 ACP - Fine to excellent condition. From the sides looks like 95% original blue, but wear to front and rear of grip frame probably leaves this closer to 85% overall. Excellent markings; fine checkered wood grips. Good mechanism and bore. Serial number #C118923. $1,950."

STANDARD 1911 COMMERCIAL GOVERNMENT MODEL WITH NUMBERED SLIDE

Colt started to stamp the slide with the receiver's serial number beginning at about serial number #C127300. This practice continued for commercial production through World War II, and all 1911 commercial pistols after about #C127300 to about #C136000 (when 1911A1 production had taken over). The first numbered slide pistols (in the #C127xxx range) had the slide numbered on the bottom of the slide rail. This only lasted a short time and the numbering was moved to behind the firing pin stop plate by serial #C128000. Subtract 20 percent for a mismatched slide number. The changes between the 1911 Commercial Government Model and the 1911A1 Commercial Government were phased in during this period. For 99-100 percent finish, add 20 to 50 percent.

EXC.	V.G.	GOOD	FAIR	POOR
3,500	2,100	1,400	900	650

FOREIGN CONTRACTS

The following foreign contract pistols are also mentioned as military pistols despite their commercial serial numbers. The majority of these pistols were used by foreign governments as military, police or other government agency sidearms.

1911 COMMERCIAL GOVERNMENT MODEL ARGENTINE CONTRACTS

Multiple contracts were awarded by Argentina between 1914 and 1948 to supply .45 caliber pistols to their armed forces, police and government agencies. These contracts totaled 21,616 pistols of which 2,151 were the 1911 model. Pistols differ from the Standard Government Model in that they are usually marked

Model 1911 Commercial Government Model Canadian Contract.

with an Argentine crest as well as the normal Colt commercial markings including the "C" prefix serial number. Colt also supplied Argentina with the 1911A1 model "MODELO 1927" that had its own serial number range of #1 to #10000 with no C prefix. Most of these pistols are well used, re-blued, had mixed parts and have import markings. Prices listed are for completely original pistols. Re-blued guns rate in the Fair to Poor range. For a finish that is 99-100 percent intact, add 20 to 100 percent.

FIRST ARGENTINE CONTRACT #C6201 TO #C6400

These pistols were delivered to the two Argentine battleships under construction at U.S. shipyards. They are rarely seen better than Good and many of them have in fact been re-blued and parts have been changed.

EXC.	V.G.	GOOD	FAIR	POOR
-	1,200	700	525	350

SECOND ARGENTINE CONTRACT #C20001 TO #C21000

EXC.	V.G.	GOOD	FAIR	POOR
1,800	1,200	750	450	300

SUBSEQUENT ARGENTINE 1911 CONTRACTS AFTER C21000

Many of these pistols have been re-blued and parts changed.

EXC.	V.G.	GOOD	FAIR	POOR
1,500	1,000	750	450	275

1911 COMMERCIAL GOVERNMENT MODEL RUSSIAN ORDER

This variation is chambered for .45 ACP and has the Russian version of "ANGLO ZAKAZIVAT" stamped on the frame (English order). There were about 51,000 of these blued pistols manufactured from 1915-1916. They are found between serial numbers #C21000 and #C89000. This variation is rarely encountered today, and a few have recently been imported and advertised. At least one example is known that bears the Finnish arsenal mark, "SA." One should be extremely cautious and verify the authenticity if contemplating a purchase, as fakes have been noted. Despite market uncertainties, demand for original pistols is high. Re-blued guns rate in the Fair to Poor range. For a finish that is 99-100 percent, add 20 to 100 percent.

EXC.	V.G.	GOOD	FAIR	POOR
5,500	3,900	2,350	1,600	1,000

1911 COMMERCIAL GOVERNMENT MODEL CANADIAN CONTRACT

This group of 5,099 pistols serial numbered between about #C3077 and #C13500 were purchased by the Canadian Government in 1914. Most observed pistols appear to be unmarked and can be identified only by a Colt factory letter. Others have been observed with the Canadian Broad Arrow property mark as well as unit markings. Often these unit markings are applied in a very rudimentary manner that detracts considerably from the appearance. (Any applied markings done

Model 1911 Commercial Government Model, British contract.

crudely, deduct between 10 and 50 percent.) Due to the nature of these markings, a Colt factory letter is probably a requirement to authenticate these pistols. Re-blued guns rate in the Fair to Poor range. For a finish that is 99-100 percent, add 20 to 100 percent.

EXC.	V.G.	GOOD	FAIR	POOR
2,5100	1,800	950	550	400

1911 COMMERCIAL GOVERNMENT MODEL BRITISH CONTRACT

This series is chambered for the British .455 cartridge and is so marked on the right side of the slide. The British "Broad Arrow" proofmark will often be found also. These pistols were made between 1915 and 1919 and follow the same numeric serial number sequence as the normal Government models, except that the "C" prefix was replaced with a "W." They are commercial series pistols. The magazine well of these .455 pistols is slightly larger than a standard caliber .45 auto pistol and will accept a .45 magazine, but a standard .45 will not accept a .455 magazine. All pistols in the #W19001 to #W19200 range as well as some in the #W29000 range are believed to be "JJ" marked above the left trigger guard bow. Add 25 percent for "JJ" marking. Some pistols in the #C101000 to about #C109000 range have RAF marks as well as a welded ring in the lanyard loop. Most RAF pistols have been refinished and many have been converted to .45 cal. by changing the barrels. Converted guns are usually considered no better than Good condition. Re-blued guns rate in the Fair to Poor range. For a finish of 99-100 percent add 20 to 50 percent. Add 25 percent for RAF guns. For an incorrect barrel, deduct 35 percent.

EXC.	V.G.	GOOD	FAIR	POOR
3,400	2,100	1,000	750	600

NORWEGIAN KONGSBERG VAPENFABRIKK PISTOL MODEL 1912

Serial numbers #1 to #96. Finding one of these pistols in better than good condition is an extremely rare occurrence. These pistols are so scarce that almost any price would not be out of order for an original pistol. For 99-100 percent finish, add 20 to 30 percent.

EXC.	V.G.	GOOD	FAIR	POOR
7,500	4,600	2,800	2,000	1,500

NORWEGIAN KONGSBERG VAPENFABRIKK PISTOL MODEL 1914

Serial numbered #97 to #32854. For 99-100 percent finish, add 20 to 50 percent.

EXC.	V.G.	GOOD	FAIR	POOR
1,500	1,200	900	700	600

NOTE: The following advertisement appeared during the Spring of 2007 on *ColtAutos.com*:

"COLT NORWEGIAN MODEL 1914 Serial number #19302 Price $1,695.00. Description: .45 ACP caliber. 90 to 90% finish – all matching numbers. Correct magazine. 1928 dated."

NORWEGIAN KONGSBERG VAPENFABRIKK MODEL 1914 – COPY

Serial numbers #29615 to #30535. Waffenamt marked on slide and barrel. CAUTION: Fakes have been reported. Any Waffenamt-marked pistol outside this serial range is probably a counterfeit. For 99-100 percent finish, add 20-30 percent.

EXC.	V.G.	GOOD	FAIR	POOR
4,500	3,500	2,500	2,000	1,500

FRENCH CONTRACT

About 5,000 pistols were delivered, serial numbered between #C17800 and #C28000. These pistols are very seldom seen. For condition 99-100 percent, add 20 to 30 percent.

EXC.	V.G.	GOOD	FAIR	POOR
4,500	3,000	1,500	900	700

ENTER THE 1911A1

Combat experience during World War I suggested a number of changes to the basic 1911 type Government Model, though none of them affected the single link locking mechanism or general construction. The improved model, designated the "A1," was developed from 1923 to 1924 and had the military nomenclature "M1911A1." It was approved in 1926, although series production did not officially commence until more than a decade later with essential and visible changes. (Different manufacturers brought these changes on line at slightly different times, so the dates in the below list are not firm for every gun.) These changes included the following:

- The rear of the butt was more curved, or perhaps it just appears so because the mainspring housing was arched and knurled. After 1943, it was serrated for a better feel.
- The front edge of the butt was chamfered behind the trigger for greater finger clearance and comfort.
- In the pre war years, the hammer spur was shortened and, following 1944, changed to flat sided.
- The grip safety tang was lengthened to protect the hand from the hammer spur's recoil.
- The trigger was made slightly smaller or shorter and it was grooved or knurled for a better grip.
- The double diamond with checkering pattern on the grips was changed to full checkering, and after

1939 the standard grips were changed to plastic.

- The taper sided round front sight was changed to parallel sided (ramped and serrated after 1943).
- The standard U-Notch rear sight changed to a square notch after 1943.
- The blued finish was changed to Parkerized or DuLite after 1941.

The A1, then, served the U.S. Army until it was replaced in 1985 by the 9mm Pistol M9, the Beretta 92F, though there were, and still are, many shooters who champion the older design.

Production of the 1911A1 was confined to Colt until the U.S. entered the Second World War in 1941 and then the manufacturing difficulties (i.e., production volume) that had been evident in 1917 recurred. The solution was identical: recruit additional manufacturers. The principal participants were Remington-Rand, Ithaca Gun and Union Switch & Signal. These guns can be identified by their individual markings, with the names stamped on the rear side of the barrel side.

The Commercial Government Models made by Colt from 1911 until 1926 may be the finest pistols that Colt ever produced. The civilian configurations of the 1911 and 1911A1 (once all of the changes were in place for that model) were known as the "Government Models." They were identical to the military models, with the exception of the fit, finish and markings. However, commercial production of the 1911A1 pistols was halted when WWII started. Therefore, production changes to the 1911A1 pistols were not carried over to contemporary commercial pistols.

The "C" serial number prefix designated the commercial series until 1950, when it was changed to a "C" suffix. Government Model pistols were polished and blued until about serial number #C230,000, when the top, bottom, and rear were matte finished. The words "Government Model" as well as the usual "Verified Proof" mark were stamped on all but about the first 500 pistols when post-war production commenced at #C220,000.

Some of the first 500 pistols following World War II also lacked the verified proof mark. These first post-war pistols used some leftover military parts such as triggers and stocks. Pre-war pistols all had checkered walnut grips. Post-war pistols generally had plastic grips until the "mid-range" serial when wood grips returned. There were a number of different commercial models manufactured. They are individually listed.

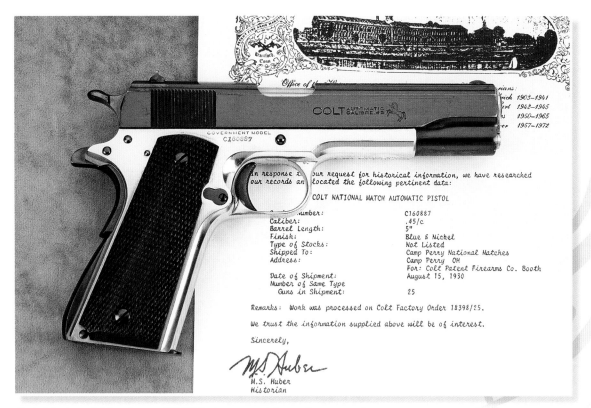

Colt National Match, pre-WWII vintage, without Swartz safety.

NOTE: For Colt Military Model 1911A1 pistols see a complete listing with photos, prices, technical data and history in the *Standard Catalog of Military Firearms* from Krause/F&W Publications.

PRE-WORLD WAR II 1911A1 COMMERCIAL GOVERNMENT MODEL

Manufactured by Colt from 1925 to 1942 from about serial number #C136000 to #C215000. Only a few pistols from serial #C202000 to #C215000 were shipped domestically, as most were sold to Brazil or renumbered into military models. (See Model 1911A1 Commercial to Military Conversions.")

STANDARD 1911A1 COMMERCIAL GOVERNMENT MODEL, DOMESTIC SALES

These pistols have numbered slides, no foreign markings, no Swartz safeties and no additions whatsoever. For 99-100 percent finish, add 30 to 60 percent.

EXC.	V.G.	GOOD	FAIR	POOR
2,500	1,600	1,150	750	500

STANDARD 1911A1 COMMERCIAL GOVERNMENT MODEL, EXPORT SALES

Usually found with a foreign crest or the foreign inscription of a county such as Argentina or Brazil, this pistol has a numbered slide. Some variations with the foreign markings are more rare than the standard domestic pistols and have a developed local followings who have raised their prices considerably. Argentine pistols do not yet have the collector interest that the others or the "Standard" domestic pistols have. Four factors have probably reduced collector interest in Argentine Colt pistols compared to the rest:

1. Most of the Argentine marked pistols have recently been imported and have the legally required import markings.
2. Many of the Argentine marked pistols have been advertised and sold in the wholesale trade publications at utility prices.
3. Most of the recent import pistols from Argentina have been refinished or are in "well used" condition.
4. Most of the recent import pistols from Argentina have had some parts changed or swapped with other pistols and are not in original condition.

The few Argentine pistols that remain in original and excellent or better condition usually sell for less than their "plain Jane" counterparts, and they sell for much less than the rarer Brazilian and Mexican pistols. For 99-100 percent finish, add 20 to 30 percent.

ARGENTINE COLT MADE 1911A1 MODEL PISTOLS WITHOUT SWARTZ SAFETIES

EXC.	V.G.	GOOD	FAIR	POOR
1,100	800	650	550	450

BRAZILIAN, MEXICAN, AND OTHER SOUTH AMERICAN (EXCEPT ARGENTINA) COLT-MADE 1911A1 COMMERCIAL GOVERNMENT MODEL PISTOLS

For 99-100 percent finish, add 20 to 100 percent.

EXC.	V.G.	GOOD	FAIR	POOR
6,500	4,500	2,800	1,700	1,000

NATIONAL MATCH CALIBER .45 PRE-WWII (WITHOUT SWARTZ SAFETIES)

The National Match Commercial pistol was introduced by Colt at the 1930 National Matches at Camp Perry. Production began in 1932. The right side of the slide was marked "National Match" and the mainspring housing had no lanyard loop. The National Match modifications to the standard pistol, as described in Colt literature included: "A tighter barrel, better sights, and a hand polished action." The "tighter barrel" probably amounted to a tighter fit between the barrel bushing and barrel. The hand polishing of the action probably produced a greatly improved trigger pull, but overall, the barrel slide lockup was probably only superficially improved. Colt also advertised a "Selected Match Grade" barrel. Advertising indicated that scores using the National Match pistols improved greatly and they probably did to a degree, but most of the improvement was probably due to the improved (wider) sights and improved trigger pull. The very first pistols had fixed sights, but by about serial number #C177000 the "Stevens Adjustable Rear Target Sight" was available. Both fixed and adjustable sights were available thereafter throughout production. The total number of National Match pistols with each type of sight is not known, but one author (Kevin Williams, *Collecting Colt's National Match Pistols*) estimates that the percentage of adjustable-sight-equipped National Match pistols may have been only 20 percent.

The Colt National Match pistol is not referred to here as a "1911A1" because this pistol lacks the military lanyard loop that is present in all Standard Government Models. This is simply a matter of personal preference. Also note however that "Colt National Match" pre-war pistols are also "Government models" as the receiver was marked as such throughout production.

WITH ADJUSTABLE SIGHTS

EXC.	V.G.	GOOD	FAIR	POOR
4,800	2,900	1,700	1,050	900

NOTE: Finish 99-100 percent add 30 to 60 percent.

FIXED SIGHTS

EXC.	V.G.	GOOD	FAIR	POOR
3,700	2,500	1,400	900	750

NOTE: The following advertisement appeared on *ArmChairGunShow.com* in the Spring of 2007:

"Colt - National Match - adjustable sight - .45 ACP - Excellent condition. - Probably about 97% original blue, taking on a plum cast; excellent markings, mech. and bore. Replaced plastic grips. Slide and frame serial numbers do not match. Serial number #C221247. $3,650."

PRE-WORLD WAR II FIRING PIN AND HAMMER/SEAR SWARTZ SAFETIES

The "Swartz Safeties" are a pair of devices that Colt installed in 1911A1 Commercial Government Models and 1911A1 Commercial National Match pistols in the late 1930s and early 1940s. Swartz Safeties are referred to in Colt factory letters as the "NSD" (New Safety Device).

The first device, a firing pin block that was actuated by the grip safety, prevented the firing pin from moving forward unless the grip safety was squeezed. The Swartz firing pin block safety can be observed by pulling the slide back all the way and looking at the top of the frame. A 1911A1 pistol equipped with the Swartz safety will have a second pin protruding upward, next to the conventional disconnector pin. This second pin pushes a spring loaded piston in the rear part of the slide that is visible when the slide is pulled back and the slide is viewed from underneath. This piston, in turn, blocks the firing pin when relaxed.

The second Swartz safety device, the hammer/sear safety prevented a possible unsafe half cock position. The hammer/sear safety is usually built into pistols equipped with the Swartz firing pin block safety. The sear safety can sometimes be detected by the drag marks of the notched sear on the round portion of the hammer that the sear rides on. Pulling the hammer all the way back will expose these drag marks if they are visible. Presence of the drag marks, however, does not ensure that the Swartz-modified sear safety parts are all present. Disassembly may be required to verify the correct parts are all present.

From serial number #C162000 to #C215000 about 3,000 total National Match pistols were made with and without the Swartz safeties. The number of National Match pistols having the Swartz safeties is unknown.

Argentine Model 1911A1 with Swartz safety.

However, only a few pistols below serial number #C190000 had the safeties installed and of the pistols made after #C190000, most were Standard Models shipped to Brazil and Argentina. The Brazilian pistols were without the safeties or the cutouts. The Argentine pistols were shipped in two batches of 250 pistols each. Both of these Argentine batches appear to have had the safeties installed as a number of them have recently been re-imported into the U.S.

Probably fewer than half of the total Colt production of National Match pistols had the Swartz safeties. The total number of pistols (both Standard Government Model and National Match) shipped with Swartz safeties is probably much less than 3,000. And probably much less than half of the total Colt made National Match pistols had the Swartz safeties. Swartz safeties were also installed in late Super .38 and Super Match .38 pistols.

STANDARD 1911A1 COMMERCIAL GOVERNMENT MODEL MARKED PISTOL WITH NUMBERED SLIDE & SWARTZ SAFETIES

"Swartz safeties," no foreign markings. Fixed sights only, no additions whatsoever. Rare, seldom seen. For 99-100 percent finish, add 20 to 50 percent.

EXC.	V.G.	GOOD	FAIR	POOR
3,750	2,500	1,900	1,150	850

NATIONAL MATCH CALIBER PRE-WORLD WAR II .45 WITH SWARTZ SAFETIES

Serial number #C186000 to #C215000 probably fewer than 1,500 pistols. Colt would rework fixed sight equipped pistols on a repair order with a Stevens adjustable sight. Therefore, a Colt letter showing that the pistol was originally shipped with adjustable sights is in order for any adjustable sight equipped pistol. For 99-100 percent finish, add 30 to 60 percent.

STEVENS ADJUSTABLE SIGHTS

EXC.	V.G.	GOOD	FAIR	POOR
6,200	3,550	2,400	1,350	1,000

FIXED SIGHTS

EXC.	V.G.	GOOD	FAIR	POOR
4,700	2,750	1,700	1,050	800

STANDARD 1911A1 PRE-WORLD WAR II GOVERNMENT MODEL EXPORT SALES

Equipped with the Swartz Safeties and normally a foreign crest or foreign inscription, mainly from Argentina. The vast majority of these foreign contract Swartz Safety equipped pistols were shipped to Argentina, but Argentine pistols do not have the collector interest that the others or the plain domestic pistols have. Although we have mentioned this before, it is worthwhile mentioning again that four factors probably reduce collector interest in the Colt-made

*Model 1927
Argentine .45.*

Argentine pistols compared to other models used or sold domestically:

1. Most of the Argentine-marked pistols have recently been re-imported and have the legally required Import Markings.

2. Many of the Argentine-marked pistols have been advertised and sold in the wholesale trade publications at utility prices.

3. Most of the recent import Argentine pistols have been refinished or are in "well used" condition.

4. Most of the recent import pistols from Argentina have had some parts changed or swapped with other pistols and are not in original condition.

The few of these Argentine Swartz equipped pistols that remain in original and excellent or better condition usually sell for less than their "plain Jane" domestic counterparts, and they sell for much less than the much rarer Brazilian and Mexican pistols. Perhaps these depressed prices represent a bargain for collectors with an eye to the future when the supply of these extremely rare pistols dries up. A 100 percent re-blue depresses the condition of the pistol to Fair or Poor. For 99-100 percent finish, add 20 to 30 percent.

EXC.	V.G.	GOOD	FAIR	POOR
1,400	1,050	900	650	550

NORMAL BRAZILIAN AND MEXICAN PISTOLS (W/SWARTZ SAFETIES)

These pistols do not normally have Swartz safeties, but if any were found, they would be expected to sell for at least the amount listed. For 99-100 percent finish, add 20 to 30 percent.

EXC.	V.G.	GOOD	FAIR	POOR
9,500	7,000	4,000	2,500	1,200

ARGENTINE CONTRACT PISTOLS "MODELO ARGENTINO 1927 CALIBRE .45"

These pistols were delivered to Argentina in 1927. The right side of the slide is marked with the two line inscription "EJERCITO ARGENTINO COLTS CAL .45 MOD. 1927." The left side is marked "COLTS PT. F.A. MFG. CO....etc." There is also the Argentine National Seal and the "rampant colt." Serial numbers were #1 to #10000 stamped on top of the slide under the mainspring housing. Verified proof, Assembler's mark and Final inspectors mark under left stock by upper bushing. None had Swartz safeties. Most of these pistols were re-blued and this depresses collector value to the Fair to Poor category, depending upon appearance. The abundance of these and other re-finished Argentine pistols has depressed the prices of all original finish Argentine pistols. For 99-100 percent finish, add 20 to 50 percent.

Post-WWII 1911A1 Commercial Government Model.

EXC.	V.G.	GOOD	FAIR	POOR
1,000	700	500	400	300

MILITARY TO COMMERCIAL CONVERSIONS

Some of the 1911 Military pistols brought home by GIs were subsequently returned to the Colt factory for repair or refinishing. If the repair included a new barrel, the pistol would have been proof fired and a normal Verified proof mark affixed to the trigger guard bow in the normal commercial practice. If the pistol was refinished between about 1920 and 1942, the slide would probably be numbered to the frame again in the normal commercial practice. Slides were numbered on the bottom disconnector rail during part of 1920, and after that they were numbered under the firing pin stop plate. These pistols are really re-manufactured Colts of limited production and should be valued at least that of a contemporary 1911A1 commercial pistol. Only pistols marked with identifiable Colt markings should be included in this category. These guns are very seldom seen. For 99-100 percent finish, add 30 percent. For pistols without VP or numbered slide usually cannot be authenticated, deduct 60 percent.

EXC.	V.G.	GOOD	FAIR	POOR
1,900	1,300	975	550	425

REWORKS OF COLT 1911 AND 1911A1 COMMERCIAL GOVERNMENT MODEL PISTOLS

Since Colt rework records have been lost, reworked and refinished pistols without identifiable Colt-applied markings are probably not verifiable as Colt reworks, and should be considered re-finished pistols of unknown pedigree. The standard rule of thumb is that the value of a reworked or refinished pistol is equivalent to a similar original pistol in Poor condition.

Many beginning collectors start by buying a pistol with either no original finish or one that has been refinished. The first thing they ask is where can I get it refinished, and second is how much will it cost? A quality restoration will often cost $1,000, and that added to an initial cost of purchase, for example, $600, will produce a pistol that might sell for $1,000 to $1,200. The lesson is that the cost of rework and refinish will seldom be recovered when the pistol is sold. Since these are no longer original pistols, their prices are much closer to that of a utility shooter and depend a lot on their overall appearance. A professionally restored example might sell for as high as $1,100; a poorly refinished example would, on the other hand, probably

Colt Ace Model .22 Pistol.

rank with the import-marked refinished pistols and sell for a disappointing $400 or so.

POST WORLD WAR II COMMERCIALLY PRODUCED, DOMESTIC SALES, 1946-1969

SERIAL NUMBERS #C220000 TO ABOUT #C220500

No "Government Model" marking, a few have no verified proof. Many parts are leftover military. For 99-100 percent finish, add 20 to 50 percent.

EXC.	V.G.	GOOD	FAIR	POOR
2,300	1,650	1,150	950	750

SERIAL NUMBERS #C220500 TO ABOUT #C249000

Verified proof and "Government Model" marking. Many parts are leftover military in the first few thousand pistols. No foreign markings.

EXC.	V.G.	GOOD	FAIR	POOR
1,450	950	650	535	450

For 99-100 percent finish, add 20 to 30 percent. Deduct 30 percent for foreign markings.

SERIAL NUMBERS #249500-C TO ABOUT #335000-C

Verified proof and "Government Model" marking. No foreign markings. For 99-100 percent finish, add 20 to 30 percent. Deduct 30 percent for foreign markings.

EXC.	V.G.	GOOD	FAIR	POOR
1,100	900	625	500	400

SERIAL NUMBERS #255000-C TO ABOUT #258000-C

Slide factory roll marked "Property of the State of New York," verified proof and "Government Model" marking. A few leftover military parts are still used. A few pairs of pistols remain as consecutive pairs. 250 pistols total. For 99-100 percent finish, add 20-50 percent. Add 10 percent for consecutive pairs.

EXC.	V.G.	GOOD	FAIR	POOR
1600	900	600	550	450

SERIAL NUMBERS #334500-C TO ABOUT #336169-C

"BB" (Barrel Bushing) marked. About 1000 pistols. Verified proof and "Government Model" marking. For 99-100 percent finish, add 20 to 50 percent.

EXC.	V.G.	GOOD	FAIR	POOR
1,375	900	700	575	450

THE ACE AND SERVICE MODEL ACE

ACE MODEL .22 PISTOL

Starting on June 21, 1913, the U.S. Military along with Springfield Armory and Colt Patented Firearms Manufacturing Co. attempted to develop a .22-cal. rimfire pistol that could be used for training purposes.

After all, the .45 ACP was an expensive round to fire. By 1927, the military became convinced that a pistol identical to the standard Service Pistol but in .22 rimfire was impractical and dropped the idea. In 1930 Colt purchased advertising that, in effect, requested the shooting public to let the company know if they would be interested in a .22 rimfire pistol built similar to the Government Model. The response must have been positive because in 1931 the Colt Ace appeared on the market.

The Ace uses the same frame as the Government Model with a highly modified slide and a heavy barrel. It is chambered for the .22 LR cartridge only. The size is the same as the larger caliber version, and the weight is 36 oz. The operation is straight blowback. The Ace has a 10-round detachable magazine and features the Improved Ace Adjustable Target Sight. The markings on the left side of the slide are the same as on the Government Model; the right side reads "COLT ACE .22 LONG RIFLE." At first the Army purchased a few pistols (totaling 206) through 1936. The Army concluded that the function of the Ace was less than perfect, as they concluded the .22 rimfire lacked the power to consistently and reliably operate the slide. Approximately 11,000 Ace pistols were manufactured, and in 1941 they were discontinued. Many owners today find that although the Ace is somewhat selective to ammunition, with full power loads, it is a highly reliable pistol when properly cleaned and maintained. For 99 to 100 percent finish, add 33 percent.

EXC.	V.G.	GOOD	FAIR	POOR
2,500	1,750	1,100	1,000	900

NOTE: The following advertisement was placed on *ColtAutos.com* during the winter of 2006-07:

"COLT ACE Serial number #5671 Price $2,795. Description: .22 LR Caliber. 98% Original blue."

PRE-1945 SERVICE MODEL ACE .22 RF PISTOL

In 1937 Colt introduced this improved version of the Ace Pistol. It utilizes a floating chamber invented by David "Carbine" Williams, the firearm's designer, who also invented the Short Stroke Gas Piston that is the basis of the M1 carbine while serving time on a Southern chain gang. Colt's advertised that this pistol with its floating chamber would give the Service Model Ace the reliability and, some would argue most importantly, the "feel" of a .45 Auto. Today, owners of Service Model Ace pistols find that they require regular maintenance and cleaning in order to keep the close fitting floating chamber from binding. Furthermore,

fouling appears to be much worse with some brands and types of ammunition. Most owners feel that although the perceived recoil of the Service Model Ace is noticeably greater than that of the Ace, it falls far short of a .45 Auto's recoil. The serial number is prefixed by the letters "SM." The external configuration is the same as the Ace, and the slide is marked "COLT SERVICE MODEL ACE .22 LONG RIFLE." Most were sold to the Army and some on a commercial basis. There were a total of 13,803 manufactured before production ceased in 1945. For 99 to 100 percent finish, add 20 to 30 percent for both models below. Add 20 percent for "US PROPERTY" marking.

BLUED PISTOLS, BEFORE ABOUT SERIAL NUMBER #SM3840

EXC.	V.G.	GOOD	FAIR	POOR
6,000	3,000	2,000	1,600	1,350

PARKERIZED PISTOLS, AFTER ABOUT SERIAL NUMBER #SM3840.

EXC.	V.G.	GOOD	FAIR	POOR
3,000	2,000	1,500	1,000	700

NOTE: The following advertisement appeared on *GunBroker.com* in March of 2007:

"Colt Service Model Ace .22 caliber, 5 inch blue. New in the original box with papers!"

The gun sold for $1375.

SERVICE MODEL ACE POST-WAR

Introduced in 1978 this model is similar to the pre-war model. Production ceased in 1982. For 99-100 percent finish, add 20 to 30 percent.

EXC.	V.G.	GOOD	FAIR	POOR
1,100	950	875	800	600

NOTE: The following advertisement appeared during the Spring of 2007 on *ColtAutos.com*:

"SM Ace - Caliber: 22 LR, serial number #SM14066, Price: $1,100. Description: Up for sale is a Post War 1978 Service Model ACE. I wish I had the box. This gun is mint, since no box I will rate it at 95%+. Must ship to FFL. Buyer pays all shipping, insurance and transfer fees. Normal three day inspection from the date and time it is received by your dealer. Funds are to be Postal Money Order ONLY. Pictures on request."

CONVERSION UNITS .22-.45, .45-.22

In 1938, Colt released a .22 caliber conversion unit. With this kit, one who already owned a Government Model could simply switch the top half and fire inexpensive .22 rimfire ammunition. The unit consists of a slide marked "Service Model Ace," barrel with floating

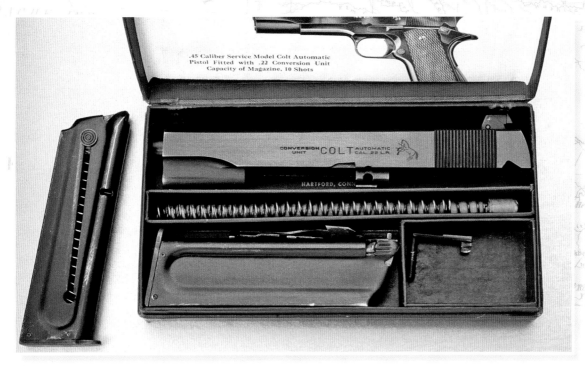

Ace post-war conversion unit.

chamber, ejector, slide lock, bushing, recoil spring 10-shot magazine and box. The Conversion Units feature the Stevens adjustable rear sight. Later that same year, a kit to convert the Service Model Ace to .45 ACP was offered. In 1942 production of these units ceased. The .22 kit was reintroduced in 1947; the .45 kit was not brought back. For 99-100 percent finish, add 20 to 30 percent. Subtract 20 percent if box is missing. Be alert, as sometimes a conversion unit is found on a Service Model Ace receiver and a Service model Ace upper is sold as a "Conversion Unit." Conversion Units are ALWAYS marked "CONVERSION UNIT." Service Model Ace pistols lack the Conversion Unit marking.

PRE-WAR AND POST-WAR "U" NUMBERED SERVICE MODEL ACE CONVERSION UNIT, .22-.45

The pre-war conversion units were serial numbered #U1 to #U2000. For 99-100 percent finish, add 20 to 30 percent.

EXC.	V.G.	GOOD	FAIR	POOR
900	650	550	500	450

POST-WAR CONVERSION UNITS

These were serial numbered #U2001 to #U2670. For 99-100 percent finish, add 20 to 30 percent.

EXC.	V.G.	GOOD	FAIR	POOR
650	550	500	450	425

NOTE: The following advertisements for different types of conversion units were placed on *ColtAutos.com* during the Winter of 2006-07:

"COLT CONVERSION UNIT, COLT MASTER SIGHT Price $495. Description: .22 LR caliber. With Box and instructions."

"COLT FIXED SIGHT CONVERSION UNIT Price $695. Description: .22 LR caliber. Rare and unusual. Very few manufactured. As new in box."

"DAY CONVERSION UNIT 5-1/2" BARREL Price $695. Description: .22 LR caliber. 98% Original blue with magazine adapter for Colt 1911 similar to a S&W 41, with no floating chamber. A true competition conversion unit. Very unusual."

"KART CONVERSION UNIT 5-1/2" BARREL Price $795. Description: .22 LR caliber. 98% Original blue with magazine. For Colt 1911. A competition conversion unit. Used by USMC for small bore competition. Similar to a S&W 41, with no floating chamber."

PRE-WAR SERVICE MODEL ACE (RE-)CONVERSION UNIT, .45-22

To convert the SMA .22 Cal. to .45 Cal. serial number #1 to #SN 112. Watch out for fakes. For 99-100 percent finish, add 20 to 30 percent.

*The first of the
.38 Supers, the
1929 Model.*

EXC.	V.G.	GOOD	FAIR	POOR
3,500	2,500	1,500	750	550

POST-WAR .22 CONVERSION UNIT – UN-NUMBERED

30 percent premium for Stevens adjustable sights, 1946 only. For 99-100 percent finish, add 20 to 30 percent.

EXC.	V.G.	GOOD	FAIR	POOR
400	350	250	225	175

MILITARY SHOOTING MATCH PISTOLS

SUPER .38 PRE-WWII 1929 MODEL

This pistol is identical in outward physical configuration to the .45 ACP Colt Commercial and was designed to replace the long obsolete Model 1902. It is chambered for the .38 Super cartridge and has a magazine that holds nine rounds. The right side of the slide is marked "COLT SUPER .38 AUTOMATIC" in two lines, followed by the "Rampant colt." The last few thousand pre-war Super .38 pistols made had the Swartz Safety parts installed, but some pistols were assembled post-war with leftover parts. These post-war assembled pistols did not have the Swartz safeties installed, but most (possibly all) had the cutouts. In 1945, 400 pistols were purchased by the U.S. Government. These 400 pistols bear the "GHD" acceptance mark as well as the Ordnance crossed cannons. (GHD and Ordnance marked add 30 to 50 percent. A factory letter is probably necessary here.) Some collectors feel that post-war assembly and post-war chemical tank blueing adds a premium, others feel that it requires a deduction. Post-war assembly may add 15 percent or it may deduct 15 percent. For 99-100 percent finish, add 33 percent. For Swartz Safeties add 20 percent.

EXC.	V.G.	GOOD	FAIR	POOR
3,600	2,400	1,400	1,100	800

*Super Match .38,
Model of 1935.*

*Model 1911A1 Military
National Match .45.*

SUPER MATCH .38 PRE-WWII 1935 MODEL

Only 5,000 of these specially fit and finished target-grade pistols were manufactured. They have fixed sights or the Stevens adjustable sights, and the top surfaces are matte-finished to reduce glare. Twelve hundred of these pistols were purchased and sent to Britain in 1939, at the then costly rate of $50 per unit. Adjustable sights. The last few thousand pre-war Super .38 pistols made had the Swartz safety parts installed, but some pistols were assembled post-war with leftover parts. These post-war assembled pistols did not have the Swartz safeties installed, but most (possibly all) had the cutouts. In 1945, 400 pistols were purchased by the U.S. Government. These 400 pistols bear the GHD acceptance mark as well as the Ordnance crossed cannons. GHD and Ordnance marked add 30-50 percent. A factory letter is probably necessary here. Swartz Safeties add 20 percent. Some collectors feel that post-war assembly and post-war chemical tank bluing adds a premium, others feel that it requires a deduction. Post-war assembly may add 15 percent or it may deduct 15 percent. For 99-100 percent finish, add 20 to 75 percent for both models.

ADJUSTABLE SIGHTS

EXC.	V.G.	GOOD	FAIR	POOR
7,500	4,200	3,000	1,800	1,200

FIXED SIGHTS

EXC.	V.G.	GOOD	FAIR	POOR
6,000	3,850	2,850	1,600	1,150

MILITARY NATIONAL MATCH .45 PISTOL

Rebuilt from service pistols at Springfield Armory between 1955 and about 1967 and at Rock Island in 1968. These pistols were built and rebuilt each year with a portion being sold to competitors by the National Rifle Association. Each year improvements were added to the rebuild program. Four articles in the *National Rifleman* – August 1959, April 1963, June 1966, and July 1966 – document these pistols. Many parts for these pistols have been available and many "lookalike" pistols have been built by basement armorers. Pistols generally came with a numbered box and shipping papers. Prices listed are for pistols with numbered box or papers. Less box and papers deduct 30 percent. When well-worn, these pistols will offer little over a standard pistol. Early pistols are much less commonly seen, but seem to be less sought after since they look largely like normal issue pistols. For 99-100 percent finish, add 20 to 30 percent.

EXC.	V.G.	GOOD	FAIR	POOR
1,500	1,075	775	600	475

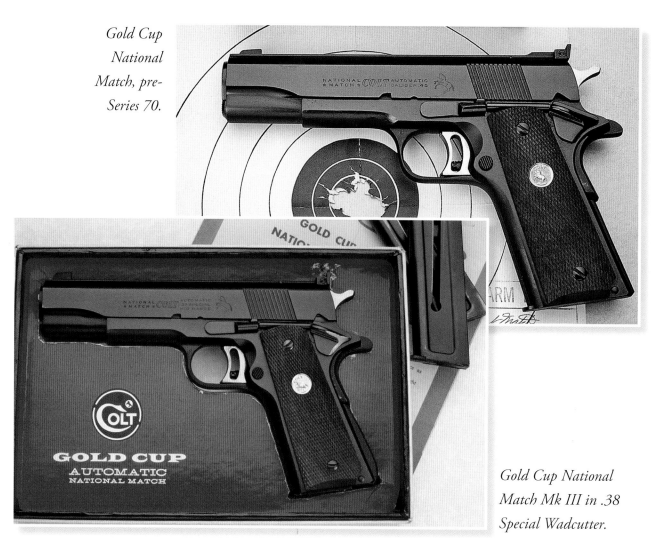

Gold Cup National Match, pre-Series 70.

Gold Cup National Match Mk III in .38 Special Wadcutter.

MILITARY NATIONAL MATCH PISTOLS (DRAKE SLIDE)

In 1964, Springfield Armory used some of these specially machined and hardened slides to build the Military National Match pistols that year. That year's pistol is perhaps the most identifiable NM pistol due to its unique slide marking. However, Drake was only the supplier of the slides that year. Colt supplied the slides in the following year (1965). For 99-100 percent finish, add 20 to 30 percent.

EXC.	V.G.	GOOD	FAIR	POOR
1,550	1,100	790	610	485

GOLD CUP NATIONAL MATCH (PRE-SERIES 70)

This model is chambered for the .45 ACP, features the flat mainspring housing of the 1911, and has a match grade barrel and bushing. The parts were hand fitted, and the slide has an enlarged ejection port. The trigger is the long version with an adjustable trigger stop, and the sights are adjustable target type. The finish is blued, with checkered walnut grips and gold medallions. The slide is marked "Gold Cup National Match," and the serial number is prefixed by the letters "NM." This pistol was manufactured from 1957 to 1970. For 99-100 percent finish, add 20 to 30 percent.

EXC.	V.G.	GOOD	FAIR	POOR
1,100	850	625	500	400

GOLD CUP MKIII NATIONAL MATCH

This pistol is identical to the Gold Cup .45 except that it is chambered for the .38 Mid-Range Wad Cutter round. It was manufactured from 1961 until 1974. For 99-100 percent finish, add 20 to 30 percent.

EXC.	V.G.	GOOD	FAIR	POOR
1,050	875	600	450	350

1911A1 AMU (ARMY MARKSMANSHIP UNIT)

For Army modified pistols deduct 70 percent.

EXC.	V.G.	GOOD	FAIR	POOR
2,700	2,250	1,450	900	400

Ballester-Molina.

LICENSED AND UNLICENSED FOREIGN-MADE 1911A1 AND VARIATIONS

ARGENTINE D.G.F.M.

Direccion General de Fabricaciones Militares made at the F.M.A.P. (Fabrica Militar de Arms Portatiles [Military Factory of Small Arms]). Licensed copies serial number #24000 to #112494. Parts are generally interchangeable with Colt made 1911A1 type pistols. Most pistols were marked "D.G.F.M. - (F.M.A.P.)." Late pistols were marked FM within a cartouche on the right side of the slide. These pistols are found both with and without import markings, often in excellent condition, currently more often in refinished condition, and with a seemingly endless variety of slide markings. None of these variations have yet achieved any particular collector status or distinction, unless new in box. A new in the box DGFM sold at auction not long ago for $1,200. In fact many of these fine pistols have and continue to be used as the platforms for the highly customized competition and target pistols that are currently popular. A refinished gun drops its collector category to Fair/Poor. For 99-100 percent finish or NIB add 10 to 30 percent.

EXC.	V.G.	GOOD	FAIR	POOR
575	475	400	350	300

ARGENTINE-MADE BALLESTER-MOLINA

Unlicensed, Argentine redesigned versions. Parts are NOT interchangeable with Colt except for the barrel and magazine. These pistols are found both with and without import markings. Pistols without import markings usually have a B prefix number stamped on the left rear part of the mainspring housing and are often in excellent to new original condition. The vast majority of currently available pistols are found in excellent, but refinished condition. Only the pistols with no import markings that are in excellent-to-new original condition have achieved any particular collector status. Most of these pistols that are being sold today are being carried and shot rather than being collected. A re-finished gun drops its collector category to Fair/Poor. For 99-100 percent finish, NIB add 10 to 30 percent.

EXC.	V.G.	GOOD	FAIR	POOR
600	375	300	215	190

BRAZILIAN MODELS 1911A1 (ITAJUBA AND IMBEL)

Made by "Fabrica de Itajuba" in Itajuba, Brazil and the Imbel Model 973 made by "Industriade Material Belico do Brazil" in Sao Paulo, Brazil. The Itajuba is a true copy of the Colt 1911A1, and the Imbel is also believed to be a true copy. However, an Imbel has yet to be examined by the author. This model is far too rarely seen in the U.S. to establish a meaningful value scale.

SERIES 70-80, 1991A1S, MODEL O, EAGLES, NINES AND HORSES

The venerable Model 1911A1 was manufactured by Colt (and others during World War II) until 1971. Shortly after the war, Colt introduced a new gun, the Commander, which was based on the M-1911A1 Government design. This gun was essentially a shortened version of the A1 and was manufactured with a 4.25-inch barrel. Formerly, a 5-inch barrel had been the standard for full size semi-autos. The new gun was the first to feature an aluminum frame. It was a startling innovation at the time because the handgun mindset was mostly limited to steel. Nevertheless, the shooting public readily accepted the Commander.

Subsequently, Colt produced the same pistol with a steel frame and named this more traditional model a "Combat Commander." Ever since, the term "Commander" has been used to designate 1911s that have 4.25-inch barrels. (The aluminum-framed gun was eventually, but not immediately, dubbed the "Lightweight Commander.")

Not long afterwards, Colt introduced a pistol with a 3.5-inch barrel, looking to develop a firearm that would satisfy the concealed carry market. Colt called this gun the "Officer's Model." It had a shorter length overall frame and used lightweight six-round magazines. This model name is used today to denote the smallest versions of particular models, versions with shorter barrels and frames.

In the 1970s, the MK IV Series 70 Government Model superseded the standard Government Model. The main modifications in the new model were a slightly heavier slide and a slotted collet barrel bushing.

In 1983 Colt introduced its MK IV Series 80 models, which had an additional passive firing pin safety lock that did not allow the pistol to fire if the trigger was not pulled to the end of its travel. Although some people feel that the change had a negative effect on trigger pull, it is probably a necessary evil in a highly litigious world. Still, it has not been completely accepted by higher level competition shooters who want a "decent trigger pull" on their firearms. (An identical firing pin safety mechanism is also used by the way

in high-capacity pistols from Para Ordnance.) At this time, the half-cock notch was also redesigned.

In the 1990s, Colt developed an "Enhanced Series" of 1911s. These were of course modified Series 80 pistols, with several factory alterations that many serious shooters would previously have performed by a custom gunsmith. The alterations included a beavertail grip safety, beveled magazine well, flared ejection port and a notch underneath the rear of the trigger guard, which allowed the pistol to sit lower in the shooter's hand.

At the beginning of 1992 another change was made and the resulting model was designated the 1991A1. Colt then recommended this pistol, with its flat mainspring housing, as an updated version of their classic 1911. Included in the series were the Government models, the Commander, the Officer's model, the Gold Cup and the Combat Elite.

All of these enhancements were the result of Colt's desire to meet shooters' demand for a more customized pistol. Colt selected several of the most popular modifications to incorporate in their new and enhanced models. The changes included a beavertail safety grip, a slotted Commander style hammer, a relief cut under the trigger guard, a beveled magazine well, a slightly longer trigger, a flat top rib and angled slide serrations. Consequently, from its earliest incarnation – which the casual observer would with difficulty distinguish from the latest – the Model 1911A1 may be the most modified handgun in the world.

The .38 Super, by the way, was introduced in 1929 in the famous Colt Government Model 1911 auto pistol. At the time of its introduction, the .38 Super cartridge was the most powerful auto pistol cartridge in the world, able to shoot through car doors and the "bulletproof" vests of the day and therefore a gangster favorite, and Colt was the only major American gun maker who produced .38 Super pistols. Ironically, the superb qualities of the .38 Super led to the development of an even more famous cartridge, the .357 Magnum.

The .38 Super is still one of the most powerful and flat-shooting cartridges available for auto loading pistols. Although it gradually fell into disuse following World War II, it has been resurrected for guns with slightly longer barrels in IPSC shooting.

Mk IV Series 70 Gold Cup National Match.

THE SERIES 70S
AND SERIES 80S

MKIV SERIES 70 GOVERNMENT MODEL

This model is essentially a newer version of the 1911A1. It has the prefix "70G" from 1970-1976, "G70" from 1976 to 1980, and "70B" from 1980-1983, the year production ceased. This model is offered in blue or nickel plate and has checkered walnut grips with the Colt medallion. It is chambered for .45 ACP, .38 Super, 9mm and 9mm Steyr (for foreign export only).

NIB	EXC.	V.G.	GOOD	FAIR	POOR
600	500	400	300	250	200

NOTE: The following advertisement appeared on *ColtAutos.com* during the Winter of 2007:

"1911A1 Caliber: 45, SN:, Price: $850. Description: Excellent condition 70 Series Colt 1911 in 45 ACP. Gun appears to never have been fired. Polished blue inside and out. No wear of any kind. Split collet barrel NM barrel bushing, rare. Just one Colt magazine. No box, just the gun, but what a gun it is."

MKIV SERIES 70 GOLD CUP
NATIONAL MATCH

This is the newer version of the 1957 National Match pistol. It features a slightly heavier slide and Colt Elliason sights. The chambering is .45 ACP only. An Accurizer barrel and bushing was introduced on this model. It was manufactured from 1970 to 1983.

NIB	EXC.	V.G.	GOOD	FAIR	POOR
800	700	600	550	500	400

NOTE: The following advertisement appeared on *ColtAutos.com* during the Spring of 2007:

"Gold Cup National Match – Series '80 Colt MK IV - Caliber: 45 ACP, serial number SN099xx, Price: $825, Description: stainless steel with original Colt clip. This gently used 95% Colt has been a gem in my collection almost 20 years. Features five inch barrel, wide grooved adj. trigger, Pachmayer grips and Colt-Eliason rear sight."

SERIES 70 1911 SERVICE
MODEL WORLD WAR I

Introduced in 2004 this model is a reproduction of the famous World War I 1911 model with the original roll marks, inspector marks, and straight mainspring housing with lanyard loop. Double diamond walnut grips plus other WWI features. Two magazines, each holding seven rounds, were originally included with each new pistol.

NIB	EXC.	V.G.	GOOD	FAIR	POOR
990	775	-	-	-	-

THE GUNSITE SERIES

SERIES 70 GUNSITE PISTOL

This is truly a shooter's firearm. It was a joint effort, led by Colt's Lt. Gen. William M. Keys, USMC (Ret.), Gunsite's Owen "Buz" Mills and Col. Bob Young USMC (Ret.). It features a 5-inch barrel, Gold Cup serrations on front strap, Heinie front sight and Novak rear sight. Introduced in 2004, it is available in blue or stainless steel. It features the Series 70 firing system, Smith & Alexander metal grip safety with palm swell, serrated flat mainspring housing dehorned all around. Thin rosewood grips and short aluminum trigger with 4- to 4.5-lb. pull. Part numbers were #O1070CGP Stainless Steel and #O1980CGP Blued Carbon Steel. Purchase of a Series 70 Gunsite in any of the three configurations came with a $100 coupon toward training at the Gunsite training school, located outside Paulden, AZ.

NIB	EXC.	V.G.	GOOD	FAIR	POOR
1,400	1,100	-	-	-	-

NOTE: The following advertisement appeared on *AuctionArms.com* in March of 2007:

"*Colt Gunsite Model 0 .45 ACP 1911A1. I am the original owner of this firearm. It shoots flawlessly. I am selling due to some other aspirations. I have all the original papers and box. A solid 98% plus gun. Light muzzle edge and rear grip safety wear. I have shot less than 300 rounds through it. These have not been produced since 2005. It is a last year – 2005 – production pistol. It is serial number #O133CGP. The 133rd off the bench has to be somewhat significant. A very nice collectible firearm. Best of all, it is a Colt!*"

The gun attracted a high bid of $900 but failed to meet the seller's reserve of $1,224.

Lt. Gen. William Keys, co-designer of the Colt Gunsite Pistol.

Colt Gunsite Pistol.

Commander in .38 Super.

Pre-Series 70 Commander.

SERIES 70 GUNSITE PISTOL COMMANDER (#O9840CGP)

The same gun as the Series 70 Gunsite but with a 4.25-inch barrel.

NIB	EXC.	V.G.	GOOD	FAIR	POOR
1,400	1,100	-	-	-	-

SERIES 70 GUNSITE CCO – CONCEALED CARRY OFFICER

Similar to the original .45 ACP Government Model Colt Gunsite Pistol. Novak rear sights with Heinie front sight, S&A grip safety, extended safety, short trigger, Gunsite rollmarks and 4.25 inch barrel. An alloy Officers model frame with undercut and front serrations with a Commander length slide. It will have the factory Colt Commander hammer and sear and a non-MIM extractor. Stocks and magazines factory standard. Retail is usually at or below $1,000.

NIB	EXC.	V.G.	GOOD	FAIR	POOR
1,100	950	-	-	-	-

MK IV SERIES 80 GOVERNMENT MODEL

This model was introduced in 1983. It is, for all purposes, the same externally as the Series 70. The basic difference is the addition of a new firing pin safety on this model. Beginning in 1997 Colt offered this model with fixed white dot sights. .22 conversion units generally sell for around $500-$750 in Excellent to NIB condition.

BLUED

NIB	EXC.	V.G.	GOOD	FAIR	POOR
650	500	400	350	300	250

NICKEL PLATED

NIB	EXC.	V.G.	GOOD	FAIR	POOR
750	600	500	375	300	250

STAINLESS STEEL

NIB	EXC.	V.G.	GOOD	FAIR	POOR
675	625	500	400	325	275

POLISHED STAINLESS STEEL

NIB	EXC.	V.G.	GOOD	FAIR	POOR
750	650	550	450	350	300

MK IV SERIES 80 GOLD CUP NATIONAL MATCH

Externally the same as the Series 70 Gold Cup with the new firing pin safety.

BLUED

NIB	EXC.	V.G.	GOOD	FAIR	POOR
850	725	600	500	350	250

STAINLESS STEEL

NIB	EXC.	V.G.	GOOD	FAIR	POOR
925	775	650	500	400	300

POLISHED STAINLESS STEEL

NIB	EXC.	V.G.	GOOD	FAIR	POOR
975	850	725	600	450	350

*Combat Commander,
nickel finish.*

*Combat Commander,
blued finish.*

COMMANDER

The Commander was produced in response to requests for a lighter pistol than the M1911A1, yet capable of firing the .45 ACP. It is a shortened version – its overall length is 7.75 inches – of the basic Government model manufactured from 1949 until 1998 and has a 4.25-inch barrel, a strong, but lightweight aluminum alloy frame, and a rounded spur combat style hammer. The slide remained steel, so the total weight of the Commander is 27.5 oz. As a natural consequence, the recoil was increased and the new Commander required some skill to extract the best from it under field conditions. The serial numbers have the suffix "LW." The gun is chambered for .45 ACP, 9mm and .38 Super. (The latter two were discontinued.) A number of guns were chambered for .32 ACP for sale in Italy. The guns were subsequently upgraded to 1992 Enhanced, M1991A1, M1991 Model O and XS Model O standards. The M1991A1 variant (1993 to 1998) was offered from 1997 in stainless steel, the sights being changed to fixed three-dot combat pattern.

NIB	EXC.	V.G.	GOOD	FAIR	POOR
700	550	450	350	300	200

COMBAT COMMANDER

The Combat Commander was produced from 1971 to 1999 in response to complaints from some quarters about the excessive recoil and rapid wear of the aluminum alloy-framed Commander. This model, however, is simply a Commander with a steel frame. The Combat Commander weighs 33 oz. and is offered in blue or satin nickel with walnut grips. The guns were subsequently upgraded to 1992 Enhanced standards.

NIB	EXC.	V.G.	GOOD	FAIR	POOR
700	550	475	375	300	200

NOTE: The following advertisement appeared on *GunBroker.com* in the Spring of 2007:

"This is a Stainless Colt Combat Commander Series 80 in 45 ACP. It is in very good condition and comes with

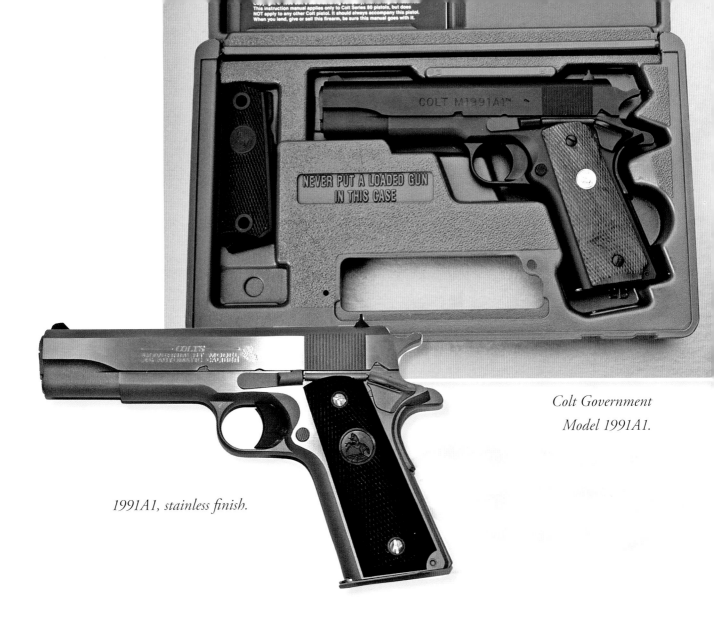

Colt Government Model 1991A1.

1991A1, stainless finish.

everything seen in the photos to include Hogue wrap around grips, 5 original Colt magazines and Scorpion carry case with storage pouch and magazine pouches. Definitely in need of a cleaning."

The gun sold for $760.

THE 1991A1S
COLT GOVERNMENT MODEL 1991A1

Introduced in 1992, this Colt Government Model is designed to resemble the original GI service issue 1911 Government Model. Flat mainspring housing. Offered in .45 ACP with a 5-inch barrel, seven round magazine, black composition grips and a special Parkerized finish. In 1996 this model was also chambered for the 9 x 23 cartridge. This pistol was offered in stainless steel beginning in 1996. Add $50 to the above prices for stainless.

NIB	EXC.	V.G.	GOOD	FAIR	POOR
550	450	350	300	150	125

M1991A1 COMMANDER

Chambered for the .45 ACP this model has all of the same features as the standard M1991A1 with a slightly shorter 4.25 inch barrel. In 1997 Colt offered this model in stainless steel with fixed white dot sights. Add $100 to the NIB price.

NIB	EXC.	V.G.	GOOD	FAIR	POOR
700	550	400	300	225	125

M1991A1 COMPACT

Chambered for the .45 ACP this model has a 3.25-inch barrel. It is 1.5 inches shorter than the standard M1991A1 model and .375 inches shorter in height. Its magazine holds six rounds. Guns made after 1997, constructed of stainless steel, had three-dot combat sights. In 1997 Colt offered this model in stainless steel with fixed white dot sights. Add $50 to the NIB price.

NIB	EXC.	V.G.	GOOD	FAIR	POOR
550	400	250	200	150	125

Mk IV Series 80
Officer's ACP.

OFFICER'S .45 ACP

In the mid-1970s, Rock Island Arsenal developed the General Officer's Model pistol, a shortened M1911A1 for issue to general officers of the U.S. Army and Air Force. Unavailable to the public, there was nevertheless a demand for it, and Colt responded by developing its own version. Like the Rock Island original, it has a 3.5-inch barrel and weighs 37.0 oz. It is chambered for six rounds of .45 ACP and has checkered walnut grips. The Officer's ACP was introduced in 1985 and production lasted for 10 years. It was offered in a number of finishes, each of which is now considered at a different value level.

BLUED
NIB	EXC.	V.G.	GOOD	FAIR	POOR
625	500	400	325	250	200

MATTE BLUED
NIB	EXC.	V.G.	GOOD	FAIR	POOR
600	475	375	300	225	200

SATIN NICKEL
Discontinued 1985.
EXC.	V.G.	GOOD	FAIR	POOR
450	350	275	200	150

STAINLESS STEEL
NIB	EXC.	V.G.	GOOD	FAIR	POOR
750	625	450	350	300	250

OFFICER'S .45 ACP LIGHTWEIGHT

This is an aluminum alloy frame version that weighs 24.0 oz. It was introduced in 1986 and discontinued about 10 years later.
NIB	EXC.	V.G.	GOOD	FAIR	POOR
675	550	450	375	300	200

CONCEALED CARRY OFFICER'S MODEL

This gun features a lightweight aluminum frame with stainless steel Commander slide. The barrel length is 4.25 inches and it is chambered for .45 ACP. It is fitted with a lightweight trigger, combat style hammer and Hogue grips. The weight is approximately 34.0 oz. Introduced in 1998, it remained in the Colt line until 2001.
NIB	EXC.	V.G.	GOOD	FAIR	POOR
800	650	-	-	-	-

ENHANCED GOVERNMENT MODELS

In 1992, Colt introduced a new set of features for its Model 1911A1 series pistols. Under consideration and in development for several years, these new features were prompted by many years of shooter thoughts, complaints and ideas: a flattop slide, angled rear slide serrations, scalloped ejection port, combat style hammer, beavertail grip safety, relief cut-under trigger guard and longer trigger. The models that are affected by the upgrade are the Delta Gold Cup, Delta Elite, Combat Elite, Government Model, Combat Commander, Lightweight Commander, Officer's ACP and the Officer's ACP Lightweight.

DELTA GOLD CUP

Introduced in 1992, the Delta Gold Cup is chambered for the 10mm Auto Pistol cartridge, features a 5-inch barrel, stainless steel finish, adjustable Accro sights, special trigger and black rubber wrap-around grips. Includes all of the "Enhanced" model features.
NIB	EXC.	V.G.	GOOD	FAIR	POOR
1000	825	700	600	400	200

Delta Elite.

DELTA ELITE

Introduced in 1987, this model is chambered for the 10 mm Norma pistol cartridge, which was new at that time. It was the first pistol in this caliber to be made by a major gunmaker. This was something of a gamble by Colt, since the 10mm cartridge had been trying to gain a foothold for about 10 years without much success (and has never really caught on since, though it's an excellent cartridge)... It is basically an M1911A1 that is offered in blue or stainless steel. The grips are black neoprene with the Delta medallion. It features a high-profile three-dot combat sight system. The slide is marked "Delta Elite" over "-Colt Auto-" the components being separated by a large triangle (for the Greek letter Δ, "delta"). A motif of a red triangle inside a circle was molded into the wrap-around Neoprene grips.

BLUED

NIB	EXC.	V.G.	GOOD	FAIR	POOR
700	525	425	350	300	250

STAINLESS STEEL

NIB	EXC.	V.G.	GOOD	FAIR	POOR
750	575	450	375	300	250

POLISHED STAINLESS STEEL

NIB	EXC.	V.G.	GOOD	FAIR	POOR
850	675	550	425	350	250

NOTE: The following advertisement appeared on *GunBroker.com* in March of 2007:

"Colt Delta Elite, 5 inch barrel Blue, 10 mm, 98% all original."

The gun sold for $925.

COMBAT ELITE

This is a specialized, variant Government Model prepared for practical shooting pistol competition. The Combat Elite has a 5-inch barrel and adjustable Accro sights. It is chambered either in .45 ACP or .38 Super. Weighing 38 oz., it has an eight-round magazine for the .45 ACP and a nine-round magazine for the smaller .38 Super. The finish can be either blue or matte stainless steel, and no distinction has yet be determined for values between the finishes.

NIB	EXC.	V.G.	GOOD	FAIR	POOR
775	625	500	400	300	200

COMBAT TARGET MODEL

Introduced in 1996 this 5-inch barreled 1911 model features a fitted barrel, Gold Cup style trigger, tuned action, flat top slide, relieved ejection port, skeletonized hammer, wide grip safety, high cut trigger guard, beveled magazine well and adjustable sights. Offered in both blue and stainless steel, the weight is 39 oz. In 1996 this model was also chambered for the new 9 x 23 cartridge as well as the .45 ACP and the .38 Super. Add $50 for the stainless steel version. In 1997 Colt expanded this Target Model to include a number of different variations. They are listed below.

NIB	EXC.	V.G.	GOOD	FAIR	POOR
800	650	550	500	400	200

COMBAT COMMANDER TARGET

Chambered for .45 ACP with a barrel length of 4.25 inches. Its finish is stainless steel and weight is 36 oz. The Commander has all other Combat Target features.

NIB	EXC.	V.G.	GOOD	FAIR	POOR
800	675	575	500	400	200

COMBAT TARGET OFFICER'S .45 ACP

Fitted with a 3.5-inch barrel and chambered for .45 ACP, this gun has a stainless steel finish and its weight

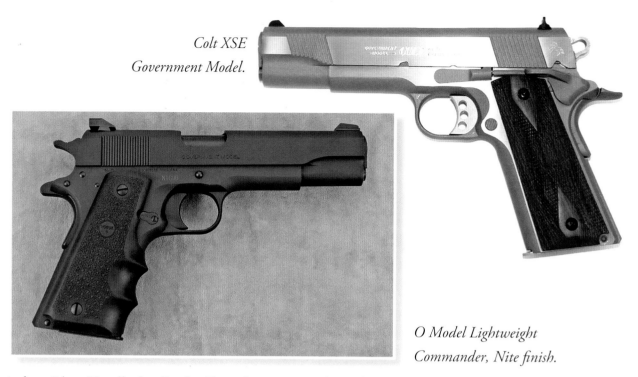

Colt XSE Government Model.

O Model Lightweight Commander, Nite finish.

is about 34 oz. Has all other Combat Target features.

NIB	EXC.	V.G.	GOOD	FAIR	POOR
800	675	575	500	400	200

SPECIAL COMBAT GOVERNMENT

This model is intended for IPSC shooting and for self- or home defense. A single action pistol that features a 5-inch barrel, double diamond rosewood grips, extended ambidextrous thumb safety and steel checkered mainspring housing with extended magazine well. Chambered for the .45 ACP and .38 Super cartridges. Adjustable Bomar rear sight. Magazine capacity is eight rounds. Choice of hard chrome or blue and satin nickel finish.

NIB	EXC.	V.G.	GOOD	FAIR	POOR
2,000	1,500	-	-	-	-

On *ImpactGuns.com*, March 2007, a tricked out Colt Special Combat Government .38 Super two tone was offered for $1,400.99. The description read:

"This competition ready 45 ACP (now also in .38 Super) comes with three hole aluminum trigger, S&A grip safety, custom tuned action, polished feed ramp, throated barrel, flared ejection port, cut out commander hammer, two eight round magazines, extended thumb safety, Bomar rear and Heinie dovetail front sight, and S&A magazine guide. Fully accurized and shipped with a certified target attesting to its exceptional precision. FEATURES: 5 inch" barrel length 8.5 inch overall length. Single action. Extended ambidextrous thumb safety. Steel checkered mainspring housing with extended magazine well." A hard chromed, fully accurized .45 ACP with five inch barrel and 8.5 inch length overall was offered for $1,411.99 and shipped with a certified target "attesting to its exceptional precision."

XSE SERIES MODEL O PISTOLS

Introduced in 1999, these single action models are an enhanced version of the Colt 1911 and feature front and rear slide serrations; checkered, double diamond rosewood grips; adjustable McCormick trigger; three dot dovetail rear sights and fixed blade front sight; ambidextrous manual safety; enhanced tolerances; aluminum frame and a stainless steel slide. All models are chambered for .45 ACP with 8 + 1 round capacity.

O-MODEL GOVERNMENT (#O1070XSE)

Fitted with a 5-inch barrel and eight-round magazine. Stainless steel finish single action semi automatic holds seven rounds. Service hammer and smooth trigger. Length overall 8.5 inches. Weight 36 oz. The blued, carbon steel model is #O1980XSE.

NIB	EXC.	V.G.	GOOD	FAIR	POOR
1,100	825	-	-	-	-

O-MODEL CONCEALED CARRY OFFICER'S (#O9850XS)

Fitted with a 4.25-inch barrel and seven round magazine.

NIB	EXC.	V.G.	GOOD	FAIR	POOR
1,100	825	-	-	-	-

O-MODEL COMMANDER (#O4012XS)

Fitted with a 4.25-inch barrel and 8 + 1 capacity. Front and rear slide serrations. Checkered, double diamond rosewood grips. Extended ambidextrous thumb safety. Fixed sights with elongated hammer slot and combat style hammer. New roll marking and enhanced tolerances.

NIB	EXC.	V.G.	GOOD	FAIR	POOR
1,100	825	-	-	-	-

NOTE: The following advertisement appeared on *GunBroker.com* in March of 2007:

"Colt Combat Commander XSE. New! Awesome! This Colt Combat Commander is the 'XSE' Series, indicating super-high tolerances, fit and finish. I've never seen a tighter, better slide-to-frame fit on a Colt 1911! This is as good as it gets!! FEATURES: Front and rear slide serrations. Checkered, double diamond, rosewood grips. Extended ambidextrous thumb safeties. Fixed sights. Combat hammer. New roll marking and enhanced tolerances. 8 + 1 round capacity for .45 caliber. Single action. The XSE Series features front and rear serrations, extended ambidextrous thumb safeties and adjustable aluminum trigger. Full-length guide rod, polished flats and bright stainless magwell. Two 8 round magazines, factory case, lock, manual and warranty card. New and unfired!"

The gun sold at $875.

O-MODEL COMMANDER LIGHTWEIGHT (#O4860XS)

Fitted with a 4.25-inch barrel and eight-round magazine. The weight is about 26 oz. (The Commander was given the "Lightweight" tag later, principally for marketing reasons.) Also available in a special "Nite" finish for tactical applications.

NIB	EXC.	V.G.	GOOD	FAIR	POOR
1,100	825	750	-	-	-

1991 SERIES MODEL O PISTOLS

This pistol series was introduced in 1991 and was designed to replace the standard Colt 1911 series pistols. It remains in the Private Security Support Center line up to this day. These single action guns feature checkered grips, a smooth aluminum trigger, fixed sights, a beveled magazine well and the standard Colt thumb safety plus a service style grip safety. They were chambered for the .45 ACP cartridge in seven-round magazines. With a cartridge in the chamber, the shooting configuration is 7 + 1.

O-MODEL GOVERNMENT MATTE (#O1991)

Fitted with a 5-inch barrel for an 8.5-inch length overall. A blued finish; carbon steel frame and slide; double diamond rosewood grips and spur hammer.

NIB	EXC.	V.G.	GOOD	FAIR	POOR
870	650	-	-	-	-

O-MODEL GOVERNMENT STAINLESS (#O1091)

Fitted with a 5-inch barrel for an 8.5-inch length overall. A stainless steel finish on stainless steel frame and slide; rubber grips and spur hammer.

NIB	EXC.	V.G.	GOOD	FAIR	POOR
920	700	-	-	-	-

O-MODEL COMMANDER MATTE (#O4691)

Fitted with a 4.25-inch barrel for a 7.75-inch length overall. A blued finish carbon steel frame and slide with double diamond rosewood grips and commander style hammer.

NIB	EXC.	V.G.	GOOD	FAIR	POOR
870	650	-	-	-	-

O-MODEL COMMANDER STAINLESS (#O4091U)

Fitted with a 4.25-inch barrel for a 7.75-inch overall length. Stainless steel finish with stainless steel frame and slide; rubber composite grips and commander style hammer.

NIB	EXC.	V.G.	GOOD	FAIR	POOR
920	700	-	-	-	-

O-MODEL GOLD CUP

This model has the same features as the O-Model Commander with the addition of a 5-inch barrel with a stainless steel frame and slide. The slide top is slightly rounded. Magazine capacity is eight rounds. Weight is about 39 oz. Introduced in 1999.

NIB	EXC.	V.G.	GOOD	FAIR	POOR
1,400	1,050	-	-	-	-

DEFENDER

This single-action semi-automatic pistol was introduced in 1998 as a compact personal defense version of the M1911A1, part of the 1992 "Enhanced" series. It remained in the line up as of 2007 and features a lightweight aluminum alloy frame and stainless steel slide; a lightweight trigger, a skeleton hammer and three-dot combat style sight. Fitted with a 3-inch barrel, it is chambered for 7 + 1 (seven rounds in the magazine and one in the chamber) of either the .45 ACP or .40 S&W cartridges. Rubber wrap-around grips. Weight is

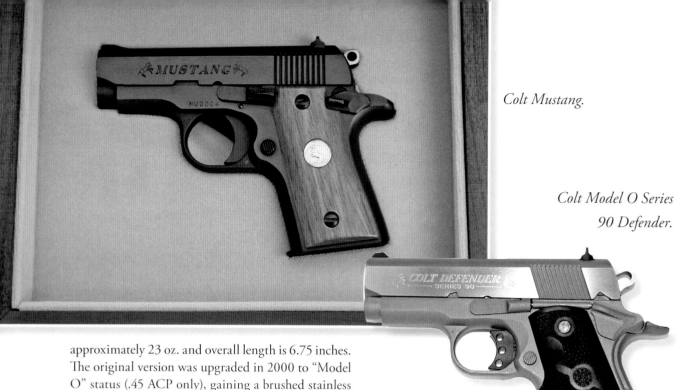

Colt Mustang.

Colt Model O Series 90 Defender.

approximately 23 oz. and overall length is 6.75 inches. The original version was upgraded in 2000 to "Model O" status (.45 ACP only), gaining a brushed stainless finish, a skeleton trigger, a beveled magazine well, an extended safety catch and a beavertail grip safety lever.

NIB	EXC.	V.G.	GOOD	FAIR	POOR
840	650	475	-	-	-

NOTE: The following advertisement appeared on *GunBroker.com* in March of 2007:

"This is a NEW IN BOX Colt Defender 07000D Compact 1911A1 in .45ACP. It is all stainless, 3 inch bbl, rubber grips with finger grooves, fixed white dot sights front and rear , 6.75 inch OAL, 22.5 oz. empty weight, adj alum trigger, combat hammer, two 7 round stainless mags, hard plastic foam lined case, lock, all papers and warranty."

The gun sold at $769.

COLT DEFENDER MODEL O (#O7000D)

This model takes the place of Defender and was introduced in 2000. It has a brushed stainless finish with a 3-inch barrel. Skeletonized composite trigger, beveled magazine well, extended thumb safety and upswept beavertail with palm swell. Chambered for .45 ACP only.

NIB	EXC.	V.G.	GOOD	FAIR	POOR
950	700	-	-	-	-

DOUBLE EAGLES, NINES AND HORSES

DOUBLE EAGLE

The Double Eagle (1989 to 2000) was the first automatic pistol produced by the reorganized Colt Manufacturing Company, Inc., and it broke new ground. It was the first double action pistol to be commercially offered by Colt. The basic M1911 action was allied with a double action trigger mechanism with a decocking lever protruding from under the left grip above the magazine release. This allowed the hammer to be safely lowered with a round in the chamber and without touching the trigger. An automatic firing pin lock disengages only during the last stages of trigger movement.

The Double Eagle shared the general appearance of the M1911A1 Government Model, but the trigger guard was shaped for a two hand hold and the front strap was grooved. In addition, the trigger was a slender pivoting lever instead of the familiar sliding blade. This short lived Mark I (designated retrospectively) was replaced in 1991 by the "Mk II/Series 90" version, which provided the basis for several variants. However, the Double Eagle was not particularly successful. Full size guns, chambered for the Norma 10mm Auto or .45 ACP, were eight inches long, had five inch barrels and weighed about 39 oz. without the detachable eight round magazine. Made largely of stainless steel, they had fixed three dot sights and black checkered Xenoy grips.

NIB	EXC.	V.G.	GOOD	FAIR	POOR
500	425	350	300	250	200

DOUBLE EAGLE OFFICER'S MODEL

This is a compact version of the double action Double Eagle pistol chambered for .45 ACP only. It was built from 1991 to 1997. A short lived version, the Double Eagle Officer's Lightweight was produced from 1992 to 1993. It was little more than a standard Officer's ACP with an aluminum alloy frame, reducing weight considerably.

NIB	EXC.	V.G.	GOOD	FAIR	POOR
480	425	375	300	250	200

NOTE: The following advertisement appeared on *ColtAutos.com* during the Spring of 2007:

"Double Eagle/Officer's ACP - Caliber: 45, serial number #df05708, Price: $775, Description: Colt Double Eagle. Stainless 3.5 inch barrel. Good condition with minor holster blemish/wear. Black Colt grips."

DOUBLE EAGLE COMBAT COMMANDER

Based on the standard Double Eagle design but with a slightly shorter 4.25 inch barrel, the Double Eagle Combat Commander fits between the standard model and the smaller Officer's Model. Available in .45 ACP and .40 S&W (1993) this model weighs about 36 oz., holds eight rounds, has white dot sights and checkered Xenoy grips. The finish is matte stainless steel. It was produced from 1991 to 1997.

NIB	EXC.	V.G.	GOOD	FAIR	POOR
625	550	500	400	300	200

DOUBLE EAGLE FIRST EDITION

This version of the double action Double Eagle pistol is chambered for 10mm Auto and is furnished with a Cordura holster, double magazine pouch and three magazines, as well as a zippered black Cordura case.

NIB	EXC.	V.G.	GOOD	FAIR	POOR
700	650	550	475	375	300

POCKET NINE

This double action semi-automatic pistol is chambered for the 9mm cartridge and was made from 1999 to 2001. The frame is aluminum alloy, the slide is stainless steel and the barrel length is 2.75 inches. The Pocket Nine's magazine capacity is six rounds and it was fitted with standard wrap-around rubber grips and a bobbed hammer. The overall length is 5.5 inches and the weight is approximately 17 oz. with slide grooves milled diagonally and three dot combat style sights.

NIB	EXC.	V.G.	GOOD	FAIR	POOR
550	450	325	-	-	-

TAC NINE

Introduced in 1999 and discontinued in 2001, this double action only semi-automatic is chambered for the 9mm Parabellum cartridge. It has a 2.75 inch barrel with an aluminum alloy frame and stainless steel slide. A bonus are the glow-in-the-dark tritium night sights. Wrap-around rubber grips are standard and the finish is black oxide. Enhanced tolerances. Weight is about 17 oz.

NIB	EXC.	V.G.	GOOD	FAIR	POOR
725	575	-	-	-	-

MUSTANG

This is a more compact version of the .380 Government Model and between 1987 and 1999 it achieved considerable popularity as a home defense pistol and as an off duty police weapon. It has a 2.75-inch barrel and a five-round detachable magazine. The Mustang was made available blued, nickel-plated or with a matte stainless steel finish. For nickel finish add 10 percent; for stainless steel add 10 percent.

NIB	EXC.	V.G.	GOOD	FAIR	POOR
350	300	250	200	175	125

MUSTANG POCKETLITE

A lightweight (approximately 12.5 oz.) version of the .380 Mustang that features a blued aluminum alloy receiver … and consequent greater recoil due to its lighter weight. The finish is blued only, and it has synthetic grips. It was introduced in 1987 and production ceased in 2000.

NIB	EXC.	V.G.	GOOD	FAIR	POOR
450	300	250	200	175	125

NOTE: The following advertisement appeared in the Spring of 2007 on *GunsAmerica.com*:

"Colt Mustang PocketLite .380 4 magazines … New DeSantis Pocket holster, new spring, hex screws and metal guide rod. Great Shooter … Plus Freight Price $695."

MUSTANG PLUS II

This version of the Mustang pistol features the 2.75-inch barrel with the longer grip frame that accommodates a seven round magazine. It was introduced in 1988, discontinued in 1999 and is offered in blue, as well as stainless steel. For stainless steel add 10 percent.

NIB	EXC.	V.G.	GOOD	FAIR	POOR
385	300	250	200	175	125

NOTE: The following advertisement appeared on *GunsAmerica.com* in the Spring of 2007:

"Colt Mustang II cased with manual. Used, but like new. $799."

The late,
lamented Colt All
American 2000.

GOVERNMENT POCKETLITE LW

Similar to the Mustang but fitted with a 3.25-inch barrel and a seven round magazine. This model has an aluminum frame and stainless steel slide. Fixed sights. Black composition grips. Weight is approximately 15 oz.

NIB	EXC.	V.G.	GOOD	FAIR	POOR
450	300	250	200	175	125

PONY

Introduced in 1997, this tiny semi-automatic pistol is chambered for the .380 ACP. It is fitted with a 2.75 inch barrel and a bobbed hammer. It is double action only and the six round magazine was released by a push button behind the trigger. Slide retraction grooves were vertical. The grips are black composition. Sights are a ramp front with fixed rear. Finish is Teflon or brushed stainless steel; the hammer was bobbed and the grips were black composition. The overall length is 5.5 inches and the weight about 19 oz.

NIB	EXC.	V.G.	GOOD	FAIR	POOR
475	400	300	-	-	-

NOTE: The following advertisement appeared in the Spring of 2007 on Sam Lisker's *ColtAutos.com*:

"Colt's Pony - Caliber: .380, serial number #CPA0166XX , Price: $3,350.00, Description: Colt prototype "Colt's Pony" in .380 caliber. Very rare and highly collectible, no box."

PONY POCKETLITE

Same as the Pony but with aluminum alloy and stainless steel frame to lighten the weight. Weight is approximately 13 oz.

NIB	EXC.	V.G.	GOOD	FAIR	POOR
550	475	350	275	-	-

NOTE: The following advertisement appeared in the Spring of 2007 on Sam Lisker's *ColtAutos.com*:

"Pony Pocket Lite - caliber: 380, serial number #nr04895, Price: $650.00, Description: Colt, semi auto pistol, model-pony pocket lite, 380 acp aluminum frame, stainless steel slide, 6rd mag, absolutely pristine, $650. Plus $20 S&H."

ALL AMERICAN MODEL 2000

Actually introduced in 1992, the Model 2000 is a departure for Colt from its traditional service style semi-automatic pistols. Chambered for the 9mm, the Model 2000 is a double-action-only pistol with a 4.5 inch barrel and a choice between a lightweight polymer frame or heavier, recoil-absorbing aluminum alloy frame. The polymer frame model weighs 29 oz. while the aluminum alloy frame weighs 33 oz. Grips are black composition and sights are the white dot style. It was dropped from the Colt line in 1994.

This pistol, built from 1991 to 1994, actually represented a major change of direction for Colt, which abandoned John Browning's well-tested dropping barrel and adopting instead a design by C. Reed Knight and

Eugene Stoner that used a rotating barrel to lock the breech. The frame of the pistol was polymer while the barrel and slide were steel. The barrel had lugs at the breech end, which locked into recesses in the slide. There was also a bottom lug on the barrel, which engaged with a helical cam track in a "cam block" on the frame. The rear end of the slide acted as the breechblock and carried a self-cocking firing mechanism. The trigger was connected to the sear, both being fitted with roller bearings to reduce friction, and a magazine carrying 15 rounds of 9mm Parabellum fit into the butt. There were no manual safety devices, and the only external lever was the slide stop. A notable feature was that this was entirely a self-cocking (or double action only) weapon.

Offered with polymer or aluminum-alloy frame, the pistol was loaded in the usual manner. On pulling the trigger, the sear engaged with the striker and forced it back against a spring. Towards the end of the trigger movement, a cam and roller caused the end of the sear to drop and release the striker, which was driven forward by the spring to fire the cartridge in the chamber.

The recoil force drives the barrel and slide back, locked together by the barrel lugs engaging in the slide recesses. During this movement, the bottom lug on the barrel was drawn through the helical cam path in the frame, rotating the barrel through 30 degrees and so freeing the barrel lugs from the slide. The barrel stopped and the slide continued rearward, extracting the empty case and loading the recoil spring beneath the barrel. On the return stroke, a round was chambered and the barrel was then rotated back into the locked position. When the trigger was released, the sear automatically re-engaged with the striker, ready for the next shot.

The axial movement of the barrel produced very good accuracy. The roller bearings in the trigger mechanism produced a very smooth double-action pull comparable to the best type of revolver. But for all its apparent virtues, it proved to be one of the most embarrassing failures in the company's history. It met with very little enthusiasm, as there were stories of poor quality control and suggestions that the 9mm Parabellum would never be a popular caliber in the U.S. Sales were poor, and the company was losing money on the design. By 1994, production ceased.

NIB	EXC.	V.G.	GOOD	FAIR	POOR
450	400	350	300	250	200

NOTE: The following advertisement appeared on ColtAutos.com during the Spring of 2007:

"All American - Caliber: 9 mm, serial number #pf10847, Price: $550, Description: gun is in original case with paper work, one of the first built, was prototype made for testing purposes with two clips."

.380 SERIES 80 GOVERNMENT MODEL

This is a single-action, blowback-operated semi-automatic pistol chambered for the .380 ACP cartridge. It has a 3.25-inch barrel and a seven round magazine. The sights are fixed. It is available either blued, nickel plated, or stainless steel. It has synthetic grips and was introduced in 1985. For nickel finish add 10 percent; for stainless steel add 10 percent.

NIB	EXC.	V.G.	GOOD	FAIR	POOR
350	300	250	200	175	125

NOTE: The following advertisement appeared on GunsAmerica.com in the Spring of 2007:

"Colt Government .380 2nd Edition 1984 Pair Engraved: cased, unfired with gold engraving. Only 1,000 made. $2,450."

COLT CZ40 (AKA COLT Z40)

Introduced in 1998, this double-action .40 S&W pistol was built for Colt by manufacturer CZ (Ceska Zbrojovka) in the Czech Republic. The CZ40 designation was later used by CZ for a pistol virtually identical to the Colt/CZ pistol; some collectors have taken to calling the Colt/CZ model the Colt Z40 to avoid confusion. It is fitted with a 4-inch barrel and has black polymer grips. The frame is alloy with a carbon steel slide with blue finish. The magazine capacity is ten rounds. Weight is approximately 34 oz. Supposedly only 800 units were manufactured before the Colt/CZ partnership went kablooey.

NIB	EXC.	V.G.	GOOD	FAIR	POOR
750	600	-	-	-	-

THE COLT WOODSMAN: THREE VERSIONS
BY BOB RAYBURN

The original Colt .22 Target Model was designed by John Moses Browning and improved by engineers at Colt Firearms prior to the start of production in 1915. Major design updates were made in 1947 and again in 1955. Those three sets of designs constitute what collectors call the three series of Woodsman pistols. The First Series refers to all those built on the frame used prior to and during World War II. The Second Series includes all versions built on the second frame design from 1947 until 1955. Third Series Woodsman means the third frame design as used from 1955 to the end of production in 1977.

Each of the three series had a Target Model, a Sport Model and a Match Target Model. All models are very similar: the Sport Model, for example, is merely the Target Model with a short barrel and, in some cases, different sights or grips. The Match Target is nearly the same as the Sport or Target Model, but with a heavier, slab sided barrel, a squared-off frame at the front of the receiver to mate with the heavy barrel, and improved sights. In the post-war years only, there were also three quite similar economy models: the Challenger, the Huntsman and, finally, the Targetsman. The actions of the economy models are identical to the higher end models of the same period internally; they lack only some of the exterior refinements.

Curiously, these guns were not assembled in strict numerical sequence as one would ordinarily expect. Furthermore, even when changes were made, old parts were used up at the same time new parts were being introduced. As a result, there is no hard and fast serial number dividing line for any particular feature, and serial number overlaps of several thousand are all too common.

All models of the Woodsman line, in all three series, are discussed here, but there are numerous variations in detail that are primarily of interest to highly specialized collectors. For more details see Bob Rayburn's *Colt Woodsman Pocket Guide*, a 96-page pocket-sized guide to the Colt Woodsman line, available for $10 (including shipping) from Bob Rayburn [P.O. Box 97104W, Tacoma, WA 98497] on line at *www.colt22.com* or *www.coltwoodsman.com*.

The values listed here are for the pistol only, without extras, for guns in the middle of each condition range. These are guidelines to the prevailing retail values for the collector or shooter who is buying it as the end user, not what one might expect to receive from a gun dealer who is buying it to resell. Furthermore, within the Excellent and Very Good condition categories, there is a considerable spread in value, especially for the older and more collectible versions. Excellent, for example, means 98 percent or more original blue, but a very nice pre-Woodsman with 100 percent of the original blue would likely be worth twice as much to a serious collector as one with only 98 percent. At the other end of the condition scale, in the Fair and Poor categories, the individual values of component parts become

significant, and effectively set a floor value. A Poor condition, rusty, pitted pre-Woodsman or First Series Match Target would still have good value if it included the original magazine and grips in nice condition, for example.

In addition, there are sometimes rare variations within the broad categories that can significantly enhance the value. Include the original crisp condition box, instructions and tools, and the value goes up more, especially for high condition early guns. On the other hand, rust, pitting (even very minor), re-bluing, or other non-factory modifications will significantly reduce the values from those listed in the Very Good category or better.

NOTE: Major Robert Rayburn, USAF retired, supplied notes on the military versions of the Colt Woodsman. Colt Woodsman pistols with military markings are relatively rare. The total number used by the U.S. military was quite small, and many of those never received any government markings. Often the only way to determine a military connection is by requesting a historical letter by serial number from Colt Firearms.

FIRST SERIES WOODSMAN

In 1915 the intended market for John M. Browning's pistol was the dedicated target shooter, so there was only one model: the Colt .22 LR Automatic Target Pistol. That model, however, proved to be very popular not only with target shooters, but also with hunters, trappers, campers and other outdoorsmen … and women. The management at Colt noticed their sales figures, of course, and decided to give the pistol a new name that more closely reflected its widespread use. "The Woodsman" was the name chosen, and that roll mark was added to the side of the receiver in 1927, at approximately serial number #54000.

To further satisfy the broader market, Colt introduced a Sport Model in 1933, and the Match Target Model in 1938. The compact and beautifully balanced Sport Model was a near perfect "kit gun" for the outdoorsman, and the Match Target was designed for the special needs of serious target shooters.

Approximately 54,000 pre-Woodsman (all with 6.63-inch barrels) and a combined total of approximately 110,000 Woodsman marked Sport and Target Models were produced in the first series. The Sport Model and Target Model were serial numbered together after the Sport Model was added to the line in 1933, so it is not

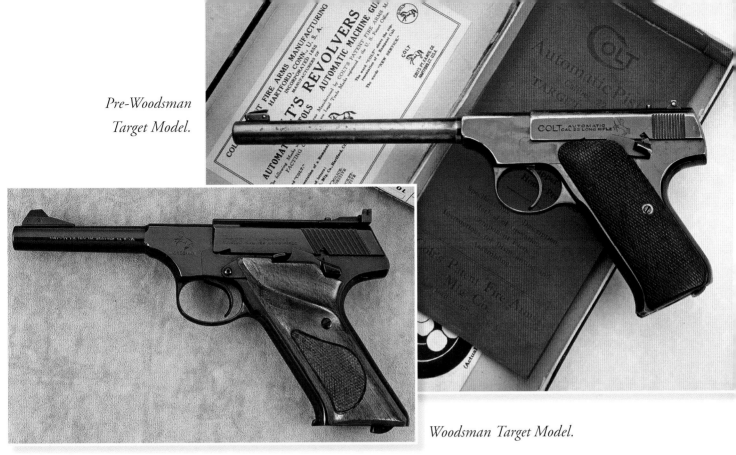

Pre-Woodsman Target Model.

Woodsman Target Model.

possible to easily determine how many of each were manufactured. It is safe to say that the Target Model far outnumbered the Sport Model.

During the war years of 1942 to 1945 the Match Target was the only Woodsman model built, and virtually the entire production was for the U.S. military.

PRE-WOODSMAN

This model was made for a dozen years, from 1915 to 1927. It has a 10-round magazine capacity, blue finish, checkered walnut grips and 6.63 inch barrel. It was designed for .22 LR standard velocity ammunition. The rear sight is adjustable for windage, the front sight for elevation. Up to approximately serial number #31000 the barrel was a very thin, so-called "pencil barrel." The barrel weight and diameter were increased slightly in 1922 to what collectors now call the "medium weight barrel." There were also numerous small changes in the grips, magazines, and markings over the years. Approximately 54,000 were made in all variations.

EXC.	V.G.	GOOD	FAIR	POOR
1,400	900	400	250	200

WOODSMAN TARGET

Initially this was exactly the same as the later pre-Woodsman, with the exception of "The Woodsman" marking on the side of the receiver. Later there were small changes in the sights, trigger and markings. In

1934 the barrel profile was again modified to a larger diameter, heavier barrel. This third and final pre-World War II barrel profile lacked the fillet, or step down, that was present on the earlier pencil and medium barrels, and is therefore commonly referred to as the "straight taper" barrel.

A significant modification occurred in 1932 when a new, heat treated mainspring housing and stiffer recoil spring were phased in to allow the use of the increasingly popular high velocity .22 LR ammunition. While this change has been widely reported to have taken place at serial number #83790, it was actually phased in over a period of time and a range of serial numbers, spanning at least #81000 to #86000, within which range both standard and high speed versions can be found. Fortunately, Colt changed the marking on the back of the mainspring housing to allow visual differentiation. Colt also sold a conversion kit to modify the older guns for use with high velocity ammunition. The kit consisted of a new style mainspring housing, a stiffer recoil spring and a coil type magazine spring for use in the very early guns that had a Z-type magazine spring.

EXC.	V.G.	GOOD	FAIR	POOR
1,100	750	400	250	200

NOTE: The following advertisement appeared on *ColtAutos.com* during the Spring of 2007:

"Colt Woodsman - Caliber: .22, serial number

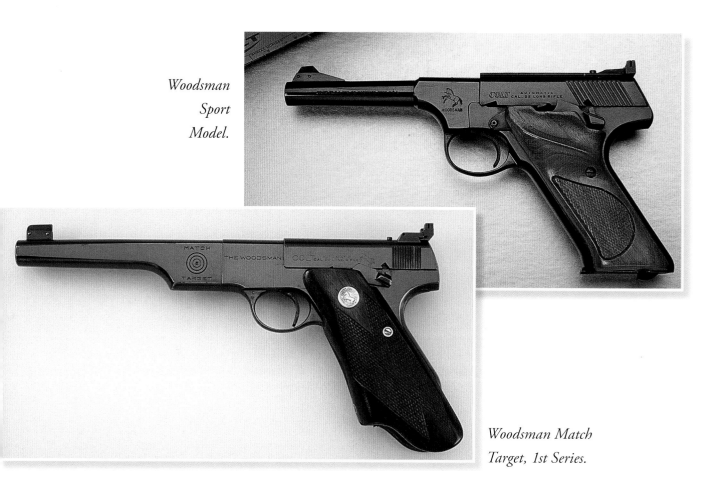

Woodsman Sport Model.

Woodsman Match Target, 1st Series.

#58094, Price: $800. Description: Wood-checked grip. Barrel reads "Colt's PT FA MFG CO HARTFORD, CT U.S.A." over "PAT'D DEC.22, 1903, AUG 27, 1918, SEPT 3, 1918." Good bluing with some holster wear."

WOODSMAN SPORT

With the Woodsman proving to be increasingly popular with outdoorsmen of all types, Colt decided to market a Woodsman better suited for a "take along" gun for hiking, camping and perhaps even family outings. This was accomplished in 1933 by merely shortening the barrel from 6.63 to 4.5 inches, and announcing the new Sport Model. Other than barrel length, the only difference between the Target Model and the Sport Model was an adjustable front sight on the Target Model and a fixed front sight on the Sport Model. Later, a front sight adjustable for elevation would be an available option for the Sport Model. Colt called this arrangement "Target Sights," and indeed it was the same front sight used on the Target Model. A First Series Sport Model with an adjustable front sight will command a premium of approximately 25 percent over the values listed.

EXC.	V.G.	GOOD	FAIR	POOR
1,400	1,000	500	250	200

NOTE: The following advertisement was placed on *GunsAmerica.com* in the Spring of 2007:

"Woodsman 1st Model Sport .22, 4 inch barrel, 97+% in original black box with papers and tools. $1,550."

WOODSMAN MATCH TARGET

Colt introduced the Match Target Woodsman in 1938, with its own serial number series beginning at #MT1, and continuing until 1944 with serial number #MT16611. The new features included larger grips, a heavier barrel 6.63 inches in length and a rear sight fully adjustable for both windage and elevation. To signify its intended market a Bullseye Target icon was rollmarked onto the side of the barrel. That led to its nickname of "Bullseye Match Target." The elongated, one piece wrap-around walnut grips also picked up a nickname, due to their unusual shape. Unfortunately, the so-called "Elephant Ear" grips are somewhat fragile and often broken. Many of the serious target shooters of the day replaced them with custom grips with thumb rest and palm swell, and the original grips were set aside and eventually lost or discarded. For those reasons the original grips are often missing, and that severely affects the price that collectors will pay. Values listed assume original one-piece walnut wrap-around Elephant Ear grips with no cracks, repairs, or modifications, and a correct Match Target marked magazine. The values

Woodsman Match Target, 1st Series, with factory box.

listed for Fair and Poor condition are primarily salvage value, and reflect the high value of original Elephant Ear grips and Match Target marked magazines for spare parts. Approximately 11,000 were produced for the civilian market from 1938 to 1942.

EXC.	V.G.	GOOD	FAIR	POOR
3,000	1,600	750	650	550

WOODSMAN MATCH TARGET 1ST SERIES (CUSTOM): ENGRAVED, CUSTOMIZED WOODSMAN MATCH TARGET, 1ST SERIES.

NOTE: The following advertisement appeared in the Summer of 2006 on *ColtAutos.com*:

"Match Target - Caliber: .22, serial number MT2692, Price: $1,800. Description: Colt Match Target in very good condition have serial numbered sight in target and original box however the box is not in good shape."

MILITARY WOODSMAN MATCH TARGET

After the United States entered World War II at the end of 1941, civilian production at Colt was stopped and the total effort was devoted to the military. Slightly more than 4,000 First Series Match Target Woodsmans were delivered on U.S. Government contract from 1942 to 1944. Most of them, but not all, had serial numbers above #MT12000. With possible rare exceptions they all had U.S. Property or U.S. military markings, standard blue finish, 6.63 inch barrel, and extended length plastic stocks. These plastic stocks are sometimes

erroneously called Elephant Ear stocks. The military plastic stocks are still relatively easy to find, and are still relatively inexpensive. Since they will fit any First Series Colt Woodsman, these stocks are often used as replacement grips on non-military guns. Since the military guns had plastic grips, rather than the costly and desirable Elephant Ear grips, the salvage value in the Fair and Poor condition range is less than that for the civilian model.

EXC.	V.G.	GOOD	FAIR	POOR
3,200	1,800	850	550	350

SECOND SERIES WOODSMAN

After World War II Colt – and virtually all U.S. hard goods manufacturers – entered a lengthy period of clearing up government contracts and retooling for the civilian market. Consequently, the Woodsman pistol line was extensively revised and modernized.

Second series guns began appearing near the end of 1947, although no appreciable numbers were shipped until 1948. The Second Series Woodsman had essentially the same action and many of the same internals as the first series guns, but were larger and heavier, with a longer grip frame. New features included a magazine safety, automatic slide stop when the magazine was emptied, fully adjustable rear sight, heavier barrels and a six inch barrel length on the Target and Match Target Models, rather than 6.63 inch, as

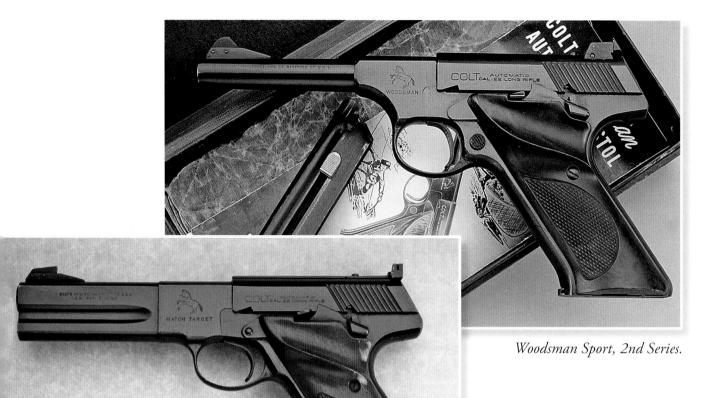

Woodsman Sport, 2nd Series.

Woodsman Match
Target, 2nd Series.

on the first series. Other new features included a push
button magazine release just aft of the trigger guard,
like that on the large frame Government Model semi-
automatics, a lanyard ring concealed in the butt, and
a provision for attaching a plastic grip adapter to the
backstrap, thereby accommodating different size hands.
Elevation adjustment was incorporated into the rear
sight of all Woodsman models, and the adjustable front
sight was replaced with a fixed blade. Serial numbers
were restarted at #1-S, and are intermixed for all three
models. Approximately 146,000 of the three models
were produced.

In 1950 Colt added the Challenger to the line of
second series pistols, the first of its economy models.
Internally the Challenger is nearly identical to the
Woodsman pistols of the same era, but it lacks most
of the external refinements introduced with the second
series. It has no magazine safety, automatic slide stop,
adjustable sights, push button magazine release, lanyard
ring or grip adapters. It was available with either a 6 or
4.5 inch barrel, and had its own serial number series

beginning with #1-C. Approximately 77,000 were
produced.

WOODSMAN TARGET (6-INCH BARREL)

EXC.	V.G.	GOOD	FAIR	POOR
750	550	300	250	150

WOODSMAN SPORT (4.5-INCH BARREL)

EXC.	V.G.	GOOD	FAIR	POOR
850	600	350	250	150

WOODSMAN MATCH TARGET
(6-INCH BARREL)

EXC.	V.G.	GOOD	FAIR	POOR
1,000	650	450	350	150

WOODSMAN MATCH TARGET
(4.5-INCH BARREL)
Introduced in 1950.

EXC.	V.G.	GOOD	FAIR	POOR
1,200	750	500	350	150

Colt Challenger.

CHALLENGER (6-INCH BARREL)

EXC.	V.G.	GOOD	FAIR	POOR
550	350	250	200	150

CHALLENGER (4.5-INCH BARREL)

EXC.	V.G.	GOOD	FAIR	POOR
550	350	250	200	150

U.S. MARINE CORPS MATCH TARGET

On December 10, 1947 Colt shipped 50 Woodsmans to the Depot Quartermaster, U.S. Marine Corps in Philadelphia. Another 50 were shipped to the same destination five days later. The 100 pistols in these two shipments were among the very first of the postwar, second series Woodsmans, and all were six inch Match Target models. Some bore single digit serial numbers, and all serial numbers in these shipments were under #400.

EXC.	V.G.	GOOD	FAIR	POOR

Too rare to price.

U.S. MARINE CORPS SPORT

In 1953 2,500 Woodsman Sport Models were sold to the U.S. Marine Corps. Half, 1,250, were shipped to the Marine Corps Supply Annex, Barstow, California on June 30th. The other 1,250 shipped to the Marine Corps Supply Depot at Camp Lejeune, North Carolina on July 17th. The serial numbers in both shipments were around #130000-S. This version is seldom found intact, although many have turned up that have been destroyed by the government prior to being sold as scrap metal.

EXC.	V.G.	GOOD	FAIR	POOR

Too rare to price.

U.S. AIR FORCE TARGET

In June, 1949 Colt contracted with the U.S. government to deliver 950 Woodsman Target pistols. These were to be the standard commercial model, modified with a fixed 0.10 inch front sight blade integral with the ramp base, and a semi-fixed rear sight. In addition the following components were to be omitted: slide stop, magazine safety, lanyard loop, grip adapters and screwdriver. Just 925 of these pistols were shipped to the Transportation Officer, Ogden Air Material Area, Ogden, Utah. In those cold war days the USAF was flying nuclear armed bombers over the arctic regions to provide a response should an attack come from the USSR, the Union of Soviet Socialist Republics. Colt's packing list indicates that the pistols were for use in Arctic Survival Kits. The other 25 pistols in the contract were sent to the Springfield Ordnance Depot. Serial numbers of all 950 pistols were in the #64000-S to #65000-S range. Many of these guns were later declared surplus and sold to U.S. citizens via the DCM program. They had no military markings of any type. Almost all of these pistols are in near new condition. For pistols in DCM box with papers in excellent condition add 25 percent.

EXC.	V.G.	GOOD	FAIR	POOR
1900	1500	-	-	-

U.S. COAST GUARD MATCH TARGET

There were at least three post-World War II Woodsman shipments to the U.S. Coast Guard: 25 pistols on June 23, 1955, 30 on December 21, 1955 and 50 on February 5, 1958. All were Match Target models with 6-inch barrels.

EXC.	V.G.	GOOD	FAIR	POOR

Too rare to price.

Woodsman Match Target, 3rd Series.

THIRD SERIES WOODSMAN

In 1955 Colt once again redesigned the Woodsman line. The most obvious change was in the location of the magazine release, which was returned to the heel of the butt, just as on first series guns. Other changes were made over time in the markings, grips, sights and trigger. The Sport, Target and Match Target models continued. The Challenger was replaced by the very similar Huntsman, with either a 4.5- or 6-inch barrel.

In 1959 the Targetsman was added to the line. The Targetsman differs from the Huntsman only in having an adjustable rear sight and a thumbrest on the left grip panel, and was available with a six inch barrel only. All Third Series models had black plastic grips until 1960, and checkered walnut grips thereafter. The Huntsman has no thumb rest on the grips. All other Third Series models have a thumb rest on the left grip panel.

It is difficult or perhaps impossible to determine how many of each model were produced in the third series, due to a very complex serial numbering scheme. Approximately 1,000 Third Series Sport, Target and Match Target Models were numbered at the end of the second series serial number range, from #146138-S to #147138-S. Numbers were then restarted at #160001-S, so there are no post-WWII Woodsmans with numbers in the #148xxx-S to #159xxx-S range. The Challenger serial numbers, meantime, reached approximately #77143-C prior to the Challenger being replaced by the Huntsman (note the C suffix, for Challenger). The Huntsman initially continued in the Challenger serial number series, although numbers skipped forward to #90000-C before restarting. The Targetsman, when added to the line early in 1959, joined the Huntsman in

using the -C suffix serial numbers, which were by then up to #129300-C.

Then, in 1969, when Woodsman serial numbers had reached #241811-S and the -C numbers had reached #194040-C, Colt decided to integrate the serial numbers for all versions of the Woodsman, Huntsman and Targetsman and restart numbering again. This time they started with #001001S. That worked fine until numbers reached #099999S, and rolled over to #100000S. Numbers used in 1951 to 1952 were then being inadvertently duplicated, with one small exception: the earlier guns had a -S suffix while the later ones had only an S (no hyphen before the S). Apparently that was not enough of a distinction to satisfy federal regulations, so by the time Colt discovered the error after approximately 1,330 had already been numbered, the existing "double headers" were hand stamped with an S prefix, in addition to the S suffix, in order to salvage them. Serial numbers were then restarted yet again, this time at #300000S, and continued to #317736S, when production ended.

WOODSMAN TARGET (6-INCH BARREL)
EXC.	V.G.	GOOD	FAIR	POOR
700	450	300	250	150

WOODSMAN SPORT (4.5-INCH BARREL)
EXC.	V.G.	GOOD	FAIR	POOR
800	500	300	250	150

WOODSMAN MATCH TARGET (6-INCH BARREL)
EXC.	V.G.	GOOD	FAIR	POOR
900	650	450	350	150

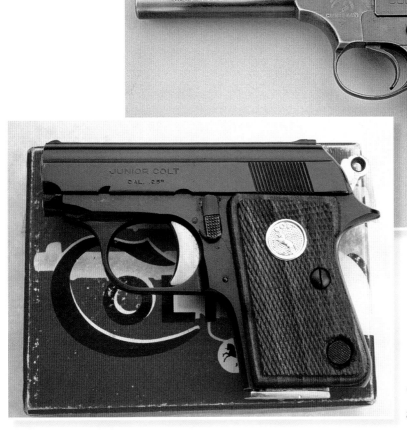

Colt Huntsman.

*Colt Junior as
made by Astra.*

WOODSMAN MATCH TARGET (4.5-INCH BARREL)

Added to the line in 1950.

EXC.	V.G.	GOOD	FAIR	POOR
1,000	750	500	350	150

NOTE: The following advertisement appeared in the Spring of 2007 on *ColtAutos.com*:

"COLT WOODSMAN 3rd SERIES 4.5 inch MATCH TARGET Serial number #309405-S Description: .45 ACP caliber. Absolutely as new in box. Price $1,295."

HUNTSMAN (4.5- OR 6-INCH BARREL)

EXC.	V.G.	GOOD	FAIR	POOR
500	350	250	200	150

TARGETSMAN (6- OR THE RARE 4.5-INCH BARREL)

EXC.	V.G.	GOOD	FAIR	POOR
550	400	250	200	150

COLT JUNIOR POCKET MODEL

This diminutive unit is only 4.5 inches long overall and weighs 12 oz. Colt did not manufacture this pistol, but rather had it made for them by Astra in Spain. The pistol was introduced in 1958 chambered for .25 ACP. One year later a .22 Short version appeared. Both had external hammers and detachable six-round magazines. The passage of the 1968 Gun Control Act made import of a weapon of this size illegal, so Colt discontinued its relationship with Astra. The pistol was re-introduced in 1970 as an American-made product and was produced for two more years. Production ceased in 1972. Astra also made this pistol and called it the Cub. For .22 Short add 25 percent.

NIB	EXC.	V.G.	GOOD	FAIR	POOR
300	250	200	175	125	75

NOTE: The following advertisement appeared in the Spring of 2007 on *GunsAmerica.com*:

"COLT JUNIOR .25 ACP, here is a CONSECUTIVE NUMBERED PAIR of 1973 production Juniors, they are NIB and appear to have never been fired, retaining 99+% of the orig. blue, xlnt checkered walnut stocks with Rampant Colt medallions, orig. nickel finish magazines, orig. lift lid wood-grain boxes with labels, includes instruction sheet and warranty card, s/n OD 10644x & OD 10644x. Price $1,295."

Colt Cadet, also known as Colt .22 Auto.

Colt .22 Target.

Colt 1911A1 built by Remington-Rand.

CADET .22 (AKA COLT .22 AUTO)

Introduced in 1994 this .22 caliber semi-automatic pistol, the "new Woodsman," is offered with a 4.5-inch bull barrel topped by a ventilated rib., stainless steel finish and polymer grips. Sights are fixed and the magazine capacity is 11 rounds. The overall length is 8.63 inches and the weight is approximately 33 oz. The gun was renamed "Colt .22 Auto" in 1995.

NIB	EXC.	V.G.	GOOD	FAIR	POOR
250	200	165	125	75	50

COLT .22 TARGET

Introduced in 1995 this model features a 6-inch bull barrel with removable front sight and adjustable rear sight. Black composite monogrip stock and stainless steel finish. The weight is a hefty 40.5 oz.

NIB	EXC.	V.G.	GOOD	FAIR	POOR
325	275	225	150	100	75

U.S. MILITARY SERIES AUTOMATIC PISTOLS

COLT 1911 MANUFACTURE

These 1911 series pistols are marked "MODEL OF 1911 U.S. ARMY" or "MODEL OF 1911 U.S. NAVY" on the right slide, and "UNITED STATES PROPERTY" on the left front frame ...until about serial number #510000. Then, they are marked above the trigger, right. Serial numbers are located on the right front frame until serial number #7500, then above the trigger, right. These pistols normally have a high polish and fire blue small parts until serial number #2400, at which time the finish changed to non-reflective dull blue. Double diamond grips are used throughout. Look for the dimpled magazine catch from serial numbers #1 to #3189, the dimpled/slotted magazine catch from serial number #3190 to about #6500, and slotted magazine catch thereafter.

Lanyard loop magazine (three types) predominates until about serial number #127000. Add five percent if

Type I (Step Base) magazine.

Type 1: stepped base until about serial number #4500,

Type 2: keyhole base until about serial number #35000 and

Type 3: plain base.

Thereafter, a two tone non-looped magazine was used through the end of 1911 model production.

NOTE: Because there were many variations in the early pistols, virtually all of which affect their rarity and value, several valuation groups follow. For condition 99-100 percent add 20 to 70 percent.

BELOW SERIAL NUMBER #101

Large "UNITED STATES PROPERTY" and other unique features. High polish mirror finish with brilliant fire blue parts. Unmarked fully blued barrel.

EXC.	V.G.	GOOD	FAIR	POOR
37,500	20,000	15,000	10,000	6,000

THREE DIGIT "MODEL OF 1911 U.S. ARMY" MARKED SLIDE, SERIAL NUMBERS #100 THROUGH #500

High polish mirror finish with brilliant fire blue parts. Unmarked fully blued barrel until SN 400. An "H" (with serifs) marked on back of the barrel hood (sometimes called "barrel overhang" or "barrel extension") until #500.

EXC.	V.G.	GOOD	FAIR	POOR
16,500	11,000	6,500	4,000	3,000

THREE DIGIT "MODEL OF 1911 U.S. NAVY" MARKED SLIDE, SERIAL NUMBERS #501 THROUGH #1000

This fully blued pistol is extremely rare in its original condition. High polish mirror finish with brilliant fire blue parts. An "H" (with serifs) marked on back of the barrel hood (sometimes called "barrel overhang" or "barrel extension"). Some seemingly original early Navy pistols have been observed with the later dull finish. Note that below serial number #2400, pistols with the later fine finish are likely to have been re-finished. Buyers should be very wary. However, most (or all) of the small number of observed Navy pistols in this first batch are reported to have the later dull (fine) finish and do not have fire blue parts. The later dull finish in this range where mirror and fire blue is expected, equal to Poor condition.

EXC.	V.G.	GOOD	FAIR	POOR
20,000	15,000	10,000	6,000	4,500

FOUR DIGIT "MODEL OF 1911 U.S. ARMY" MARKED SLIDE WITH FIRE BLUE PARTS

Very rare in original condition. Serial numbers #1001 to #1500 and #2001 to #2400 only. High polish mirror finish with brilliant fire blue parts. Barrel is "H" marked (with serifs) on the rear of the barrel hood. The only documented original early pistols below #2400 with the later dull (fine) finish are a very small group of test pistols in the #1201 to about #1600 range. Pistols below #2400 with the later "fine" finish are likely to have been re-finished. Buyers should be exceptionally wary. Later dull finish in this range less 65 percent. Unless documented test pistol less 25 percent.

EXC.	V.G.	GOOD	FAIR	POOR
12,000	8,000	5,000	3,000	2,000

FOUR DIGIT "MODEL OF 1911 U.S. ARMY" MARKED SLIDE WITHOUT FIRE BLUE PARTS

Five groups #2401 to #2500, #3801 to #4500, #5501 to #6500, #7501 to #8500, and #9501 to #9999. Dull (fine), no fire blue small parts. An "H" with serifs was marked on the rear of the barrel hood until #7500. After #7500 no serifs.

EXC.	V.G.	GOOD	FAIR	POOR
6,000	4,550	3,400	2,450	1,675

1913 PRODUCTION U.S. MARINE CORPS SERIAL NUMBERS #3501 TO #3800

Rarely seen and, when such a gun is discovered at a gun show or in an old garage, is often well used.

EXC.	V.G.	GOOD	FAIR	POOR
12,000	8,000	6,000	3,500	3,000

FOUR DIGIT "MODEL OF 1911 U.S. NAVY" MARKED SLIDE WITH FIRE BLUE PARTS

Extremely rare in original condition. Fire blue parts and high polish from SN 1501 to SN 2000 only. Barrel is fully blued and H with serifs marked on rear of hood. The only documented original pistols (below SN 2400) with the later dull ("fine") finish are a very small group of test pistols in the serial number #1201 to about #1600 range. However most or all of the reported pistols of this second NAVY batch (serial number #1501 to #2000) have the high polish and fire blue parts. Below #2400, pistols with the later dull ("fine") finish are likely to have been re-finished. Buyers should be exceptionally wary. Later dull finish in this range where mirror and fire blue are expected equal to Poor condition. Unless documented test pistol then less 25 percent.

EXC.	V.G.	GOOD	FAIR	POOR
21,000	15,000	8,000	5,000	3,500

Model 1911 US Army with marked slide.

Five-digit Model of 1911 US Navy with marked slide.

FOUR DIGIT "MODEL OF 1911 U.S. NAVY" MARKED SLIDE WITHOUT FIRE BLUE PARTS

Barrel is fully blued and "H" marked on rear of hood. The "H" has serifs until #7500, then no serifs. This pistol was issued in groups #2501 to #3500, #4501 to #5500, #6501 to #7500 and #8501 to #9500. All pistols should have the later dull finish.

EXC.	V.G.	GOOD	FAIR	POOR
10,200	5,700	3,900	2,325	1,675

FIVE DIGIT "MODEL OF 1911 U.S. ARMY" MARKED SLIDE

No fire blue, and dull finish. Circled horse on left rear of slide until about serial number #20000. An "H" (without serifs) is marked on rear of barrel hood until somewhere below about serial number #24xxx. A "P" (without serifs) is marked on the rear of barrel hood and the "H" is visible through the ejection port from about #24200 to about #24900. "H"-"P" (horizontal) visible through eject port from #24900 to about #110,000. (There is considerable uncertainty as to the barrel marking in the #19xxx to #242xx range as too few original pistols have been examined.) For an "H" on the back of the hood add 15 percent. For a "P" on the back of the hood add 30 percent.

EXC.	V.G.	GOOD	FAIR	POOR
4,500	3,500	2,500	2,000	1,150

1913 PRODUCTION SERIAL NUMBERS #36401 TO #37650 USMC SHIPMENT

Slide marked "MODEL OF 1911 U.S. ARMY" on ALL ORIGINAL USMC shipped pistols. (Any "USMC" marked 1911 pistol should be considered a FAKE!) These pistols are rarely seen and often well used when they are found. Extremely rare in high condition.

EXC.	V.G.	GOOD	FAIR	POOR
6,100	4,700	3,350	2,300	1,600

FIVE DIGIT "MODEL OF 1911 U.S. NAVY" MARKED SLIDE

Four serial numbered groups: #10501 to #11500, #12501 to #13500, #38001 to #44000 and #96001 to #97537.

EXC.	V.G.	GOOD	FAIR	POOR
6,800	5,300	3,300	2,400	1,500

SIX DIGIT "MODEL OF 1911 U.S. NAVY" MARKED SLIDE WITH SERIAL NUMBERS #109501 TO #110000

These 500 Navy-marked pistols were shipped to the Brooklyn Navy Yard for the Naval Militia and are more often found than most other batches – curious because of their low overall number. These are the only Navy-marked pistols to bear the "JMG" cartouche.

EXC.	V.G.	GOOD	FAIR	POOR
7,000	4,800	3,000	2,400	1,550

Model 1911 made by
Springfield Armory.

1911 Government
Model made by Colt.

SPRINGFIELD ARMORY "MODEL OF 1911 U.S. ARMY"

Dull, rust blued finish. All external parts are identifiable as Springfield manufactured by the shape. Most pistols have a combination of "S" marked and unmarked parts. Made in these serial numbered groups: #72571 to #83855, #102597 to #107596 and #113497 to #120566. Models in the #72571 to #75000 serial number range have a short stubby hammer: add 15 percent.

EXC.	V.G.	GOOD	FAIR	POOR
7,250	5,000	3,500	2,500	1,500

REMINGTON UMC "MODEL OF 1911 U.S. ARMY"

Dull finish, all parts must be Remington-made. Most examples appear to have a significantly deteriorated finish, probably due to poor surface preparation. EEC accepted and marked. Mainspring housing "E" marked, barrels "P" marked. Most pistols show a thinning finish as well as flaking, but with little apparent wear. These pistols are numbered in their own block from #1 to #21676 in large gothic letters. Almost never seen in extremely good condition. Beware of re-finished pistols masquerading as original. Very late pistols show a one-line right side marking, add 15 percent.

EXC.	V.G.	GOOD	FAIR	POOR
6,200	4,000	3,000	2,100	1,600

1915-1918 SPRINGFIELD SUSPENDED SERIAL NUMBERS REASSIGNED TO COLT

These receivers were apparently shipped as replacement parts (incomplete pistols) because they lack an Ordnance acceptance mark. Springfield's unused assigned serial numbers (#128617 to #133186) were re-assigned to Colt when Springfield ceased production of 1911 pistols. These receivers were apparently numbered and used as needed until late 1917 when a new series of serial numbers was assigned (#210387 through #215386) These receivers are found with almost every post-1911 slide.

EXC.	V.G.	GOOD	FAIR	POOR
4,600	3,400	2,500	1,700	1,200

SIX DIGIT COLT 1915 TO 1918 "MODEL OF 1911 U.S. ARMY" MARKED SLIDE

A dull blue finish. Vertically oriented "P H" or "H P" marked on barrel, visible through the eject port from about serial number #110000 to #425000. Slides marked "MODEL OF 1911 U.S. ARMY" on all original USMC shipped pistols. (Any "USMC" marked 1911 pistol should be considered a FAKE.)

EXC.	V.G.	GOOD	FAIR	POOR
3,800	2,500	1,800	1,500	1,100

NOTE: The following advertisement appeared in the Spring of 2007 on *ColtAutos.com*:

"*Colt 1911 Government Issue circa 1918 - Caliber: .45,*

Model 1911 made by North American Arms of Montreal, Quebec.

Modelo Argentino 1927.

serial number #382509, Price: $3,500 obo, Description: This is a very nice weapon tracing back to a 1918 manufacture date. It is a 'Model 1911 of U.S. Army.' It is an original weapon with some holster wear on the finish. Included is a U.S. flap holster and a clip, pictures available."

The following categories are listed relative to the previously-listed "Six Digit" serial numbered Colt 1915 to 1918 "MODEL OF 1911 U.S. ARMY" marked slide:

1916 PRODUCTION

- with "S" marked frame, slide and barrel add 60 percent
- with partial "S" marked frame, slide or barrel add 35 percent
- with normally marked frame, slide, and barrel add 20 percent
- #151187 to #151986 USMC shipment add 45 percent (Often well used.)

1917 PRODUCTION

- #185801 to #186200 USMC shipment add 45 percent (Often well used.)
- #209587 to #210386 USMC shipment add 45 percent (Often well used.)
- #210387 to #215386 replacement frames add 45 percent (Rarely seen.)

- #215387 to #216186 USMC shipment add 45 percent (Rarely seen.)
- #216187 to #216586 ARMY transferred from USMC add 15 percent (Rarely seen.)
- #216587 to #217386 USMC shipment add 45 percent (Rarely seen.)
- #223953 to #223990 NAVY (ARMY marked) add 15 percent
- #232001 to #233600 NAVY (ARMY marked) add 15 percent

1918 TO 1919 PRODUCTION WITH EAGLE OVER NUMBER ACCEPTANCE MARK

Often called the "Black Army" because the coarse wartime finish appeared almost black. The black finish started about serial number #375000. No inspector's cartouche from about #302000 to end of 1911 production at about #625000. Barrel marked with letters "H" and "P" through about #425000. "HP" with a common leg, horizontal orientation visible through ejection port from about #425000 to end of 1911 production. (If flaking present deduct 25 percent, watch out for re-blue if no flaking present.)

EXC.	V.G.	GOOD	FAIR	POOR
3,900	2,500	1,700	1,250	900

NORTH AMERICAN ARMS OF MONTREAL QB "1911"

Made for the U.S. but none were actually delivered to the Army. Fewer than 100 pistols assembled from parts. Very rarely seen. Numbered on trigger under left grip and on left rear slide. Similar to five digit Colt "ARMY" marked slide, but add 500 percent. So few of these pistols have been sold publicly that these prices are intended as a rough guide only.

EXC.	V.G.	GOOD	FAIR	POOR
26,000	20,000	16,000	10,000	7,300

FOUR DIGIT X NUMBERED RE-WORK

These pistols were renumbered when their original serial numbers were either defaced, obliterated or became too light to read during rebuilding or re-finishing. The four digit X prefix serial numbers (#X1000 through #X4385) were assigned after World War I (in 1924) and were used by Springfield through 1953. All are considered "Arsenal Re-finished" and even this "official" re-work dramatically reduces their collector value.

EXC.	V.G.	GOOD	FAIR	POOR
1,350	1,100	800	750	600

"MILITARY TO COMMERCIAL CONVERSIONS"

We have mentioned this elsewhere, but it bears repeating here. Many 1911 military pistols that were taken home by U.S. GIs were subsequently returned to the Colt factory by their owners for repair or re-finishing. If the repair included a new barrel, the pistol would have been proof fired and a normal verified proof mark affixed to the trigger guard bow in the normal commercial practice. If the pistol was re-finished between 1920 and 1942, the slide would probably be numbered to the frame again in the normal commercial practice. Slides were numbered on the bottom disconnector rail during part of 1920, and after that they were numbered under the firing pin stop plate. These pistols are really a re-manufactured Colt pistol of limited production and should be valued at least that of a contemporary 1911A1 commercial pistol. (Pistols without VP or numbered slide usually cannot be authenticated, deduct 60 percent). Very seldom seen.

EXC.	V.G.	GOOD	FAIR	POOR
2,100	1,500	1,200	950	750

1911 COLT "NRA" MARKED PISTOL

An unknown number of shipped Colt 1911 pistols were taken from stores and sold to NRA members. These pistols ranged from about serial number #70000 to the high #150000 range. Pistols were marked N.R.A. under the serial number or at the right front of the frame. The number is unknown, perhaps 300. Both crude and clever fakes abound. So few of these rare pistols have been sold publicly that these prices are intended as a rough guide only.

EXC.	V.G.	GOOD	FAIR	POOR
6,600	4,200	2,700	1,800	1400

1911 SPRINGFIELD (NRA MARKED PISTOL)

An unknown number of shipped Colt 1911 pistols were taken from stores and sold to NRA members. These pistols ranged from about serial number #70000 to the high #129000 range. Pistols were marked N.R.A. under the serial or at the right front of the frame. The number of N.R.A. marked Springfields is unknown, but based on observed pistols, it is perhaps 600. Both crude and clever fakes abound. Note that at one time these NRA marked pistols sold for about twice what a normal Springfield sold for, but lately, the very few examples sold seem to have sold for about the same price as a normal Springfield. This trend may reflect the inability to document the originality of the NRA marking as well as the ease with which such a mark can be counterfeited.

EXC.	V.G.	GOOD	FAIR	POOR
7,250	6,100	3,600	2,500	1,500

COLT FOREIGN MILITARY CONTRACTS

These foreign contract pistols are included as military pistols despite their commercial serial numbers. These pistols were sold by Colt to foreign governments as military, police or other government agency sidearms. Many of these pistols have recently been imported into the USA, but only a few have been in collectible, original condition. Most have, at one time or another, been re-finished and sold at utility prices. Consequently the prices that the handful of original pistols sell for have been kept down by their poorer relations. These original-finish pistols, when found, may be some of the few remaining bargains out there. Pistols were shipped to Mexico, Philippines, Shanghai, Haiti and elsewhere, but specific prices for these variations are not practical because they are so seldom seen.

ARGENTINE ARMY MODELO 1927

Serial numbered #1 through #10000. Marked "EJERCITO ARGENTINO. Colts Cal.45 MOD.1927" on the right slide, and "Colts Pt. F.A. MFG. Co....etc."

on the left slide. VP marked under left stock. Serial numbered on top of slide, under mainspring housing. Most of these pistols have been re-blued and original finish pistols are very rare. Prices shown are for original pistols and the common re-blued pistols would be equal to the Fair/Poor categories, depending on appearance.

EXC.	V.G.	GOOD	FAIR	POOR
1,000	700	500	400	300

ARGENTINE ARMY "SIST.COLT CAL. 11.25MM MOD 1927"

Serial numbers extend to over #112000. Made in Argentina under Colt license. This is a high quality 1911A1 copy with parts that generally interchange with Colt's 1911A1s. Marked "SIST.COLT CAL.11.25mm MOD 1927" on the right slide, and "D.G.F.M.-(F.M.A.P.)." on the left slide. Serial numbered on top of slide, frame, and barrel. Many of these pistols have been re-blued, although original finish pistols are often seen. Prices shown are for original pistols and the more common re-blued pistols would be equal to the Fair/Poor categories, depending on appearance.

EXC.	V.G.	GOOD	FAIR	POOR
700	600	500	400	325

ARGENTINE NAVY, COAST GUARD, AIR FORCE, OR ARMY CONTRACT "GOVERNMENT MODEL"

Pistols serial numbered from about #C130000 to about #C190000. Marked "ARMADA NACIONAL," "MARINA ARGENTINA," "AERONAUTICA ARGENTINA" or "EJERCITY ARGENTINA" on the right slide, and "COLTS PT. F.A. MFG. CO.... etc." on the left slide. VP marked on left trigger guard bow. Serial numbered and marked as were normal commercial pistols. Most of these pistols have been re-blued and original finish pistols are seldom seen. Prices shown are for original pistols and the common re-blued pistols would be equal to the Fair/Poor categories, depending on appearance.

EXC.	V.G.	GOOD	FAIR	POOR
750	600	500	400	300

ARGENTINE NAVY, COAST GUARD, AIR FORCE OR ARMY PISTOLS

Serial numbered through about #112000. Marked "ARMADA NACIONAL," "MARINA ARGENTINA," "AERONAUTICA ARGENTINA" or "EJERCITY ARGENTINA" on the right slide, and "D.G.F.M.-(F.M.A.P.)." on the left slide. Most of the recent imports of these pistols have been re-blued

and collectable original finish pistols are seldom seen except when from older collections. Prices shown are for original pistols, and the common re-blued pistols would be equal to the Fair/Poor categories, depending on appearance.

EXC.	V.G.	GOOD	FAIR	POOR
550	450	350	270	225

ARGENTINE NAVY "GOVERNMENT MODEL" WITH SWARTZ SAFETY

Serial numbered from about #C199000 to about #C2010001. Marked "REPUBLICA ARGENTINA, ARMADA NACIONAL-1941" on the right slide, and "COLTS PT. F.A. MFG. CO....etc." on the left slide. VP marked on left trigger guard bow. Serial numbered and marked as were normal 1941 commercial pistols. Most or all of these pistols have the Swartz safeties. Most of these pistols were re-blued or Parkerized when imported, and original finish collectable pistols are very rare. Prices shown are for original pistols, and the common re-blued pistols would be equal to the Fair/Poor categories, depending on appearance.

Note that the very rare Swartz safeties (only a few thousand total were produced) in these pistols are under-appreciated by most collectors, and make this variation highly undervalued, especially for the few original finish pistols. The Swartz firing pin block safety can be observed by pulling the slide back all the way and looking at the top of the frame. A Swartz safety equipped 1911A1 pistol will have a second pin protruding up, next to the conventional disconnector pin. This second pin pushes a spring-loaded piston in the rear part of the slide that is visible when the slide is pulled back and the slide is viewed from underneath. This piston, in turn, blocks the firing pin when relaxed. A second Swartz safety (the Swartz Sear Safety) is usually built into pistols equipped with the Swartz firing pin block safety. The sear safety can sometimes be detected by the drag marks of the notched sear on the round portion of the hammer that the sear rides on. Pulling the hammer all the way back will expose these drag marks if they are visible. Presence of the drag marks however, does not insure that the Swartz modified sear safety parts are all present.

EXC.	V.G.	GOOD	FAIR	POOR
1,700	1,200	900	700	500

BRAZILIAN ARMY CONTRACT "GOVERNMENT MODEL"

Pistols serial numbered from about #C190000 to

about #C214000. Marked "EJERCITO BRAZILIA" on the right slide, and "COLTS PT. F.A. MFG. CO…. etc." on the left slide. VP marked on left trigger guard bow. Serial numbered and marked as were normal commercial pistols. Only a few of these complete pistols have made it to the USA, but many slides were sold as surplus parts when Brazil converted from .45 caliber to 9mm. Most or all of these slides have been re-blued and original finish pistols are very rarely seen. Prices shown are for original pistols, and the common re-blued pistols would be equal to the Poor category or below, depending on appearance. Separate slides would have the value of a high quality "after market" part.

EXC.	V.G.	GOOD	FAIR	POOR
1,500	1,100	900	700	500

COLT 1911A1 MANUFACTURE

TRANSITION MODEL OF 1924 (SERIAL NUMBERED #700001 TO #710000)

Some very early Transition pistols (#700004 and #700009) have been observed to have matching numbered slides. The number of pistols so numbered is not known, but if enough pistols surface, the serial number range may eventually be deduced. A pistol with a matching numbered slide will probably bring a premium. These were made in 1924. All were accepted by Walter T. Gordon and marked with the "G," which forms the outer circle as seen through about #7022000. A second type has an outer circle around the "G." Brushed blue finish, all 1911A1 features (arched mainspring housing, short checkered trigger, long tang on grip safety, trigger finger cutouts, full checkered walnut grips, etc.). However, they retained the "MODEL OF 1911 U.S. ARMY" slide marking. No verified proof or final inspector's mark on trigger guard bow, interlaced "H P" and "K" marked barrel, and serifed "H" over firing pin stop plate. (Add 20 to 30 percent for 99 to 100 percent finish.)

EXC.	V.G.	GOOD	FAIR	POOR
6,200	4,500	3,200	2,000	1,300

FIRST TRANSITION MODEL OF 1937 (SERIAL NUMBERED #710001 TO ABOUT #711001)

Numbered slide under firing pin stop plate. No "P" marking on frame or slide. Brushed blue finish, all 1911A1 features (arched mainspring housing, short checkered trigger, long tang on grip safety, trigger finger cutouts, full checkered walnut grips, etc.). However,

they retained the "MODEL OF 1911 U.S. ARMY" slide marking. Verified proof and final inspector's mark on trigger guard bow. "COLT .45 AUTO" marked magazine floor plate with flattened letters and "COLT .45 AUTO" marked barrel. Extremely rare. Pistols with mis-matched number (but still second type 1937 slide) deduct 40 percent. (Add 30 to 40 percent for 99 to 100 percent finish.) So few of these pistols have sold publicly that these prices are intended as a rough guide only.

EXC.	V.G.	GOOD	FAIR	POOR
8,000	6,500	5,000	4,000	2,200

SECOND TRANSITION MODEL OF 1937 (SERIAL NUMBERED #711001 TO ABOUT #712349)

Numbered slide under firing pin stop plate. "P" marking on frame and top of slide. Brushed blue finish, all 1911A1 features (arched mainspring housing, short checkered trigger, long tang on grip safety, trigger finger cutouts, full checkered walnut grips, etc.). However, they retained the "MODEL OF 1911 U.S. ARMY" slide marking. Verified proof and final inspector's mark on trigger guard bow. "COLT .45 AUTO" marked magazine floor plate with flattened letters and "COLT .45 AUTO" marked barrel. Extremely rare. Pistols with mis-matched number (but still second type 1937 slide) deduct 40 percent. (Add 30 to 40 percent for 99 to 100 percent finish.) So few of these rare pistols have sold publicly that these prices are intended as a rough guide only.

EXC.	V.G.	GOOD	FAIR	POOR
8,000	6,500	5,000	4,000	2,200

1911A1, 1938 PRODUCTION (SERIAL NUMBERED #712350 TO #713645)

Numbered slide under firing pin stop plate. "P" marking on frame and top of slide. No markings on right side of slide. Brushed blue finish, all 1911A1 features (arched mainspring housing, short checkered trigger, long tang on grip safety, trigger finger cutouts, full checkered walnut grips, etc.). Right side of receiver is marked "M1911A1 U.S. ARMY" forward of the slide stop pin, and "United States Property" behind the slide stop pin. Verified proof and final inspector's mark on trigger guard bow. Most are "H" marked on left side by magazine catch. "COLT .45 AUTO" marked magazine floor plate with flattened letters and "COLT .45 AUTO" marked barrel. Extremely rare. Pistols with mis-matched number (but still second type 1937 slide) deduct 40 percent. (Add 50 to 100 percent for

99 to 100 percent finish.) So few of these rare pistols have been sold publicly that these prices are intended as a rough guide only. All Military .45 cal. pistols after #710000 were officially M1911A1s, although they were first called Improved M1911.

EXC.	V.G.	GOOD	FAIR	POOR
20,000	15,000	10,000	6,000	4,500

1911A1, 1939 PRODUCTION (1939 NAVY: SERIAL NUMBERED #713646 TO #717281)

Numbered slide under firing pin stop plate. "P" marking on frame and top of slide. No markings on right side of slide. Brushed blue finish. Shortened hammer. Right side of receiver is marked "M1911A1 U.S. ARMY" forward of the slide stop pin, and "United States Property" behind the slide stop pin. Verified proof "VP" and final inspector's mark on triggerguard bow. Full checkered walnut grips. Most are "H" marked on left side by magazine catch. "COLT .45 AUTO" marked magazine floorplate with flattened letters, and "COLT .45 AUTO" marked barrel. Extremely rare. Pistols with mis-matched serial numbers (but still second type 1937 slide) deduct 25 percent. (Add 20 to 30 percent for 99 to 100 percent finish.)

EXC.	V.G.	GOOD	FAIR	POOR
5,000	3,500	2,500	2,000	1,400

1911A1, 1940 PRODUCTION (CSR: SERIAL NUMBERED #717282 TO #721977)

Look for the numbered slide under the firing pin stop plate. "P" marking on frame and top of slide. No markings on right side of slide. Brushed blue finish. Shortened hammer. Right side of frame is marked "M1911A1 U.S. ARMY" forward of the slide stop pin, and "United States Property" behind the slide stop pin. Verified proof "VP" and final inspector's mark on trigger guard bow. "CSR" (Charles S. Reed) marked on left side below slide stop. "COLT .45 AUTO" marked magazine floor plate with flattened letters, and "COLT .45 AUTO" marked barrel. Full checkered walnut grips but some pistols may have early brittle plastic grips. Extremely rare. Pistols with mis-matched number, but still second type 1937 slide, deduct 25 percent. Add 20 to 30 percent value for 99 to 100 percent finish.

EXC.	V.G.	GOOD	FAIR	POOR
5,100	3,500	2,500	1,800	1,350

1911A1, 1941 PRODUCTION (RS AND EARLY WB: SERIAL NUMBERED #721978 TO #756733)

Numbered slide under firing pin stop plate. "P" marking on frame and top of slide. No markings on right side of slide. Brushed blue finish through about serial number #736000. Parkerizing was used thereafter until the end of Colt production. Any Colt pistol after about #737000 with a blued finish is likely to be a FAKE. Shortened hammer. Right side of frame is marked "M1911A1 U.S. ARMY" forward of the slide stop pin, and "United States Property" behind the slide stop pin. Verified proof and final inspector's mark on trigger guard bow. "RS" (Robert Sears) marked on left side below slide stop starting at about #723000, ending about #750500. After about #750500, pistols were marked "WB" (Waldemar S. Broberg). "COLT .45 AUTO" marked magazine floorplate with flattened letters, and "COLT .45 AUTO" marked barrel. Early pistols may have wood grips, later pistols have hollow back (without ribs) plastic grips. Prices are for blued finish. Parkerized finish less 25 percent. Extremely rare. Pistols with mis-matched number (but still second type 1937 slide) deduct 20 percent. (Subtract 5 percent to 10 percent for British proofs, most collectors prefer virgin pistols. Add 20 to 50 percent for 99 to 100 percent finish.)

EXC.	V.G.	GOOD	FAIR	POOR
4,250	2,950	2,000	1,500	1,200

MODEL OF 1911A1, 1942 PRODUCTION (WB: SERIAL NUMBERED #756733 TO ABOUT #856100)

Numbered slide under firing pin stop plate. All subsequent Colt made 1911A1 pistols have a "P" marking on frame and top of slide. No markings on right side of slide. Parkerized finish. Shortened hammer. Right side of frame is marked "M1911A1 U.S. ARMY" forward of the slide stop pin, and "United States Property" behind the slide stop pin. Colt plastic stocks with narrow concave rings and hollow backs with no ribs through serial number #803000, wide rings around screws and hollow backs with ribs thereafter. A number of originals in the #820000 range have been observed with 1911 type slide stops. This is a good example of a seemingly out of sequence part that would often be changed by someone with a hair trigger trying to make his pistol "Like the Book" when in reality they would be messing up an original rare variation. Verified proof and final inspector's mark on trigger guard bow, and "COLT .45 AUTO" marked barrel. "WB" (Waldemar S. Broberg) marked on left side below slide stop. "COLT .45 AUTO" marked magazine floor plate with flattened letters, sand blasted bottom. (Subtract 5 to 10 percent for British proofs, most collectors seem to prefer virgin pistols.

Add 20 to 30 percent for 99 to 100 percent finish.)

EXC.	V.G.	GOOD	FAIR	POOR
2600	1900	1500	1200	875

1911A1, 1942 NAVY

A total of 3,982 pistols were shipped to naval supply depots in Oakland, Ca., and Sewalls Point, Va. They were serial numbered #793658 to #797639. Numbered slide under firing pin stop plate. "P" marking on frame and top of slide. No markings on right side of slide. Parkerized finish. Shortened hammer. Right side of frame is marked "M1911A1 U.S. ARMY" forward of the slide stop pin, and "United States Property" behind the slide stop pin. Verified proof "VP" and final inspector's mark on trigger guard bow. "WB" (Waldemar S. Broberg) marked on left side below slide stop. "COLT .45 AUTO" marked magazine floor plate with flattened letters, sand blasted bottom, and "COLT .45 AUTO" marked barrel. (Subtract 5 to 10 percent for British proofs, most collectors seem to prefer virgin pistols. Add 20 to 30 percent for 99 to 100 percent finish.)

EXC.	V.G.	GOOD	FAIR	POOR
3,100	2,000	1,700	1,400	1,000

1911A1, SINGER MANUFACTURING CO., EDUCATIONAL ORDER 1941

MODEL 1911A1 SINGER MFG:

Model 1911A!, made by Singer.

Exactly 500 pistols accepted and shipped. "JKC" (John K. Clement) marked on left side below slide stop. At least two un-numbered (and not marked United States Property) pistols were made and retained by employees. Slightly dull blue finish, brown plastic hollow-back grips, unmarked blue magazine, wide spur hammer, checkered slide stop, thumb safety, trigger, and mainspring housing. About 100 of the original 500 are known to exist in collections. These are very rare and most highly desired. Exercise caution when contemplating a purchase as fakes, improved, and re-blued models abound. Be extra cautious with an example that is 98 percent or better. (Add 50 percent for 99 to 100 percent finish. Original pistols un-numbered or numbered with out of sequence numbers subtract 50 percent to 70 percent. Subtract 5 to 10 percent for British proofs, most collectors seem to prefer virgin pistols. Re-blued, restored subtract 90 percent to 95 percent.)

EXC.	V.G.	GOOD	FAIR	POOR
36,000	25,000	17,500	14,000	9,000

ROCK ISLAND ARSENAL REPLACEMENT NUMBERS

Serial numbered #856101 to #856404. Replacement numbers issued to allow a pistol whose number had been defaced or worn away during re-finishing to be numbered again. Very rare; only one is actually known to exist in a collection.

EXC.	V.G.	GOOD	FAIR	POOR
1,500	1,200	900	750	600

1911A1, MILITARY 1943 PRODUCTION (GHD MARKED: SERIAL NUMBERED #867000 TO ABOUT #1155000)

Colt had its own serial numbers assigned within this range, but in addition, Colt duplicated Ithaca's serial numbers between #865404 and #916404 as well as Remington Rand's between #916405 and #958100 and US&S's between #1088726 and #1092896. Numbered slide under firing pin stop plate until about #1140000. "P" marking on frame and top of slide. Parkerized. Right side of frame is marked "M1911A1 U.S. ARMY" forward of the slide stop pin, and "United States Property" behind the slide stop pin. Verified proof and final inspector's mark on trigger guard bow. "GHD" (Guy H. Drewry) marked on left side below slide stop. Plain blued or contract magazine, and "COLT .45 AUTO" marked barrel. Colt plastic stocks with wide rings around screws. (Subtract 5 to 10 percent for British proofs, most collectors prefer virgin pistols. Add 20 to 30 percent for 99 to 100 percent finish.) Colt in Ithaca or Remington Rand range add 10 percent, Colt in US&S range add 20 percent.

PRE (APPROX.) #1140000 WITH MATCHING SLIDE

EXC.	V.G.	GOOD	FAIR	POOR
2,350	1,650	1,200	900	750

POST (APPROX.) #1140000 WITH MATCHING SLIDE

EXC.	V.G.	GOOD	FAIR	POOR
2,000	1,550	1,225	1,000	875

1911A1, COMMERCIAL TO MILITARY CONVERSIONS, 1943 PRODUCTION

(A few were WB marked, but most were GHD marked. Serial numbered #860003 to about #867000.)

Numbered slide under firing pin stop plate. "P" marking on frame and top of slide. Commercial markings on right side of slide. Parkerized finish over previously blued finish. The original commercial serial number peened and re-stamped with military numbers.

Most have the Swartz grip safety cutouts in slide and frame, but not the Swartz parts. None of the commercial to military conversions have the Swartz "sear safety." No slides marked "NATIONAL MATCH" have been reported. If any exist, a non-marked slide pistol would command a premium. Shortened hammer. Right side of frame is marked "M1911A1 U.S. ARMY" forward of the slide stop pin, and "United States Property" behind the slide stop pin. Verified proof "VP" and final inspector's mark on trigger guard bow. "GHD" (Guy H. Drewry) marked on left side below slide stop. "COLT .45 AUTO" marked magazine floor plate with flattened letters, sand blasted bottom. Colt plastic stocks with wide rings around screws. (Subtract 5 to 10 percent for British proofs, most collectors seem to prefer virgin pistols. Add 20 to 30 percent for 99 to 100 percent finish. Add 10 to 30 percent for non-marked slide.)

EXC.	V.G.	GOOD	FAIR	POOR
3,100	2,150	1,750	1,500	1,000

1911A1, MILITARY WITH COMMERCIAL SLIDE. 1943 PRODUCTION (GHD MARKED: SERIAL NUMBERED #867000 TO ABOUT #936000)

Perhaps a few hundred total. Numbered slide under firing pin stop plate. "P" marking on frame and top of slide. Commercial markings on right side of slide. Parkerized finish over previously blued finish (slide only). Most have the Swartz grip safety cutouts in slide but not in frame. None have the Swartz parts. Frames are generally new military manufacture. Shortened hammer. Right side of frame is marked "M1911A1 U.S. ARMY" forward of the slide stop pin, and "United States Property" behind the slide stop pin. Verified proof "VP" and final inspector's mark on trigger guard bow. "GHD" (Guy H. Drewry) marked on left side below slide stop. May have "COLT .45 AUTO" marked magazine floor plate with flattened letters with sand blasted bottom or plain blued magazine. Colt plastic stocks with wide rings around screws. Barrels marked "COLT .45 AUTO." (Subject 5 to 10 percent for British proofs, most collectors seem to prefer virgin pistols.) (Add 20 to 30 percent for 99 to 100 percent finish.)

EXC.	V.G.	GOOD	FAIR	POOR
3,000	2,400	1,900	1,400	900

1911A1, CANADIAN BROAD ARROW/ C MARKED 1943 PRODUCTION (GHD MARKED: SERIAL NUMBERED #930000 TO ABOUT #939000)

Marked with the "C" broad arrow Canadian Property mark on the left rear of the slide and left of the receiver above the magazine catch. A total of 1,515 pistols Numbered slide under firing pin stop plate. "P" marking on frame and top of slide. Commercial markings on right side of slide on a few, otherwise blank. Parkerized finish. Right side of frame is marked "M1911A1 U.S. ARMY" forward of the slide stop pin, and "United States Property" behind the slide stop pin. Verified proof "VP" and final inspector's mark on trigger guard bow. "GHD" (Guy H. Drewry) marked on left side below slide stop. All appear to have British proofs except a few pistols in "Fair" condition that were sold at auction a couple of years ago. These pistols without British proofs were apparently used in Canadian prisons and recently released. Beware non-British marked Canadian pistols in better than "Good" condition, as at least one of these same former prison pistols has appeared for sale in "New" condition. Barrels marked "COLT .45 AUTO." Most have plain blued magazine. Colt plastic stocks with wide rings around screws. (Add 30 percent for 99 to 100 percent finish. Add 25 percent for numbered commercial marked slide.)

EXC.	V.G.	GOOD	FAIR	POOR
2500	1900	1500	1200	900

1911A1, MILITARY 1944 PRODUCTION (GHD MARKED: SERIAL NUMBERED #1155000 TO ABOUT #1208673 AND #1609529 TO #1720000)

Un-numbered slide. "P" marking on frame and top of slide. Parkerized. Right side of frame is marked "M1911A1 U.S. ARMY" forward of the slide stop pin, and "United States Property" behind the slide stop pin. Verified proof "VP" and final inspector's mark on trigger guard bow. "GHD" (Guy H. Drewry) marked on left side below slide stop. Barrels marked "COLT .45 AUTO." Plain blued or contract magazine. Colt plastic stocks with wide rings around screws. (Subtract 5 to 10 percent for British proofs, most collectors seem to prefer virgin pistols. Add 20 to 30 percent for 99 to 100 percent finish.)

EXC.	V.G.	GOOD	FAIR	POOR
2,000	1,550	1,225	1,000	875

1911A1, MILITARY 1945 (GHD ACCEPTANCE MARK, SERIAL NUMBERED #1720000 TO #1743846 AND #2244804 TO #2368781)

Un-numbered slide. "P" marking on frame and top of slide. Parkerized. Right side of frame is marked "M1911A1 U.S. ARMY" forward of the slide stop pin,

1911A1, made by Ithaca.

and "United States Property" behind the slide stop pin. Verified proof "VP" and final inspector's mark on trigger guard bow. "GHD" (Guy H. Drewry) marked on left side below slide stop. Plain blued or contract magazine. Early barrels marked "COLT .45 AUTO," later examples marked with a "C" in a square. Colt plastic grips with wide rings around screws. (Subtract 5 to 10 percent for British proofs, most collectors seem to prefer virgin pistols. Add 20 to 30 percent for 99 to 100 percent finish.)

EXC.	V.G.	GOOD	FAIR	POOR
2,000	1,550	1,225	1,000	875

1911A1, MILITARY 1945 JSB ACCEPTANCE MARK

Around serial number #2360600 a small number of pistols (perhaps a few thousand) were acceptance marked under the authority of John S. Begley, a civilian employee of the Ordnance Department who had the title "Army Inspector of Ordnance." Un-numbered slide. "P" marking on frame and top of slide. Parkerized. Right side of frame is marked "M1911A1 U.S. ARMY" forward of the slide stop pin, and "United States Property" behind the slide stop pin. Verified proof "VP" and final inspector's mark on triggerguard bow. "JSB" (John S. Begley) acceptance mark on left side below slide stop. Plain blued or contract magazine. Barrels marked with a "C" in a square. Colt plastic grips with wide rings around screws. Extremely rare! Subtract 5 to 10 percent for British proofs, most collectors seem to prefer virgin pistols. Add 30 to 50 percent for 99 to 100 percent finish.

EXC.	V.G.	GOOD	FAIR	POOR
5,900	4,200	3,000	2,200	1,600

1911A1, MILITARY 1945 NO ACCEPTANCE MARK

(Un-inspected and usually no Ordnance wheel.) Very rare and are usually found around serial number #2354000. Un-numbered slide. "P" marking on frame and top of slide. Parkerized. Right side of frame is marked "M1911A1 U.S. ARMY" forward of the slide stop pin, and "United States Property" behind the slide stop pin. Verified proof "VP" and final inspector's mark on trigger guard bow. Plain blued or contract magazine. Barrels marked with a "C" in a square. Colt plastic grips with wide rings around screws. Very rare. These pistols may not have been delivered but they may have been sold commercially. Add 20 to 30 percent for 99 to 100 percent finish.

EXC.	V.G.	GOOD	FAIR	POOR
1,750	1,400	950	650	450

ITHACA GUN CO. 1943 TO 1945 PRODUCTION

FJA inspected, un-numbered slide. Right side of frame is marked "M1911A1 U.S. ARMY" forward of the slide stop pin, and "United States Property" behind the slide stop pin. Plastic Keyes Fibre grips, stamped trigger, flat sided hammer, late pistols had serrated flat sided hammer, HS marked barrel, contract magazine. A few early pistols had an "I" prefix Serial Number. A few into the 1.28 million range had the "M1911A1 U.S. ARMY" on the right side of the slide. A few thousand early pistols were made with reclaimed World War I Colt frames ("H" marked on top of frame, and heart shaped cutouts). Add 50 percent for Colt frame. (Subtract 5 to 10 percent for British proofs, most collectors seem to prefer virgin pistols.) (Add 30 to 40 percent for 99 to 100 percent finish. Add 20 percent for "M1911A1

Colt 1911A1 built by Remington-Rand.

U.S. ARMY" marked slide, but only in the proper serial number range. Add 15 percent for DuLite finish, below about #905000. Add 150 percent for "I" prefix.) Recently discovered shipping documents show certain pistols going to Navy units and Airfield orders, however it is still too early to determine the associated premium for these shipments.

EXC.	V.G.	GOOD	FAIR	POOR
1,700	1,300	1,000	800	600

REMINGTON RAND CO. 1942 TO 1943 PRODUCTION

"NEW YORK" (Type I) marked slide. FJA inspected, un-numbered slide. Right side of frame is marked "M1911A1 U.S. ARMY" forward of the slide stop pin, and "United States Property" behind the slide stop pin. DuLite (blued over sand blasting) finish. Plastic Keyes Fibre grips with no rings around screws. Milled trigger, flat sided hammer, "COLT .45 AUTO" marked barrel, contract magazine. Fine checkered mainspring housing. (Subtract 5 to 10 percent for British proofs, most collectors seem to prefer virgin pistols. Add 30 to 50 percent for 99 to 100 percent finish. Pistols shipped after 1942 (after serial number #921699) seem to be less desirable. Subtract 15 percent.)

EXC.	V.G.	GOOD	FAIR	POOR
3,000	2,000	1,500	1,200	900

REMINGTON RAND CO. 1943 PRODUCTION

Large "N.Y." (Type II) marked slide. FJA inspected, un-numbered slide. Right side of frame is marked "M1911A1 U.S. ARMY" forward of the slide stop pin, and "United States Property" behind the slide stop pin.

DuLite (blued over sand blasting) finish. Plastic Keyes Fibre grips with small rings around screws. Stamped trigger, flat sided hammer, "HS" marked barrel, contract magazine. Fine checkered mainspring housing. Note that there appears to be considerable overlap of features near the 1 million serial range. (Subtract 5 to 10 percent for British proofs, most collectors seem to prefer virgin pistols. Add 30 to 50 percent for 99 to 100 percent finish.)

EXC.	V.G.	GOOD	FAIR	POOR
2,100	1,500	1,150	950	750

REMINGTON RAND CO. 1943 TO 1945 PRODUCTION

Small "N. Y." (Type III) marked slide. "FJA" inspected, un-numbered slide. Right side of frame is marked "M1911A1 U.S. ARMY" forward of the slide stop pin, and "United States Property" behind the slide stop pin. Parkerized (phosphate over sand blasting) finish. Plastic Keyes Fibre grips with small rings around screws. Stamped trigger, flat-sided hammer, "HS" marked barrel, contract magazine. Serrated mainspring housing. (Subtract 5 to 10 percent for British proofs, most collectors prefer virgin pistols. Add 40 percent for 99 to 100 percent finish.)

EXC.	V.G.	GOOD	FAIR	POOR
1,400	1,100	900	825	750

REMINGTON RAND CO. 1942 TO 1945 PRODUCTION

Exceptionally rare, Numbered Presentation pistol (all observed are Type III) marked slide. They were usually disposed of as giveaways to contracting personnel and employees, however several remained in the company safe long after World War II concluded until they were eventually sold. No inspector, un-numbered slide. The only frame marking is a two or three digit number above trigger right. Parkerized (phosphate over sand blasting) finish. Plastic Keyes Fibre grips with small rings around screws. Stamped trigger, flat sided hammer, "HS" marked barrel, contract magazine. Serrated mainspring housing. (Add 30 percent for 99 to 100 percent finish. Add 10 to 20 percent for original box.)

EXC.	V.G.	GOOD	FAIR	POOR
3,500	2,500	1,800	1,400	1,200

REMINGTON RAND CO. 1942 TO 1945 PRODUCTION

Also quite rare and collectible, these Presentation pistols feature ERRS prefix; all observed are Type III marked slide. They were usually disposed of as giveaways to contracting personnel and employees, however several remained in the company safe long after WWII until they were eventually sold. No inspector, un-numbered slide. The only frame marking is a two or three digit number with the "ERRS" prefix above trigger right. Parkerized (phosphate over sand blasting) finish. Plastic Keyes Fibre grips with small rings around screws. Stamped trigger, flat sided hammer, "HS" marked barrel, contract magazine. Popular wisdom seems to be that "ERRS" meant "Experimental Remington Rand"; however, there seems to be no evidence to support that notion. The true meaning of ERRS may never be known. (Add 30 percent for 99 to 100 percent finish. Add 10 percent to 20 percent for original numbered box.) Some ERRS pistols were DuLite blued and some were "P" proofed, too few to establish an accurate premium.

EXC.	V.G.	GOOD	FAIR	POOR
3,500	2,800	2,200	1,800	1,250

UNION SWITCH SIGNAL CO.

Swissvale, Pennsylvania. A total of 55,000 pistols were delivered in 1943. US&S pistols have become one of the most sought after of all the 1911/1911A1 pistols.

UNION SWITCH SIGNAL CO. 1943 PRODUCTION TYPE I

No "P" on frame or slide. From serial number #1041405 to about #1060000 with probable overlap. RCD inspected, un-numbered slide. Right side of frame is marked "M1911A1 U.S. ARMY" forward of the slide stop pin, and "United States Property" behind the slide stop pin. DuLite (blued over sand blasting) finish.

Plastic Keyes Fibre grips with or without rings around screws. Stamped, blued trigger, flat-sided hammer, "HS" marked barrel, contract magazine. Checkered mainspring housing. (Add 30 to 40 percent for 99 to 100 percent finish.)

EXC.	V.G.	GOOD	FAIR	POOR
4,000	3,000	2,400	1,800	1,400

UNION SWITCH SIGNAL CO. 1943 PRODUCTION TYPE II

"P" on top edge of slide. From about serial number #1060000 to about #1080000 with probable overlap. RCD inspected, un-numbered slide. Right side of frame is marked "M1911A1 U.S. ARMY" forward of the slide stop pin, and "United States Property" behind the slide stop pin. DuLite (blued over sand blasting) finish. Plastic Keyes Fibre grips with or without rings around screws. Stamped, blued trigger, flat sided hammer, "HS" marked barrel, contract magazine. Checkered mainspring housing. (Add 30 to 40 percent for 99 to 100 percent finish.)

EXC.	V.G.	GOOD	FAIR	POOR
4,000	3,000	2,400	1,800	1,400

UNION SWITCH SIGNAL CO. 1943 PRODUCTION TYPE III

"P" on frame and slide in the normal locations. From about SN 1080000 to 1096404 with probable overlap. RCD inspected, un-numbered slide. Right side of frame is marked "M1911A1 U.S. ARMY" forward of the slide stop pin, and "United States Property" behind the slide stop pin. DuLite (blued over sand blasting) finish. Plastic Keyes Fibre grips with or without rings around screws. Stamped, blued trigger, flat sided hammer, "HS" marked barrel, contract magazine. Checkered mainspring housing. (Add 30 to 40 percent for 99 to 100 percent finish.)

EXC.	V.G.	GOOD	FAIR	POOR
4,000	3,000	2,400	1,800	1,400

UNION SWITCH SIGNAL CO. 1943 PRODUCTION. EXP.

About 100 pistols total. ("EXP" followed by a one or two digit number on receiver partially under right grip.) These pistols usually have some apparent defect, which may have caused them to be rejected and written off. They were believed to have been disposed of as giveaways to contracting personnel and employees. No inspector, no Ordnance mark un-numbered slide. Some pistols were finished with the DuLite process (blued over sand blasting) that closely resembled the finish of the

*Union Switch
Signal 1911A1, left
and right views.*

delivered military pistols. The "EXP" and serial number marking was hand applied and is partially obscured by the right stock panel. Other EXP marked pistols were blued over such heavy buffing that the pistols have an amateur look about them. This, along with the crudeness of the markings, might lead one to question the authenticity of the blued EXPs. However, most evidence indicates that they are indeed genuine US&S made pistols. Popular wisdom seems to be that "EXP" meant "Experimental"; however, there seems to be no evidence to support that notion. Plastic Keyes Fibre grips with or without rings around screws. Stamped, blued trigger, flat-sided hammer, "HS" marked barrel, contract magazine. Checkered mainspring housing. (Add 30 to 40 percent for 99 to 100 percent finish. Subtract 50 percent for blued or buffed.) Most observed have type II slides.

EXC.	V.G.	GOOD	FAIR	POOR
5,200	3,750	2,800	2,200	1,700

SEVEN DIGIT X NUMBERED RE-WORK

These pistols were renumbered when their original serial numbers were either defaced, obliterated, or became too light to read during rebuilding or re-finishing. The seven digit X prefix serial numbers (#X2693614 through #X2695212) were assigned to various arsenals from 1949 to 1957. Some of the re-works are done in small batches and are more distinctive and collectable than the four digit X numbers. Each batch of pistols may have unique characteristics as they are done at different times by various arsenals. All are considered "Arsenal Re-finished."

EXC.	V.G.	GOOD	FAIR	POOR
1,100	850	700	500	350

MILITARY ARSENAL RE-WORK

Many 1911/1911A1 pistols were re-worked/re-furbished at government arsenals such as Augusta Arsenal (AA), Rock Island Arsenal (RIA), Springfield Armory (SA), Raritan Arsenal (no mark) and others. Some arsenals applied an identification/ inspection mark to each pistol rebuilt, but others did not mark them in any way. Some of the re-works were sold through the NRA and sales/shipping papers identify the serial number of the pistol Most of these pistols also had shipping boxes. An original shipping box and papers will almost certainly cause the price to increase by $200. (A fake box is worth about $2.00, and most

*Military National
Match .45*

of the boxes seen and advertised as originals are indeed fakes.) Some re-worked pistols appear to have most or all original parts, but have been re-finished and Parkerized. A few pistols went through a rebuild facility and carry the rebuild facility's mark, but appear to be original pistols and were not re-finished or rebuilt. Most rebuilt pistols have new plastic stocks as well as a new barrel. Each batch of rebuilt pistols may have unique characteristics as they are done at different times by various arsenals. Therefore it is often impossible to determine when a pistol was re-worked, if it has been altered since it left the rebuild facility, or even if it was re-worked in a government facility. Consequently, although re-worked pistols are considered collectable, they are likely to remain at the bottom of the collectable price structure for the foreseeable future. (Add up to $100 for original box, add up to $100 for numbered shipping papers.) Prices shown are for government facility marked (AA, RIA, SA, etc.) re-works, equivalent to Poor condition if no Government facility markings, unless with original numbered box and papers. Add $2.00 for fake box. Completely original pistols with re-work marks on them, like their original pistol category, but less 20 percent.

EXC.	V.G.	GOOD	FAIR	POOR
850	700	575	500	400

STATE OF NEW YORK GOVERNMENT MODEL

250 pistols in the serial number range of about #255000-C to about #258000-C with factory roll mark "PROPERTY OF THE STATE OF NEW YORK" and verified proof "VP" and "GOVERNMENT MODEL" markings. A few of the parts were leftover military. This is a state militia pistol. (99 to 100 percent finish, add 33 percent. For the few consecutive pairs known add 15 percent premium. A few match pistols were made by Al Dinan in the early 1960s; add 15 percent.)

EXC.	V.G.	GOOD	FAIR	POOR
2,300	1,500	1,100	800	500

MILITARY NATIONAL MATCH .45

These are .45 caliber pistols rebuilt from service pistols at Springfield Armory between 1955 and about 1967. In 1968 the last year of the program, all rebuilding took place at Rock Island Arsenal. These pistols were built and rebuilt each year with a portion being sold to competitors by the NRA. Each year improvements were added to the rebuild program. Four articles in the *American Rifleman* NRA magazine document these pistols well: August, 1959; April, 1963; June, 1966; and July, 1966. Many parts for these pistols have been available and many "look-alike" pistols have been built by basement armorers. Pistols generally came with a numbered box or papers. Add 40 percent for numbered box and papers. When well worn these pistols offer little advantage over a standard well worn pistol. Pistols must be in original match condition to qualify as Military National Match pistols.

EXC.	V.G.	GOOD	FAIR	POOR
1,400	1,000	875	750	550

COLT'S LONG GUNS

THE PATERSON LONG GUNS (1837-1847)

Although the Colt name is perhaps most closely associated with revolving handguns, some of the first revolving cylinder guns out of Colt's Paterson, New Jersey plant were rifles and shotguns. Unfortunately, these guns were afflicted with some of the same flaws as the early Paterson handguns: designs that were not quite perfected and black powder residues that quickly fouled the guns' actions. While not a commercial success, these earliest Colt revolving long guns nevertheless had their part to play in the Colt story.

MODEL NO. 1 RING LEVER RIFLE

This was actually the first firearm manufactured by Colt; the first revolver appeared a short time later. There were 200 single action First Models produced in 1837 and 1838. Its browned octagonal barrel is 32 inches long; the rest of the finish is blued. The stock is varnished walnut and includes a cheekpiece inlaid with Colt's trademark. The ring lever located in front of the frame is pulled to rotate the eight shot cylinder and cock the concealed hammer. The rifle is chambered for .34, .36, .38, .40 and .44 caliber percussion. Look for the four horseheads cheekpiece stock inlay. The cylinder is roll engraved and the barrel is stamped "COLT'S PATENT/PATENT ARMS MFG. CO., PATERSON N. JERSEY." This model has a top strap over the cylinder – a feature Sam Colt generally eschewed – and an internal hammer. They were made both with and without an attached loading lever. The latter is worth approximately 10 percent more.

EXC.	V.G.	GOOD	FAIR	POOR
-	-	60,000	20,000	-

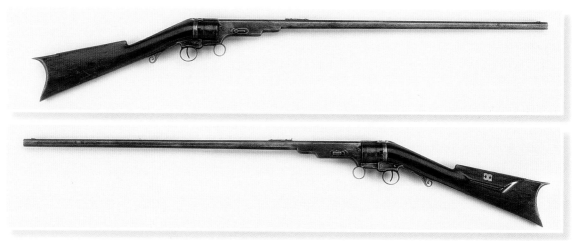

Paterson 1st Model Ring Lever Rifle.

Paterson 2nd Model Ring Lever Rifle.

MODEL NO. 2 RING LEVER RIFLE

This single action model is similar in appearance to the First Model, even down to the concealed hammer, and its mechanism is identical. The major difference is the absence of the top strap or bridge over the cylinder. Neither does it have a trademark stamped on the cheekpiece or the four-horseheads inlay. Look for a snake and star terminal device on the barrel marking, and a house in the horseman, centaur and stag cylinder roll scene. The Model No. 2, offered with a 28 or a 32 inch octagonal barrel, is chambered for .44 caliber percussion and holds eight shots, although a few held as many as ten. About 500 were produced from 1838 to 1841. The earliest had a square back cylinder and no loading lever. Later production models rounded off the cylinder rear, included a loading lever on the barrel lug and even escalloped a cutout on the frame's recoil shield for applying percussion caps to the cylinder. The presence of an attached cheekpiece would add approximately 10 percent to the value.

EXC.	V.G.	GOOD	FAIR	POOR
-	-	40,000	12,500	-

MODEL 1839 CARBINE

The most popular of Colt's Paterson longarms, this single action model has no cocking ring, instead featuring an exposed hammer for cocking and rotating the six shot cylinder. It is chambered for .525 smoothbore and comes standard with a 24 inch round barrel, although other barrel lengths have been discovered. The finish is blued, with a browned barrel and a varnished walnut stock. All cylinders were scroll-rolled with a three panel

Martial-marked Paterson Model 1839 Carbine.

design: a hunter with a trophy lion, ships battling on the high seas and the battle of Bunker Hill. The earliest cylinders were squareback with no loading lever. Mid-production began including loading levers and late production rounded off the cylinder backs. The barrel is stamped "PATENT ARMS MFG. CO. PATERSON, N.J.-COLT'S PT." There were 950 manufactured from 1838 to 1841. Early models without a loading lever would merit an additional 25 percent. The U.S. military purchased 360 and stamped "WAT" on the stock. These would be worth twice what a standard model would bring. Anyone considering the purchase of one would be well advised to proceed with extreme caution.

EXC.	V.G.	GOOD	FAIR	POOR
-	-	25,000	9,500	-

Paterson Model 1839 Shotgun. Though it's been refinished and had its barrel shortened, it's a rarity in any condition.

Paterson Model 1839-1850 Carbine.

MODEL 1839 SHOTGUN

This exposed hammer smoothbore shotgun is similar in appearance to the 1839 Carbine. Chambered for 16 gauge or 0.62 caliber, it holds six shots. It has a Damascus pattern barrel, and the most notable difference is a long 3.5 inch (instead of a 2.5 inch) cylinder. Only 262 of these were made from 1839 to 1841. The markings are the same as on the Carbine.

EXC.	V.G.	GOOD	FAIR	POOR
-	-	25,000	10,000	-

MODEL 1839/1850 CARBINE

In 1848 Colt acquired a number of Model 1839 Carbines (approximately 40) from the state of Rhode Island. To make them marketable, they were refinished and the majority were fitted with plain, but brightly polished cylinders having integral ratchets around the arbor hole. The Carbine's barrel length is 24 inches and caliber .525. Expect a browned barrel, a polished cylinder, blued frame, case hardened furniture and varnished walnut stock.

EXC.	V.G.	GOOD	FAIR	POOR
-	-	35,000	12,500	-

ANTIQUE COLT LONG GUNS

Sam Colt had always been interested in applying his revolving cylinder to long guns as well as handguns, but for whatever reason – perhaps because of the excessive black powder residue left behind following a shot from the cap and ball loads of the day – the revolver concept was never quite realized in long guns.

Following the Civil War, the lucrative U.S. firearms market changed direction. Not only did military sales decline – not totally, but there were no longer armies of hundreds of thousands in the field – but the self-enclosed breechloading cartridge replaced muzzleloading in almost all of its forms.

With the success of its Singe Action Army handguns, Colt was endowed with the cash flow to experiment and produced numerous rifle and shotgun designed to compete at the high end of marksmanship and quality. Unfortunately, with a subsequent flood of inexpensive foreign guns, most of Colt's designs did not stand the tests of time and corporate profitability.

Berdan Single Shot Rifle.

MODEL 1854 RUSSIAN CONTRACT MUSKET

In 1854 Colt purchased a large number of U.S. Model 1822 flintlock muskets, altering them for percussion cap ignition and rifling the barrels. The reworked muskets are dated 1854 on the barrel tang and at the rear of the lockplate. In most instances the original manufactory marks, such as Springfield or Harpers Ferry at the rear of the lockplate have been removed while the U.S. and eagle between the hammer and bolster remain. The percussion nipple bolster is marked "COLT'S PATENT." Some examples have been noted with the date 1858. Barrel length 42 inches; caliber .69; lock and furniture burnished bright; walnut stock oil finished.

EXC.	V.G.	GOOD	FAIR	POOR
-	-	4,000	1,500	750

Breechloading examples made in two styles are also known. Production of this variation is believed to have taken place only on an experimental basis.

EXC.	V.G.	GOOD	FAIR	POOR
-	-	6,500	2,500	1,000

BERDAN SINGLE SHOT RIFLE

This is a scarce rifle on today's market: approximately 30,200 were manufactured, but nearly 30,000 of them were sent to Russia. Produced from 1866 to 1870, it is a trapdoor type action with shells inserted from the top; chambered for .42 centerfire. The standard model has a 32.5 inch barrel; the carbine, just 18.25 inches. The finish is blued, with a walnut stock. This rifle was designed and the patent held by Hiram Berdan, Commander of the Civil War "Sharpshooters" Regiment. Berdan Single Shots were actually the Colt company's first cartridge arm. The 30,000 rifles and 25 half stocked carbines that were sent to Russia were lettered with Russian Cyrillic script. The few examples made for American sale have Colt's name and Hartford address on the barrel.

RUSSIAN RIFLE ORDER

30,000 manufactured.

EXC.	V.G.	GOOD	FAIR	POOR
-	2,500	1,000	450	

RUSSIAN CARBINE ORDER

25 manufactured.

EXC.	V.G.	GOOD	FAIR	POOR
-	6,000	3,000	1,250	

U.S. RIFLE SALES

100 manufactured.

EXC.	V.G.	GOOD	FAIR	POOR
-	5,000	2,250	1,250	

U.S. CARBINE SALES

25 manufactured.

EXC.	V.G.	GOOD	FAIR	POOR
-	9,500	4,500	2,000	

Colt-Franklin Military Rifle.

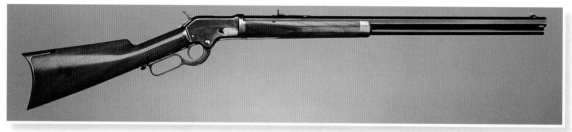

The Colt-Burgess.

Colt-Burgess Carbine.

COLT-FRANKLIN MILITARY RIFLE

Although the patents were held by William B. Franklin, a vice president of the company and former U.S. Army general who specialized in ordnance, this rifle was not a successful venture for Colt. It was a bolt-action rifle with a primitive, gravity-fed box magazine holding nine rounds that interfered with effective sighting. Chambered for the .45-70 government cartridge, it has a blued barrel that measured 32.5 inches long, with a walnut stock. The rifle has the Colt Hartford barrel address and is stamped with an eagle's head and U.S. inspectors marks. Only 50 of these rifles were produced in 1887 and 1888, and it is believed that they were prototypes intended for government sales, which did not materialize and production ceased

EXC.	V.G.	GOOD	FAIR	POOR
-	8,000	4,500	2,000	-

COLT-BURGESS LEVER ACTION RIFLE

This gun, brought to Colt by gun designer Andrew Burgess, was Colt's only attempt to compete with Winchester for the lever action rifle market. It is said that when Winchester started to produce revolving handguns for prospective marketing, Colt dropped the Burgess from its line. This legend has never been satisfactorily documented, but nevertheless some proof does exist, most notably in the form of several prototype Winchester centerfire revolvers. The Burgess rifle is chambered for .44-40 with a 25.5-inch barrel and a 15-shot tubular magazine. The Carbine version has a 20.5-inch barrel and 12-shot magazine. The finish is blued, with a case colored hammer and lever while the stock is walnut with an oil finish. The Colt Hartford address is on the barrel, and "Burgess Patents" is stamped on the bottom of the lever. A total of 3,775 rifles were manufactured: 1,219 with round barrels and 2,556 with octagonal barrels. There were also 2,593 carbines. The Burgess was produced from 1883 to 1885.

RIFLE
Octagonal barrel.

EXC.	V.G.	GOOD	FAIR	POOR
-	-	3,500	1,500	550

RIFLE
Round barrel.

EXC.	V.G.	GOOD	FAIR	POOR
-	-	3,500	1,500	550

CARBINE

EXC.	V.G.	GOOD	FAIR	POOR
-	-	5,000	2,000	950

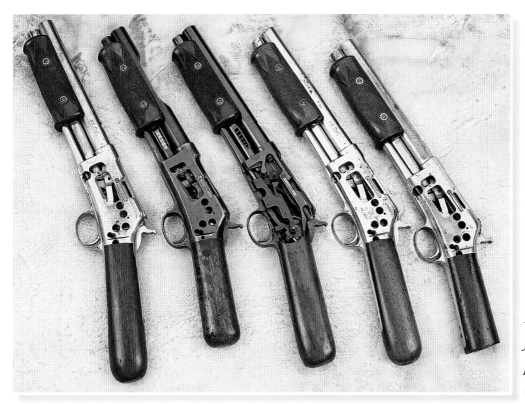

Colt Lightning Magazine Rifle factory cutaways, probably made for use by jobbers.

BABY CARBINE
Lighter frame and barrel (RARE).

EXC.	V.G.	GOOD	FAIR	POOR
-	-	6,000	2,500	1,150

NOTE: The following Burgess rifle was listed on *AntiqueGuns.com* in the Spring of 2007:

"Colt Burgess Rifle was restored many years ago. It has a rare 25.5 inch round barrel. Only 1,213 were produced with round barrels. The bore is shiny and it has a 15 shot magazine tube. Rifling is pronounced. The metal finish is blued with fine surface pitting here and there. The wood is 2x or better, very nice figure. Action smooth and crisp. Overall, a solid and desirable, scarce and shootable piece. Serial number #57XX from about 1885. This is antique as an old lever action. Overall a solid gun; hard to find in any condition."

The seller opened bidding at $2,500, offered to sell it immediately for $4,500 and estimated its true collector value at $8,500.

LIGHTNING SLIDE ACTION MEDIUM FRAME
This was the first slide action rifle Colt produced. It was chambered for .32-20, .38-40 and .44-40, and was intended to be a companion piece to the Single Action Armys of the same calibers. The rifle has a 26-inch barrel with 15-shot tube magazine; the carbine, a 20-inch barrel with 12-shot magazine. The finish is blued, with case colored hammer; the walnut stock is oil finished; the forend is usually checkered. The Colt name and Hartford address are stamped on the barrel along with the patent dates. There were approximately 89,777 manufactured between 1884 and 1902.

Considering that modern copies of the Medium Frame Lightning Rifle are today available from Taurus, United States Fire Arms, AWA and Beretta, it might fairly said that the Lightning rifle is a bigger success today than it was 125 years ago!

RIFLE

EXC.	V.G.	GOOD	FAIR	POOR
-	2,500	1,250	750	400

Medium-frame Lightning Magazine Rifle.

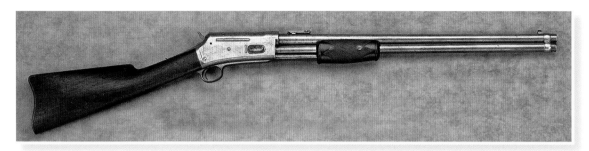

Medium-frame Lightning Saddle Ring Carbine.

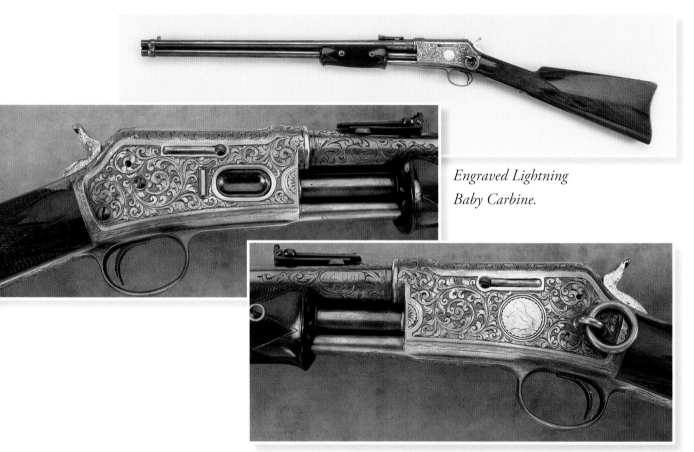

Engraved Lightning Baby Carbine.

CARBINE

EXC.	V.G.	GOOD	FAIR	POOR
-	3,500	1,750	800	500

MILITARY RIFLE OR CARBINE

.44-40 caliber, short magazine tube, bayonet lug and sling swivels.

EXC.	V.G.	GOOD	FAIR	POOR
-	4,250	2,000	1,000	600

BABY CARBINE

One pound, lighter version of standard carbine.

EXC.	V.G.	GOOD	FAIR	POOR
-	5,000	2,500	1,250	750

NOTE: The following advertisement appeared in the Spring of 2007 on *AntiqueGunList.com*:

"Colt Lightning Baby Carbine 44-40. This gun has been totally redone, engraved and nickel plated. New wood butt stock and fore end. A really nice engraved job and had a brand new barrel put on it. A beautiful show piece or hang on the wall and look at it. Manufactured in 1889. Serial #336XX. $5,525."

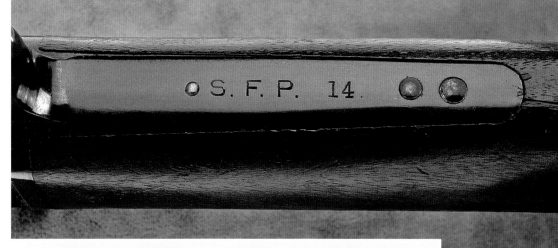

San Francisco Police Lightning Rifle.

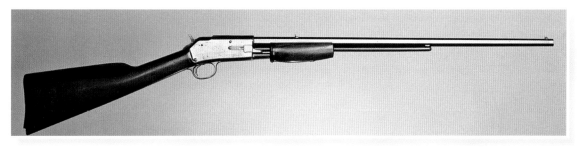

Colt Lightning Magazine Rifle, small frame.

SAN FRANCISCO POLICE RIFLE

.44-40 caliber, #SFP1 to #SFP401 on bottom tang.

EXC.	V.G.	GOOD	FAIR	POOR
-	3,250	1,250	800	500

NOTE: The following advertisement appeared in the Spring of 2007 on *AntiqueGunList.com*:

"Colt Rifle .44-40 pump action Lightning Rifle Round Barrel British Proof Mark. This gun was manufactured in 1886, and has 90% original blue. This is the early gun with no dust cover. It has a little slide lock in trigger guard. Nice checkered forearm grips nice butt stock; an excellent bore in excellent working condition. Serial #184XX $4,350."

And this advertisement appeared in the Summer of 2007 on *ArmChairGunShow.com*:

"Colt - Lightning medium frame pump action rifle with scarce bolt lock feature - .38 Cal. (i.e., .38 WCF or 38-40); 26" round barrel. Good condition. Brown patina, thinning on receiver and front of barrel, with wear on top of bolt, muzzle and edges; some pecking around pins and screws; very good markings. Barrel and magazine tube have even light pitting over most of the surface. Standard rifle features with original rear semi-buckhorn sight, home made Rocky Mountain style front sight. Very good mech; distinct rifling in dark pitted bore. Stocks are sound with buttstock sanded long ago with minor usage marks and no finish, while 2 piece forearm has 50% varnish remaining. - Early type with 1883 patent dates only on barrel. Scarce factory original bolt locking safety lever mounted in front of trigger guard (prevents operation of pump when activated). About 1887. Serial number #136689. $1,850."*

LIGHTNING SLIDE ACTION SMALL FRAME

This rifle is chambered for the .22 short and long and was the second model of Lightning rifle that Colt introduced. The standard barrel length is 24 inches; the finish is blued with a case colored hammer. The stock is walnut; some were checkered and some were not. The barrel is stamped with the Colt name and Hartford address and the patent dates. There were 89,912 manufactured between 1887 and 1904.

EXC.	V.G.	GOOD	FAIR	POOR
2,750	1,250	700	500	300

Colt Lightning Magazine Rifle, large frame.

Colt Model 1883 Double Barrel Shotgun.

LIGHTNING SLIDE ACTION LARGE FRAME

This rifle is similar in appearance to the medium frame Lightning, though larger in size. It is chambered in larger rifle calibers of the era, from .38-56 up to .50-95 Express. The larger calibers are more desirable from a collector's standpoint. The rifle has a 28-inch barrel; the carbine, a 22-inch barrel. The finish is blued, with a case colored hammer. The stock is oiled walnut; the forend, checkered. The Colt name and Hartford address are stamped on the barrel along with the patent dates. This rifle is quite large and has come to be known as the "Express Model." Colt manufactured 6,496 between 1887 and 1894. The Large Frame Lightning Rifle is considered extremely desirable today, and shootable examples, especially those chambered for the "Express"-type cartridges, may command values well in excess of those shown. It's just one of those things.

RIFLE

28-inch octagonal barrel.

EXC.	V.G.	GOOD	FAIR	POOR
-	5,500	2,000	750	500

RIFLE

28-inch round barrel.

EXC.	V.G.	GOOD	FAIR	POOR
-	5,000	1,750	750	500

CARBINE

22-inch barrel.

EXC.	V.G.	GOOD	FAIR	POOR
-	7,500	3,500	1,500	750

BABY CARBINE

22-inch barrel; one pound lighter.

EXC.	V.G.	GOOD	FAIR	POOR
-	10,000	5,000	2,250	950

MODEL 1878 DOUBLE-BARREL SHOTGUN

This shotgun is chambered in 10 or 12 gauge and has 28-, 30- or 32-inch barrels. It is a sidelock double trigger hammer gun with case colored locks and breech. The barrels are browned and Damacus patterned. The checkered walnut stock is varnished or oil finished. Colt's Hartford address is stamped on the barrel rib, and Colt's name, on the lock. This is regarded as one of the finest shotguns made in America in this era, although Colt had difficulty competing with the less expensive European imports of the day. They ceased production after only 22,690 were manufactured between 1878 and 1889. For a fully engraved model add 300 percent.

EXC.	V.G.	GOOD	FAIR	POOR
-	2200	1500	850	350

MODEL 1883 DOUBLE BARREL SHOTGUN

This model is a hammerless boxlock, chambered for 10 or 12 gauge, with double triggers.. The barrels are 28, 30 or 32 inches. The frame and furniture are case colored; the barrels are browned with a Damascus pattern. The checkered walnut stock is varnished or oil finished. Colt's Hartford address is stamped on the barrel rib. "Colt" is stamped on each side of the frame. Again, as in the Model 1878, this double-barrel is rated as one of the finest of all American made shotguns. There were many special orders and they, of course,

Rare, rare, rare. Colt Double Barrel Rifle in .45-70.

Model 1855 Side Hammer Sporting Rifle, 1st Model.

require individual appraisal. Colt manufactured 7,366 between 1883 and 1895. For fully engraved model add 300 percent.

EXC.	V.G.	GOOD	FAIR	POOR
-	2750	1800	1000	450

NOTE: The following advertisement appeared on *ColtAutos.com* in the Spring of 2007:

"COLT MODEL 1883 DOUBLE BARREL SHOTGUN Serial number #2007 Price $3,495. Description: 10 gauge. Excellent 85% case color, 95% Damascus barrels. Very good wood."

DOUBLE BARREL RIFLE

Because only 35 were manufactured, the double barrel rifle is one of the rarest of all Colt firearms and is a prize for the Colt collector. They were said to be the special interest of Caldwell Hart Colt, Samuel Colt's son, who was an avid arms collector, and most of the 35 guns produced undoubtedly wound up in his collection or those of his friends. This gun is chambered for .45-70 or one of the larger variations thereof. It is an exposed hammer sidelock with double triggers. The locks, breech and furniture are case-colored; the barrels, browned or blued. The barrels are 28 inches in length, and the checkered stock was oil finished or varnished walnut. The barrel rib is stamped with the Colt name and Hartford address. The locks are also stamped "Colt." Colt manufactured the 35 guns over the period 1879 to 1885

NOTE: One must exercise extreme caution when dealing with this model, because quite a few model 1878 shotguns have been converted into double rifles.. In fact, the James D. Julia auction house sold a Colt double rifle in October, 2006 at the Center of New Hampshire Holiday Inn in Manchester, New Hampshire. The reported selling price was $51,175.

EXC.	V.G.	GOOD	FAIR	POOR
-	35,000	20,000	12,000	5500

COLT/ROOT SIDE HAMMER LONG GUNS (AKA MODEL 1855)

Although they were functionally excellent for their time, Lieutenant Colonel Colt's Hartford Side Hammers – the pistols and the long guns – were not very successful on the commercial market. Other than the original Patersons, they were, in fact, the least successful models developed during Colt's life.

About 18,300 long guns of all styles were produced as Side Hammers. The most common caliber was .56. Today, these guns are highly collectible.

1855 SPORTING RIFLE 1ST MODEL

This is a six-shot revolving rifle chambered for .36 cal. percussion. It comes with a 21-, 24-, 27- or 30-inch

Model 1855 Side Hammer 1st Model Carbine and 1855 Colt-Root Revolver, in case.

Model 1855 Side Hammer 1st Model Carbine and 1855 Colt-Root Revolver, right view.

Model 1855 Side Hammer Half Stock Sporting Rifle.

round barrel that is part octagonal where it joins the frame. The stock is walnut with either an oil or varnish finish. The frame, hammer, and loading lever are case colored; the rest of the metal is blued. The hammer is on the right side of the frame. The 1st Model has no fore end, and an oiling device is attached to the barrel underlug. The trigger guard has two spur like projections, one in front and one in back of the bow. The roll engraved cylinder scene depicts a hunter shooting at five deer and is found only on this model. A cleaning rod is mounted along the left side of the barrel. The standard stampings are "COLT'S PT./1856" and "ADDRESS S. COLT HARTFORD, CT U.S.A."

EARLY MODEL

Low serial numbers with a hand-engraved barrel marking "ADDRESS S. COLT HARTFORD, CT U.S.A."

EXC.	V.G.	GOOD	FAIR	POOR
-	-	15,000	5,500	1,500

PRODUCTION MODEL

EXC.	V.G.	GOOD	FAIR	POOR
-	-	12,000	3,000	1,000

1855 1ST MODEL CARBINE

Identical to the 1st Model Rifle but offered with a 15-inch or 18-inch barrel.

EXC.	V.G.	GOOD	FAIR	POOR
-	-	9,500	3,000	1,000

Several carbines named after Sam Colt's friend, firearms engineer and (following Sam's death in 1862) Colt company president Elias K. Root (not Elihu K. Root, as has been reported) have been presented for auction in recent years. The James D. Julia auction house sold a Root Carbine in October, 2006 at the Center of New Hampshire Holiday Inn in Manchester, New Hampshire:

". . .Probably unique Colt Root Transition Carbine .40 cal. (only 10 Root Carbines made in this caliber). This with smooth cylinder and exterior oiler of the 1st mod. and with the full wood fore grip of the 2nd mod.. Only such example known to us. (Hutchinson)"

This Root sold for $21,000.

1855 HALF STOCK SPORTING RIFLE

Although this rifle is similar in appearance and finish to the 1st Model, there are some notable

*Model 1855
Side Hammer
Full Stock
Military Rifle.*

differences. It features a walnut forend that protrudes halfway down the barrel. There are two types of trigger guards; a short projectionless one or a long model with a graceful scroll. The six shot model is chambered for .36 or .44 cal., while the five shot model is chambered for .56 cal. The cylinder is fully fluted. The markings are "COLT'S PT/1856" and "ADDRESS COL. COLT/ HARTFORD CT. U.S.A." Approximately 1,500 were manufactured between 1857 and 1864.

EXC.	V.G.	GOOD	FAIR	POOR
-	-	9,500	3,500	1,000

1855 FULL STOCK MILITARY RIFLE

This model holds six shots in its .44 cal. chambering; five shots when chambered for .56 cal.. It is another side hammer revolving rifle and it resembles the Half Stock model. The barrels are round and partly octagonal where they join the frame. They come in lengths of 21, 24, 27, 31 and 37 inches. The hammer and loading lever are case colored; the rest of the metal parts are blued. The walnut buttstock and full length forend are oil finished, and this model has sling swivels. The cylinder is fully fluted. Military models have provisions for affixing a bayonet and military style sights, and bear the "U.S."

martial mark on guns that were actually issued to the military. The standard stampings found on this model are "COLT'S PT/1856" and "ADDRESS COL. COLT. HARTFORD, CT. U.S.A." An estimated 9,300 were manufactured between 1856 and 1864.

The 1855 Full Stock Military Rifle was the first weapon adopted and used by Col. Berdan's Sharpshooters during the Civil War. That's right; it was used as a long-range sniper's rifle. The legend that these rifles fell out of favor partly because troops occasionally shot off their fingers with them – an accidental consequence of gripping the rifle ahead of the cylinder with the off-hand when firing – appears to be true, judging from contemporary diaries. At any rate, the Colt/Root rifle was rapidly discarded in favor of the Sharps breechloader.

MARTIALLY MARKED MODELS

EXC.	V.G.	GOOD	FAIR	POOR
-	-	25,000	9,500	2,000

WITHOUT MARTIAL MARKINGS

EXC.	V.G.	GOOD	FAIR	POOR
-	-	8,000	3,500	1,000

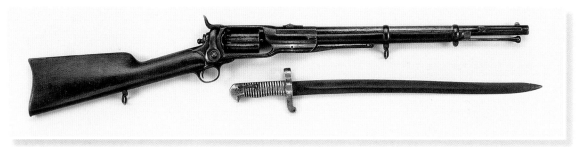

Carbine with bayonet.

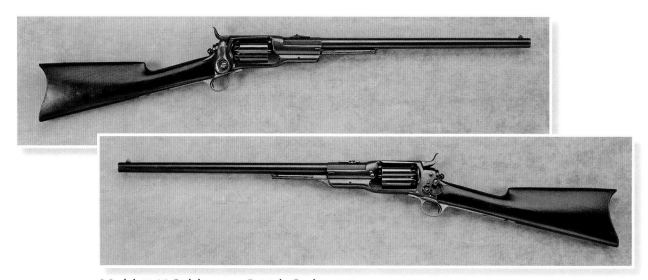

Model 1855 Sidehammer British Carbine.

1855 FULL STOCK SPORTING RIFLE

With a few notable exceptions, this model is similar in appearance to the military model. There is no provision for attaching a bayonet; there are no sling swivels; and it has sporting style sights. The buttplate is crescent shaped. This model has been noted chambered for .56 cal. in a five shot version, and chambered for .36, .40, .44 and .50 cal. in the six shot variation. They are quite scarce in .40 and .50 cal. and will bring a 10 percent premium. The standard markings are "COLT'S PT/1856" and "ADDRESS COL. COLT HARTFORD, CT. U.S.A." Production of this model was quite limited (several hundred at most) between the years 1856 and 1864.

EXC.	V.G.	GOOD	FAIR	POOR
-	-	10,500	4,000	1,000

MODEL 1855 REVOLVING CARBINE

This model is similar in appearance to the 1855 military rifle. The barrel lengths of 15, 18 and 21 inches plus the absence of a fore end make the standard carbine model readily identifiable. The markings are the same. Approximately 4,400 were manufactured between 1856 and 1864.

EXC.	V.G.	GOOD	FAIR	POOR
-	-	9,500	4,000	1,000

MODEL 1855 ARTILLERY CARBINE

Model 1855 Sidehammer Artillery Identical to the standard carbine but only chambered for .56 cal. It has a 24 inch barrel, a full length walnut forend and a bayonet lug.

EXC.	V.G.	GOOD	FAIR	POOR
-	-	17000	5500	1500

MODEL 1855 BRITISH CARBINE

This is a British-proofed version with barrel lengths from 21 to 30 inches. It has a brass trigger guard and buttplate and is only chambered for .56 caliber. This variation is usually found in the #10000 to #12000 serial number range.

EXC.	V.G.	GOOD	FAIR	POOR
-	-	9,000	3,750	1,000

Model 1855 Sidehammer Revolving Shotgun.

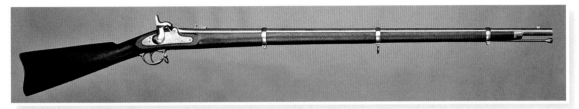

Model 1861 Single Shot Rifled Musket.

MODEL 1855 REVOLVING SHOTGUN

This model very much resembles the Half Stock Sporting Rifle but was made with a 27-, 30-, 33- and 36-inch smoothbore barrel. It has a five shot cylinder chambered for .60 or .75 caliber (20 or 10 gauge). The revolving shotgun has a case colored hammer and loading lever; the rest of the metal is blued, with an occasional browned barrel noted. The butt stock and fore end are of walnut, either oil or varnish finished. This model has no rear sight, but the small trigger guard has the caliber stamped on it. Some have been noted with the large scroll trigger guard; this feature adds 10 percent to the value. The rarest shotgun variation would be a full stocked version in either gauge, and qualified appraisal would be highly recommended. This model is serial numbered in its own range, #1 to #1100. They were manufactured from 1860 to 1863.

.60 CALIBER (20 GAUGE)

EXC.	V.G.	GOOD	FAIR	POOR
-	-	8,000	3,500	1,000

.75 CALIBER (10 GAUGE)

EXC.	V.G.	GOOD	FAIR	POOR
-	-	8,000	3,500	1,000

NOTE: The following advertisement appeared on *GunsAmerica.com* in the Spring of 2007:

"Colt 1855 Revolving Shotgun .60 caliber, 27 inch round barrel. Serial number #49x. Some original finish left. Mechanically very good. Stock has no cracks. Has typical handling marks. Excellent specimen. Original cleaning rod is intact with gutta percha shield. Bore and cylinder are in good shape. Asking $6,495."

MODEL 1861 SINGLE SHOT RIFLED MUSKET

With the advent of the Civil War, the army of the Union needed military arms. Colt was given a contract to supply 112,500 1861 pattern percussion single shot muskets. Between 1861 and 1865, 75,000 were delivered. They have 40-inch rifled barrels chambered for .58 caliber. The musket is equipped with military sights, sling swivels and a bayonet lug. The metal finish is bright steel, and the stock is oil finished walnut. Military inspector's marks are found on all major parts. "VP" over an eagle is stamped on the breech along with a date. The Colt address and a date are stamped on the lock plate. A large number of these rifles were altered to the Snyder breech loading system for the Bey of Egypt.

PRODUCTION MODEL

EXC.	V.G.	GOOD	FAIR	POOR
-	7000	5500	2000	450

MODERN ERA LONG GUNS INCLUDING SPORTER AND AR15

COLTEER I-22

This is a single-shot bolt action rifle chambered for .22 LR or .22 Magnum. It has a plain uncheckered walnut stock, 20 inch barrel, and adjustable sights. There were approximately 50,000 manufactured between 1957 and 1966.

EXC.	V.G.	GOOD	FAIR	POOR
400	300	175	125	90

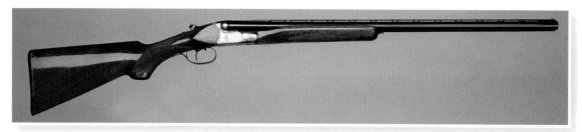

Colt Double Barrel Shotgun.

STAGECOACH

Here's a semi-automatic, saddle ring carbine. It is chambered for .22 LR and has a 16.5 inch barrel and a 13 shot tubular magazine. The stock is fancy walnut, and the receiver has the classic Colt stagecoach holdup scene roll engraved on it. There were approximately 25,000 manufactured between 1965 and 1975.

EXC.	V.G.	GOOD	FAIR	POOR
450	350	200	150	100

COURIER

This model is similar to the Stagecoach, with a pistol grip stock and beaver tail forearm. It was manufactured between 1970 and 1975.

EXC.	V.G.	GOOD	FAIR	POOR
450	350	200	125	90

COLTEER

This is a less expensive version of the Stagecoach. It features a 19.5 inch barrel, has a 15 shot tubular magazine, and is stocked in a plainer grade walnut. There is no roll engraving. Approximately 25,000 were manufactured between 1965 and 1975.

EXC.	V.G.	GOOD	FAIR	POOR
450	350	200	125	90

COLT "57" BOLT-ACTION RIFLE

This rifle was manufactured for Colt by the Jefferson Mfg. Co of New Haven, Connecticut. It utilizes a Fabrique Nationale Mauser action and has a checkered American walnut stock with a Monte Carlo comb. The rifle is offered with adjustable sights. It is chambered for .243 or .30-06. There is also a deluxe version that features higher grade wood. There were approximately 5,000 manufactured in 1957. For the deluxe version, add 20 percent.

EXC.	V.G.	GOOD	FAIR	POOR
550	450	350	300	225

COLTSMAN BOLT-ACTION RIFLE

The Coltsman was manufactured for Colt by Kodiak Arms. It utilizes either a Mauser or Sako action. The rifle is offered in .243, .308, .30-06 and .300 Winchester Magnum. It has a barrel length of 22 or 24 inch in the Magnum chambering. The stock is checkered American walnut. There were approximately 10,000 manufactured between 1958 and 1966. There is a deluxe version that features a higher grade, skipline checkered walnut stock and rosewood forend tip; this is called "The Coltsman Custom" (add 50 percent).

EXC.	V.G.	GOOD	FAIR	POOR
650	550	450	350	250

COLTSMAN PUMP SHOTGUN

This pump gun was manufactured by Jefferson Arms utilizing an aluminum alloy frame made by Franchi. It is chambered for 12, 16, and 20 gauge shells and has a 26- or 28- inch plain barrel. There were approximately 2,000 manufactured between 1961 and 1965.

EXC.	V.G.	GOOD	FAIR	POOR
350	300	275	200	150

NOTE: The following advertisement appeared on *GunsAmerica.com* in the Spring of 2007:

"I have a Colt Coltsman 12 gauge pump shotgun made in about 1963. The gun is almost like new with handling marks on stock otherwise like new has rampant colt under forearm and barrel marked 'COLT,S PT.F.A.MFG. CO.HARFFORD CT. U.S.A. ---12 GAUGE 3------- MOD----' Bottom of the action is marked 'Action Made In France.' Serial number #9045x. Near as I can tell they only made 2,000 in 12,16 and 20 gauge. Asking $650."

SEMI-AUTOMATIC SHOTGUN

This shotgun was manufactured for Colt by the firm of Luigi Franchi in Italy. It features an aluminum alloy receiver and is chambered for 12- or 20-gauge shells. The barrel length is 26, 28, 30 or 32 inches with either ventilated rib or plain barrel options. A deluxe version, The Custom Auto, features a fancy walnut stock and a hand engraved receiver (add 25 percent). There were approximately 5,300 manufactured between 1962 and 1966.

EXC.	V.G.	GOOD	FAIR	POOR
375	325	300	225	175

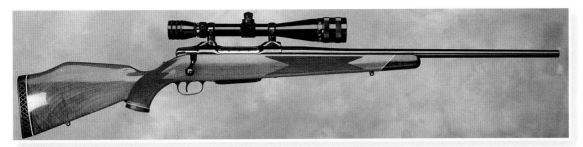

Colt-Sauer Bolt Action Rifle.

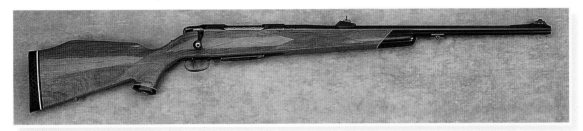

Colt-Sauer Grand African.

Colt Light Rifle.

DOUBLE-BARREL SHOTGUN (1960S VINTAGE)

During 1961 and 1962, Colt had approximately 50 side by side shotguns made for them by a French gun manufacturer. They have the Colt name on the breech area of the barrels and are in the serial number #467000 to #469000 range. There is little information available on this gun, and Colt never went past the test market stage.

EXC.	V.G.	GOOD	FAIR	POOR
1,000	750	650	500	400

SAUER BOLT-ACTION RIFLE

This was a high-quality and unique rifle manufactured for Colt by the firm of J.P. Sauer & Son of Germany. The rifle features a non-rotating bolt that makes the Colt Sauer action smoother functioning than most. It has a 24-inch barrel, skipline checkered walnut stock with rosewood forend tip, pistol grip cap and recoil pad. There are five basic configurations: the Standard Action, chambered for .25-06, .270 Winchester and .30-06; the Short Action, chambered for .22-250, .243 Winchester and .308 Winchester; the Magnum Action, chambered for 7mm Remington Magnum, .300 Winchester Magnum and .300 Weatherby Magnum; and finally the "Grand Alaskan" and the "Grand African," heavier versions chambered for .375 Holland & Holland Magnum and .458 Winchester Magnum, respectively. These rifles were all discontinued by Colt in 1985. For Standard Action add $50; for Magnum Action add $200; for Grand Alaskan add $400; for Grand African add $450.

SAUER SHORT ACTION

EXC.	V.G.	GOOD	FAIR	POOR
1500	1150	775	600	500

NOTE: The following advertisement appeared on *ColtAutos.com* in the Spring of 2007:

"Colt Sauer Sporting Rifle - Caliber: 25-06, serial number #CR13136, Price: $1600. Description: Like new, fired only 6 rounds. No dings or scratches."

COLT LIGHT RIFLE

Introduced in 1999, this bolt-action rifle was offered in both long- and short-action calibers from .243 to .300 Win. Mag. Fitted with a 24-inch barrel

Colt-Sharps Rifle.

and an adjustable trigger; the stock is black synthetic. Action and barrel are matte black. The long-action rifle weighs about 6 lb. and the short action rifle about 5.4 lb. Adjustable trigger. No sights. This rifle was not a commercial success; the effect of firing a .300 Win Mag in a 6-lb. rifle may provide some clue as to why.

NIB	EXC.	V.G.	GOOD	FAIR	POOR
600	495	365	-	-	-

SAUER DRILLING

This is a rather unique firearm and one with which many American enthusiasts are not familiar, a three-barrel gun. It features a side by side shotgun in 12 gauge above a .30-06 or .243 rifle barrel. The name "Drilling" is based on the German word for three (*drei*), as this is where the concept was developed. These guns are quite popular in Europe where the game preserve style of hunting is prevalent, but have relatively little use in America where our hunting seasons do not often overlap in a manner that would make the three-barrel concept practical. The Sauer Drilling has 25-inch barrels with pop-up sights for the rifle barrel and is nicely engraved. It was discontinued by Colt in 1985.

EXC.	V.G.	GOOD	FAIR	POOR
4,500	3,250	2,250	1,500	1,100

COLT-SHARPS RIFLE

Introduced in 1970 as the last word in sporting rifles, the Colt-Sharps is a falling block action that was advertised as a modern Sharps-Borchardt. This undertaking was first-class all the way. The finish is high polish blue with a deluxe grade hand checkered walnut stock and forend. This rifle is chambered for .17 Remington, .22-250, .243, .25-06, 7mm Remington Magnum, .30-06 and .375 Holland & Holland Magnum. To complete it as a high-end "ensemble buy," the Colt-Sharps was offered cased with accessories. This model was manufactured between 1970 and 1977.

NIB	EXC.	V.G.	GOOD	FAIR	POOR
3,500	2,900	1,500	850	500	300

NOTE: The following advertisement was shown on *GunsAmerica.com* during the spring 2007:

"As New in box, rare Colt Sharp's Sporting rifle, Single shot drop action, 30-06, with carry case, serial numbered to Rifle. This comes with all the original equipment, patches, brushes, screwdriver kit, cleaning rod, swing swivels and sling. All original paperwork including test target. Also included as original equipment, a Leupold 3x9 Gold Ring Scope. Not a scratch or wear on the rifle. This rifle is perfect for hunting or for a collector. $3,995."

AR-15 AND SPORTER RIFLES

There are three different and distinct manufacturing cycles that not only affect the value of these rifles, but also the legal consequences of their modifications. Note that the "ban" mentioned below refers to the Federal Assault Weapons Band (AWB), a provision of the Violent Crime Control and Law Enforcement Act of 1994. The ban was allowed to "sunset" (i.e., expire without renewal) in 2004. During the ban, "pre-ban" rifles reached unprecedented spikes in value. When the ban expired, values decreased, though not quite to their pre-ban levels.

Pre-Ban Colt AR-15 Rifles (Pre-1989): Fitted with bayonet lug, flash hider and stamped AR-15 on lower receiver. Rifles that are New in the box (NIB) have a *green label*. It is legal to modify this rifle with any AR-15 upper receiver. These are the most desirable models because of their pre-ban features, though this desirability has lessened somewhat because of the ban's lapse.

Colt Sporters (Post-1989, Pre-September 1994): This transition model has no bayonet lug, but it does have a flash hider. There is no AR-15 designation stamped on the lower receiver. Rifles that are NIB have a *blue label*. It is legal to modify this rifle with upper receivers made after 1989, i.e. no bayonet lug. These rifles are less desirable than pre-ban AR-15s.

Colt Sporters (Post-September 1994): This rifle has

Colt AR-15 Sporter.

no bayonet lug, no flash hider and does not have the AR-15 designation stamped on the lower receiver. Rifles that are NIB have a *blue label*. It is legal to modify this rifle only with upper receivers manufactured after September 1994. These rifles are the least desirable of the three manufacturing periods because of their lack of pre-ban military features and current manufacture status.

PRICING NOTE: It is estimated that the value of pre-ban AR-15s have declined 10 to 15 percent since the Assault Weapons ban has lapsed. The pricing status of the AR-15 Sporter is still volatile. As if to emphasize that volatility, a 9mm AR-15 Sporter with 16-inch barrel noted as "Green Label – Unfired" was recently (2007) listed on *ImpactGuns.com* for $2,999.99.

Also note that, although it is popular to modify AR-15-type guns to suit one's own tastes, doing so lessens their value in the eyes of many collectors. Highest values for Colt AR-15s are realized for 100% factory guns in Excellent or better condition.

AR-15 SP-1 SPORTER (MODEL #6000)

This rifle, a semi-automatic firing from a closed bolt, was introduced into the Colt product line in 1964. It is similar in appearance and function to the military version, the M-16. Chambered for the .223 cartridge. It is fitted with a standard 20-inch barrel with no forward assist, and no case deflector, but – curiously – with a bayonet lug. Weight is about 7.5 lb. It was dropped from production in 1985.

NIB	EXC.	V.G.	GOOD	FAIR	POOR
1,650	1,100	900	700	600	400

NOTE: The following advertisement appeared on *GunBroker.com* in March of 2007:

"*Colt SP1 AR15 SP-1 AR-15 PreBan 1982 6 digit serial number. An outstanding example of the 1982 state-of-the-art in Colt's military weaponry. You get what you see - all original parts as it came off the assembly line. Excellent condition. Includes 1 mag. 6-digit serial number 20775x.*"

The gun sold for $980.

AR-15 SP-1 SPORTER W/COLLAPSIBLE STOCK (MODEL #6001)

Same as above but fitted with a 16-inch barrel and folding stock. Weighs approximately 5.8 lb. Introduced in 1978 and discontinued in 1985.

NIB	EXC.	V.G.	GOOD	FAIR	POOR
1,800	1,200	1,000	750	650	425

AR-15 CARBINE (MODEL #6420)

Introduced in 1985 this model has a 16-inch standard weight barrel. All other features are the same as the previous discontinued AR-15 models. This version was dropped from the Colt product line in 1987.

NIB	EXC.	V.G.	GOOD	FAIR	POOR
1,450	1,200	900	750	600	400

AR-15 CARBINE 9MM (MODEL #6450)

Same as above, chambered for 9mm cartridge. Weighs 6.3 lb.

NIB	EXC.	V.G.	GOOD	FAIR	POOR
1,300	1,150	1,000	800	700	400

AR-15A2 SPORTER II (MODEL #6500)

Introduced in 1984 this was an updated version with a heavier barrel and forward assist. The AR sight was still utilized. Weighs approximately 7.8 lb.

NIB	EXC.	V.G.	GOOD	FAIR	POOR
1,450	1,100	950	750	550	400

AR-15 A2 Government Carbine.

AR-15A2 GOVERNMENT MODEL CARBINE (MODEL #6520)

Added to the Colt line in 1988 (and still in the Law Enforcement line up in the summer of 2007) this rifle has a 16.1-inch (41 cm) standard barrel (six groove rifling twist with a right-hand turn of 1:7). For the first time this carbine featured a case deflector and the improved A2 rear sight with dual apertures (0-200m and 300-800m) adjustable for windage and elevation. Adjustable front sight and sight radius of 14.5 inches (37 cm). This model is fitted with a four-position telescoping buttstock so its length varies from 32 (81 cm) to 35 inches (89 cm). Weighs about 5.8 lb. (2.63 kg) empty. Front barrel lug allows for easy mounting of a variety of optional accessories. Cartridge case deflector available for left hand shooters. Standard carbine handguards with heat shield. Ejection port cover protects the chamber from dust and grime. Muzzle compensator reduces muzzle climb and helps eliminate flash and dust signatures. Fixed carrying handle.

NIB	EXC.	V.G.	GOOD	FAIR	POOR
1,600	1,300	1,000	800	700	500

AR-15A2 GOVERNMENT MODEL (MODEL #6550)

This model was introduced in 1988 as the rifle equivalent to the Carbine. It features a 20-inch A2 barrel, forward assist and case deflector, but still retains the bayonet lug. Weighs about 7.5 lb. Discontinued in 1990. (U.S. Marine Corps model.)

NIB	EXC.	V.G.	GOOD	FAIR	POOR
2,300	2,000	1,250	950	700	500

AR-15A2 H-BAR (MODEL #6600)

Introduced in 1986 this version features a special 20-inch heavy barrel. All other features are the same as the A2 series of AR15s. Discontinued in 1991. Weighs about 8 lb.

NIB	EXC.	V.G.	GOOD	FAIR	POOR
1,650	1,450	1,250	850	700	500

AR-15A2 DELTA H-BAR (MODEL #6600DH)

Same as above but fitted with a 3x9 scope and detachable cheekpiece. Dropped from the Colt line in 1990. Weighs about 10 lb.

NIB	EXC.	V.G.	GOOD	FAIR	POOR
1,900	1,750	1,300	1,000	850	600

SPORTER LIGHTWEIGHT RIFLE

This lightweight model has a 16-inch barrel and is finished in a matte black. It is available in either a .223 Rem. caliber (Model #6530) that weighs 6.7 lb., a (Model #6430) 9mm caliber weighing 7.1 lb., or a (Model #6830) 7.65x39mm that weighs 7.3 lb. The .223 is furnished with two, five round box magazines as is the 9mm and 7.65x39mm. A cleaning kit and sling are also supplied with each new rifle. The buttstock and pistol grip are made of durable nylon and the handguard is reinforced fiberglass and aluminum lined. The rear sight is adjustable for windage and elevation. These newer models are referred to simply as Sporters. They are *not* fitted with a bayonet lug and the receiver block has different size pins. The Model 6830 will bring about $25 less than the above prices. For post-9/94 guns deduct 30 percent.

NIB	EXC.	V.G.	GOOD	FAIR	POOR
950	850	750	600	400	300

SPORTER TARGET MODEL RIFLE (MODEL #6551)

This 1991 model is a full size version of the Lightweight Rifle. The Target Rifle weighs 7.5 lb. and has a 20-inch barrel. Offered in .223 Rem. caliber only, with target sights adjustable to 800 meters. New rifles are furnished with two, five-round box magazines, sling and cleaning kit. For post-September 1994 guns deduct 30 percent.

Colt Match Target Competition H-BAR.

NIB	EXC.	V.G.	GOOD	FAIR	POOR
1,200	1,100	850	650	400	300

SPORTER MATCH TARGET H-BAR (MODEL #6601)

This 1991 variation of the AR-15 is similar to the Target Model but has a 20-inch heavy barrel (six grooves, right hand rifling, one turn in seven inches) chambered for the .223 caliber. With a black anodized receiver and black oxide barrel, the 6601 is a semi automatic, gas operating locking bolt rifle that weighs eight lb. It has target type rear sights adjustable out to 800 meters and the front sight's post is adjustable for elevation. The carry handle is fixed. It is supplied with two, five round box magazines, sling and cleaning kit. Overall length is 39 inches. For post-September 1994 guns deduct 35 percent.

NIB	EXC.	V.G.	GOOD	FAIR	POOR
1,300	1,150	1,000	650	400	300

MATCH TARGET H-BAR COMPENSATED (MODEL #6601C)

This is the same gun as the regular Sporter H-Bar with the addition of a compensator (muzzle brake) to reduce recoil and muzzle rise.

NIB	EXC.	V.G.	GOOD	FAIR	POOR
1,250	900	750	-	-	-

SPORTER MATCH DELTA H-BAR (MODEL #6601 DH)

Same as above but supplied with a 3 x 9 scope. Weighs about 10 lb. Discontinued in 1992.

NIB	EXC.	V.G.	GOOD	FAIR	POOR
1,400	1,200	1,100	850	600	400

SPORTER MATCH TARGET COMPETITION H-BAR (MODEL #6700)

Introduced in 1992, the Competition H-Bar is available in .223 caliber with a 20-inch heavy barrel counterbored for accuracy (six rifling grooves, right hand twist, one turn in nine inches). The carry handle is detachable and target sights adjust out to 800 meters; in addition, the front sight post is adjustable for elevation. With the carry handle removed the upper receiver is dovetailed and grooved for Weaver-style scope rings. This model weighs approximately 8.5 lb. and is 39 inches long. New rifles are furnished with two five-round box magazines, although it handles all AR15/M16 high capacity magazines and drums. A sling and cleaning kit are usually included. For post-September 1994 guns deduct 35 percent.

NIB	EXC.	V.G.	GOOD	FAIR	POOR
1,150	1,000	900	700	500	350

NOTE: The following advertisement appeared in March of 2007 on *GunBroker.com*:

"Colt Model 6700 Match Target Comp. AR-15. You are bidding on a Colt Model 6700 Match Target Competition AR-15, with a 20 inch H-Bar barrel with a 1 in 9 twist chambered in 5.56 NATO/.223 Rem. caliber. Removable carry handle with ½ minute hooded national match sights by Compass Lake Engineering, also a National Match Front Sight Post, it has a float tube by Compass Lake Engineering and a Rock River Two-Stage National Match Trigger, three 20 round Colt Mags, one 9 round Colt mag, Front Hand Guard and Buttstock Balance weights, Sling and carry case. This gun is ready for a CMP or NRA match, This gun has had approximately 2,000 rounds put through it."

This altered, non-factory gun had a reserve of $1,075 but attracted no bids.

SPORTER COMPETITION H-BAR SELECT W/SCOPE (MODEL #6700CH)

This variation, also new for 1992, is identical to the Sporter Competition with the addition of a factory mounted scope. The rifle has also been selected for accuracy and comes complete with a 3-9X rubber armored variable scope, scope mount, carry handle with iron sights, and nylon carrying case. The flattop receiver allows for low scope mounting.

NIB	EXC.	V.G.	GOOD	FAIR	POOR
1,200	1,100	-	-	-	-

Colt AR-15A3 Tactical Carbine.

MATCH TARGET COMPETITION H-BAR COMPENSATED (MODEL #6700C)

Same as the Match Target with a compensator. Competition semi automatic rifle chambered for .223 Remington, with 20-inch heavy barrel, black finish and black stock. These Match Target Rifles have the accuracy and dependability needed to live up to the reputation of their predecessors as one of the greatest rifles of all time. Designed to meet government specifications, the Match Target family of rifles are, according to Colt, "... excellent examples of the responsible role Colt plays in the future of firearms. They are easy to field strip, and feature comfortable, accurate shooting. Match Target rifles are enhanced with heat dissipating ribbed hand guards, cartridge case deflectors and adjustable sights. They are ideal for competition shooting, varmint hunting and general target shooting. The Colt Match Target is second to none." An optional flat top receiver allows for removable carry handle with built in target style rear sights, and easy mounting of optics

NIB	EXC.	V.G.	GOOD	FAIR	POOR
1,250	900	-	-	-	-

AR-15A3 CARBINE FLATTOP HEAVYWEIGHT/MATCH TARGET COMPETITION (MODEL #6731)

This semi-auto, gas operated, locking bolt variation in the Sporter series features a heavyweight 16-inch barrel (six grooves 1 turn in 9 inches) with flat-top receiver chambered for the .223 cartridge. It is equipped with a fixed buttstock. Adjustable post front sight for elevation; rear sight adjusts to 800m. Flattop receiver allows for low scope mounting. Overall length is 34.5 inches. Weight is about 7.1 lb. For post-9/94 guns deduct 10 percent.

NIB	EXC.	V.G.	GOOD	FAIR	POOR
1,100	900	750	600	400	300

AR-15A3 TACTICAL CARBINE (MODEL #6721)

This version is similar to the above semi-auto and was still in the Law Enforcement line-up in the summer of 2007. It is a gas operated locking bolt model with the exception of the butt stock, which is telescoping and adjusts to four positions thus giving an overall length of 32 to 35 inches (81 to 89 cm). Chambered for 5.56mm (.223 Rem.) cartridges (it also accepts the NATO M855/SS109 and U.S. M193) and has a 16.1-inch (41 cm) heavy barrel and weight of about 7 lb. (3.2 kg). Six right hand rifling grooves, 1 turn in 9 inches (229 mm). Detachable carrying handle allows mounting of various tactical sighting systems. Front sight is adjustable; rear target sight features dual apertures (0-200m, 300-600m) and adjusts for windage and elevation. Sight radius 14.5 inches (37 cm). Straight-line construction disperses recoil straight back to the shoulder, increasing handling capabilities, especially during repeated fire. A four-position sliding buttstock allows the weapon to adapt to users of different sizes and physical characteristics as well as various firing positions and clothing variations. Most of these guns were designed for law enforcement only (LEO). Two 20-round magazines are standard; a 30 round magazine is optional. Can be field stripped without special tools. Standard carbine hand guards with heat shield. Cartridge case deflector for left hand shooting. Muzzle compensator helps reduce muzzle climb and eliminate flash and dust signatures. Ejection port cover protects the chamber from dust and grime. Front barrel lug allows for easy mounting of a variety of accessories. Only 134 rifles are pre-ban.

NIB	EXC.	V.G.	GOOD	FAIR	POOR
1,400	1,200	1,000	800	600	400

SPORTER H-BAR ELITE/ACCURIZED RIFLE (MODEL #6724)

This 43-inch, nine-shot M16 variation accommodates the full range of 5.56mm/.223 Rem. ammunition, including the NATO M855/SS109 and U.S. M193, utilizing a rifling twist of six grooves right hand 1 turn in 9 inches (229mm). It was introduced

*Colt Sporter H-BAR Elite, aka
the Colt Accurized Rifle.*

Colt Law Enforcement Carbine.

in 1996 and features a free floating 24 inch stainless steel match barrel with an 11 degree target crown and special, smooth Teflon coated trigger group. The tubular handguard is all-aluminum with twin swivel studs. Flat top receiver allows for scope mounting. Multi-lug rotary locking bolt Weight is approximately 9.26 lb.

NIB	EXC.	V.G.	GOOD	FAIR	POOR
1,200	900	700	550	400	300

COLT AR-15 (XM16E1)

This rifle was made upon request for foreign government contracts and is very rare, especially in Excellent to Very Good condition. A potential collector should proceed with caution. This variation will command a premium price over the standard AR-15 rifle. Secure a competent appraisal before a sale.

CARBINE A3 16 M4 MT6400C

One of Colts latest version of the AR15, with a factory muzzle brake. It is very hard to find! This post ban model features a pinned lightweight carbine style flat top stock and muzzle brake. True M4 hand guards, front side sling mount, one nine round magazine included and a detachable handle. Matte black semi auto; gas operated with multi lug rotary locking nut. 5.56mm/.223 Rem. with nine round magazine. Barrel is 16.1 inches long with 6 groove right hand rifling, 1 turn in 7 inches. Smooth trigger; adjustable front sight (elevation) and rear sights (windage and elevation);

sight radius 14.75 inches; 7.3 lb. and 35 inches length overall.

NIB	EXC.	V.G.	GOOD	FAIR	POOR
1,150	900	650	500	350	250

LAW ENFORCEMENT CARBINE (LE6920)

This law enforcement weapon system features many of the combat proven advantages of the military M4 and was still included in the Law Enforcement line-up in 2007. Straight-line construction disperses recoil straight back to the shoulder, increasing handling capabilities, especially during repeated fire. Unique direct gas operating system eliminates conventional operating rod and results in fewer and lighter components. Bird cage style upper receiver. With the four position buttstock (allows the weapon to adapt to users of different sizes and physical characteristics as well as various firing positions and clothing variations) fully retracted, LE6920 is 30.4 inches (76.2 cm) in length and weighs only 5.95 lb. (2.67 kg), ideal for tactical deployment and traditional patrol. At maximum extension, the length is 34.6 inches (88 cm). This carbine is available with a step-cut 16.1-inch barrel that allows it to accept the M203 40mm grenade

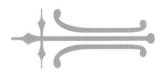

Colt Law Enforcement M4 Carbine.

launcher for non-lethal options. The hand guard has dual insulated aluminum shielding for more effective heat protection. Accommodates the full range of 5.56 mm ammunition, including NATO M855/SS109 and U.S. M193, utilizing a rifling twist of 1 turn in 7 inches (178mm). Cartridge case deflector allows easy right and left hand operation. Muzzle compensator reduces muzzle climb, helps eliminate flash and dust signatures. Ejection port cover protects chamber from dust. Flat top receiver allows for removable carrying handle and easy mounting of accessories. Two 20 round magazines included with purchase; 30 round magazines are optional. Adjustable front sight and target style rear sight features dual apertures (0-200m and 300-600m) and adjusts for both windage and elevation. Carrying handle.

Law Enforcement Model LE6921 is even shorter. The barrel length is 14.5 inches (37 cm) and length overall with the four position buttstock is 29.8 to 33.0 inches (76 to 84 cm). The LE6921 weighs 5.65 lb. (2.56 kg).

NIB	EXC.	V.G.	GOOD	FAIR	POOR
1,700	1,200	-	-	-	-

LAW ENFORCEMENT M4 CARBINE (R0977)

In the Law Enforcement and Private Security line-ups, Colt says its M4 Carbine is the weapon of choice according to today's law enforcement concepts of rapid deployment, mobility and increased firepower. It can be comfortably carried, yet instantly available. Direct gas operating system with locking bolt eliminates the conventional operating rod for fewer and lighter components. Accommodates the full range of 5.56mm ammunition, including NATO M855/SS109 and U.S.

M193, utilizing a rifling twist of 1 turn in 7 inches (178mm). Straight-line construction disperses recoil straight back to the shoulder, increasing handling capabilities, especially during repeated fire. Four position sliding buttstock – from 29.8 (75.7 cm) to 33 inches (83.8 cm) – allows the weapon to adapt to users of different sizes and physical characteristics as well as various firing positions and clothing variations. Barrel is 14.5 inches (36.8 cm) long; muzzle velocity 2,900 fps (884 m/sec); and effective range is 600 meters. Rate of fire in full auto is 700 to 950 rpm. Cartridge case deflector allows easy operation in both right and left hand shooting positions. Muzzle compensator helps reduce muzzle climb and eliminate flash and dust signatures. Ejection port cover protects the chamber from dust. Flat top receiver allows for removable carrying handle and easy mounting of accessories such as the M203 40mm Grenade Launcher, which mounts without modification. Target style rear sight features dual apertures (0-200m and 300-600m) and adjusts for both windage and elevation. Magazine capacity is 30 rounds. Weight without magazine is 5.9 lb. (2.68 kg). Variations include:

- R0977: Flat top, detachable handle: Firing modes in Safe, Semi and Full Auto
- R0979: Flat top, detachable handle: Firing modes in Safe, Semi Auto and Burst
- R0777: Flat top, fixed handle: Firing modes in Safe, Semi and Full Auto
- R0779: Flat top, fixed handle: Firing modes in Safe, Semi Auto and Burst

Pricing is not given as civilian ownership is prohibited.

Colt M16A4 on duty with U.S. Marine in streets of Fallujah, Iraq.

LAW ENFORCEMENT M4
COMMANDO (R0933)

A part of the Law Enforcement line-up as of 2007, the Commando is Colt's compact 5.56 mm (.223 Rem.) with a four position sliding buttstock - 26.8 (68.1 cm) to 30 in (76.2 cm) – and an 11.5 inch (29.2 cm) long barrel. It shares most of the characteristics of the M16A3/M4 group of weapons: direct gas operating system, straight line construction, cartridge case deflector, muzzle compensator, ejection port cover, flat top receiver, 30 round magazine, adjustable front sight and target style rear sight with dual apertures (0-200m and 300-600m). Accommodates the full range of 5.56mm ammunition, including NATO M855/SS109 and U.S. M193, utilizing a rifling twist of 1 turn in 7 inches (178mm). Weight without magazine is 5.38 lb. (2.44 kg) and barrel length is 11.5 inches (29.2 cm). Muzzle velocity listed at 2,612 fps (796 m/sec) and an effective range of 600 meters. Rate of fire in full auto is 700 to 950 rpm. Variations include:

- R0933: Flat top, detachable handle: Firing modes in Safe, Semi and Full Auto
- R0935: Flat top, detachable handle: Firing modes in Safe, Semi Auto and Burst
- R0733: Flat top, fixed handle: Firing modes in Safe, Semi and Full Auto
- R0733: Flat top, fixed handle: Firing modes in Safe, Semi Auto and Burst

Pricing is not given as civilian ownership is prohibited.

MILITARY ISSUE M16 AND BEYOND

M16 ASSAULT RIFLE

The M16 rifle has a great many variations and configurations. Some of these variations are available to the collector and others are so rare as to be, for practical purposes, unavailable because of cost or simple difficulty to locate. As collecting these guns is a rather rarified activity, pricing is not given, and data is given for reference purposes only.

Please keep in mind that the M16 series of rifles is comprised of two main parts: the upper receiver and lower receiver. The upper receiver is not considered a firearm by the ATF and is not registered. Nor is the upper receiver marked or serial numbered to the lower receiver. Conversely, the lower receiver is serial numbered and marked with its model designation. It is therefore quite possible for upper receivers to be matched to lower receivers that are not in an original factory configuration. In order to be factory original, both upper and lower receivers must be configured at the factory prior to shipment. This is sometimes impossible to determine. It is therefore highly recommended that an expert be consulted prior to a purchase to help determine originality.

On early models, the "A" suffix usually means it has a forward assist and the "B" suffix usually means it has a burst mode. Model numbers began with the 600 series, then the 700 series, which are based on the M16A2. The 800 series models are grenade launchers (M203). The 900 series models have flat top upper receivers and removable carry handles.

The following are model designations with Colt nomenclature:
* XM16 became the M16
* XM16E1 became the M16A1
* M16A1E1 became the M16A2
* M16A2E4 became the M16A4

M203 grenade launchers retail for about $4,500 NIB, but launchers made by AAI will bring $15,000 because of their rarity.

As a general rule, "U.S. PROPERTY" marked guns will bring a premium, in some cases a substantial premium, depending on model and configuration. These premiums will be so stated where applicable.

The M16 was also produced by GM's Hydramatic division and Harrington & Richardson, Inc. Manufacturing began in late 1968. M16s from either supplier are rarely encountered. Rifles made by H&R will bring about 85 percent of a comparable Colt M16, while the Hydramatic rifles will bring almost double that of a Colt M16. This premium does not apply to rifles that have been re-welded.

The Colt M16 comes in a variety of configurations (upper receivers), some of which are mentioned here. It is important to note (as we have above discussed) that these configurations are based on being matched with the same lower receiver. In the case of civilian ownership, the lower receiver is the registered part of the firearm as far as the Bureau of Alcohol, Tobacco, Firearms and Explosives (BATFE) is concerned. Therefore, it is possible, with a registered lower receiver, to interchange upper receiver components to a wide variety of different configurations, from 9mm to .223 LMG uppers, for instance. Be aware that this interchangeability works best with Colt parts.

THE 600 SERIES

COLT/ARMALITE AR-15/M16 MODEL 601

This rifle was first produced in 1960 and many variants followed. Chambered for the 5.56x45mm cartridge it has a 20.8 inch barrel with flash hider. Magazine capacity is 20 or 30 rounds. Weight is seven pounds. Rate of fire is 800 rounds per minute. It was formerly used extensively in Vietnam and is now a standard military and police weapon around the world. Some were marked "COLT AR-15 PROPERTY OF US GOVT. M15 CAL 5.56MM" on left side of magazine housing, but early guns were not even marked "US Property." There is a wide variation in prices and models. Prices listed below are for the standard Colt/Armalite rifle. For Armalite only marked rifles no price given because of rarity. For Colt only marked rifles deduct $2,000.

PRE-1968
EXC.	V.G.	FAIR
-	-	-

PRE-1986 CONVERSIONS, FOR OEM A1 ADD 40 PERCENT
EXC.	V.G.	FAIR
-	-	-

PRE-1986 DEALER SAMPLES
EXC.	V.G.	FAIR
-	-	-

COLT MODEL 602
This U.S. ("US PROPERTY") model was fitted with a 20-inch barrel. It has no forward assist. Select fire is available in full or semi-automatic.

EXC.   V.G.   FAIR

-          -   -

COLT MODEL 603 (M16A1)

This U.S. ("US PROPERTY") model has a 20-inch barrel with forward assist. Barrel has a 1-in-12 twist rate. Select fire is available in full- or semi-automatic.

PRE-1968
EXC.   V.G.   FAIR

-          -   -

PRE-1986 CONVERSIONS, FOR OEM A1 ADD 40 PERCENT
EXC.   V.G.   FAIR

-          -   -

PRE-1986 DEALER SAMPLES
EXC.   V.G.   FAIR

-          -   -

COLT MODEL 604 (M16)

This U.S. ("US Property") Air Force model has a 20 inch barrel with a 1-in-12 twist. No forward assist. Select fire is available in full- or semi-automatic.

PRE-1968
EXC.   V.G.   FAIR

-          -   -

PRE-1986 CONVERSIONS, FOR OEM A1 ADD 40 PERCENT
EXC.   V.G.   FAIR

-          -   -

PRE-1986 DEALER SAMPLES
EXC.   V.G.   FAIR

-          -   -

COLT MODEL 605A CAR-15 CARBINE

This U.S. ("US PROPERTY") version is the short barrel (10-inch) model of the rifle with a forward assist. Select fire is available in full or semi-automatic.

PRE-1968
EXC.   V.G.   FAIR

-          -   -

PRE-1986 OEM/COLT
EXC.   V.G.   FAIR

-          -   -

PRE-1986 DEALER SAMPLES
EXC.   V.G.   FAIR

-          -   -

COLT MODEL 605B

This U.S. ("US PROPERTY") version is the same as above but with these select fire settings: semi-auto, full auto and three round burst. No forward assist.

PRE-1968
EXC.   V.G.   FAIR

-          -   -

PRE-1986 CONVERSIONS, FOR OEM A1 ADD 40 PERCENT
EXC.   V.G.   FAIR

-          -   -

PRE-1986 DEALER SAMPLES
EXC.   V.G.   FAIR

-          -   -

COLT MODEL 606

This is the export version of the Model 616.

PRE-1968
EXC.   V.G.   FAIR

-          -   -

PRE-1986 CONVERSIONS, FOR OEM A1 ADD 40 PERCENT
EXC.   V.G.   FAIR

-          -   -

PRE-1986 DEALER SAMPLES
EXC.   V.G.   FAIR

-          -   -

COLT MODEL 606B

As above, but with burst version.

PRE-1968
EXC.   V.G.   FAIR

-          -   -

PRE-1986 CONVERSIONS, FOR OEM A1 ADD 40 PERCENT
EXC.   V.G.   FAIR

-          -   -

PRE-1986 DEALER SAMPLES
Exc.V.G.   Fair

-          -   -

COLT MODEL 607

This U.S. ("US PROPERTY") version is an SMG with sliding buttstock and 10 inch barrel. Designed for use by tank, helicopter, and APC crews. Length with stock closed is 26 inch, with stock extended about 28.7 inch. Weight is about 5.3 lb.

EXC.	V.G.	FAIR
-	-	-

PRE-1986 CONVERSIONS, FOR OEM A1 ADD 40 PERCENT

EXC.	V.G.	FAIR
-	-	-

PRE-1986 DEALER SAMPLES

EXC.	V.G.	FAIR
-	-	-

COLT MODEL 608 SURVIVAL RIFLE

This rifle was built in prototype only and its design was for use by aviation personnel. Fitted with a 10 inch barrel, cone shaped flash suppressor, short fixed buttstock, round handguard, no forward assist, no bayonet lug and short pistol grip. Overall length is 29 inch. Weight was slightly more than 4.7 lb. Designed to be broken down to fit the standard USAF seat pack. Fewer than 10 manufactured.

PRE-1968

EXC.	V.G.	FAIR
-	-	-

PRE-1986 OEM/COLT

EXC.	V.G.	FAIR
-	-	-

PRE-1986 DEALER SAMPLES

EXC.	V.G.	FAIR
-	-	-

COLT MODEL 609 (XM177E1)

This is a U.S. Army version of the Commando with an 11.5 inch barrel with a 1-in-12 twist rate. This model has a forward assist. Select fire in full-auto or semi-auto.

PRE-1968

EXC.	V.G.	FAIR
-	-	-

PRE-1986 OEM/COLT

EXC.	V.G.	FAIR
-	-	-

PRE-1986 DEALER SAMPLES

EXC.	V.G.	FAIR
-	-	-

COLT MODEL 610 (GAU-5/A)

This is the U.S. Air Force version of the XM177 Commando with 10 inch barrel, A 1-in-12 twist and no forward assist. Select fire in full-auto or semi-auto.

PRE-1968

EXC.	V.G.	FAIR
-	-	-

PRE-1986 OEM/COLT

EXC.	V.G.	FAIR
-	-	-

PRE-1986 DEALER SAMPLES

EXC.	V.G.	FAIR
-	-	-

COLT MODEL 613

This is export version of the 603.

PRE-1968

EXC.	V.G.	FAIR
-	-	-

PRE-1986 CONVERSIONS, FOR OEM A1 ADD 40 PERCENT

EXC.	V.G.	FAIR
-	-	-

PRE-1986 DEALER SAMPLES

EXC.	V.G.	FAIR
-	-	-

COLT MODEL 614

This is the export version of the Model 604.

PRE-1968

EXC.	V.G.	FAIR
-	-	-

PRE-1986 CONVERSIONS, FOR OEM A1 ADD 40 PERCENT

EXC.	V.G.	FAIR
-	-	-

Pre-1986 dealer samples

EXC.	V.G.	FAIR
-	-	-

COLT MODEL 616

This U.S. ("US PROPERTY") version is fitted with a 20 inch heavy barrel with 1-in-12 twist rate. No forward assist. Select fire in full- or semi-auto.

PRE-1968

EXC.	V.G.	FAIR
-	-	-

PRE-1986 CONVERSIONS, FOR OEM A1 ADD 40 PERCENT

EXC.	V.G.	FAIR
-	-	-

PRE-1986 DEALER SAMPLES

EXC.	V.G.	FAIR
-	-	-

COLT MODEL 619

This is the export version of the 609.

PRE-1968

EXC.	V.G.	FAIR
-	-	-

PRE-1986 CONVERSIONS, FOR OEM A1 ADD 40 PERCENT

EXC.	V.G.	FAIR
-	-	-

PRE-1986 DEALER SAMPLES

EXC.	V.G.	FAIR
-	-	-

COLT MODEL 621

This U.S. ("US Property") version is fitted with a 20 inch heavy barrel with 1-in-12 twist. It is fitted with a forward assist. Select fire in full- or semi-auto.

PRE-1968

EXC.	V.G.	FAIR
-	-	-

PRE-1986 CONVERSIONS, FOR OEM A1 ADD 40 PERCENT

EXC.	V.G.	FAIR
-	-	-

Pre-1986 dealer samples

EXC.	V.G.	FAIR
-	-	-

COLT MODEL 629 (XM177E2)

This is the U.S. Army version of the Commando with 11.5 inch barrel with 1-in-12 twist. Sliding butt stock. Fitted with a forward assist. Select fire in full- or semi-auto. Equipped with a 4.5 inch flash suppressor. Weight is about 6.2 lb. without magazine.

PRE-1968

EXC.	V.G.	FAIR
-	-	-

PRE-1986 OEM/COLT

EXC.	V.G.	FAIR
-	-	-

PRE-1986 DEALER SAMPLES

EXC.	V.G.	FAIR
-	-	-

COLT MODEL 630 (GAU-5/A/B)

This is the U.S. Air Force version of the XM177E1 with 11.5 inch barrel with 1-in-12 twist. No forward assist. Select fire in full or semi-auto.

PRE-1968

EXC.	V.G.	FAIR
-	-	-

PRE-1986 OEM/COLT

EXC.	V.G.	FAIR
-	-	-

PRE-1986 DEALER SAMPLES

EXC.	V.G.	FAIR
-	-	-

COLT MODEL 639

This is the export version of the Model 629.

PRE-1968

EXC.	V.G.	FAIR
-	-	-

PRE-1986 OEM/COLT

EXC.	V.G.	FAIR
-	-	-

PRE-1986 DEALER SAMPLES

EXC.	V.G.	FAIR
-	-	-

COLT MODEL 645 (M16A2)

This model is an improved variation of the M16A1 Standard Rifle with a 1-in-7 barrel twist and a heavier 20 inch barrel. A case deflector is mounted on the right side. Sights are an improved version of the standard M16 type. Forward assist. Improved flash suppressor, buttstock and pistol grip. First produced in 1982. See list of M16A2 modifications on prior page.

PRE-1968

EXC.   V.G.   FAIR

-       -   -

PRE-1986 OEM/COLT

EXC.   V.G.   FAIR

-       -   -

PRE-1986 DEALER SAMPLES

EXC.   V.G.   FAIR

-       -   -

COLT MODEL 646 (M16A3)

This is the U.S. ("US PROPERTY") version of the M16A3 except that there is no three-round burst but full auto and semi-auto.

COLT MODEL 649 (GAU-5/A/A)

This is the U.S. Air Force version of the XM177E2 with 11.5 inch barrel with 1-in-12 twist rate and no forward assist. Select fire with full-auto and semi-auto. Equipped with a 4.5 inch flash suppressor.

PRE-1968

EXC.   V.G.   FAIR

-       -   -

PRE-1986 OEM/COLT

EXC.   V.G.   FAIR

-       -   -

PRE-1986 DEALER SAMPLES

EXC.   V.G.   FAIR

-       -   -

COLT MODEL 651

This is the export version of the rifle with 14.5 inch barrel.

PRE-1968

EXC.   V.G.   FAIR

-       -   -

PRE-1986 CONVERSIONS

For OEM A1 add 40 percent.

EXC.   V.G.   FAIR

-       -   -

PRE-1986 DEALER SAMPLES

EXC.   V.G.   FAIR

-       -   -

COLT MODEL 652

This is the export version of the rifle with 14.5 inch barrel and no forward assist.

PRE-1968

EXC.   V.G.   FAIR

-       -   -

PRE-1986 CONVERSIONS, FOR
OEM A1 ADD 40 PERCENT

EXC.   V.G.   FAIR

-       -   -

PRE-1986 DEALER SAMPLES

EXC.   V.G.   FAIR

-       -   -

COLT MODEL 653

This is the export version of the rifle with 14.5 inch barrel and sliding buttstock.

PRE-1968

EXC.   V.G.   FAIR

-       -   -

PRE-1986 CONVERSIONS, FOR
OEM A1 ADD 40 PERCENT

EXC.   V.G.   FAIR

-       -   -

PRE-1986 DEALER SAMPLES

EXC.   V.G.   FAIR

COLT MODEL 655 (SNIPER)

This was a U.S. ("US PROPERTY") prototype version with a 20 inch barrel with a 1-in-9 twist rate. It has a forward assist. The upper receiver has a high profile scope mount and was to have been fitted with a Leatherwood Realist scope and Sionics suppressor. Select fire with full- or semi-auto.

COLT MODEL 656 (SNIPER)

Same as above but with a special low profile upper receiver with no carry handle and low profile scope mount.

700 SERIES – EXPORT VERSIONS OF THE M16A2

The A2 Military serial numbers are in the #6000000 range (yes, that is six million!), while A2 Civilian models are in the #8000000 (again, numbers in the millions!).

COLT MODEL 701 EXPORT RIFLE

This is the M16A2 with 20 inch barrel and all the A2 features. Weight is about 7.5 lb.

COLT MODEL 703 TEST MODEL

This is a test model with a gas piston designated the M703/16A2. Test model used an AK type bolt and carrier. Test model is not priced.

COLT MODEL 703 EXPORT RIFLE

[There are two different types of 703s. Colt used the same model designation twice. See above.] Select fire with semi-, three round burst and full-auto. The Export Model is an M16A2 style rifle.

PRE-1968

EXC.	V.G.	FAIR
-	-	-

PRE-1986 OEM/COLT

EXC.	V.G.	FAIR
-	-	-

PRE-1986 DEALER SAMPLES

EXC.	V.G.	FAIR
-	-	-

COLT MODEL 707 EXPORT RIFLE

This is a M16A2 with 20 inch A1 style barrel with 1-in-7 twist rate. Select fire with semi-auto and three-round burst. Weight is about 7.5 lb.

PRE-1968

EXC.	V.G.	FAIR
-	-	-

PRE-1986 CONVERSIONS, FOR OEM A1 ADD 40 PERCENT

EXC.	V.G.	FAIR
-	-	-

PRE-1986 DEALER SAMPLES

EXC.	V.G.	FAIR
-	-	-

COLT MODEL 711 EXPORT RIFLE

This model is the same as the M16A2 but fitted with M16A1 sights and standard weight M16A1 barrel.

PRE-1968

EXC.	V.G.	FAIR

PRE-1986 CONVERSIONS, FOR OEM A1 ADD 40 PERCENT

EXC.	V.G.	FAIR
-	-	-

PRE-1986 DEALER SAMPLES

EXC.	V.G.	FAIR
-	-	-

COLT MODEL 713 EXPORT RIFLE

This model is fitted with an M16A1 upper receiver with case deflector 20 inch A1 barrel with 1-in-7 twist. Buttstock is A2 type. The compensator is A2 type with A2 lower receiver with select fire in semi-auto and three-round burst. Weight is about 7 lb.

PRE-1968

EXC.	V.G.	FAIR
-	-	-

PRE-1986 CONVERSIONS, FOR OEM A1 ADD 40 PERCENT

EXC.	V.G.	FAIR
-	-	-

PRE-1986 DEALER SAMPLES

EXC.	V.G.	FAIR
-	-	-

COLT MODEL 723 EXPORT CARBINE

This model is an M16A2 carbine with lightweight 14.5 inch barrel, M16A1 sights, and telescoping stock. Select fire in semi-auto and full-auto.

PRE-1968

EXC.	V.G.	FAIR
-	-	-

PRE-1986 CONVERSIONS, FOR OEM A1 ADD 40 PERCENT

EXC.	V.G.	FAIR
-	-	-

PRE-1986 DEALER SAMPLES

EXC.	V.G.	FAIR
-	-	-

COLT MODEL 725 EXPORT CARBINE

Same as the Model 723 with semi-auto and three round burst select fire.

PRE-1968

EXC.	V.G.	FAIR
-	-	-

PRE-1986 CONVERSIONS, FOR OEM A1 ADD 40 PERCENT

EXC.	V.G.	FAIR
-	-	-

PRE-1986 DEALER SAMPLES

EXC.	V.G.	FAIR
-	-	-

COLT MODEL 727 CARBINE

This is the M16A2 version of the M4 Carbine. Fitted with a 14.5 inch barrel capable of accepting the M203 grenade launcher. Rifling twist is 1-in-7. Sliding buttstock. Rate of fire is 700 to 950 rounds per minute. Select fire in semi-auto and full auto. Weight is about 5.65 lbs without magazine.

PRE-1968

EXC.	V.G.	FAIR
-	-	-

PRE-1986 CONVERSIONS, FOR OEM A1 ADD 40 PERCENT

EXC.	V.G.	FAIR
-	-	-

PRE-1986 DEALER SAMPLES

EXC.	V.G.	FAIR
-	-	-

COLT MODEL 733 EXPORT COMMANDO

This model is the M16A2 Commando with an 11.5 inch barrel, M16A1 sight and telescoping butt.

PRE-1968

EXC.	V.G.	FAIR
-	-	-

PRE-1986 OEM/COLT

EXC.	V.G.	FAIR
-	-	-

PRE-1986 DEALER SAMPLES

EXC.	V.G.	FAIR
-	-	-

COLT MODEL 741 EXPORT HEAVY BARREL

This is an M16A2 with 20 inch heavy barrel that is magazine fed. Designed as a SAW (Squad Automatic Weapon). Weight is about 10 lb.

PRE-1968

EXC.	V.G.	FAIR
-	-	-

PRE-1986 CONVERSIONS, FOR OEM A1 ADD 40 PERCENT

EXC.	V.G.	FAIR
-	-	-

PRE-1986 DEALER SAMPLES

EXC.	V.G.	FAIR
-	-	-

COLT MODEL 750 LMG (SEE RAPID FIRE COLTS – MACHINE GUNS)

COLT MODEL 720 M4 (ORIGINAL VERSION)

This is a short barrel version of the M16 with collapsible stock. Chambered for 5.56x45mm cartridge. It is fitted with a 14.5 inch barrel and has a magazine capacity of 20 or 30 rounds. Its rate of fire is 800 rounds per minute. The weight is about 5.6 lb. Marked "COLT FIREARMS DIVISION COLT INDUSTRIES HARTFORD CONN USA" on the left side of the receiver, with "COLT M4 CAL 5.56MM" on the left side of the magazine housing. In use with American military forces as well as several South American countries.

PRE-1968

EXC.	V.G.	FAIR
-	-	-

PRE-1986 CONVERSIONS OR OEM/COLT (RARE)

EXC.	V.G.	FAIR
-	-	-

PRE-1986 DEALER SAMPLES

EXC.	V.G.	FAIR
-	-	-

900 SERIES

COLT MODEL 920 – M4

This model is the current U.S. ("US PROPERTY") version of the flat top carbine with 14.5-inch barrel with a 1-in-7 twist rate, forward assist, sliding buttstock, and A2 improvements. Select fire with three-round burst and semi-auto.

COLT MODEL 921 – M4A1

This U.S. ("US PROPERTY") model is the same

as the Model 920, except it is full auto with no burst feature.

COLT MODEL 945 – M16A4

This U.S. ("US PROPERTY") version is the flat top version of the M16A2. It is currently supported in the Colt Military line up as the fourth generation of the M16 weapon system. Colt says, "The M16A4 Rifle still represents the world standard by which all other weapons of this class are judged. Its combat proven performance is verified by the fact that over 8 million M16 weapon systems have been produced and placed in military service throughout the world … [and] the U.S. Marine Corps considers there to be '… no finer service rifle in the world today.'"

The Colt M16A4 Rifle, now in production, features a performance identical to the M16A2. Physical differences between the two include a removable carrying handle with an integral rail mounting system on the M16A4. When the carrying handle is removed, any accessory with a rail grabber, such as an optical sight, can be mounted. The M16A4 barrel is designed to accept the M203 Grenade Launcher, which offers the user both point and area firing capabilities. All US and NATO rifle grenades can be fired without any supplementary equipment.

According to Colt, "The new concepts of rapid deployment, mobility and increased firepower play a major part in the overall strategy of modern warfare. Increased emphasis is now put on small tactical units that are able to 'get in and out' fast. Increased need for a lightweight, highly dependable, accurate service rifle with added firepower therefore exists. The Colt M16A4 Rifle is the ultimate in 5.56mm."

SPECIALTY SERIES

COLT CAR-15 MODEL M1 HEAVY ASSAULT RIFLE

This was a prototype with a heavy AR-15 20 inch barrel. Fires from a closed bolt. Uses standard M16 magazines. Weight without magazine is about 7.6 lb. Semi- or full-auto fire. Rate of fire is approximately 800 to 850 rounds per minute.

COLT CAR-15 MODEL M2 BELT-FED HEAVY ASSAULT RIFLE

Similar to the M1 version with the addition of a removable belt feeding mechanism designed by Rob Roy. Weight is about 8.3 lb. Also feeds from standard M16 magazines. Fewer than 20 M2s were built.

PRE-1968
EXC.	V.G.	FAIR
-	-	-

PRE-1986 OEM/COLT
EXC.	V.G.	FAIR
-	-	-

PRE-1986 DEALER SAMPLES
EXC.	V.G.	FAIR
-	-	-

COLT M231 FIRING PORT WEAPON

This gun was never assigned a Colt model number but was fitted with a 15.6-inch barrel and a 1-in-12 twist rate. It fired from an open bolt in full auto only. It had no sights or buttstock. All original Colt firing port guns have an "F" prefix as part of the serial number and are marked "US PROPERTY."

PRE-1968
EXC.	V.G.	FAIR
-	-	-

PRE-1986 OEM/COLT
EXC.	V.G.	FAIR
-	-	-

PRE-1986 DEALER SAMPLES
EXC.	V.G.	FAIR
-	-	-

COLT ACR ADVANCED COMBAT RIFLE

This model was built in prototype only and was designed to fire special duplex cartridges. It was fitted with a 20 inch barrel, flattop receiver with special rib designed by Aberdeen Human Engineering Labs. It has a sliding buttstock with a hydraulic buffer. Select fire in full- or semi-auto.

COLT CMG-1

One prototype was built of this model. It was a belt-fed light machine gun designed by Rob Roy and fitted with a 20 inch barrel with a 1-in-12 twist. Rate of fire of 650 rounds per minute. Weight is about 12.5 lb. Fires from an open bolt. Designed to be used as a tripod mount, bipod mount, vehicle mount or solenoid fixed machine gun.

COLT CMG-2

This was an improved version of the CMG-1 designed by George Curtis and Henry Tatro. Approximately six were produced, five in 5.56 NATO and one in 7.62 NATO. It was fitted with a 20 inch quick change barrel with a 1-in-8.87" twist for the 68 gr. GX- 6235 bullet. Hydraulic buffer in buttstock. Bipod. Weight was about 15 lb. Cycle rate is about 650 rounds per minute. It is fed by a 150 round belt fed drum magazine. These prototypes were built by Colt between 1967 and 1969.

PRE-1968

EXC.	V.G.	FAIR
-	-	-

PRE-1986 OEM/COLT

EXC.	V.G.	FAIR
-	-	-

PRE-1986 DEALER SAMPLES

EXC.	V.G.	FAIR
-	-	-

M16 RIMFIRE CONVERSION KITS

There are several different conversion kits featuring different designs both adapted by the U.S. military. Both of these kits use a 10-round magazine but are not interchangeable with each other. The first is the Rodman design, known as the Air Force Model, built by OK Industries, New Britain, CT and the second is the M261 built by the Maremont Corp., Saco, ME. TM 9-6920-363-12 was issued with the M261 conversion kit. The Atchisson Mark I and Mark II kits and the Atchisson Mark III made by Jonathan Ciener, Inc., are also used by military forces in the U.S. as well as by foreign governments. The Ciener kit was introduced in about 1988 and is designed to be used in both the M16 and AR15 rifles, both semi-automatic fire and full auto fire. Rate of fire is between 700 and 800 rounds per minute in the M16.

Colt also built a conversion kit produced for commercial sale but this kit was not adopted by the military.

CIENER KIT MARK III

EXC.	V.G.	GOOD	FAIR	POOR
200	150	-	-	-

RAPID FIRE COLTS

COLT THOMPSON SUBMACHINE GUNS

TEXT AND PRICES BY NICK TILOTTA

THOMPSON MODEL 1921AC/ 21A, 1921/28 NAVY

The first Thompsons to come to market were the Model 1921s, manufactured by Colt Patent Firearms for Auto Ordnance Corporation in New York, NY. Between March 1921 and April 1922, 15,000 Thompsons were built. Of those 15,000 manufactured, only about 2,400 weapons still exist in a transferable state today. "Transferable," meaning weapons that can be bought, sold or traded legally within the U.S.

Three models of the Model 1921 were produced. The Model 1921A had a fixed front sight and a rate of fire of 800 rounds per minute. The Model 1921AC has a Cutts compensator instead of a fixed front sight and an 800 rounds per minute rate of fire. The Model 1928 Navy was fitted with a Cutts compensator and a heavier actuator that reduced the rate of fire to 600 rounds per minute. All of these Navy models had the number "8" stamped crudely over the number "1" on the left side of the receiver.

Of the 15,000 Colt Model 1921s produced, approximately 25 percent were Model 1921As, 33 percent were Model 1921ACs and 41 percent were 1928 Navys. A handful of Model 1927s were manufactured by Colt and left the factory as semiautomatics. However, the BATFE considers these guns machine guns and requires that all federal firearms rules apply. Consequently, these Model 1927s are quite rare and represent only about one percent of the total production. Unless they may have been used in some famous or gangster related, notorious manner, they do not seem to sell for the same dollar figures that the machine guns do.

All Colt-manufactured Thompsons were bright blued; none were Parkerized. All had walnut stocks, grips, and forearms manufactured by Remington. With the exception of a few prototypes, all Colt Thompsons were chambered for the .45 ACP cartridge. All internal parts were nickel plated and all barrels were finned. All weapons had a Lyman rear sight assembly. A removable rear stock was standard. All weapons were marked with a "NEW YORK, USA" address on the right side of the receiver. "COLT PATENT FIREARMS" was marked on the left side of the receiver. These Colt Thompsons would accept a 20 or 30 round box magazine as well as a 50 round "L" drum or 100 round "C" drum. Their weight is about 10.75 lb. The prices given below are for original Colt guns with original parts and finish.

NOTE: Model 1921As, early serial numbers, previous ownership and documentation can dramatically add to the prices below. In addition, missing components, re-barreled weapons, etc, will see a substantial reduction in price, as these original components are almost extinct. Re-finishing or re-bluing will result in a substantial reduction in value by as much as 50 percent.

For Thompsons with historical background such as Texas Ranger or gangster guns prices can exceed 50 percent to 100 percent of what is suggested here, with documentation.

PRE-1968

EXC.	V.G.	FAIR
35,000	25,000	20,000

THOMPSON MODEL 1928AC (COMMERCIAL)/1928A1 MILITARY

The next limited run of Thompsons came just before and right at the beginning of World War II. This version is called the Model 1928AC or Commercial model. These weapons were assembled by Savage Arms in Utica, NY, using original Colt internal components. The receivers were still marked with the New York address but void of any "Colt" markings. Most weapons were simply marked "MODEL 1928." The first of these guns have blued receivers and blued barrels. The second run had Parkerized receivers and blued barrels. These guns are quite rare and command premium prices.

MACHINEGUNS

COLT GATLING GUN

Invented by American Dr. Richard J. Gatling in 1861, this is a multi-barrel (6 to 10 barrels) hand-cranked machine gun. Several different models were developed and built in the 1860s and some were actually used in the American Civil War. Some of these early guns were chambered for .58 caliber, while a few others were chambered for one inch shells.

The classic Gatling gun is the Model 1874 chambered for the .45-70 cartridge. There are several other models such as the Model 1879, Model 1881, the Model 1892, Model 1895 and the Model 1903. Some of these guns were tripod mounted while others were mounted on gun carriages, and still others were deck mounted for ship-board use. Some of the Gatling guns have exposed barrels while others are enclosed in a brass jacket. The Model 1877 "bulldog" is fitted with five 18 inch barrels enclosed in a brass jacket. The Model 1893 Police has six 12 inch barrels in .45-70 and weighs about 75 lb. These guns are marked with a brass plate on top of the receiver, "GATLING'S/BATTERY/GUN 9 (PATENT DATES) MADE BY COLT'S/PT. FIRE ARMS MFG. CO./HARTFORD, CONN. U.S.A."

As an interesting aside, Gatling guns are still in use by military forces but are now electrically powered (GEC M134/ GAU-2B Minigun) and capable of a rate of fire of 6,000 rounds per minute using the 7.62 x 51 cartridge.

Values for these guns are difficult to establish. Gatling guns in excellent condition in .45-70 caliber can bring between $75,000 and $200,000 perhaps more, depending upon the interest and pocket-size of the potential collector. In fact, the James D. Julia auction house sold a tripod mounted Colt Gatling gun in October, 2006 at the Center of New Hampshire Holiday Inn in Manchester, New Hampshire for $55,200.

COLT MODEL 1895

Designed by John Browning and built by Colt, this is a gas operated air cooled belt fed gun chambered for the .30-03, 6mm U.S.N. and .30-40 cartridges as well as the .30-06 (called the Model 1906 cartridge) in later applications. Rate of fire is about 450 rounds per minute. Called the "potato digger" because of its back and forth motion and proximity to the ground. This was the first non-mechanical firing machine issued to the U.S. military. It saw limited use during the Spanish-American War, the Boxer Rebellion and as a training gun during World War I. (See also Colt/Marlin Model 1914/1915.)

NOTE: The .30-03 cartridge was the original and earlier version of the .30-06 cartridge. Guns chambered for the older .30-03 cartridge will function and fire the .30-06 cartridge (although accuracy suffers) but the reverse is not true. Sometimes the .30-03 cartridge is referred to as the .30-45. Both of these cartridges replaced the older .30-40 Krag as the official military round.

Colt-manufactured Model 1874 Gatling Gun on caisson.

Model 1874 Gatling Gun, closeup of manufacturer's insignia.

PRE-1968 (RARE)

EXC.	V.G.	FAIR
25,000	23,000	21,000

PRE-1986 CONVERSIONS

EXC.	V.G.	FAIR
18,000	16,000	15,000

COLT MAXIM 1904

This belt fed machine gun was originally chambered for the .30-03 cartridge and then altered to the .30-06. Built on the standard Maxim M1900 pattern. Barrel length is 28.5 inch. Rate of fire is about 500 rounds per minute. Fed by a 250 round cloth belt. Primarily used as a training gun during World War I. A total of 287 of these guns were produced. Weight is approximately 75 lb.

PRE-1968 (VERY RARE)

EXC.	V.G.	FAIR
40,000	35,000	30,000

PRE-1986 CONVERSIONS

EXC.	V.G.	FAIR
30,000	27,500	25,000

MODEL 1909 BENET-MERCIE MACHINE RIFLE

Developed by the French firm Hotchkiss and built in the U.S. by Colt and Springfield Armory, this air cooled gas operated automatic rifle is fed by a 30-round metal strip. Chambered for the .30-06 cartridge. Rate of fire was about 400 rounds per minute. Weight of gun was about 27 lb. This gun was equipped with a Model 1908 Warner & Swasey telescope. It was used (well, available for use) against Mexican bandits in 1915 and 1916 by the U.S. Army, and in France during the early stages of World War I. However, it did not prove to be reliable and was soon replaced by the Hotchkiss and Vickers guns. About 670 were produced by both Colt and Springfield.

PRE-1968 (RARE)

EXC.	V.G.	FAIR
15,000	13,000	11,000

COLT/MARLIN MODEL 1914/1915

This was a Browning design that was first produced in 1895; it was nicknamed the "Potato Digger" because of its swinging arm bolt driver. It was air cooled and fired a variety of calibers both for the military and commercial sales. The Model 1914 was converted to fire the .30-06 cartridge. Rate of fire was about 450 rounds per minute. Barrel length was 28 inches. Belt fed by 250 round cloth belt. The Model 1915 had cooling fins added to the barrel. The gun was built from 1916 to 1919.

PRE-1968

EXC.	V.G.	FAIR
25,000	22,500	20,000

PRE-1986 CONVERSIONS

EXC.	V.G.	FAIR
18,000	16,000	14,000

COLT-VICKERS MODEL 1915

This gun is similar to the British Vickers but built by Colt in Hartford, CT. Many of these Colt Model 1915 guns were rebuilt aircraft guns. About 12,000 were produced by Colt during the period 1915 to 1918 but few of these were original Colt built ground guns and many of those were destroyed after the war. Therefore, original Colt-Vickers ground guns are very rare and quite desirable.

PRE-1968 (ORIGINAL COLT GROUND GUN)

EXC.	V.G.	FAIR
27,000	25,000	22,000

PRE-1968 (COLT RE-BUILT AIRCRAFT GUN)

EXC.	V.G.	FAIR
17,000	15,000	13,000

PRE-1986 CONVERSIONS

EXC.	V.G.	FAIR
17,000	15,000	13,000

BROWNING M1917 & M1917A1

Based on John M. Browning's original automatic weapon design it was chambered for the .30-06 cartridge. This water cooled gun is fitted with a 23.8-inch barrel and has a rate of fire of 500 rounds per minute using a cloth belt. Its empty weight for the gun only is 33 lb. The M1917A1 tripod weighs about 53 lb. Marked "US INSP BROWNING MACHINE GUN US CAL 30 MODEL OF 1917." This gun was produced by various manufacturers from 1917 to 1945. About 56,000 were built prior to the end of World War I although few saw actual combat service. In the mid 1930s, a few minor modifications were made to the gun and it became known as the Model 1917A1. These modifications follow.

The most important legacy of the Model 1917 Browning is that it led to the use of this gun as the air cooled Model 1919. During its production life the gun was built by Colt, Remington and Westinghouse.

EXC.	V.G.	FAIR
35,000	32,500	30,000

PRE-1986 CONVERSIONS (NON-MARTIAL CURRENT U.S. MANUFACTURE)

EXC.	V.G.	FAIR
18,000	16,000	14,000

BROWNING .30 AIRCRAFT M1918

This was a M1917 water cooled gun modified to air cooled for aircraft use. The water jacket was removed and replaced with a slotted barrel jacket and spade grips. This model is referred to as the M1918M1.

BROWNING .30 AIRCRAFT M1918 FIXED

As above but made as new in the same configuration with spade grips.

BROWNING .30 AIRCRAFT M1919 FLEXIBLE

Same as M1918 but newly made with spade grips.

BROWNING M1919A1

First deployed in 1931, this gun was a M1919 tank gun modified for ground use. It was fitted with a removable butt with a hand grip under the receiver. The barrel jacket was slotted. The front sight was mounted on the front of the receiver. Chambered for the .30-06 cartridge. Barrel length is 18 inches. Fed with a 250 round cloth belt. Cycle rate of about 600 rounds per minute. Weight is about 40 lb. with tripod.

BROWNING M1919A2

Introduced in 1931, this gun was intended for cavalry use. The front sight was mounted on the barrel jacket. There was no butt stock. The gun was issued with the M2 tripod. Otherwise, this model is an improved M1919A1.

BROWNING M1919A3

There were 72 trial samples built. This gun was essentially a M1919A2 with the front sight moved back to the receiver.

BROWNING M1919A4

This air cooled gun is chambered for the .30-06 cartridge and fitted with a 23.8 inch barrel. It has a rate of fire of 500 rounds per minute and is fed with a cloth belt. Weight is about 31 lb. Marked "BROWNING M1919M4 US CAL .30" on the left side of the receiver. First produced in 1934, it is still in use today. There were

a number of earlier variations of this model beginning with the M1919 aircraft gun and several improvements leading to the A4 version. The Model 1919 was used in World War II as an infantry weapon, tank gun and even on aircraft (M2). It has seen service all over the world in untold conflicts. Many arms experts think of the A4 version as the definitive .30 caliber machine gun.

PRE-1968

EXC.	V.G.	FAIR
25,000	22,500	20,000

PRE-1986 CONVERSIONS (NON-MARTIAL CURRENT U.S. MANUFACTURE)

EXC.	V.G.	FAIR
15,000	12,500	11,000

PRE-1986 DEALER SAMPLES

EXC.	V.G.	FAIR
12,000	11,000	10,000

BROWNING M1919A5

This gun is an modified version of the M1919A4 for use with the M3 light tank. It was fitted with a special bolt retracting slide. Weight is about 30 lb.

BROWNING M1919A6

This model is a M1919A4 fitted with a shoulder stock, flash hider and bipod. Its weight is 32 lb. Produced from 1943 to 1954. Marked "US INSP BROWNING MACHINE GUN US CAL 30" on the left side of the receiver.

PRE-1968

EXC.	V.G.	FAIR
25,000	22,500	20,000

PRE-1986 CONVERSIONS (NON-MARTIAL CURRENT U.S. MANUFACTURE)

EXC.	V.G.	FAIR
15,000	12,500	10,000

PRE-1986 DEALER SAMPLES

EXC.	V.G.	FAIR
12,000	11,000	9,000

BROWNING .30 AIRCRAFT M2

This gun was designed for airplane use in 1931. Its rate of fire is higher than the ground gun version: 1,200 to only 1,000 rounds per minute. Chambered primarily for the .30-06 cartridge but some were chambered for the .303 British round for that country's use. The gun is fed from either the left or right side as determined by the situation. It was originally designed in two configurations; as a flexible gun (for an observer) with hand grips and hand trigger or as a fixed or wing type with a back plate without hand grips. The recoil buffer in the flexible type is horizontal while the fixed gun has a vertical type buffer. Weight is about 21 lb. The barrel length is 23.9 inches.

PRE-1968
EXC.	V.G.	FAIR
22,000	20,000	18,500

PRE-1986 CONVERSIONS (NON-MARTIAL CURRENT U.S. MANUFACTURE)
EXC.	V.G.	FAIR
17,000	15,000	12,500

PRE-1986 DEALER SAMPLES
EXC.	V.G.	FAIR
10,000	8,000	7,000

BROWNING TANK M37
This gun is a version of the M1919A4 adopted for tank use. Feed mechanism was designed to be used from either side.

PRE-1968
EXC.	V.G.	FAIR
25,000	22,500	20,000

PRE-1986 CONVERSIONS (NON-MARTIAL CURRENT U.S. MANUFACTURE)
EXC.	V.G.	FAIR
17,000	15,000	12,500

PRE-1986 DEALER SAMPLES
EXC.	V.G.	FAIR
10,000	8,000	7,000

MG 38
Similar in appearance to the Model 1917 (water cooled) but with several modifications such as an improved bolt handle. The MG 38 is fitted with a pistol grip back plate while the MG 38B has a double grip (spade type) black plate. Fed from a 250 round belt. Weight of MG 38 is about 35 lbs, while the MG 38B weighs about 36.5 lb. The barrel length is 24 inches. This gun was utilized for several different purposes and therefore has different tripods depending on the application. Rate of fire is between 400 and 650 rounds per minute.

MODEL 1924
A commercial version of the Model 1917. Some interior modifications.

MODEL 1928
A commercial version of the Model 1917 with interior modifications.

PRE-1968
EXC.	V.G.	FAIR
35,000	32,500	30,000

PRE-1986 CONVERSIONS (NON-MARTIAL CURRENT U.S. MANUFACTURE)
EXC.	V.G.	FAIR
16,000	14,000	12,000

PRE-1986 DEALER SAMPLES
EXC.	V.G.	FAIR
12,000	11,000	10,000

MG 40
This is the commercial version of the M2 .30 caliber aircraft gun.

PRE-1968
EXC.	V.G.	FAIR
22,000	20,000	18,500

PRE-1986 CONVERSIONS (NON-MARTIAL CURRENT U.S. MANUFACTURE)
EXC.	V.G.	FAIR
17,000	15,000	12,500

PRE-1986 DEALER SAMPLES
EXC.	V.G.	FAIR
10,000	8,000	7,000

BROWNING .50 M1921
Introduced in 1925, this heavy machine gun is water cooled and recoil operated. Chambered for the .50 Browning cartridge. Rate of fire is about 450 rounds per minute. Barrel length is 36 inches. Fed by a cloth belt. Weight of gun is 66 lb.

BROWNING .50 M1921A1
An improved version of the M1921 with a compound leverage cocking handle.

BROWNING .50 M2

Introduced in 1933, this gun is an improved version of the M1921 with a water jacket that extends past the muzzle. Fitted with spade grips and fed from either side. Early guns had a 36 inch barrels later guns were fitted with a 45 inch barrel. Intended for anti-aircraft use with a special mount for that purpose. Weight of gun was 100 lb. while the tripod weighed about 375 lb. Cycle rate is about 650 rounds per minute. Fed by a 110 round metal link belt.

BROWNING M2/M2HB .50

This is an air-cooled .50 caliber machine first produced in 1933. It has a 44.5 inch barrel and weighs about 84 lb. Its rate of fire is 500 rounds per minute. It is belt fed. Marked "BROWNING MACHINE GUN CAL 50 M2" on the left side of the receiver. Approximately three million were produced. The gun was produced by Colt, FN, Ramo, Saco and Winchester.

In use today by U.S. armed forces in the Middle East, the Browning .50 is one of the most widely used and successful heavy machines ever produced. Besides being utilized as an aircraft, ground and vehicle weapon, the M2 is also used as an anti-aircraft gun in single, twin and four-barrel configurations. The M2 was additionally configured as a water-cooled gun for sustained fire. The commercial designation for this model was the MG 52A. Widely used throughout the world and is still in use today and still in production in the UK, USA, and Belgium.

The .50 caliber cartridge was first adopted in 1923 after extensive research by John M. Browning, Winchester and Colt. The cartridge, like many with military applications, has a wide variety of variations.

For original M2 water cooled guns add $10,000 to pre-1968 prices.

PRE-1968
EXC.	V.G.	FAIR
30,000	27,500	25,000

PRE-1986 CONVERSIONS (NON-MARTIAL CURRENT U.S. MANUFACTURE)
EXC.	V.G.	FAIR
25,000	22,500	20,000

BROWNING AUTOMATIC RIFLE (BAR)

This is gas operated light machine gun chambered for the .30-06 cartridge. It is fitted with a 23.8 inch barrel and a 20-round magazine, it weighs about 16 lb. Its rate of fire is 500 rounds per minute. Marked "BROWNING BAR M1918 CAL 30" on receiver it was produced from 1917 until 1945, but saw service in the Korean War.

This Browning designed rifle was built by Colt, Marlin and Winchester. It has several variations from the original M1918 design. About 50,000 Model 1918 BARs saw service in Europe during World War I. The M1918A1 was first built in 1927 and has the buttplate hinged shoulder support. The bipod has spiked feet and is attached to the gas cylinder. It, too, is select fire. Weight for the M1918A1 is 18.5 lb. The M1918 A2 was first built in 1932 and is fitted with a bipod with skid feet attached to the flash hider. There is a monopod beneath the buttstock. The rear sight is from a Browning M1919A4 machine gun and is adjustable for windage. This version has a rate of fire regulator that sets the rate between 450 and 650 rounds per minute. Weight for this variation is 19.5 lb. During World War II approximately 188,000 Model 1918A2 BARs were produced. The last version is called the M1922 and was built in limited numbers. It is similar to the M1918 but with a heavily finned barrel. The bipod is attached to the barrel. Barrel length is 18 inch with rate of fire of 550 rounds per minute.

PRE-1968
EXC.	V.G.	FAIR
30,000	28,000	26,000

PRE-1986 CONVERSIONS
EXC.	V.G.	FAIR
22,500	20,000	18,000

PRE-1986 DEALER SAMPLES
EXC.	V.G.	FAIR
17,500	15,000	12,000

COLT LMG (RO-750)

First introduced in early 1986, this M16A2 light machine gun was designed as a squad automatic weapon (SAW). SAWs are designed to provide a more sustained fire capability than the standard M16 rifle. Similar in appearance to the M16A2 rifle, this model features a 20 inch heavy hammer forged barrel upper made by Diemaco with square handguard and vertical handgrip. The lower receiver fires from an open bolt full auto only and is marked, "SAFE AND FIRE." The fixed stock houses a hydraulic buffer and special spring

Colt 9mm Submachine Gun.

to reduce the rate of fire to about 600 to 750 rounds per minute. Weight is 12.75 lb. Fed by a standard 30 round M16 magazine or other high capacity devices such as the 100-round Beta C magazine. In use by the U.S. Marine Corp. and other military forces in Central and South America and the Middle East. The Colt LMG was also utilized by the Canadian forces supplied by Colt licensee Diemaco of Canada.

Still in production, but under the reintroduced name of Colt Automatic Rifle (now in its Military line up) with changes to the bipod, removal of the front carry handle, and improvements in the handguard heat shield as well as a flat top upper. It is estimated by knowledgeable sources that there are less than 20 transferable examples in this country.

PRE-1968

EXC.	V.G.	FAIR
-	-	-

PRE-1986 OEM (VERY RARE)

EXC.	V.G.	FAIR
22,500	20,000	18,000

9MM SUBMACHINE GUN (RO635/RO639)

In the Law Enforcement line-up this 9mm Submachine Gun is a lightweight, compact weapon with the same straight line construction and design of the M16. Coupled with the low recoil of 9mm ammunition, it provides accurate fire with less muzzle climb, especially in full auto, which facilitates ease of training and improves accuracy. The 9mm SMG fires with gas operating system from blowback/closed bolt position, and is equipped with a four position sliding buttstock – 25.6 (65 cm) to 28.9 inches – and is readily field stripped without special tools. Operation and training are similar to that of the M4 Carbine and M16 Rifle. The barrel is 10.5 inches (26.7 cm) long and weight without a magazine is 5.75 lb. (2.61 kg). Cartridge case deflector, bird-cage flash hider, ejection port cover, front barrel lug (for mounting accessories), adjustable front sight, rear target sight adjusts for windage and elevation (short range 0-50m, and long range (50-100m), effective range is 100 meters, magazine capacity 32 rounds and rate of fire is 700 to 1,000 rpm. Muzzle velocity is 1,300 fps (396 m/sec).

The R0635 is the fixed handle gun with safe, semi-auto and full-auto modes. The R0639 is the fixed handle gun with safe, semi-auto and burst modes (no full-auto).

SECTION VII

COLT'S CUSTOM SHOP & COMMEMORATIVES

Colt Gold Cup Trophy.

COLT CUSTOM SHOP

The Colt Custom Shop has developed numerous models over the years that are available to the public. The basis of these offerings are standard Colt Models upgraded to perform special functions, to have a special "look and feel" or even perhaps to commemorate a specific event or public celebration.

SPECIAL COMBAT GOVERNMENT MODEL (COMPETITION)

This is a competition-ready semi-automatic. Chambered for the .45 ACP it comes fitted with a skeletonized trigger, upswept grip safety, custom tuned action, polished feed ramp, throated barrel, flared ejection port, cutout commander hammer, two eight round magazines, hard chromed slide and receiver, extended thumb safety, Bomar rear sight, Clark dovetail front sight, and flared magazine funnel. The pistol has been accurized and is shipped with a certified target.

NIB	EXC.	V.G.	GOOD	FAIR	POOR
1,450	1,100	800	500	300	200

SPECIAL COMBAT GOVERNMENT MODEL (CARRY)

This model has all of the same features as the

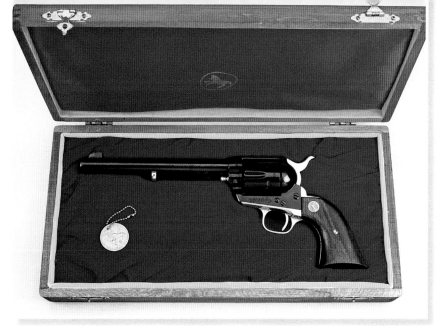

*125th Anniversary
Edition Peacemaker.*

competition model except that it has a royal blue finish, special bar dot night sights and an ambidextrous safety. It has also been accurized and shipped with a certified target.

NIB	EXC.	V.G.	GOOD	FAIR	POOR
1,250	900	700	400	300	200

GOLD CUP COMMANDER

Chambered for the .45 ACP, the pistol has these features: heavy duty adjustable target sights, beveled magazine well, serrated front strap, checkered mainspring housing, wide grip safety, Palo Alto wood grips and stainless steel or royal blue finish.

NIB	EXC.	V.G.	GOOD	FAIR	POOR
875	775	650	600	500	375

GOLD CUP TROPHY

Introduced in 1997 and chambered in .45 ACP, this model features a 5-inch barrel with a choice of stainless steel or blue finish. Its purpose was to give competitive shooters a gun that they could take directly from the dealer's shelf to the firing line. It includes several custom features such as skeletonized hammer and adjustable trigger. Adjustable rear sight, wrap-around rubber grips and flat grooved top rib on the side are standard. The pistol has been accurized and is shipped with a target. Magazine capacity is seven or eight rounds. Weight is approximately 39 oz. Add $60 for stainless steel finish.

NIB	EXC.	V.G.	GOOD	FAIR	POOR
1,000	800	-	-	-	-

125TH ANNIVERSARY EDITION PEACEMAKER

Introduced in 1998 this model features a "V" shaped rear sight with two line patent date. Barrel is 4.75 inches and it is chambered for .45 Colt cartridge. The cylinder is the second generation type and the hammer is knurled. Frame and hammer are case colored with blue barrel. Grips are two piece walnut with oil finish. Special serial number range #SA74000 to #SA75999. Suggested Retail Price: $1,615.

NIB	EXC.	V.G.	GOOD	FAIR	POOR
1700	1400	-	-	-	-

NOTE: This advertisement was found in the spring 2007 on *AntiqueGunList.com*:

"Colt SAA 2nd Generation 125th Anniversary .45 cal blue gun with a gold back strap trigger guard and hammer comes in a wood box a modern gun that has to be shipped to an FFL or a C&R ask all questions on this sold as is Serial number #12XX. $1,550."

CUSTOM ANACONDA

Custom tuned action, Magna-Ported barrel, with Elliason rear sight. The contoured trigger is polished smooth. Comes with Pachmayr grips and brushed stainless steel finish.

NIB	EXC.	V.G.	GOOD	FAIR	POOR
1150	975	800	-	-	-

ANACONDA HUNTER

Comes with a Leupold 2X scope, heavy duty mounts, cleaning accessories, both walnut and rubber grips, in a hard case. Furnished only with an 8-inch barrel.

NIB	EXC.	V.G.	GOOD	FAIR	POOR
1350	1100	850	-	-	-

ULTIMATE PYTHON

Custom tuned action with both Elliason and Accro sighting systems. Both rubber and walnut grips are included. Bright stainless steel or royal blue finish. Available only with 6-inch barrel.

NIB	EXC.	V.G.	GOOD	FAIR	POOR
1,350	1150	900	-	-	-

Python Elite.

PYTHON ELITE

This model has a hand-tuned .357 Magnum action with a choice of 4- or 6-inch barrel with adjustable rear sight and red ramp front sight. On the 4 inch barrel model grips are rubber service, while on the 6 inch model they are rubber target style. Finish is stainless steel or royal blue. Weight is about 38 oz. with 4 inch barrel and 43 oz. with 6 inch barrel.

NIB	EXC.	V.G.	GOOD	FAIR	POOR
1,350	1,150	900	-	-	-

BOBBED DETECTIVE SPECIAL

First offered in 1994 this model features a bobbed hammer, a front sight with night sight, and honed action. Available in either chrome or blue finish.

NIB	EXC.	V.G.	GOOD	FAIR	POOR
625	575	-	-	-	-

LIMITED CLASS .45 ACP

Designed for tactical competition. Supplied with a parkerized matte finish, lightweight composite trigger, extended ambidextrous safety, upswept grip safety, beveled magazine well, fully accurized and shipped with a signed target. Introduced in 1993.

NIB	EXC.	V.G.	GOOD	FAIR	POOR
1,600	1,200	775	-	-	-

COMPENSATED MODEL .45 ACP

This competition pistol has a hard chrome receiver, bumper on magazine, extended ambidextrous safety, blue slide with full profile BAT compensator, Bomar rear sight, and flared funnel magazine well. Introduced in 1993.

NIB	EXC.	V.G.	GOOD	FAIR	POOR
1,850	1,350	900	-	-	-

COMPENSATED .45 ACP COMMANDER

Introduced in 1998 and limited to 500 pistols. This model is fitted with a full length guide rod, extended beavertail safety, skeletonized hammer, Novak style sights, and checkered walnut double diamond grips.

NIB	EXC.	V.G.	GOOD	FAIR	POOR
1,850	1,350	900	-	-	-

NITE LITE .380

Supplied with a bar dot night sight, special foil mark on barrel slide, Teflon coated alloy receiver, stainless slide, high capacity grip extension magazine and a standard magazine. Shipped with a soft carrying case. Introduced in 1993.

NIB	EXC.	V.G.	GOOD	FAIR	POOR
750	600	500	-	-	-

STANDARD TACTICAL MODEL

Built for the 20th anniversary of International Practical Shooting Confederation (IPSC) competition shooting in 1996. Built on the Colt Government model with round top slide and chamber for .45 ACP. Many special features special serial numbers. Limited to 1,500 pistols.

NIB	EXC.	V.G.	GOOD	FAIR	POOR
1,650	1,350	900	-	-	-

SUPERIOR TACTICAL MODEL

Same as above but built on an enhanced frame with many custom features. Special serial numbers limited to 500 pistols.

NIB	EXC.	V.G.	GOOD	FAIR	POOR
1,850	1,450	1,000	-	-	-

DELUXE TACTICAL MODEL

Same as above but with added features. Limited to 250 pistols.

NIB	EXC.	V.G.	GOOD	FAIR	POOR
2,000	1,550	1,100	-	-	-

LEW HORTON DISTRIBUTING SERIES

Following is a list of special edition Colt pistols and revolvers produced by the Colt Custom Shop exclusively for Lew Horton Distributing, which specializes in special edition and custom guns. These handguns are listed to provide the reader with an idea of the number of limited edition Colts sold by Horton and the year they were produced with the retail price. (Lew Horton Distributing, P.O. Box 5023, Westboro, MA 01581 (508) 366-7400 *www.lewhorton.com*).

GOLD CUP U.S. SHOOTING TEAM

This is a limited edition Gold Cup .45 ACP with special blue, sights, grips. The U.S. Shooting Team logo is rolled on the slide. Limited to 500 pistols and built for Horton.

Suggested Retail Price: $1,025

MCCORMICK COMMANDER

This is a limited edition pistol made for Horton in 1995 and limited to 100 pistols. It has many special features. The slide is engraved and there is a gold rampant colt on the slide.

Suggested Retail Price: $1,125

NOTE: This advertisement appeared on *GunBroker.com* in March of 2007:

MCCORMICK OFFICER

This Horton exclusive pistol has factory installed McCormick parts and a hard chrome finish. A total of 500 guns were built in 1995.

Suggested Retail Price: $950

MCCORMICK FACTORY RACER

This is a limited edition pistol for Horton. It is a full size government model with hard chrome finish, special barrel, trigger safety and other custom features. Each gun is rollmarked "McCORMICK FACTORY RACER" on the slide. Special serial numbers from #MFR001 to #MFR500.

Suggested Retail Price: $1,100

COLT CLASSIC .45 SPECIAL EDITION

This Horton model is limited to 400 pistols and features a royal blue polish with special "CLASSIC .45" gold etched on the slide. Pearlite grips.

Suggested Retail Price: $960

COLT COMMEMORATIVES

The field of commemoratives is fascinating and can be terribly frustrating, depending on one's motives and point of view. For someone who collects things from purely an aesthetic sense, commemoratives are quite desirable. Most are embellished and have had great care put into their fit and finish. They are attractively cased, and their proliferation makes acquisition relatively simple, except of course financially.

On the other hand, the collector who has an eye for the investment or resale potential of his acquisitions has usually found that the commemorative market has been "soft" for some years and, as investments, the items in his or her collection have not done well.

Traditionally, the secondary market for commemorative Colt single actions has not kept pace with that for regular factory-production SAAs. This is no longer the case, at least not to the extent it has been in the past. Colt SAA commemoratives are, for the most part, 2nd Generation guns, and they have appreciated in value just as all 2nd Generation SAAs have. It seems that the value of these guns doesn't lie in their commemorative status as much as it does in their 2nd Generation status. In fact, many of these commemoratives are used as shooters! This severely limits their collectibility, but not perhaps their desirability. (Note that the values given below are for Mint, NIB, unfired guns with all original packaging and what-nots.)

The market for commemorative Scouts is fairly healthy, too, perhaps the result of a wave of '60s nostalgia. Not so for commemorative 1911s, however. The value of these guns generally lies in their mint, unfired status; once they've been fired, all bets are off. This is so perhaps because most of these guns are so dandied-up that most shooters feel they're inappropriate for everyday casual shooting in front of other people.

One final note. A number of Colt commemoratives were produced by Colt but offered for sale by private companies – in a way like those guns built for sale by Lew Horton Distributing, mentioned earlier in this chapter – to commemorate an event for instance such as the famous shoot-out at the OK Corral in Tombstone, Arizona. This publication does not cover most of these private commemoratives because it is practically impossible to determine any secondary market value. It is also difficult to construct any meaningful comprehensive list of such private offerings.

Year/Model	Issue Price	NIB	Number Mfd.
1961			
Geneseo, IL. 125th Anniversary Derringer	$28	$650	104
Sheriff's Model (Blue & Case)	130	2,250	478
Sheriff's Model (Nickel)	140	6,000	25
Kansas Statehood Cent. Frontier Scout	75	450	6,197
Colt Factory 125th Anniv. Model SAA .45	150	1,495	7,390
Pony Express Cent. Scout	80	475	1,007
Civil War Cent. Single Shot Pistol	75	175	24,114
1962			
Rock Island Arsenal Cent. Single Shot Pistol	$39	$250	550
Columbus, OH. Sesquicent. Frontier Scout	100	550	200
Ft. Findlay, OH. Sesquicent. Frontier Scout	90	650	150
Ft. Findlay Cased Pair	185	2,500	20
New Mex. Golden Anniv. Frontier Scout	80	450	1,000
West Virginia Statehood Cent. Frontier Scout	75	450	3,452
1963			
West Virginia Statehood Cent. SAA .45	$150	$1495	600
Ft. McPherson, Nebraska Cent. Derringer	29	395	300
Arizona Terr. Cent. Frontier Scout	75	450	5,355
Arizona Terr. Cent. SAA .45	150	1,495	1,280
Carolina Charter Tercent. Frontier Scout	75	450	300
Carolina Charter Tercent .22/.45 Combo.	240	1,895	251
H. Cook 1 To 100 .22/.45 Comb.	275	1,995	100
Ft. Stephenson, Oh. Sesquicent. Frontier Scout	75	550	200
Battle of Gettysburg Cent. Frontier Scout	90	450	1,019
Idaho Terr. Cent. Frontier Scout	75	450	902
Gen. J.H. Morgan Indiana Raid Frontier Scout	75	650	100
1964			
Cherry's Sport. Goods 35th Anniv. .22/.45 Combo.	$275	$1,995	100
Nevada Statehood Cent. Frontier Scout	75	450	3,984
Nevada Statehood Cent. SAA .45	150	1,495	1,688
Nevada Statehood Cent. .22/.45 Combo.	240	1,895	189
Nevada Statehood Cent. .22/.45 W/Engr. Cyls.	350	1,995	577
Nevada "Battle Born" Frontier Scout	85	450	981
Nevada "Battle Born" SAA .45	175	1,495	80
Nevada "Battle Born" .22/.45 Comb.	265	2,595	20
Montana Terr. Cent. Frontier Scout	75	450	2,300
Montana Terr. Cent. SAA .45	150	1,495	851
Wyoming Diamond Jubilee Frontier Scout	75	450	2,357
General Hood Cent. Frontier Scout	75	450	1,503
New Jersey Tercent. Frontier Scout	75	450	1,001
New Jersey Tercent SAA .45	150	1,495	250
St. Louis Bicent. Frontier Scout	75	450	802
St. Louis Bicent. SAA .45	150	1,495	200
St. Louis Bicent .22/.45 Combo.	240	1,895	250
California Gold Rush Frontier Scout	80	475	500
Pony Express Presentation SAA .45	250	1,495	1,004
Chamizal Treaty Frontier Scout	85	450	450

Year/Model	Issue Price	NIB	Number Mfd.
Chamizal Treaty SAA .45	170	1,495	50
Chamizal Treaty .22/.45 Combo.	280	1,995	50
Col. Sam Colt Sesquicent. SAA .45	225	1,495	4,750
Col. Sam Colt Deluxe SAA .45	500	2,500	200
Col. Sam Colt Custom Deluxe SAA .45	1,000	4,000	50
Wyatt Earp Buntline SAA .45	250	2,750	150
1965			
Oregon Trail Frontier Scout	$75	$450	1,995
Joaquin Murietta Frontier Scout .22/.45 Combo.	350	1,995	100
Forty-Niner Miner Frontier Scout	85	450	500
Old Ft. Des Moines Reconst. Frontier Scout	90	475	700
Old Ft. Des Moines Reconst. SAA .45	170	1,495	100
Old Ft. Des Moines Reconst. .22/.45 Combo.	290	1,995	100
Appomattox Cent. Scout	75	450	1,001
Appomattox Cent. SAA .45	150	1,495	250
Appomattox Cent. .22/.45 Combo.	240	1,895	250
General Meade Pa. Campaign Frontier Scout	75	450	1,197
St. Augustine Quadracent. Frontier Scout	85	475	500
Kansas Cowtown Series – Wichita Frontier Scout	85	450	500
1966			
Kansas Cowtown Series – Dodge City Frontier Scout	$85	$450	500
Colorado Gold Rush Frontier Scout	85	475	1,350
Oklahoma Territory Frontier Scout	85	450	1,343
Dakota Territory Frontier Scout	85	450	1,000
General Meade Pa. Campaign SAA .45	165	1,495	200
Abercrombie & Fitch "Trailblazer" – Chicago New Frontier	275	1,295	100
Abercrombie & Fitch "Trailblazer" – San Francisco New Frontier	275	1,295	100
Kansas Cowtown Series – Abilene Frontier Scout	95	450	500
Indiana Sesquicent. Frontier Scout	85	450	1,500
Pony Express 4-Square Set .45 (4 Guns)	1,400	5,995	N/A
California Gold Rush SAA .45	175	1,495	130
1967			
Lawman Series – Bat Masterson Frontier Scout	$90	$475	3,000
Lawman Series – Bat Masterson SAA .45	180	1,500	500
Alamo Frontier Scout	85	450	4,250
Alamo SAA .45	165	1,495	750
Alamo .22/.45 Combo.	265	1,895	250
Kansas Cowtown Series – Coffeyville Frontier Scout	95	450	500
Kansas Trail Series – Chisolm Trail Frontier Scout	100	450	500
WWI Series – Chateau Thierry .45 Auto	200	795	7,400
WWI Series – Chateau Thierry .45 Auto Deluxe	500	1,350	75
WWI Series – Chateau Thierry .45 Auto Sp. Deluxe	1,000	2,750	25
1968			
Nebraska Cent. Frontier Scout	$100	$450	7,001
Kansas Trail Series – Pawnee Trail Frontier Scout	100	450	501
Santa Fe Trail Frontier Scout	-	-	501
WWI Series – Belleau Wood .45 Auto	200	795	7,400
WWI Series – Belleau Wood .45 Auto Deluxe	500	1,350	75

Year/Model	Issue Price	NIB	Number Mfd.
WWI Series – Belleau Wood .45 Auto Sp. Deluxe	1,000	2,750	25
Lawman Series – Pat Garrett Frontier Scout	110	475	3,000
Lawman Series – Pat Garrett SAA .45	220	1,495	500
Gen. Nathan B. Forrest Frontier Scout	110	450	3,000
WWI Series – 2nd Battle of Marne .45 Auto	220	795	7,400
WWI Series – 2nd Battle of Marne Deluxe	500	1,350	75
WWI Series – 2nd Battle of Marne Sp. Deluxe	1,000	2,750	25
1969			
Alabama Sesquicent. Frontier Scout	$110	$450	3,001
Golden Spike Frontier Scout	135	475	11,000
Kansas Trail Series – Shawnee Trail Scout	120	450	501
Kansas Trail Series – Fort Larned Frontier Scout	120	450	501
Texas Ranger SAA .45	650	2,250	800
Texas Ranger Deluxe .45	-	-	200
Lawman Series – Wild Bill Hickok Scout	117	475	3,000
Lawman Series – Wild Bill Hickok SAA .45	220	1,495	500
WWI Series – Meuse-Argonne Deluxe	500	1,350	75
WWI Series – Meuse-Argonne Sp. Deluxe	1,000	2,750	25
Arkansas Terr. Sesquicent. Frontier Scout	110	450	3,501
California Bicent. Frontier Scout	135	450	5,001
Lawman Series – Wyatt Earp Scout	125	495	3,001
Lawman Series – Wyatt Earp SAA .45	395	2,750	501
1970			
WWII Series – European Theatre Auto	$250	$795	11,500
WWII Series – Pacific Theatre Auto	250	795	11,500
Kansas Fort Series – Ft. Hays Frontier Scout, etc.	130	425	500
Maine Sesquicent. Frontier Scout	120	450	3,001
Missouri Sesquicent. Frontier Scout	125	450	3,001
Missouri Sesquicent. SAA .45	220	490	501
1971			
NRA Centennial SAA .357 Mag.	250	1,295	5,001
NRA Centennial Gold Cup .45 Auto	250	1,295	2,500
Gen. U.S. Grant 1851 Navy	250	595	4,751
Gen. Robert E. Lee 1851 Navy	250	595	4,751
Lee - Grant Set 1851 Navy Combo.	500	1,350	251
Kansas Fort Series – Ft. Scott Frontier Scout	130	450	500
1972			
Florida Territorial Sesquicent. Frontier Scout	$125	$450	2,001
1973			
Arizona Ranger Frontier Scout	$135	$450	3,001
Peacemaker Centennial SAA .44-40	$300	$1,495	1,501
Peacemaker Centennial SAA .45	300	1,495	1,501
Peacemaker Centennial SAA .44-40/.45 Combo.	625	3,250	501
Alabama Sesquicent. SAA .45	-	-	1
1974			
none			
1975			
none			

Year/Model	Issue Price	NIB	Number Mfd.
1976			
U.S. Bicentennial Set: Python, Dragoon, SAA	$1,695	$2,995	1,776
1977			
2nd Amendment .22 Frontier Scout	$195	$450	3,020
U.S. Cavalry 200th Anniversary Pair	995	1,250	3,001
1978			
Statehood Dragoon 3rd Model	$250	$750	52
1979			
Ned Buntline SAA N.F. .45	$895	$1,295	3,000
Ohio President's Spec. Edit. .45 Auto N/A	995	250	
Tombstone Cent. .45 SAA	550	1,395	300
1980			
Drug Enforcement Agency .45 Auto	$550	$1,100	910
Olympics Ace Spec. Edition .22	1,000	1,295	200
Heritage Walker .44 Percussion	1,495	1,950	1,000
1981			
John M. Browning .45 Auto	$1,100	$995	3,000
Ace Signature Series .22	1,000	1,050	1,000
1982			
John Wayne SAA	$2,995	$2,250	3,100
John Wayne SAA Deluxe	10,000	7,500	500
John Wayne SAA Presentation	20,000	12,000	100
1983			
Buffalo Bill Wild West Show Cent. SAA	$1,350	$1,595	500
1984			
1st Edition Govt. Model .380 ACP	$425	$475	1,000
Duke Frontier .22	475	495	1,000
Winchester/Colt SAA .44-40	N/A	2,250	4,000
U.S.A. Edition SAA .44-40	4,995	3,500	100
Kit Carson New Frontier .22	550	450	1,000
2nd Edition Govt. Model .380 ACP	525	475	1,000
Officer's ACP Commencement Issue	700	795	1,000
Theodore Roosevelt SAA .44-40	1,695	1,995	500
North Amer. Oilmen Buntline SAA .45	3,900	3,500	200
1985			
Mustang 1st Edition .380ACP	$475	$450	1,000
Officer's ACP Heirloom Edition	1,575	1,550	N/A
Klay-Colt 1851 Navy	1,850	1,850	150
Klay-Colt 1851 Navy Engraved Edition	3,150	3,150	50
Double Diamond Set .357 & .45 Auto	1,575	1,795	1,000
1986			
150th Anniversary SAA .45	$1,595	$1,995	1,000
150th Anniv. Engraving Sampler	1,613	2,750	N/A
150th Anniv. Engraving Sampler .45 Auto	1,155	1,295	N/A
Texas 150th Sesquicent. Sheriff's .45	836	1,695	N/A
1987			
Combat Elite Custom Edition .45 Auto	$900	$995	500
12th Man Spirit of Aggieland .45 Auto	950	995	999
1989			
Snake Eyes Ltd. Edition 2-2.5" Python	$2,950	$1,995	500

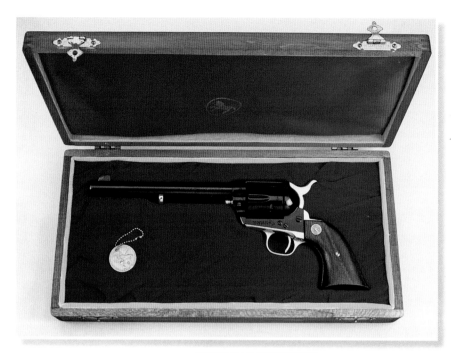

*125th Anniversary
Edition Peacemaker.*

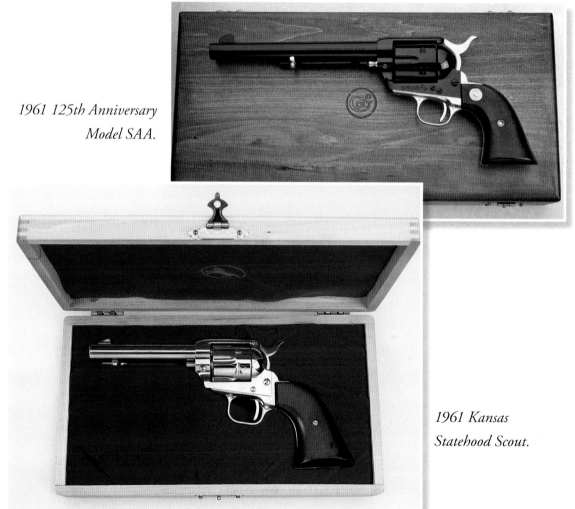

*1961 125th Anniversary
Model SAA.*

*1961 Kansas
Statehood Scout.*

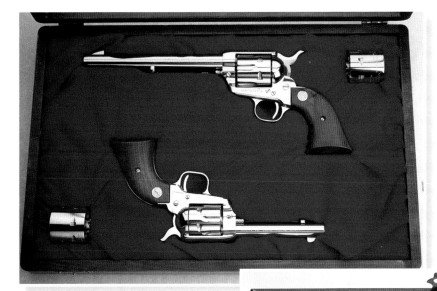

*1961-1964 Pony Express
Centennial Scout & SAA.*

*1962 Columbus OH
Sesquicentennial Scout.*

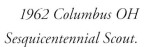

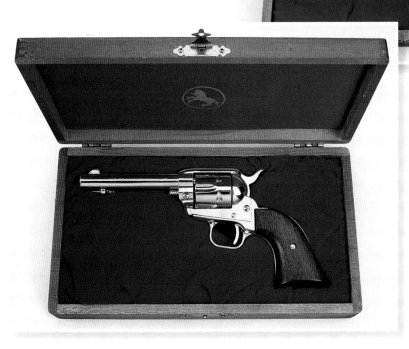

*1962 Ft Findlay OH
Sesquicentennial Scout.*

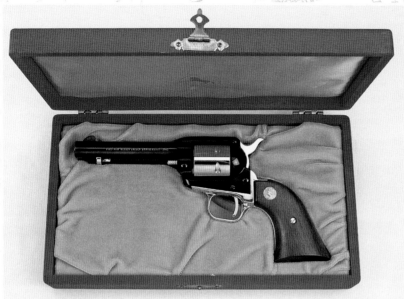

1962 New Mexico Golden Anniversary Scout.

1962 West Virginia Statehood Scout.

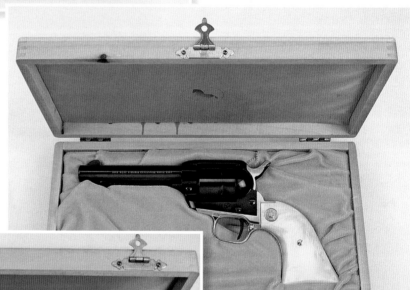

1963 Arizona Territory Centennial SAA.

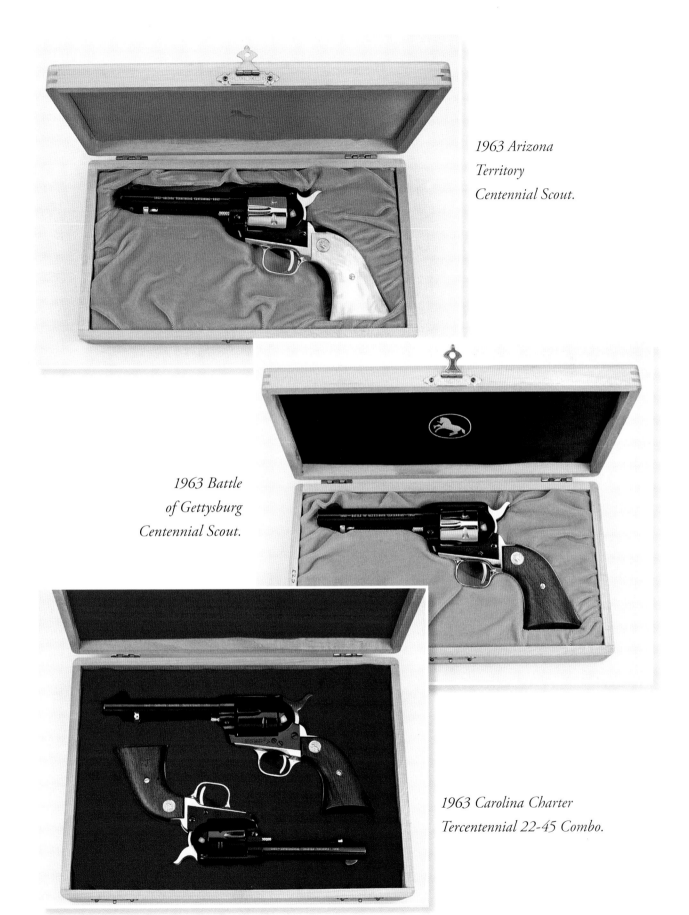

*1963 Arizona
Territory
Centennial Scout.*

*1963 Battle
of Gettysburg
Centennial Scout.*

*1963 Carolina Charter
Tercentennial 22-45 Combo.*

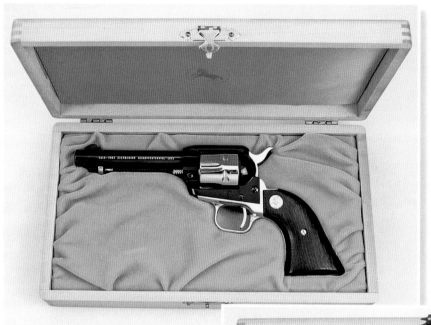

*1963 Ft
Stephenson Ohio
Sesquicentennial
Scout.*

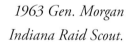

*1963 Gen. Morgan
Indiana Raid Scout.*

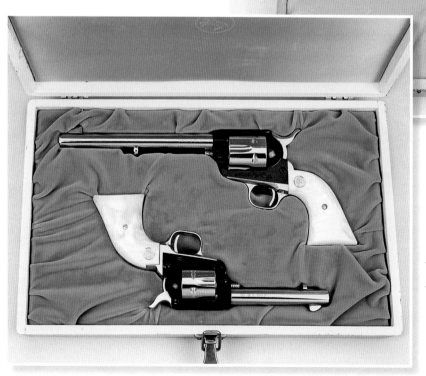

*1963 H. Cook 1 of
100 22-45 Combo.*

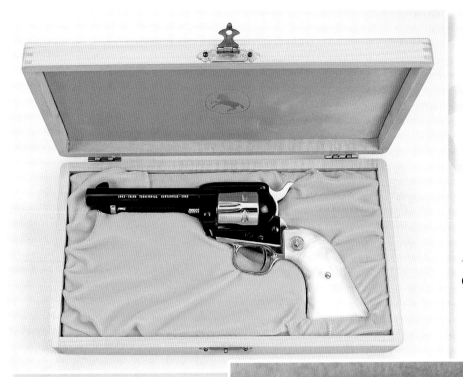

1963 Idaho Territory
Centennial Scout.

1963 West Virginia
Statehood SAA.

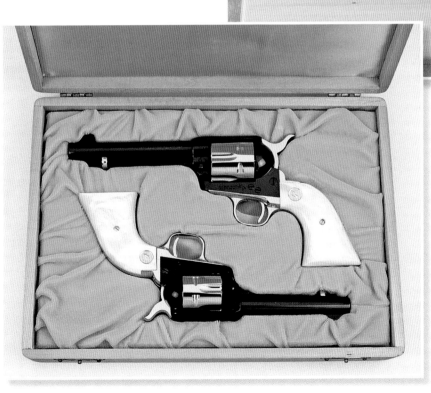

1964 Chamizal Treaty
22-45 Combo.

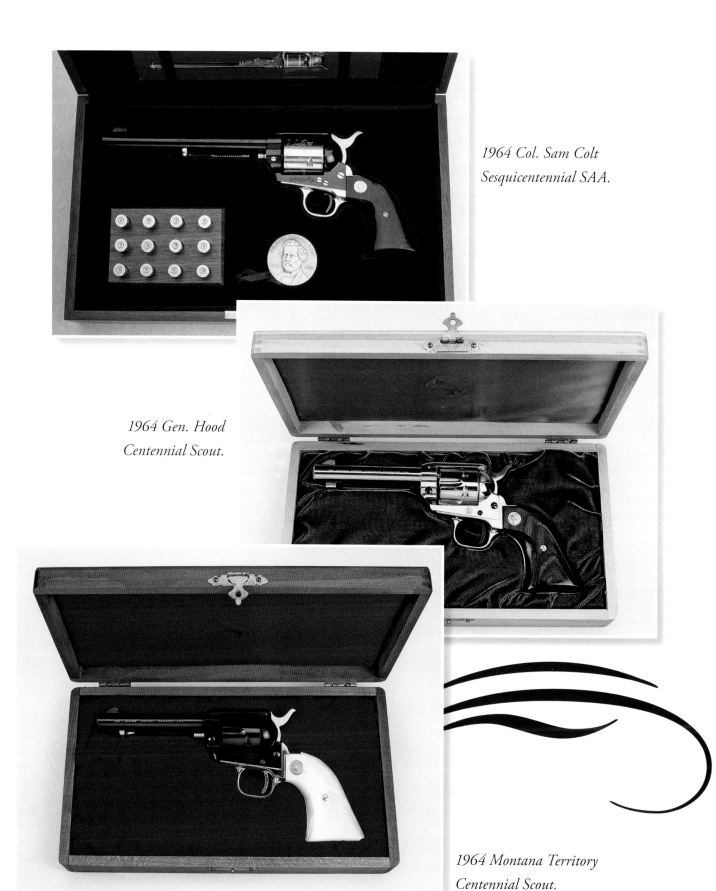

1964 Col. Sam Colt Sesquicentennial SAA.

1964 Gen. Hood Centennial Scout.

1964 Montana Territory Centennial Scout.

*1964 Nevada Battle
Born Scout.*

*1964 Nevada Statehood
Centennial 22-45 with
Extra Cylinders.*

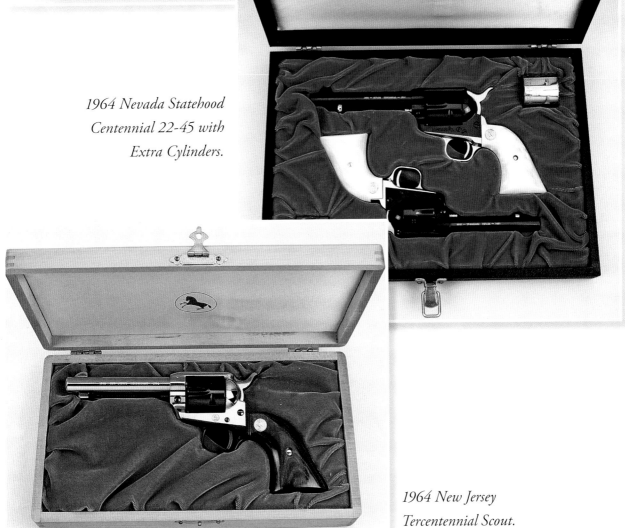

*1964 New Jersey
Tercentennial Scout.*

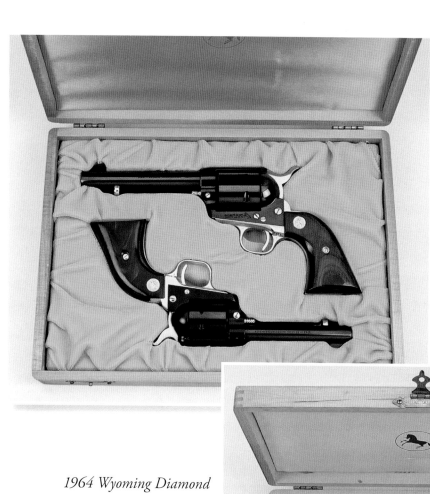

1964 St Louis Bicentennial
22-45 Combo.

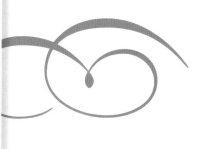

1964 Wyoming Diamond
Jubilee Scout.

1965 Appomattox
Centennial 22-45 Combo.

1965 Forty-Niner Scout.

1965 Gen. Meade Campaign Scout.

1965 Old Ft. Des Moines Reconstruction SAA 45.

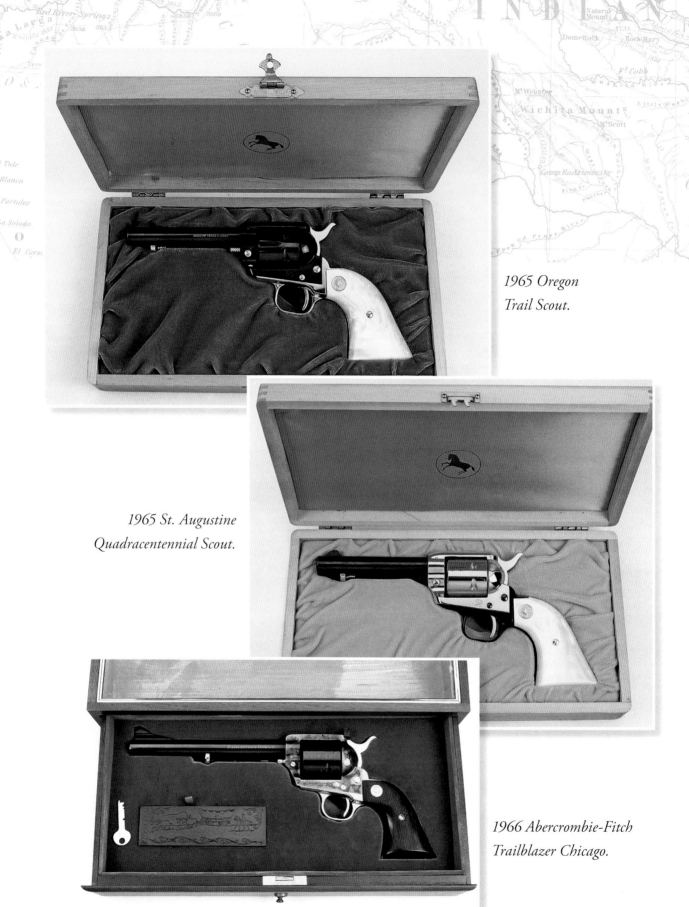

1965 Oregon
Trail Scout.

1965 St. Augustine
Quadracentennial Scout.

1966 Abercrombie-Fitch
Trailblazer Chicago.

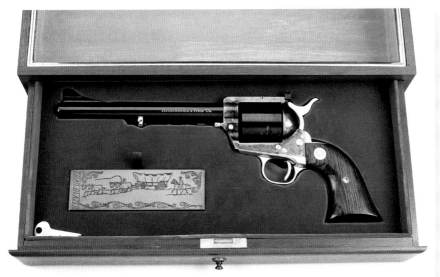

1966 Abercrombie-Fitch Trailblazer NY.

1966 Abercrombie-Fitch Trailblazer San Francisco.

1966 California Gold Rush SAA.

*1966 Colorado
Gold Rush Scout.*

*1966 Dakota
Territory Scout.*

*1966 IN Sesquicentennial
Scout.*

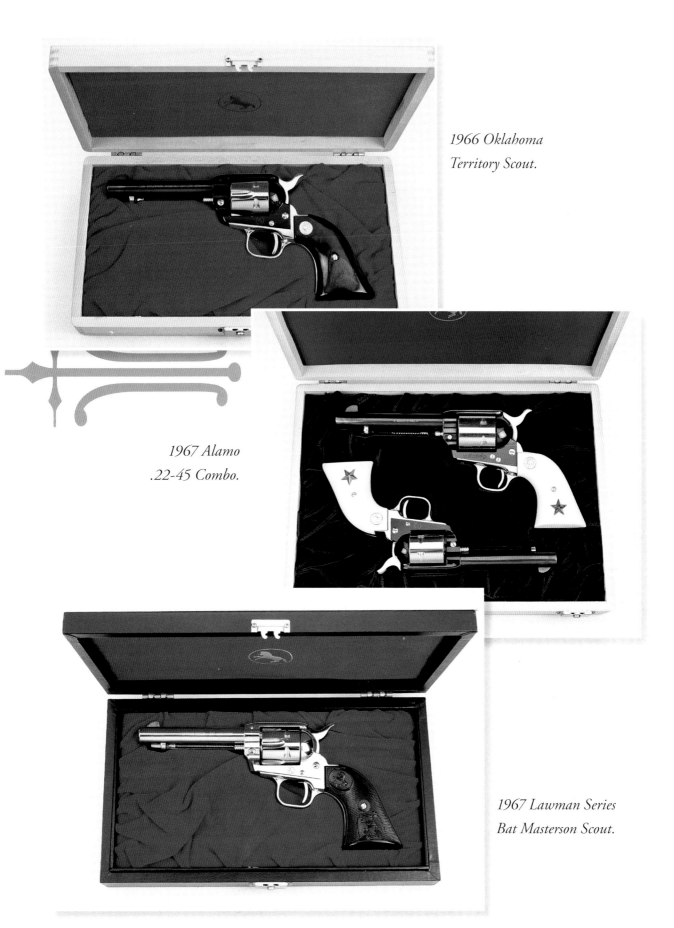

1966 Oklahoma Territory Scout.

1967 Alamo .22-45 Combo.

1967 Lawman Series Bat Masterson Scout.

1967 WWI Series Chateau-Thierry Deluxe 45 Auto.

1968 Lawman Series Pat Garrett SAA 45.

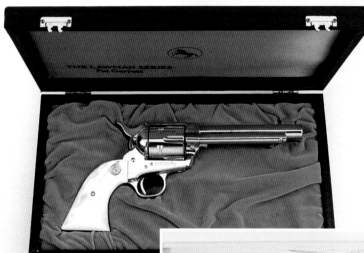

1968 Nebraska Centennial Scout.

1968 WWI Series Belleau Wood 45 Auto.

1969 Alabama Sesquicentennial Scout.

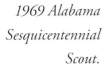

1969 Arkansas Territory Sesquicentennial Scout.

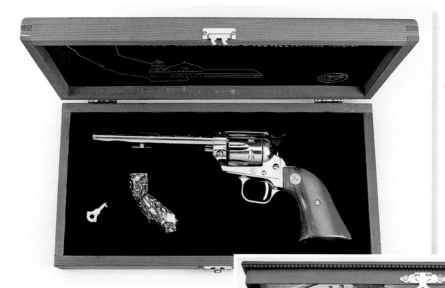

*1969 California
Bicentennial Scout.*

1969 Golden Spike Scout.

*1969 Kansas Trails
- Shawnee, Santa Fe,
Chisholm, Pawnee – Scouts.*

1969 Lawman Series Wild Bill Hickock Scout.

1969 Nathan B. Forrest Scout.

1969 WWI Series 2nd Battle of the Marne Deluxe.

1969 WWI Series Meuse-Argonne Deluxe 45 Auto.

1969 WWI Series Meuse-Argonne Deluxe.

1970 Texas Ranger SAA 45.

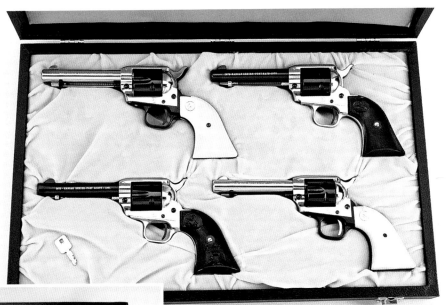

(top l-r) Ft. Riley & Ft. Hayes; (bottom l-r) Ft. Scott & Ft. Larned Scouts.

1970 Kansas Series Scouts Boxes.

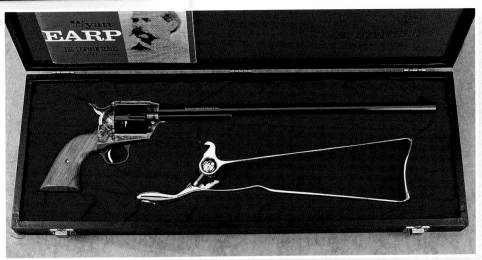

1970 Lawman Series Wyatt Earp SAA Buntline.

*1970 Maine
Sesquicentennial Scout.*

*1970 Missouri
Sesquicentennial SAA.*

*1970 WWII Series
European Theatre.*

*1970 Missouri
Sesquicentennial Scout.*

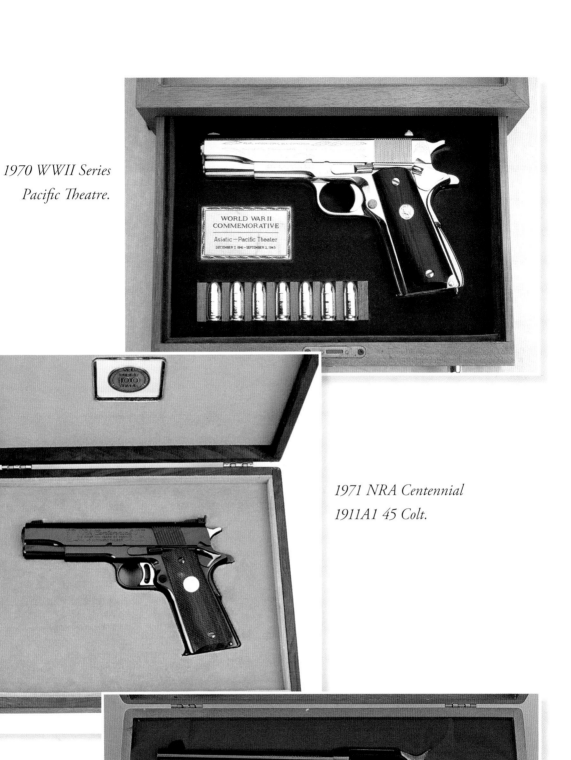

*1970 WWII Series
Pacific Theatre.*

*1971 NRA Centennial
1911A1 45 Colt.*

*1971 NRA
Centennial Gold Cup.*

*1971 NRA
Centennial SAA
357 Mag.*

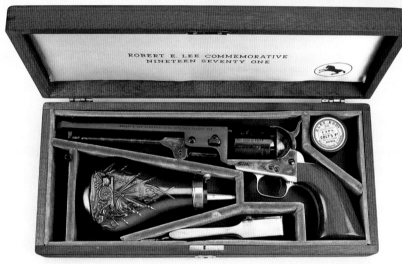

*1971 Robert E.
Lee 1851 Navy.*

*1971 Ulysses S. Grant
1851 Navy.*

1972 Arizona Ranger Scout.

1972 Centennial
Cased Set
Florida Territory
Sesquicentennial
Scout.

1973 Peacemaker
Centennial SAA 44-40.

1973 Peacemaker
Centennial Master Set.

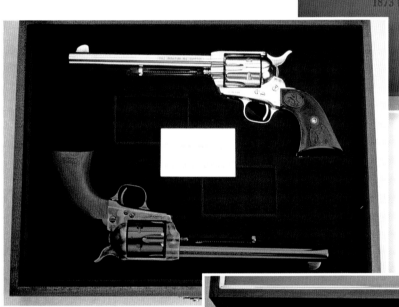

1975 Peacemaker
Centennial SAA 45.

*1976 US
Bicentennial
Python.*

*1976 US
Bicentennial Set.*

*1977 2nd
Amendment 22.*

*1979 Ned Buntline
Commemorative
New Frontier.*

*1980 Heritage Walker
44 Percussion.*

*1981 John M.
Browning 45 Auto.*

*1982 John Wayne
SAA Presentation.*

*1982 John Wayne "The
Duke" New Frontier.*

1983 Buffalo Bill
Wild West Show
Centennial SAA.

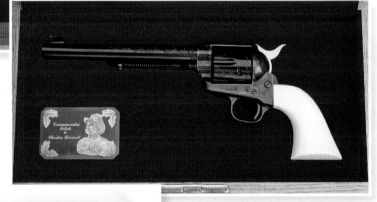

1984 Kit Carson
New Frontier 22.

1984 Theodore Roosevelt
SAA 44-40.

1984 USA Edition SAA.

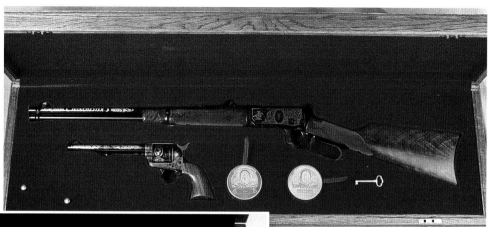

1984 Winchester-Colt SAA 44-40.

1985 Double Diamond Set .357 & .45.

1985 Mustang 1st Edition 380 ACP.

1986 Texas 150th Anniversary Sesquicentennial Sheriffs Model.

Mark IV Series 70, 2003 issue.

Colt Defender Plus.

CURRENT COLT REPLICA EDITIONS

1911 WORLD WAR I REPLICA (MODEL O1911)

This model 1911 was offered through the Colt Private Security Support Center. Colt says its current model .45 semi-automatic is a "faithful reproduction of the WWI Model 1911 U.S. Military sidearm .... In recognition of the contribution of the Colt .45, Colt reproduces it in detail, including the packaging." Based on original 1911 blueprints; Series 70 single action firing system; original rollmarks and inspector marks; 5-inch barrel with wide hood and overall length 8.5 inches; smooth, straight mainspring housing with lanyard loop; WWI manual and grip safety; tapered blade front sight and U-Notch rear sight; carbon steel frame in Carbonia blue finish; forged, knurled slide stop; WWI style screwdriver and manuals included; .45 ACP caliber two 7 round magazines; double diamond walnut grips; long, smooth steel trigger and WWI style hammer; and vertical rear slide serrations.

MKIV SERIES 70 GOVERNMENT MODEL

This is a faithful reproduction of the Series 70 pistol. "The legacy of the Government Model is well known. It is a combat proven weapon that has tirelessly served our Armed Forces in past conflicts. Colt's Series 70 pistol features the Series 70 firing system making it a faithful reproduction and throwback to Colt Government Models manufactured during the 1970's. It is a rugged and dependable single action Colt that features high maintainability and sustains repeatable accuracy." Features a 5 inch barrel, chambering for .45 ACP with 7 + 1 firing, double diamond and checkered rosewood grips, the original rollmarks, fixed sights, Series 70 firing system and available in blue (Model #O1970A1CS) or stainless steel (Model #O1070A1CS) finish. Frames are steel and length overall is 8.5 inches; spur hammer and aluminum trigger. White dot front and rear sights. Service style grip safety and standard thumb safety.

DEFENDER PLUS (MODEL O7000D)

A smaller sized frame matched to a smaller than Officer's length slide. "Colt first introduced the use of a lightweight aluminum alloy in a gun frame in 1948. Building on this experience, the Colt Defender model now offers the power and performance of a full-sized .45 ACP pistol in a compact, lightweight carry model. Small, lightweight, accurate, reliable, with excellent white dot front and rear sights, and able to withstand everyday wear and frequent practice sessions without the need for extensive maintenance." Wrap around rubber finger

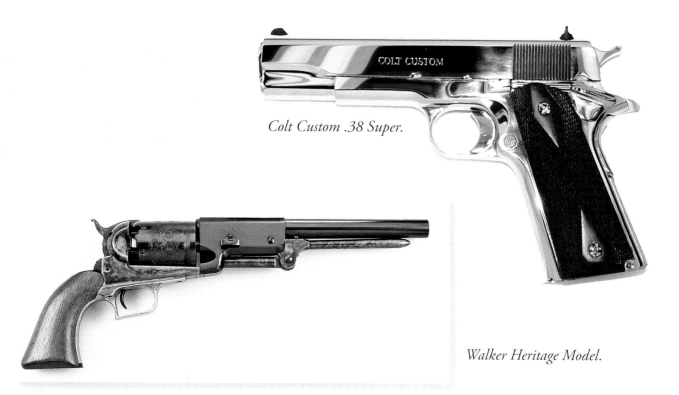

Colt Custom .38 Super.

Walker Heritage Model.

groove grips; skeletonized aluminum trigger; single action; fixed sights; chambered for .45 caliber; ultra short 3-inch barrel and combat style hammer; 6.75 inches overall length; beveled magazine well; ultra lightweight; brushed stainless frame and slide; 7 + 1 round capacity. Teflon coated receiver. Wrap around Hogue grips. Beavertail grip safety; standard thumb safety.

COLT .38 SUPER (MODELS #O2070E, #O2070ELC2, #O2570)

"The .38 Super was introduced in 1929 in the famous Colt Government Model 1911 auto pistol. At the time of its introduction the .38 Super was the most powerful auto pistol cartridge in the world. Colt is the only major American gun maker who has produced .38 Super pistols [most others having selected the .357 Magnum which was developed in response to the .38 Super]. The .38 Super is one of the most powerful and flat-shooting cartridges available for auto-loading pistols [and is finding increased popularity in pistols with longer barrels for IPSC shooting]." The .38 Super is a single action, with fixed white dot front and rear sights, a 9 + 1 capacity, beveled magazine well, standard thumb safety and service style grip safety, 5 inch barrel and 8.5 inch overall length. Available models #O2070E (stainless steel frame and finish), #O2070ELC2 (stainless steel

frame with bright stainless finish) and #O2570 (blued carbon steel). The Model ELC2 differs from the other two models in that it has a spur hammer whereas they have combat style hammers; it has double diamond and checkered rosewood grips whereas the other two have checkered rubber grips; and it has a standard grip safety whereas the other two have beavertail safeties.

REPRODUCTION COLT PERCUSSION REVOLVERS

NOTE: The revolvers listed were manufactured in a variety of styles (cylinder form, stainless steel, etc.) that affect prices. Factory engraved examples command a considerable premium over the prices listed. Labeled as "Colt Second Generation" or "Colt Blackpowder Series" revolvers, these guns were assembled in the USA from parts manufactured by Uberti of Italy. Uberti is a high-quality manufacturer; but the perception persists that these guns were actually made by Colt. This is not the case. Nevertheless their values are appreciating rapidly, perhaps because few people realize the circumstances of their manufacture.

*2nd Generation First
Model Dragoon.*

*2nd Generation Model
1848 Pocket Pistol.*

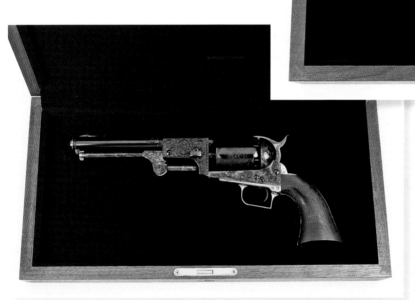

*2nd Generation Second
Model Dragoon.*

WALKER HERITAGE MODEL

Made from 1979 to 1981; serial numbers #1200 to #4120 and #32256 to #32500.

NIB	EXC.	V.G.
895	750	500

FIRST MODEL DRAGOON

Made from 1980 to 1982; serial numbers #24100 to #34500.

NIB	EXC.	V.G.
695	600	300

SECOND MODEL DRAGOON

Made from 1980 to 1982; serial numbers as above.

NIB	EXC.	V.G.
695	600	300

THIRD MODEL DRAGOON

Made from 1980 to 1982; serial numbers as above.

NIB	EXC.	V.G.
695	600	300

*2nd Generation
Third Model
Dragoon.*

*2nd Generation
Model 1851 Navy.*

*2nd Generation
Model 1860 Army.*

MODEL 1848 POCKET PISTOL

Made in 1981; serial numbers #16000 to #17851.

NIB	EXC.	V.G.
625	500	300

MODEL 1851 NAVY REVOLVER

Made from 1971 to 1978; serial numbers #4201 to #25100 and #24900 to #29150.

NIB	EXC.	V.G.
675	575	375

MODEL 1860 ARMY REVOLVER

Made from 1978 to 1982; serial numbers #201000 to #212835.

NIB	EXC.	V.G.
675	575	375

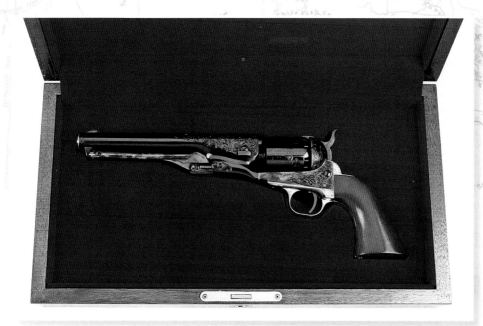

2nd Generation
Model 1861 Navy.

2nd Generation
1862 Pocket Navy.

MODEL 1861 NAVY REVOLVER

Made during 1980 and 1981; serial numbers #40000 to #43165.

NIB	EXC.	V.G.
675	575	375

MODEL 1862 POCKET PISTOL

Made from 1979 to 1984; serial numbers #8000 to #58850.

NIB	EXC.	V.G.
625	500	300

MODEL 1862 POLICE REVOLVER

Made from 1979 to 1984; serial numbers in above range.

NIB	EXC.	V.G.
NIB	EXC.	V.G.
625	500	300

*2nd Generation
Model 1862 Police.*

*Colt Blackpowder
3rd Model Dragoon.*

COLT BLACKPOWDER ARMS/ BROOKLYN, NEW YORK

As noted above, these blackpowder revolvers and rifles were made under license from Colt by Uberti.

1842 PATERSON NO. 5 HOLSTER MODEL

This model is a copy of the No. 5 Holster model and is chambered for the .36 cal. ball. Fitted with a 7.5-inch octagon barrel. Hand engraved. This is a special order revolver.

NIB	EXC.	V.G.	GOOD	FAIR	POOR
3000	-	-	-	-	-

WALKER

This .44 caliber large-frame revolver is fitted with a 9-inch barrel.

NIB	EXC.	V.G.	GOOD	FAIR	POOR
475	400	350	300	200	150

WALKER 150TH ANNIVERSARY MODEL

Marked "A Company No. 1" in gold. Introduced 1997.

NIB	EXC.	V.G.	GOOD	FAIR	POOR
600	500	-	-	-	-

WHITNEYVILLE HARTFORD DRAGOON

Similar in appearance to the Walker Colt this

Colt Blackpowder
Model 1860 Army,
fluted cylinder.

Colt Blackpowder Model 1860 Army.

revolver is fitted with a 7.5 inch barrel and a silver plated iron backstrap and trigger guard. This is a limited edition with a total of 2,400 guns built with serial numbers from #1100 through #1340.

NIB	EXC.	V.G.	GOOD	FAIR	POOR
575	450	350	300	200	150

MARINE DRAGOON

NIB	EXC.	V.G.	GOOD	FAIR	POOR
895	-	-	-	-	-

3RD MODEL DRAGOON

Another large frame revolver with 7.5 inch barrel with a brass backstrap, three screw frame, and unfluted cylinder.

NIB	EXC.	V.G.	GOOD	FAIR	POOR
475	400	350	300	200	150

3RD MODEL DRAGOON – STEEL BACKSTRAP

NIB	EXC.	V.G.	GOOD	FAIR	POOR
500	425	375	325	200	150

3RD MODEL DRAGOON – FLUTED CYLINDER

NIB	EXC.	V.G.	GOOD	FAIR	POOR
510	435	375	325	200	150

COCHISE DRAGOON

This is actually a commemorative issue Third Model with gold inlay frame and barrel with special grips.

NIB	EXC.	V.G.	GOOD	FAIR	POOR
895	-	-	-	-	-

1849 MODEL POCKET

A small-frame revolver chambered in .31 caliber with a 4-inch barrel. Fitted with one piece walnut grips.

NIB	EXC.	V.G.	GOOD	FAIR	POOR
535	375	325	275	200	150

1851 MODEL NAVY

This is medium frame revolver chambered in .36 caliber with 7.5-inch barrel. Walnut grips and case color frame.

NIB	EXC.	V.G.	GOOD	FAIR	POOR
535	375	325	275	200	150

1851 MODEL NAVY WITH DUAL CYLINDER

NIB	EXC.	V.G.	GOOD	FAIR	POOR
575	400	350	300	200	150

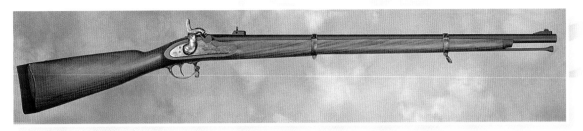

Colt Blackpowder 1861 Musket.

MODEL 1860 ARMY

This model is chamber in .44 caliber with roll engraved cylinder and one piece walnut grips. Barrel length is 8 inches.

NIB	EXC.	V.G.	GOOD	FAIR	POOR
555	375	325	275	200	150

COLT MODEL 1860 ARMY WITH DUAL CYLINDER

NIB	EXC.	V.G.	GOOD	FAIR	POOR
675	400	350	300	200	150

COLT MODEL 1860 ARMY – FLUTED CYLINDER

NIB	EXC.	V.G.	GOOD	FAIR	POOR
450	400	350	300	200	150

COLT 1860 OFFICER'S MODEL

This is a deluxe version of the standard 1860 with a special blued finish and gold crossed sabres. This is a four screw frame with 8 inch barrel and six shot rebated cylinder.

NIB	EXC.	V.G.	GOOD	FAIR	POOR
675	575	450	375	250	150

COLT MODEL 1860 ARMY GOLD U.S. CAVALRY

Features a gold engraved cylinder and gold barrel bands.

NIB	EXC.	V.G.	GOOD	FAIR	POOR
950	775	450	375	250	150

COLT MODEL 1860 ARMY – STAINLESS STEEL

NIB	EXC.	V.G.	GOOD	FAIR	POOR
575	400	350	300	200	150

COLT 1860 HEIRLOOM EDITION

This is an elaborately engraved revolver done in the Tiffany style and fitted with Tiffany style grips.

NIB	EXC.	V.G.	GOOD	FAIR	POOR
5000	-	-	-	-	-

COLT MODEL 1861 NAVY

This .36 caliber revolver features a 7.5-inch barrel with engraved cylinder, case colored frame and one piece walnut grips.

NIB	EXC.	V.G.	GOOD	FAIR	POOR
600	400	350	300	200	150

COLT MODEL 1861 NAVY GENERAL CUSTER

Same as above but with engraved frame and cylinder.

NIB	EXC.	V.G.	GOOD	FAIR	POOR
975	850	700	500	300	200

COLT MODEL 1862 POCKET NAVY

This small frame revolver is fitted with a round engraved cylinder with a 5 inch octagon barrel with hinged loading lever. Chambered for .36 cal.

NIB	EXC.	V.G.	GOOD	FAIR	POOR
550	375	325	275	200	150

COLT MODEL 1862 TRAPPER-POCKET POLICE

This small frame revolver is fitted with a 3.5-inch barrel, silver backstrap, and trigger guard. The cylinder is semi-fluted and chambered in .36 caliber.

NIB	EXC.	V.G.	GOOD	FAIR	POOR
635	375	325	275	200	150

COLT 1861 MUSKET

This Civil War musket is chambered in the .58 cal. Lockplate, hammer, buttplate, and three barrel bands. The 40-inch barrel is finished bright. The stock is a one piece oil finish affair. Bayonet and accessories are extra.

NIB	EXC.	V.G.	GOOD	FAIR	POOR
750	550	400	325	275	150

COLT 1861 MUSKET – ARTILLERY MODEL

Same as above but fitted with a 31.5 inch barrel.

NIB	EXC.	V.G.	GOOD	FAIR	POOR
750	550	400	325	275	150

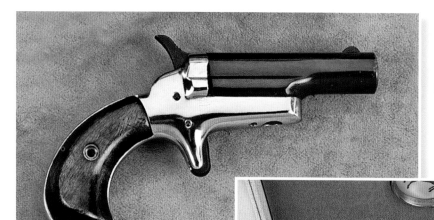

Colt Lord Model deringer.

Colt Lady Model deringer.

COLT 1861 MUSKET PRESENTATION (1 OF 1,000)

Limited to 1,000 guns these are special finished with a high polish and Colt's signature in gold on the trigger guard. Sold with special custom wooden case.

NIB	EXC.	V.G.	GOOD	FAIR	POOR
2,100	1500	750	600	450	300

COLT 1861 MUSKET PRESENTATION ARTILLERY MODEL (1 OF 1,000)

Same as above but 31.5-inch barrel.

NIB	EXC.	V.G.	GOOD	FAIR	POOR
2,100	1500	750	600	450	300

COLT GAMEMASTER .50

Introduced in 1997 this .50 cal. rifle is fitted with a 31.5 inch barrel and weighs about 13 lb. It is a sporting version of the 1861 Colt/Springfield rifle. Supposedly uncatalogued with fewer than 50 manufactured.

NIB	EXC.	V.G.	GOOD	FAIR	POOR
850	650	-	-	-	-

COLT DERINGER REPRODUCTIONS

FOURTH MODEL DERINGER

At the same time as the Single Action Army was revived, so was this deringer, which was intended largely for collectors. To allow them to be fired for amusement, however, they were chambered for .22 RF Short and eventually, some 112,000 were sold between 1959 and 1963. This gun was a copy of the Third Model except for caliber and finish, as many were elaborately engraved and finished with wood, ivory or mother-of-pearl grips. (Designed by F. Alexander Thuer, the 6.5 oz. Third Model debuted in 1875 and remained popular in .41 rimfire until 1912.)

NIB	EXC.	V.G.	GOOD	FAIR	POOR
375	350	300	-	-	-

LORD AND LADY MODEL DERINGERS

The success of the Fourth Model led to the

production of these fancy pairs, of what was actually a Fourth Model, in 1970. The Lord Deringer had a gold plated frame, blued barrel and walnut grips. The Lady Model had a gold frame and barrel, blued hammer and trigger and simulated pearl grips. Both were chambered in .22 RF Short and weighed about 6.5 oz.

NIB	EXC.	V.G.	GOOD	FAIR	POOR
500	400	-	-	-	-

AMERICA REMEMBERS SERIES AND OTHERS

America Remembers is a private enterprise specializing in somewhat gaudy commemoratives from a variety of manufacturers. They are generally considered the least collectible collectibles, if you know what we mean. Values are difficult to ascertain for these items. Where possible, we give auction listings that include a general asking price. The secondary market for these guns is difficult to determine.

COLT BUNTLINE SAA MINIATURE

"The Colt Single Action Army Buntline Miniature is licensed by Colt's Manufacturing Company, Inc. and issued by The United States Society of Arms and Armour, the antique arms affiliate of America Remembers. Flat topped frame with adjustable folding rear sight. The Classic Edition is available in a limited edition of 1500. The frame is case hardened, and the balance of the revolver is blued. Custom grips of select walnut complete this exceptional issue. The Presidential Edition, issued in a limited edition of 1500, is hand-engraved in a traditional Colt pattern. All parts are blued, except for the frame, which is case hardened. The grips are select walnut. Each miniature is fully functional. For safety reasons, no attempt should be made to fire this miniature as this could cause serious injury and damage the miniature. Closed edition."

COLT LEGENDS IN STEEL TRIBUTE REVOLVER

Only 250 of this Single Action Army were produced in .45 LC with 5.5 inch barrel and walnut grips. Delivered in lined wood display case. Handsomely decorated with 24 karat gold. Delivered in lined wood display case. Retail price $2,995.

COLT LEGACY TRIBUTE .45 PISTOL

Colt Government Model .45 ACP pistol with 5 inch barrel. Rosewood grips. Limited edition of 300. Handsomely decorated with 24 karat gold. Delivered in lined wood display case. Retail price $1,995.

COLT PATRIOTIC TRIBUTE .45 PISTOL

Colt Government Model .45 ACP with rosewood grips and 5 inch barrel. Limited edition of 500. Handsomely decorated with 24 karat gold. Delivered in lined wood display case. Retail price $1,995.

"DON'T GIVE UP THE SHIP" U.S. NAVY .45

Colt Government Model .45 ACP with rosewood grips and 5 inch barrel. Limited edition of 1,997. Handsomely decorated with 24 karat gold. Delivered in lined wood display case. Retail price $1,795.

GENERAL GEORGE S. PATTON, JR. TRIBUTE PISTOL

Colt Government Model .45 ACP with faux ivory grips and adorned with the distinctive GSP monogram seen on General Patton's favorite pistols. 5 inch barrel. Limited edition of 500. Handsomely decorated with 24 karat gold and delivered in lined wood display case. Retail price $2,195.

GENERAL GEORGE S. PATTON, JR. TRIBUTE REVOLVER

Colt Single Action Revolver (Uberti) with faux ivory grips and adorned with the distinctive GSP monogram seen on General Patton's favorite pistols. 4.75 inch barrel. Limited edition of 500. Handsomely decorated with 24 karat gold and delivered in lined wood display case. Retail price $2,295.

HERB JEFFRIES TRIBUTE REVOLVER

Born and raised in Detroit, Herb Jeffries became America's first black singing cowboy, the "Bronze Buckaroo," overturning the prevailing attitudes of his day about race, capturing the hearts of youngsters across the country, and becoming an American legend. Colt Single Action Revolver (Uberti) with pearl (bonded) grips. 5.5 inch barrel. Limited edition of 500. Handsomely decorated with 24 karat gold and delivered in lined wood display case. Retail price $1,695.

INTERPOL REVOLVER, A COLT .45 S.A.A.

Colt Single Action Army .45 LC with 4.75 inch barrel. Limited edition of 154, the same number as the number of Interpol member countries. Handsomely decorated with 24 karat gold and delivered in lined wood display case. A closed edition.

LONE STAR TRIBUTE REVOLVER

A .44 caliber 1847 Walker (Uberti) decorated with 24 karat gold on blued steel. Polished walnut grips. A limited edition of 150. Handsomely decorated with 24 karat gold and delivered in lined wood display case. Retail price $1,795.

NATIONAL RIFLE ASSOCIATION TRIBUTE PISTOL

Colt Government Model .45 ACP with rosewood grips and 5 inch barrel. Limited edition of 300. Handsomely decorated with 24 karat gold. Delivered in lined wood display case. Retail price $2,195.

THE PURPLE HEART TRIBUTE COLT .45

Colt Government Model .45 ACP with rosewood grips and 5 inch barrel. Limited edition of 250. Handsomely decorated with 24 karat gold. Delivered in lined wood display case. Retail price $1,895.

"THE HAPPY TRAILS TO YOU" ROY ROGERS TRIBUTE REVOLVER

Named in honor of Roy Rogers, America's movie, television and singing sensation. Colt Single Action .45 LC Revolver (Uberti) with pearl (bonded) grips. 5.5 inch barrel. Limited edition of 250. Lavishly decorated with 24 karat gold and delivered in lined wood display case. Retail price $1,295.

THE TEXAS RANGER TRIBUTE REVOLVER

Colt Single Action .45 LC Revolver (Uberti) with pearl (bonded) grips. 5.5 inch barrel. Limited edition of 300. Lavishly decorated with 24 karat gold and delivered in lined wood display case. Retail price $2,195.

TEXAS RANGER WALKER COLT REVOLVER

Colt blackpowder 1847 Walker revolver with a 9 inch barrel in .44 cal. Walnut grips and a limited edition of 300. Lavishly decorated with 24 karat gold and delivered in lined wood display case. Retail price $2,195.

VFW VIETNAM WAR TRIBUTE PISTOL

Colt Government Model .45 ACP with rosewood grips and 5 inch barrel. Limited edition of 300. Handsomely decorated with 24 karat gold. Delivered in lined wood display case. Retail price $2,195.

SAMUEL WALKER COLT REVOLVER

Colt blackpowder 1847 Walker revolver with a 9 inch barrel in .44 caliber. Walnut grips and a limited edition of 300. Lavishly decorated with 24 karat gold and delivered in lined wood display case. Retail price $3,495.

THE AMERICAN EAGLE

Colt Government Model .45 ACP with rosewood grips and 5 inch barrel. Limited edition of 300. Handsomely decorated with 24 karat gold. Delivered in lined wood display case. NOTE: According to an advertisement with pictures on *GunBroker.com*, the American Eagle is part of the America Remembers Series … even though the gun is not listed on the America Remembers web site. "You are bidding on a Colt 1911 commemorative pistol. It is the American Eagle (America Remembers). This is a superbly crafted pistol and is numbered in the 800 range of 2500 made. This one is new in the box and comes with the Certificate of authenticity. I am selling for a friend who is thinning out his collection." Bidding had reached $900 in March 2007.

EHLERS 1836 COLT PATERSON

This is a well done aged reproduction of the 1836 Colt Paterson revolver as produced by the United States Historical Society. Only 100 produced and is so marked. New in case with accessories and papers.

SAM HOUSTON COMMEMORATIVE COLT WALKER

This is a Sam Houston commemorative revolver as produced by the United States Historical Society.

COLT SINGLE ACTION ARMY MISSISSIPPI RIVER GAMBLER

Colt .44-40 six shot with 3-inch barrel. Grips featured dice and cards. Retail price $2,249.

HOPALONG CASSIDY COMMEMORATIVE

Premier Edition Hopalong Cassidy Single Action Colt .45. An edition of 100 issued in tribute to the legendary motion picture and television hero. It is an authorized hand-engraved reproduction of the Colt .45 owned by Hopalong Cassidy (William Boyd). A seller on *GunsAmerica.com* in Spring of 2007 asked $5,000.

USA EDITION – NEW JERSEY AND TRENTON

U.S.A. edition single action two gun set chambered for .44-40 with 7.5-inch barrels. Only 100 guns were manufactured, one for each state and one for its capitol. This set is New Jersey and Trenton.

GARIBALDI COMMEMORATIVE

There were only 106 of these sets made commemorating the famous Italian democratic revolutionary. Included glass display case.

MICHIGAN STATE POLICE COMMEMORATIVE

.45 semi-automatic commemorating the 60th anniversary of Michigan State Police.

COLT TALO DIAMOND .45 ACP

Made for Talo Distributing. Stainless finish; engraved with gold overlay with leaf and acorn design and carved grips. Adjustable trigger.

LEATHERNECK TRIBUTE EDITION

The following advertisement appeared on *GunsAmerica.com* in the Spring of 2007: "1911 Leatherneck Tribute Edition. 24 K Gold slide, trim pieces, screws, hammer. Walnut, Double Diamond Grips. Model 1991 A1. In wood and glass presentation case. 45 ACP. One of 300 guns that will be produced."

CIVIL WAR CENTENNIAL SET

The following advertisement appeared on *GunsAmerica.com* in the Spring of 2007: "These pistols are 7/8ths scaled .22 short versions of the original 1860 Army revolver. They have a blued finish with gold frame, backstrap and wedge key. Unfired and new in the presentation case. Very rare set and hard to find." Subtract 50 percent for single gun.

NIB	EXC.	V.G.	GOOD	FAIR	POOR
550	475	395	-	-	-

COLT JOE FOSS COMMEMORATIVE

This advertisement appeared on *GunsAmerica. com* in the Spring of 2007: "A Colt 1911 Joe Foss Commemorative in .45 ACP. The pistol is in NIB condition. The pistol comes with presentation case and original box from the factory. The price of the pistol is $1,850 plus shipping to the continental USA."

ALASKA PIPELINE SAA

This advertisement appeared on *GunsAmerica.com* in the Spring of 2007: "The Colt is Mint unturned and unfired. The box is mint. The knife [also in the presentation box] has a crack in the handle. Best Offer." Seller asked $1,400.

PRESIDENTIAL 1911

This advertisement appeared on *GunsAmerica.com*
in the Spring of 2007: "This is a new in the box Colt Government Model George Bush Presidential high polish stainless steel edition 45 ACP, Colt Model #0170XSEB from the Custom Shop. It is one of only 100 produced. Serial number #GB06X. Item has gold inlay with ramped Colt on slide. Beautiful coco grips. A super collector's piece." Seller asked $1,695.

COLT LIMITED EDITION 1911 TIGER

This advertisement appeared on *GunsAmerica.com* in the Spring of 2007: "Limited edition 1911 Tiger .45 semi-automatic with jungle tiger etched on both sides with serpentine Colt logo. Only 200 made with fancy zebra wood grips. New in box. Own a Colt one of a kind. This pistol has a great look! This gun is out of the custom shop and will enhance any collection." Seller asked $1,150.

OSS 1911

This ad appeared on *GunsAmerica.com* in the Spring of 2007: "Limited edition Colt 70 Series Govt. .45 ACP. OSS [Office of Strategic Services] Commemorative, 1 of 250. Gold inlaid slide and special ebony wood grips. Comes with briefcase that conceals the pistol under a flap divider, yet is very quick to access. Includes a book about the history of the OSS the first CIA." Seller asked $2,195.

SECOND AMENDMENT COMMEMORATIVE .22 COLT PEACEMAKER

From *ActionArms.com* in March 2007, this advertisement: "This gun has never been fired. It has no scratches or blemishes. It comes with the presentation case which has one nick and some light scratches. It has a 7.5-inch barrel. Barrel, frame, ejector rod assy. hammer and trigger are nickel plated. The rest is blued with pearlite stocks. The barrel is inscribed, 'The right to keep and bear arms.'"

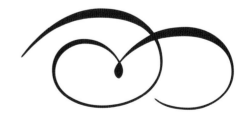

APPENDIX 1

THE COLT COLLECTOR'S ASSOCIATION, INC.

The official web site of the Colt Collector's Association, Inc. is located at *www.coltcollectorsassoc.com/index.htm.* According to the site, "The Association was founded in 1980 by a group of avid collectors of Colt firearms and Colt memorabilia. The Association was established for the purpose of promoting the collecting of all types of Colt firearms and memorabilia and to provide a means of exchanging knowledge among Colt collectors and to offer an annual show and meeting for members and guests with an emphasis on a convenient and quality location.

"The organization is now over 2,200 strong with members in all 50 states and many foreign countries. There is an annual three day show each year with the location moving from year to year to allow the different members to attend. In years past the show has been in cities like Atlanta, Houston, St. Louis, Hartford, Orange County, California, Dallas, Portland, Reston, Virginia, Saint Paul, Austin, Tampa, Kansas City and Louisville, Kentucky to name just a few. In 2007, the 28th Annual Show will be held in Reno, Nevada. The event is as much a social weekend as it is a gun show. The show itself includes some 240 tables, usually divided between 75 percent trade tables and 25 percent display tables.

"Throughout the year, the membership keeps in touch through *The Rampant Colt*, the official magazine of the Colt Collectors Association. This is a wonderful magazine full of articles, pictures and advertisements that keep the membership together as a family.

"We invite you to come and **join us today**. If you live in the United States, a one year membership is $40.00 and a life membership is $700.00. If you live outside the U.S., a one year membership is $70.00. When you join as a member, you automatically get a subscription to *The Rampant Colt* magazine. You will also receive all the information on the annual show and an entire itinerary of the three days of festivities.

"The Colt Collectors Association regrets that we cannot give you specifics as to the history or value of your particular firearm. Our organization is completely volunteer in nature and such an undertaking would be overwhelming to our current volunteers. As a member of the Association, you will receive a complete roster of members and be exposed to experts in their respective areas. Our quarterly magazine includes informative articles in all areas of Colt collecting. As a member, this will give you the opportunity to be exposed to other members and thus obtain a great deal of information about Colt firearms. In addition, you will also have access to a volunteer Historian who can help you with specific questions about your Colt firearm.

"Applicant names and city of residence will be published in our Association publication giving members an opportunity to object to an applicant being accepted as a member. Should a complaint be registered against an applicant, the [CCA] Board of Directors will review the complaint and vote on his/her acceptance. The Colt Collectors Association, Inc. is a non-profit organization incorporated in the State of Texas, and is affiliated with the National Rifle Association. It is a national organization with members throughout the United States as well as some foreign countries. The following membership benefits are offered by the CCA:

- A quality All Colt Show is sponsored annually where members can buy, sell, trade, get to know fellow collectors and exchange knowledge.
- A high quality magazine [The Rampant Colt] published quarterly in which articles solicited from members are printed. Members may also advertise at reasonable prices for items wanted or for sale.
- Membership in an organization dedicated to the preservation of Colt firearms and other products, studying the various arms and products produced by Colt as well as the history related to their development and usage.

The opportunity to increase your knowledge by contact with other members through our publication or at our annual show.

The Association is staffed by elected officers and directors who receive no salary or travel expense compensation."

To join CCA, send a check to the organization's secretary, payable to: "Colt Collectors Association, Inc." All funds must be in U.S. dollars and drawn on a U.S. bank (or International Money Order). Annual dues are based on a Calendar Year.

COLT COLLECTORS ASSOCIATION, INC.
P.O. BOX 2241
LOS GATOS, CA 95031-2241

U.S. MEMBERSHIP
$40.00 ONE YEAR
$700.00 LIFE

OUTSIDE U.S.
$70.00 ONE YEAR
$140 TWO YEARS
$800 LIFE

APPENDIX 2
RELEVANT ARMS MUSEUMS IN THE U.S.

AIR FORCE ARMAMENT MUSEUM

Museum of the U.S. Air Force dedicated to the collection, preservation, and exhibition of weapons artifacts, memorabilia and the platforms of delivery. The museum is located at 100 Museum Drive inside Eglin Air Force Base, Pensacola, Florida 32542 – Phone 904-882-4062 – *www.florida.flyer.co.uk/airforce.htm.* Hours are 9:30 am to 4:30 pm daily. Closed Thanksgiving Day, Christmas Day, New Year's Day and all federal holidays. Admission is free.

BERMAN MUSEUM OF WORLD HISTORY

A fine collection of art, historical objects and weapons (the founder, Farley Berman, an Anniston lawyer, began collecting with a .22 rifle when he was six years old) from around the world including paintings and bronzes by 19th century European and American artists and material from military campaigns. Located at 840 Museum Dr./P.O. Box 2245, Anniston, AL 36206 – Phone (256) 237-6261 – *www.bermanmuseum.org.* Museum hours are: September to May (Tues-Sat 10 am – 5 pm), June to August (Mon-Sat 10 am – 5 pm, Sun 1 pm – 5 pm) and Closed on Thanksgiving Day, Christmas Eve, Easter, Christmas Day and New Years Day.

BUFFALO BILL HISTORICAL CENTER

The Historical Center houses five internationally recognized museums including the Cody Firearms Museum, which houses the most comprehensive assemblage of American firearms in the world. The Winchester Collection, the heart of this museum, was transported from New Haven, Connecticut to Cody in 1976. Dedicated in 1991, the Cody Firearms Museum provides an expansive permanent home for the collection.

Don't expect to see only Winchester-made arms here; virtually every significant manufacturer in the world is represented. Within the exhibits, visitors are able to trace the evolution of modern firearms technology from its earliest days through today's outstanding variations.

The museum staff gladly responds to queries for information on firearms and firearms-related items. While the staff strives to respond within a reasonable amount of time, they receive a large number of requests. Please be patient about receiving a response. The curatorial staff cannot resolve gunsmithing or highly technological queries, but they can assist you with general and historical information about firearms.

The museum is located at 720 Sheridan Ave., Cody, WY 82414 – Phone 307-587-4771 – *www.bbhc.org.* Hours vary by month of year; please call or check the web site.

FRAZIER MUSEUM OF HISTORICAL ARMS

In perhaps a surprisingly small way, the Frazier is only occasionally a "gun museum" for connoisseurs and collectors interested in details of craftsmanship and minute shifts in technical engineering. Its story of arms and armor is the story of "us," what we call history.

This museum has been called "The finest arms museum in the western hemisphere." It is a "must see" that the entire family will enjoy. Exceptionally well done with superb exhibits, innovative presentations and a memorable learning experience focused on arms in the context of their use in world events. Third floor exhibits by the Royal Armories, Leeds, England are especially well done. The Frazier is located at 829 West Main St. Louisville, KY 40202 – Phone 502-412-2280 - *www.courier-journal.com/cjextra/frazier/*.

LAPORTE COUNTY HISTORICAL SOCIETY

Along with the typical local history museum, it features the Walter A. Jones Collection of Ancient Weapons. There are nearly 850 weapons on display. In addition, uniforms from the Civil War to the present day, as well as miscellaneous items brought back to La Porte County by war veterans round out this permanent exhibit at the museum. It is located at 2405 Indiana Ave., Suite 1, La Porte, Indiana 46350 – Phone 219-324-6767 – *www.laportecountyhistory.org*. Hours are Tuesday to Saturday from 10 am to 4:30 pm.

THE METROPOLITAN MUSEUM OF ART

The Metropolitan Museum has collected a vast array of armor, edged weapons and firearms, ranging from full suits of Japanese armor to minute ornamental sword fittings. The Met received its first examples of arms and armor in 1881. Galleries are also devoted to American arms from the colonial era to the late nineteenth century, and to arms from various Islamic cultures, including a distinguished series of decorated armor from fifteenth and sixteenth century Iran and Anatolia, and jewel studded weapons from the Ottoman Turkish and Mughal Indian courts.

Always among the Museum's most popular attractions, the Arms and Armor Galleries were renovated and reinstalled in 1991 to display to better effect the outstanding collection of armor and weapons of sculptural and ornamental beauty from around the world. Many objects were cleaned and restored in the course of this refurbishment, notably some late fifteenth century German shields, from which as many as five layers of paint were removed to recover their original emblems. The Met is located at 1000 5th Ave., NY, NY 10028 – Phone 212-535-7710/650-2551 – *www.metmuseum.org*. Hours are Fri/Sat (9:30 am – 9 pm), Sun/Tue/Wed/Thur (9:30 am – 5:30 pm) and Closed Monday. Also Closed on New Year's Day, Thanksgiving Day and Christmas Day.

MUSEUM OF WEAPONS AND EARLY AMERICAN HISTORY

Educational exhibits of unusual guns, Florida Civil War artifacts, swords and historical documents. "There are various weapons, from the beautiful inlaid .80 caliber Bavarian wheelock, dating to the 1500s, through the Indian War period, to the 1890s. On exhibit is one of the finest Civil War collections you will see anywhere. While we emphasize the Civil War, we want to make it clear that the display is not just weapons, but rather a harmonious blend of historically significant items, and a vivid portrayal of Americana." This privately organized and funded museum is located at 81-C King Street St. Augustine, Florida 32084 – Phone (904) 829-3727 – *www.museumofweapons.com*. Hours are 7 days a week from 9:30 am – 5:00 pm.

NATIONAL FIREARMS MUSEUM

The mission of the National Firearms Museum of the National Rifle Association is to develop and manage educational programs that promote appreciation, understanding and participation in gun collecting, and the preservation of the heritage of firearms through collection, conservation, exhibition and research as part of a nationally recognized museum in America. A superbly presented collection that will appeal to the whole family, as well as the specialist. Top rate changing exhibits with an excellent cafeteria in adjacent building.

The museum is located at the headquarters of the NRA at 11250 Waples Mill Rd., Fairfax, VA 22030 – Phone (703) 267-1600 – *www.nationalfirearmsmuseum.org*. Hours are from 10 am to 4 pm every day except major holidays.

OGDEN UNION STATION

The **Browning Firearms Museum** celebrates the genius of John M. Browning (1855 -1926), inventor of many legendary military and sporting firearms. Displays feature original guns or prototypes designed by Browning. Although many of his inventions were manufactured and sold under names such as Winchester, Remington, and Colt, they were designed in Ogden, Utah, and many of the designer's initial models and prototypes are on display in the museum. Display models include the original Browning Automatic Rifle, mainstay of the U.S. Army through 80 years, as well as the machine guns that protected US vehicles and aircraft. Displays include a reproduction of the workshop where John M. Browning used these tools to create the prototypes of some of the world's most famous firearms. There are dozens of guns on display including richly detailed handguns and rifles as well as an innovative display of miniature firearms near the entrance to the museum. Visit the John M. Browning Firearms Museum at the Ogden Union Station to see the unique and comprehensive collection of guns created by this Ogden family.

The museum is located at 2501 Wall Ave., Ogden, UT 84401 – Phone 801-393-9882 – *www.theunionstation.org*. Regular hours are Monday-Saturday from 10 am to 5 pm. Closed Sundays.

ROCK ISLAND ARSENAL MUSEUM

The Rock Island Arsenal Museum was established in 1905, making it the second oldest U.S. Army museum after West Point. The museum has been closed twice, during W.W. I and W.W. II, in order to create more space for manufacturing. It has been in its present location since 1948.

Rock Island Arsenal is an active U.S. Army factory, manufacturing ordnance and equipment for the armed forces. It is located on Arsenal Island in the Mississippi River.

The Arsenal Museum interprets the history of Arsenal Island to include the building of Fort Armstrong in 1816, the Black Hawk War, the Confederate Prison Camp 1863 to 1865, and the establishment of the Arsenal in 1862. The theme of the Museum is "People, Processes and Products." The exhibits depict the people involved in the Island's history, the manufacturing processes used at the Arsenal, and the equipment that the Arsenal has produced.

Also, included at the museum is an extensive collection of military firearms, both foreign and domestic. More than 1,100 weapons are currently on display.

Located in Building 60, the museum is open daily from 10 am to 4 pm. It is closed Thanksgiving, Christmas Eve, Christmas Day, and New Year's Day.

Other historic points of interest on Arsenal Island are the Confederate Cemetery, the Rock Island Arsenal National Cemetery, the original 19th century stone workshops, the officer's quarters along the river and the site of the first bridge built across the Mississippi.

The Mississippi River Visitor's Center is located on the west end of Arsenal Island at Lock & Dam #15, and is operated by the U.S. Army Corps of Engineers. The Visitor's Center is open daily from 9 am to 9 pm, May through September. The hours for October through April are 9 am to 5 pm. Phone (309) 794-5338 - *www.ria.army.mil/Base%20Ops/museum.htm*.

SOLDIERS & SAILORS NATIONAL MILITARY MUSEUM AND MEMORIAL

The Grand Army of the Republic (GAR) – veterans of the Union Army – conceived Soldiers & Sailors during the 1890s. It was originally built to recognize the sacrifice, valor and patriotism of the Civil War Veterans of Allegheny County, Pennsylvania. Today it honors the men and women of Pennsylvania who served the United States in its military endeavors during our country's history.

Soldiers & Sailors is the largest memorial building in the United States dedicated solely to America's fighting personnel, representing all branches of service while honoring both the career and citizen soldier. Our mission is to preserve a lasting tribute to those men and women who unselfishly gave of themselves in serving their country during American wars.

Look forward to a wonderful sampling of Civil War relics plus a fine U.S. Military small arms collection. Fort Pitt is nearby and well worth the visit, also Ft. Ligonier to understand the importance of this frontier area in the French and Indian War. The museum is located at 4141 Fifth Ave., Pittsburgh, PA 15213 – Phone 412-621-4253 *www.soldiersandsailorshall.org*. It is open Monday through Saturday from 10 am to 4 pm.

SPRINGFIELD ARMORY NATIONAL HISTORIC SITE

Mecca for U.S. martial arms collectors with superb exhibits of virtually every important small arm. Videos here are especially well done. A small selection of new and changing exhibits will justify your repeat visits (if you need an excuse). Private tours of off limits storage areas are occasionally available by prior arraignment for a fee. Web site includes schedule of special events; tours of the collection not on display; some manufacturing dates and serial number info; on line information about many collection items and archives they hold.

The Springfield Armory National Historic Site is located at Armory Square, Suite 2, Springfield, MA 01105 – Phone 413-734-8551 - *http://www.nps.gov/spar/*. Hours are seasonal: **Labor Day through Memorial Day (fall to spring),** Tuesday to Saturday, 9 am to 5 pm and *Memorial Day* **through** *Labor Day (summer only),* Tuesday to Sunday, 9 am to 5 pm. The Museum at Springfield Armory NHS is closed for the following holidays: New Year's Day, Thanksgiving Day and Christmas Day.

THE U.S. ARMY ORDNANCE MUSEUM

This military museum has about 230 large items, mostly examples of foreign countries' weapons from World War I and II, on display in the field outside the building. Inside are special displays, an extensive collection of small arms, a library and a small theater.

The museum is operated by The Ordnance Museum Foundation, Inc., which is a not-for-profit organization dedicated to support the U.S. Army Ordnance Corps Museum at Aberdeen Proving Ground. The Foundation is not a part of the U.S. Army, U.S. Army Ordnance Corps, or the Department of Defense. Therefore, as a civilian not-for-profit organization, the Foundation is able to solicit and accept tax-deductible contributions. The museum is located at Aberdeen Proving Ground, 2201 Aberdeen Blvd., Aberdeen, MD 21005 – Phone 410-278-3602 – *www.ordmusfound.org.* Hours are Monday 12 noon to 4 pm; Tuesday – Sunday 10 am – 4 pm. Closed national holidays except for Veteran's Day, Independence Day, Memorial Day and Armed Forces Day.